Classical Music Discographies, 1976–1988

**Recent Titles in
Discographies**

Thank You Music Lovers:
A Bio-Discography of Spike Jones and His City Slickers, 1941-1965
Jack Mirtle, compiler

John McCormack: A Comprehensive Discography
Paul W. Worth and Jim Cartwright, compilers

Count Basie: A Bio-Discography
Chris Sheridan, compiler

The Symphonies of Gustav Mahler
Lewis M. Smoley, compiler

V-Discs: First Supplement
Richard S. Sears, compiler

French Horn Discography
Michael Hernon, compiler

The Clef/Verve Labels: A Discography
Michel Ruppli, compiler

The Cliff Edwards Discography
Larry F. Kiner, compiler

Broadway on Record: A Directory of New York Cast Recordings
of Musical Shows, 1931-1986
Richard Chigley Lynch, compiler

The Blue Note Label: A Discography
Michael Cuscuna and Michel Ruppli, compilers

His Master's Voice/La Voce Del Padrone
Alan Kelly, compiler

Irish Folk Music: A Selected Discography
Deborah L. Schaeffer, compiler

Movie Musicals On Record: A Directory of Recordings of Motion
Picture Musicals, 1927-1987
Richard Chigley Lynch, compiler

Classical Music Discographies, 1976–1988

A Bibliography

Compiled by
Michael Gray

Discographies, Number 34

GREENWOOD PRESS
New York • Westport, Connecticut • London

For Dottie, as always

Library of Congress Cataloging-in-Publication Data

Gray, Michael H., 1946-
  Classical music discographies, 1976-1988 : a bibliography /
compiled by Michael Gray.
    p. cm.—(Discographies, ISSN 0912-334X ; no. 34)
  Includes index.
  ISBN 0-313-25942-9 (lib. bdg. : alk. paper)
  1. Music—Discography—Bibliography. I. Title. II. Series.
ML128.D56G7   1989
016.7816'8'0266—dc20   89-11861

British Library Cataloguing in Publication Data is available.

Library of Congress Catalog Card Number: 89-11861
ISBN: 0-313-25942-9
ISSN: 0912-334X

First published in 1989

Greenwood Press, Inc.
88 Post Road West, Westport, Connecticut 06881

Printed in the United States of America

The paper used in this book complies with the
Permanent Paper Standard issued by the National
Information Standards Organization (Z39.48-1984).

10 9 8 7 6 5 4 3 2 1

CONTENTS

PREFACE

This bibliography of discographies of classical music is the first
cumulative supplement in a series that began with Bibliography of
Discographies. Volume I: Classical Music 1925-1975, published by R. R.
Bowker in 1977. In addition to covering discographies published as
books, as supplements to books, or as magazine articles as in the
earlier volume, this new bibliography adds entries for record labels
citing significant numbers of classical recordings, discographies
included in dissertations and theses, and discographies appearing in
program notes on sound recordings. Although the period of coverage for
the most part is from 1976 to 1988, a number of citations for
discographies overlooked in the earlier volume are included here as
well.

RESEARCH METHOD

In gathering citations, I have relied almost exclusively on
examining the discographies themselves. Entries reported from
secondary sources are enclosed in double brackets "[[ ]]." A seven-
number annotative code identifies elements in the discography that are
likely to be important to discography users. These appear in double
parentheses "(( ))" following the citations. The symbol "((--))"
shows that the discography contained none of the coded elements. The
elements and their symbols are:

1 **Noncommercial recordings**
2 **Personnel listings**
3 **Matrix numbers**
4 **Index[es]**
5 **Release dates**
6 **Take numbers**
7 **Place and/or date of recording**

ORGANIZATION

The bibliography is divided into two parts: the body, which contains personal names and other subjects arranged in an alphabetical sequence; and the index, encompassing names of compilers, authors, editors, series titles and distinctive discography titles. The names of compilers, authors and editors have been capitalized to facilitate identification and to make scanning the entries easier. Headings for names and subjects are based on those from the Library of Congress; where appropriate, I have made cross-references linking variant subjects or name forms. In filing discographies of music from a particular country or region, I have placed discographies referring specifically to composers under the heading **COMPOSERS**, such as **COMPOSERS, BRITISH**. Discographies of music of a particular region or country, however, are found under the general heading **MUSIC**, as in **MUSIC--GREAT BRITAIN**. Discographies of record labels are filed alphabetically under the general heading **LABELS, RECORD**. Entries under a heading are filed by date of publication; within a given year of publication, monographs appear first, followed by citations filed by the month of publication. Entries for composers and their works are arranged first by general discographies, followed by discographies for a composer's works, such as symphonies, operas, etc., and within those sections by discographies of particular works. Each discography has been given a discrete alphanumeric entry code, which is used in the index of authors and series titles that concludes the volume.

ACKNOWLEDGMENTS

Many people helped me complete work on this Bibliography. Thanks are due especially to the staff of the Library of Congress, and particularly, to Sam Brylawski and Wynn Mathias of the Motion Picture, Broadcasting, and Recorded Sound Reference Staff and to Gerry Gibson of the MPBRS Division. Gary-Gabriel Gisondi and the staff of the Rodgers and Hammerstein Archives of the New York Public Library are responsible for many important entries.

Hajime Suga (Tokyo), Carlo Marinelli (Rome), Alan Poulton (London), Bill Curtis (Boston), and J.F. Weber (Utica, NY) also sent information on discographies they had compiled. David Hamilton read the entire manuscript in final draft and provided many helpful corrections.

BIBLIOGRAPHY OF DISCOGRAPHIES

ABBADO, CLAUDIO, 1933–   (Italian conductor)

A-1   [Claudio Abbado discography] in *Stereo Geijutsu*, No. 58 (February 1973): 178–179   ((7))

A-2   [Abbado discography] in *Record Geijutsu*, No. 276 (September 1973): 180   ((--))

A-3   SELVINI, Michele: Discografia in *Musica*, No. 18 (September 1980): 250–251 ((--))

A-4   [Discography] in *Record Geijutsu*, No. 393 (June 1983): 200–207 ((5, 7))

A-5   Discographische Hinweise: Claudio Abbado – Aktuelle Aufnahmen in *fono forum* (July 1987): 24   ((--))

A-6   Discographie complète in *Diapason-Harmonie*, No. 333 (December 1987): 54–55 ((--))

ABDULLAYEV, RAUF   (Azerbaijani conductor)

A-7   Discography in *Music in the USSR* (January–March 1988): 18 ((--))

ABENDROTH, HERMANN, 1883–1956   (German conductor)

A-8   SUGA, Hajime: Karl Muck and Hermann Abendroth in *LP Techno*, November 1978: 80–82; addenda in LP Techno, January 1980: 104–106 ((--))

ACADEMY OF ANCIENT MUSIC, London

A-9   Discographische Hinweise in *fono forum* (December 1985): 34   ((--))

ACADEMY OF ST. MARTIN-IN-THE-FIELDS, London

A-10 Discography in HARRIES, Meirion: *The Academy of St. Martin in the Fields.* London: Joseph, 1981: 241–264   ((--))

ACKTÉ, AINO, 1876–1944   (Finnish soprano)

A-11   WILE, Raymond: Edison disc masters: Aino Ackté in *Talking Machine Review*, No. 56-57 (February-April 1979): 1486   ((3, 7))

ADAM DE LA HALLE, ca. 1237-ca.1287   (Flemish composer)

A-12   Discographie sommaire in MAILLARD, Jean: *Adam de la Halle*. Paris: H. Champion, 1982: [213]-214   ((5))

ADAM, ADOLPHE, 1803-1856   (French composer)

GISELLE (1841)

A-13   MARINELLI, Carlo: [Discography] in Teatro dell'Opera, Roma, season 1967-68: program pp. 261-263   ((7))

A-14   MARINELLI, Carlo: [Discography] in Teatro dell'Opera, Roma, season 1971-72: program pp. 268-270   ((7))

A-15   MARINELLI, Carlo: [Discography] in Teatro La Fenice, Venice, 1977-78: program pp. 110-112   ((7))

A-16   [[[Discography] in *Giselle*. Paris: *L'Avant-Scène ballet/danse*, No. 1 (1980): 148-149]]

A-17   MARINELLI, Carlo: [Discography] in Teatro alla Scala, Milano, season d'opera e balletto, 1983-84: program pp. 29-30   ((5))

ADAM, THEO, 1926-   (German bass-baritone)

A-18   Schallplattenverzeichnis (Auswahl) in MÜLLER, Hans-Peter: *Theo Adam*. Leipzig: Deutscher Verlag für Musik, 1977: 68-[70]   ((--))

A-19   Diskographie in ADAM, Theo: *Seht, hier ist Tinte, Feder, Papier ...* Berlin: Henschelverlag, 1980: 221-222   ((--))

A-20   Diskographie in MÜLLER, Hans-Peter: *Theo Adam*. Leipzig: Deutscher Verlag für Musik, 1986:]]

A-21   Diskographie in ADAM, Theo: *Die hundertste Rolle, oder, Ich mache einen neuen Adam*. München: M. Hieber, 1987: 243-246   ((--))

ADLER, SAMUEL, 1928-   (American composer)

A-22   Selected discography in Program notes for *Exultation*. [Sound recording] New World Records NW 304, 1979: [2]   ((--))

AFFRÉ, AGUSTARELLO, 1858-1931   (French tenor)

A-23   [Discography] in *Record Collector*, IX/3 (March 1954): 61   ((--))

AGUSSOL, CHARLOTTE-MARIE PAULINE, 1863-?   (French soprano)

A-24   [Discography] in *Record Collector*, IX/3 (March 1954): 61-62   ((--))

AITKEN, HUGH, 1924-   (American composer)

A-25   Selected discography in Program notes for *Robert Davidovici, violin*.

[Sound recording] New World Records NW 334, 1987 ((--))

ALAIN, MARIE-CLAIRE, 1926-   (French organist)

A-26 Discographie disponible in *Diapason-Harmonie*, No. 326 (April 1987): 117 ((--))

ALBAN-BERG QUARTET, West Germany

A-27 BARBIER, Pierre-E.: Une carriere discographique in *Diapason-Harmonie*, No. 343 (November 1988): 59-60 ((--))

ALBANI, EMMA, 1847-1930 (Canadian soprano)

A-28 MORAN, W. R.: Emma Albani (1847-1930) The recordings in ALBANI, Emma: *Forty years of song*. New York: Arno Press, 1977: i-v ((3, 7)) [Reprinted from the 1911 ed. published without discography by Mills & Boon, London)

ALBÉNIZ, ISAAC, 1860-1909 (Spanish composer)

A-29 [[Discography] in MAST, Paul B.: *Style and structure in Ibéria by Isaac Albéniz* [Dissertation, University of Rochester, 1974] 409 pp.]]

ALBERT-SCHWEITZER QUINTETT, Germany

A-30 Discographische Hinweise in *fono forum* (May 1988): 21 ((--))

ALBRECHT, GERD, 1935-   (German conductor)

A-31 Discographie Gerd Albrecht in *fono forum* (October 1988): 26-27 ((--))

ALCHEVSKYĬ, IVAN, 1876-1917 (Ukrainian singer)

A-32 [Discography] in *Ivan Alchevskyui: spohady, materialy, lystuvannĩa*. Kiev: Muzychna Ukraïna, 1980: 253-[255] ((3, 6, 7))

ALEKSANDROV, ALEKSANDR VASILOVICH, 1883-1946 (Russian composer)

A-33 [Discography] in *A. Aleksandrov: notobibliograficheskiĭ spravochnik*. Moskva: Vses.izd-vo Sov. kompozitor, 1980: 37-[42] ((--))

ALEKSANDROV, BORIS ALEKSANDROVICH, 1905-   (Russian composer)

A-34 [Discography] in *Boris Aleksandrovich Aleksandrov: Stat'i, materialy*. Moskva: Vses. izd.vo "Sov. kompozitor", 1985: 140-143 ((--))

ALKAN, CHARLES, 1813-1888 (French composer)

A-35 HAILSTONE, Charles: *Provisional discography of works by Ch V Alkan*. 3d ed. London: The Alkan Society (c/o author, 7a Alder Road, Mortlake, London SW14 8ER) [May 1979]: 7 pp.; Addenda, May 1980: 2 pp. ((3, 5))

A-36 HAILSTONE, Charles: The Alkan Society discography in SMITH,

Ronald: *Alkan: the music.* London: Kahn and Averill; New York
Taplinger, 1987: 262-271   ((5))

ALONSO, FRANCISCO, 1887-1948   (Spanish composer)

A-37   Discografía in MONTERO ALONSO, José: *Francisco Alonso.* Madrid:
Espasa-Calpe, 1987: [124]-126   ((--))

ALWYN, WILLIAM, 1905-1985   (English composer)

A-38   CRAGGS, Stewart and POULTON, Alan: Discography in *William
Alwyn; a catalogue of his music.* [Kidderminster]: Bravura
Publications, 1985: 100-119   ((1, 7))

AMADEUS STRING QUARTET, London

A-39   Discography, Deutsche Grammophon artist information, 1980, 2 pp.
((--)

A-40   WALKER, Malcolm: Discography in SNOWMAN, Daniel: *The Amadeus
Quartet: the men and the music.* London: Robson Books, 1981: 137-
155   ((3, 6, 7))

AMELING, ELLY, 1934-   (Dutch soprano)

A-41   Discographie Elly Ameling in JONG, Janny de: *Elly Ameling: vocaal
avontuur.* Soest: Gooise Uitgeverij, 1978:   102-104   ((--))

A-42   Discography [on Philips label].   S.l.: [Philips, 198-?]   2 l.
((--))

AMOYAL, PIERRE, 1949-   (French violinist)

A-43   Discographie de Pierre Amoyal: enregistrements parus chez Erato in
Harmonie hi-fi conseil, No. 9 (May 1981): 28   ((--))

ANDA, GÉZA, 1921-1976   (Hungarian pianist)

A-44   Repertoire und Schallplatten verzeichnis in *Géza Anda: ein
Erinnerungbild.* Zürich: Autemis, 1977: 115-118   ((--))

ANDERS, PETER, 1908-1954   (German tenor)

A-45   [[[Discography] in *Stimmen die um die Welt gingen,* No. 16 (June
1987): 21-62]]

ANDERSÉN, HARALD, 1919-   (Finnish conductor)

A-46   HAAPAKOSKI, Martti: Harald Andersén levytykset in *Chorus et
psalmus.* Helsinki: Sibelius-akatemia, 1979: 268-272   ((7))

ANDERSON, MARIAN, 1902-   (American contralto)

A-47   Discography in SIMS, Janet L.: *Marian Anderson, an annotated
bibliography and discography.* Westport, CT: Greenwood Press, 1981:
235-237   ((5))

ANDRÉ, MAURICE, 1933-   (French trumpeter)

A-48   [[GRANDEMANGE, Thierry: *Discographie commentée de Monsieur Maurice André*. Paris: Sorbonne, VER de musique et musicologie, mémorie maîtrise, June 1986]]

ANDRIESSEN, HENDRICK, 1892-   (Dutch composer)

A-49   [[Discography in DOX, Thurston Jacob: *The works of Hendrick Andreissen*. [Dissertation, University of Rochester, 1970] 244 pp.]]

ANGELES, VICTORIA DE LOS, 1923-   (Spanish soprano)

A-50   Discografía de Victoria de los Angeles in FERNÁNDEZ-CID, Antonio: *Victoria de los Angeles*. Madrid: Aldus, 1970: 181-191   ((--))

A-51   Discography in ROBERTS, Peter: *Victoria de los Angeles*. London: Weidenfeld & Nicolson, 1982: 169-177   ((5))

A-52   VOISIN, Georges: Discographie in *L'Avant Scéne Opèra*, No. 78 (August 1985): 90-96   ((5, 7))

ANSELMI, GIUSEPPE, 1876-1929   (Italian tenor)

A-53   LUSTIG, Larry and WILLIAMS, Clifford: The recordings of Giuseppe Anselmi in *Record Collector*, XXXII/3-5 (April 1987): 86-96   ((3, 7))

ANSERMET, ERNEST, 1883-1969   (Swiss conductor)

A-54   [Ernest Ansermet discography] in *Record Geijutsu*, No. 342 (March 1979): 284-287   ((5, 7))

A-55   Discographie Ernest Ansermet in *fono forum* (December 1980): 18-21 ((--))

A-56   Ansermet à écouter in *Diapason*, No. 288 (November 1983): 11   ((--))

A-57   Discographie complète in HUDRY, François: *Ernest Ansermet, pionnier de la musique*. Lausanne: Editions de l'Aire, 1983: 167-193   ((7))

A-58   HUDRY, François: Enregistrements sur disques d'Ernest Ansermet in *Ernest Ansermet: 1883-1969*. Lausanne: Bibliothèque cantonale et universitaire, Association Ernest Ansermet, 1983: 230-236   ((--))

A-59   HUDRY, François: Discographie in *Ernest Ansermet: catalogue de l'oeuvre*. Lausanne: Bibliothéque cantonale et universitaire, 1983: 257-281   ((--))

ANSOV, NICOLAI PARLOVICH, 1900-1962   (Russian conductor)

A-60   Discographic references in *N. P. Ansov: literary inheritance, correspondence, reminiscences of contemporaries*. Moscow, 1978: [181]-196   ((--))

ANTHEIL, GEORGE, 1900-1959   (American composer)

A-61   Discography in WHITESITT, Linda: *The life and music of George Antheil, 1900-1959*. Ann Arbor, Mich.: UMI Research Press, 1983: [263]-270   ((1, 7)) [An adaptation of her dissertation, University of Maryland, 1981, which also contained a discography]

ApIVOR, DENIS, 1916–   (English composer)

A-62   GANDOLFI, Rosemary: Recordings of works by Denis ApIvor in *Recorded Sound*, No. 66–67 (April–July 1977): 697–698 ((1, 7))

ARGERICH, MARTHA, 1941–   (Argentinian pianist)

A-63   Discography, Deutsche Grammophon artist information, 1980, 1 p. ((--))

A-64   [Discography] in *Record Geijutsu*, No. 398 (November 1983): 222–225 ((5, 7))

ARKHIPOVA, IRINA, 1925–   (Russian mezzo–soprano)

A-65   Discography in *Music in the USSR* (October–December 1987): 11–12 ((--))

ARNOLD, MALCOLM, 1921–   (English composer)

A-66   POULTON, Alan J.: Discography in *The music of Malcolm Arnold; a catalogue.* [London; Boston]: Faber Music, 1986: 175–198 ((1, 5))

ARRAU, CLAUDIO, 1902–   (Chilean pianist)

A-67   [Claudio Arrau discography] in *Record Geijutsu*, No. 345 (June 1979): 254–256 ((5, 7))

A-68   Discography [on Philips label] S.l.: [Philips, 198–?] 3 l. ((--))

A-69   SCRAGG, T. W.: Discography in HOROWITZ, Joseph: *Conversations with Arrau.* New York: Knopf, 1982: 288–308 ((5))

A-70   [[[Discography] in HARDEN, Ingo: *Claudio Arrau: ein Interpreten-portrait.* Frankfurt/M.: Ullstein, 1983: 122–136]]

A-71   HARDEN, Ingo: Discographie Claudio Arrau in *fono forum* (February 1983): 28–29 ((5))

A-72   Discographic chronologique in *Diapason–Harmonie*, No. 327 (May 1987): 44–47 ((5))

ARRIAGA, JUAN CRISOTOMO DE, 1806–1826 (Spanish composer)

A-73   [[[Discography] in ROSEN, Barbara: *Arriaga, the forgotten genius: the short life of a Basque composer.* Tarrytown, NY: Associated Faculty Press; Reno, NV: Basque Studies Program, 1988:]]

(LES) ARTS FLORISSANTS, Paris

A-74   Discographie in WALTHER, Edith: Tête d'affiche: William Christie in *Harmonie–Panorama musique*, No. 46 (October 1984): 15 ((--))

ARUTYUNYAN, ALEXANDER (Armenian composer)

A-75   Discography in *Music in the USSR* (April–June 1986): 17 ((--))

ASHKENAZY, VLADIMIR, 1937–   (Russian pianist/conductor)

A-76   [Ashkenazy discography] in *Stereo Geijutsu*, No. 44 (January 1972): 170-171 ((--))

A-77   Discographie de Vladimir Ashkenazy in *Harmonie*, No. 137 (May 1978): 49 ((--))

A-78   COSSÉ, Peter: Vladimir Ashkenazy, Perfektion als Normalfall in *fono forum* (June 1985): 20-23 ((--))

A-79   KEHOE, John: Discography in PARROTT, Jasper: *Beyond frontiers.* New York: Atheneum, 1985: 221-233 ((--))

A-80   Selected discography in *Stereophile* (November 1988): 149 ((--))

ATTERBERG, KURT, 1887-1974 (Swedish composer)

A-81   FOREMAN, Lewis: Kurt Atterberg discography in *Recorded Sound*, No. 62 (April 1976): 539-541 ((1, 7))

AUBER, DANIEL, 1782-1871 (French composer)

OPERAS

MANON LESCAUT (1856)

A-82   [MARINELLI, Carlo: [Discography] in Ente lirico Arena di Verona, season 1984: program pp. 40-41 ((7))

AURIC, GEORGES, 1899-1983 (French composer)

A-83   ROY, Jean: À écouter, Georges Auric in *Diapason*, No. 286 (September 1983): 6 ((--))

AVISON, CHARLES, 1710-1770 (English composer)

A-84   [[Discography in STEPHENS, Norris Lynn: *Charles Avison: an eighteenth-century composer, musician, and writer.* [Dissertation, University of Pittsburgh, 1968] 349 pp.]]

BBC RADIOPHONIC WORKSHOP, London

B-1   [[Discography in BRISCOE, Desmond: *The BBC Radiophonic Workshop: the first 25 years.* London: BBC, 1983: 167]]

B.B.C. SYMPHONY ORCHESTRA, London

B-2   The BBC Symphony Orchestra--a discography in KENYON, Nicholas: *The BBC Symphony Orchestra; the first fifty years, 1930-1980.* London: BBC, 1981: [499]-508 ((1))

B-3   Sir Adrian Boult and the B.B.C. Symphony Orchestra (1932-1946) in *Vintage Light Music*, No. 35 (Summer 1983): 6-8 ((3))

See also entry for

TOSCANINI, ARTURO

BABBITT, MILTON, 1916-   (American composer)

B-4   Selected discography in Program notes for *Milton Babbitt: Philomel*. [Sound recording] New World Records NW 307, 1980 ((−−))

B-5   Discography in Program notes for *Milton Babbitt: Piano Concerto*. [Sound recording] New World Records NW 346, 1987 ((−−))

B-6   HAMILTON, David: Babbitt on records in *Opus*, II/6 (October 1986): 29 ((−−))

BACEWICZ, GRAZYNA, 1909-1969 (Polish composer)

B-7   Complete discography in ROSEN, Judith: *Grazyna Bacewicz, her life and works*. Los Angeles: Friends of Polish Music, University of Southern California School of Music, 1984: 57−62 ((−−))

BACH, CARL PHILLIP EMANUEL, 1714-1788 (German composer)

B-8   Bach's boys: some illustrious sons of an illustrious father in *Tarakan Music Letter*, IV/3 (January−February 1983): 13 ((−−))

B-9   Discographische Hinweise in *fono forum* (November 1988): 35 ((−−))

B-10   [[[Discography] in OTTENBERG, Hans−Günter: *Carl−Philipp Emanuel Bach*. Leipzig: Ottenberg, 1987]]

BACH, JOHANN CHRISTIAN, 1735-1782 (German composer)

B-11   Bach's boys: some illustrious sons of an illustrious father in *Tarakan Music Letter*, IV/3 (January−February 1983): 13 ((−−))

B-12   [[Discography in VOS, Marie Ann Heiberg: *The liturgical works of Johann Christian Bach*. [Dissertation, Washington University, 1969] 293, 264 pp.]]

BACH, JOHANN CHRISTOPH FRIEDRICH, 1732-1795 (German composer)

B-13   Bach's boys: some illustrious sons of an illustrious father in *Tarakan Music Letter*, IV/3 (January−February 1983): 13 ((−−))

BACH, JOHANN SEBASTIAN, 1685-1750 (German composer)

B-14   [J.S. Bach discography] in *Record Geijutsu*, No. 302 (November 1975): [193]−239 ((5, 7))

B-15   REDFERN, Brian: Selected discography of Bach's music in ROBERTSON, Alec: *Bach: a biography, with a survey of books, editions, and recordings*. London: C. Bingley; Hamden, CT: Linnet Books, 1977: 107−129 ((−−))

B-16   BRODER, Nathan: *The collector's Bach*. Westport, CT: Greenwood Press, 1978. 192 pp. ((−−)) [Reprinted from the 1958 ed. published by Lippincot, New York]

B-17   Beginning list of Bach recordings in LEE, Robert E. A.: *The joy of Bach*. Minneapolis: Augsburg Pub. House, 1979: 129−135 ((−−))

B-18   Discografia bachiana in RESCIGNO, Eduardo: *Bach*. Milano: Fabbri, 1980: 129−136 ((−−))

B-19   Discographie (quelques enregistrements exemplaires) in CANDÉ, Roland
        de: *Jean-Sébastien Bach.* Paris: Seuil, 1984: 483-[486]   ((--))

B-20   Diskographie in HARNONCOURT, Nikolaus: *Der musikalische Dialog:
        Gedanken zu Monteverdi, Bach und Mozart.* Salzburg: Residenz Verlag,
        1984: 290-304   ((--))

B-21   MARINELLI, Carlo: Bach: per una discografia di base in Ente autonomo
        Teatro Massimo, Quaderni, Palermo, 1985: 15-35   ((--))

B-22   LINCOLN, Stoddard: Bach: a critical discography in *Ovation*, VI/1
        (February 1985): 28-37   ((--))

B-23   Discography in FERNANDEZ, Dominique: Bach, Haendel et l'opéra
        italien in *Diapason-Harmonie*, No. 303 (March 1985): 50-54   ((--))

B-24   CHIEN, George: Teldec's 300th-birthday bash in *Fanfare*, VIII/4
        (March-April 1985): 110-114   ((--))

B-25   [[Discography in CARRUTHERS, Glen Blaine: *Bach and the piano:
        editions, arrangements, and transcriptions from Czerny to
        Rachmaninoff.* [Dissertation, University of Victoria, 1987]
        251 pp.]]

CHORAL WORKS

B-26   Recommended recordings in DAW, Stephen: *The music of Johann
        Sebastian Bach.* Rutherford, NJ: Fairleigh Dickinson University
        Press, 1981: 178-219   ((--))

B-27   KENYON, Nicholas: Bach's choral works; a discographic survey,
        part 1: introduction, B minor mass in *Opus*, II/1 (December
        1985): 14-17; [other works] in II/2 (February 1986): 10-15, 54-55
        ((5))

CANTATAS

B-28   Notice discographique in ZWANG, Philippe: *Guide pratique des
        cantates de Bach.* Paris: Laffont, 1982: 33-[37]   ((--))

CHRISTMAS ORATORIO, BWV 248

B-29   LACAS, Pierre-Paul: L'oratorio de Noël de J. S. Bach: disco-
        graphie critique in *Diapason*, No. 223 (December 1977): 28-29
        ((5)

B-30   THOMAS, Louis: Discographie comparée--Bach: L'Oratorio de Noël
        in *Harmonie*, No. 153 (December 1979): 122-129   ((--))

B-31   Discographische Hinweise: Johann Sebastian Bach: Weihnachts-
        oratorium (Gesamtaufnahmen) in *fono forum* (December 1985):
        30   ((7))

MASS IN B MINOR, BWV 232

B-32   PIEL, Jean-Marie: Discographie Bach La messe en si in
        Diapason-Harmonie, No. 324 (February 1987): 101-103   ((5))

PASSIONS

B-33   Discography in STEINITZ, Paul: *Bach's Passions*. New York: Scribner's, 1978; London: Elek, 1979: [133]-134 ((--))

ST. JOHN PASSION, BWV 245

B-34   THOMAS, Louis: Le passion selon Saint Jean [de] Jean-Sebestien Bach: discographie comparée in *Harmonie*, No. 135 (March 1978): [100]-107 ((--))

B-35   MARINELLI, Carlo: [Discography] in Teatro Massimo, Palermo, Ente autonomo Teatro Massimo, 1984-85 season: program p. 6 ((7))

ST. MATTHEW PASSION, BWV 244

B-36   MARINELLI, Carlo: [Discography] in Milano, Teatro alla Scala, season 1984-85: program pp. 59-61 ((5))

CONCERTOS

BRANDENBURG CONCERTOS, BWV 1046-1051

B-37   BENTEJAC, Annie: Bach: les six concertos brandebourgeois in *Harmonie*, No. 129 (September 1977): 108-115 ((5))

BRANDENBURG CONCERTO, No. 5, BWV 1050

B-38   CUKIER, Michel: Le 5e Brandenbourgeois de Jean-Sébstien Bach in *Diapason*, No. 245 (December 1979): 96-97 ((5))

INSTRUMENTAL OR KEYBOARD WORKS

ART OF THE FUGUE, BWV 1080

B-39   ELSTE, Martin: *Bachs Kunst der Fuge auf Schallplatten*. Frankfurt am Main: Buchhändler-Vereiningung, 1981. ((4, 5, 7))

GOLDBERG VARIATIONS, BWV 988

B-40   PIEL, Jean-Marie: Les Variations Goldberg de Bach in *Diapason*, No. 271 (April 1982): 45-47 ((--))

B-41   Discographie: "Goldbergvariationen", BWV 988 in *fono forum* (August 1985): 26-27 ((5))

SUITES, LUTE

B-42   [[[Discography] in *Luitesuite in sol klien = Suite pour luth en sol mineur BWV 995*. Bruxellis in Monte Artium: Bibliotheca Regia Belgica, 1981: [2-3]]]

ORGAN WORKS

B-43   CRAUZAT, Claude Noisette de: Jean Sébastien Bach: l'oeuvre pour orgue: discographie comparée in *Harmonie hi-fi conseil*, XVI/5 (January 1981): 38-43 ((5))

TOCCATA, ORGAN, BWV 565

B-44   BRAS, Jean-Yves: J. S. Bach--Les "100" toccata et fugue en re m
          BWV 565 in *Diapason*, No. 210 (October 1976): 32-35 ((5, 7))

SONATAS, VIOLIN & HARPSICHORD, BWV 1014-1019

B-45   PIEL, Jean-Marie: Le point sur les six Sonates pour violon et
          clavecin de Bach in *Diapason*, No. 249 (April 1980): 38-39 ((5))

SUITES, VIOLONCELLO, BWV 1007-1012

B-46   I dischi ascoltati in *Musica*, No. 42 (October 1986): 26 ((5))

WELL-TEMPERED CLAVIER, BWV 846-893

B-47   PIGEAUD, François: Le clavier bien tempere in *Harmonie*, No.
          133 (January 1978): 104-111 ((--))

BACH, P. D. Q.

See entry for

SCHICKELE, Peter

BACH, WILHELM FRIEDEMANN, 1710-1784 (German composer)

B-48   Bach's boys: some illustrious sons of an illustrious father in
          Tarakan Music Letter, IV/3 (January-February 1983): 13 ((--))

BACKHAUS, WILHELM, 1884-1969 (German pianist)

B-49   MASINI, Umberto: Discografia di Wilhelm Backhaus in *Musica*, No. 34
          (October 1984): 43-47 ((5, 7))

BACON, ERNST, 1898-   (American composer)

B-50   Published records in HORGAN, Paul: *Ernst Bacon: a contemporary
          tribute.* [s.l.: s.n. 197-]: 19-20 ((--))

B-51   Selected discography in Program notes for *William Parker recital.*
          [Sound recording] New World Records NW 305, 1980: [4] ((--))

BADINGS, HENK, 1907-   (Dutch composer)

B-52   [[Discography in DITTO, John Allen: *The four preludes and fugues,
          the Ricercar, and the Passacaglia for Timpani and Organ by Henk Badings.*
          [DMA, University of Rochester, 1979] 112 pp.]]

BAILLIE, ISOBEL, 1895-1983 (English soprano)

B-53   Discography of the commercial recordings of Isobel Baillie in her
          Never sing louder than lovely. London: Hutchinson, 1982: 161-197
          ((3, 6, 7))

BAINES, WILLIAM, 1899-1922 (English composer)

B-54   Bibliography and discography in CARPENTER, Roger: *Goodnight to*

Flamboro; the life and music of William Baines. Rickmansworth: Triad Press, 1977: 124-127 ((1))

BAIRD, TADEUSZ, 1928-1981 (Polish composer)

B-55   PAZDRO, Michel: Catalogue des oeuvres de Tadeusz Baird [includes discographic references] in *Musique en jeu*, No. 25 (November 1976): 83-86 ((--))

BAKER, JANET, 1933-   (English mezzo-soprano)

B-56   Discography [on Philips label] S.l.: [Philips, 198-?] 1 leaf. ((--))

BAKFARK, BÁLINT, 1507-1576 (Hungarian composer)

B-57   Diszkográfia in HOMOLYA, István: *Bakfark*. Budapest: Zeneműkiadó, 1982: 222 ((--))

B-58   Discography in HOMOLYA, István: *Valentine Bakfark: lutenist from Transylvania*. Budapest: Corvina, 1984: 236-237 ((--))

BALADA, LEONARDO, 1933-   (Spanish composer)

B-59   Selected discography in Program notes for *Leonardo Balada, Steel Symphony*. [Sound recording] New World Records NW 348, 1987 ((--))

BALAKIREV, MILY, 1837-1910 (Russian composer)

B-60   Discographische Hinweise Milij Balakirev (Auswahl) in *fono forum* (June 1987): [27] ((--))

BALLETS

B-61   The dancer's floor: music for the ballet in *Tarakan Music Letter*, II/5 (May-June 1981): 1, 6 ((--))

BAMBERG SYMPHONY

B-62   Discographische Hinweise in *fono forum* (December 1985): 20 ((--))

BAMPTON, ROSE, 1908-   (American soprano)

B-63   ZITMAN, Manfred: Rose Bampton in *Record Collector*, XXXIII/11-12 (November 1988): [266]-299 ((1, 3, 6, 7))

BANCHIERI, ADRIANO, 1568-1634 (Italian composer)

LA PAZZIA SENILE

B-64   MARINELLI, Carlo: [Discography] in Roma, Teatro dell'Opera, 1969 season: program p. 371 ((7))

BAND MUSIC

B-65   [[Discography in OLSON, Kenneth Elmer: *Yankee bands of the Civil War*. [Dissertation, University of Minnesota, 1971] 255 pp., 80 pp.]]

B-66   [[RASMUSSEN, Richard Michael: *Recorded concert band music,
1950-1987: a selected, annotated listing. Jefferson, NC: McFarland,
1988]]

BANSHCHIKOV, GENNADY, 1943-   **(Russian composer)**

B-67   Discography in *Music in the USSR* (July-September 1988): 63   ((--))

BARBER, SAMUEL, 1910-1981   (American composer)

B-68   Selected discography in Program notes for *Third Essay.* [Sound
recording] New World Records NW 309, 1981: [4]   ((--))

B-69   KOZINN, Alan: Samuel Barber: the recordings in *High
Fidelity/Musical America,* XXXI/6 (June 1981): 89-90; XXXI/7 (July
1981): 45-47, 65-68   ((--))

B-70   List of records in BRODER, Nathan: *Samuel Barber.* Westport, CT:
Greenwood Press, 1985: 104-107   ((--)) [Reprinted from the ed.
published by G. Schirmer, 1954]

B-71   Discography in HENNESSEE, Don A.: *Samuel Barber: a bio-
bibliography.* Westport, CT: Greenwood Press, 1985: [83]-129   ((5))
(Bio-bibliographies in music; 3)

B-72   Selected discography in Program notes for *Anthony and Cleopatra.*
[Sound recording] New World Records NW 322/4, 1985   ((--))

BARBIROLLI, SIR JOHN, 1899-1970   (English conductor)

B-73   [Discography] in *Stereo Geijutsu,* No. 56 (November 1972): 164-167
((--))

B-74   WALKER, Malcolm: A full discography in KENNEDY, Michael:
Barbirolli, conductor laureate.   New York: Da Capo Press, 1981:
[341]-402   ((1, 3, 7)) [Reprinted from the 1973 ed. published by
Hart-Davis, MacGibbon, London]

BARBLAN, OTTO, 1860-1943   (Swiss composer)

B-75   Catalogue discographique in PERINI, Élisa: *Otto Barblan, père de
l'École d'orgue de Genève: vie et oeuvre.*   Neuchâtel: Éditions de
la Baconnière, 1976: 163   ((--))

BARCE, RAMÓN, 1928-   **(Spanish composer)**

B-76   Catalogo, discografia y bibliografia in MEDINA, Angel: *Ramón Barce.*
Madrid: Arte-musicología, Servicio de Publicaciones, Universidad
de Oviedo, 1983: 206-215   ((--))

BARENBOIM, DANIEL, 1942-   **(Israeli pianist/conductor)**

B-77   Discographie DG de Daniel Barenboim, chef d'orchestre in *Harmonie,*
No. 147 (May 1979): 51; discographie [as pianist]: 49   ((--))

B-78   RATTALINO, Piero: Daniel Barenboim suona Beethoven in *Musica,* No. 27
(December 1982): 421   ((--))

BARERE, SIMON, 1896-1951   (Russian pianist)

B-79   Discographische Hinweise in *fono forum* (June 1986): 27   ((--))

BARLET, JEAN, 1862-?   (French baritone)

B-80   [Discography] in *Record Collector*, IX/3 (March 1954): 62   ((--))

BARNS, ETHEL, 1873-1948   (English violinist)

B-81   [[Discography in ENGLESBERG, Barbara J.: *The life and works of Ethel Barns: British violinist composer (1873-1948)* [Dissertation, Boston University, 1987]   317 pp.]]

BAROQUE MUSIC

See

MUSIC, BAROQUE

BARRIENTOS, MARIA, 1884-1946   (Spanish soprano)

B-82   Discografia in COLMER PUJOL, Josep M.: *Maria Barrientos.* Barcelona: Edicions de Mou Art Thor, 1984: 27-30   ((3, 7))

B-83   WILLIAMS, Clifford: Discography in *Record Collector*, XXVIII/3-4 (July 1983): 87-92; Addenda in XXX/10-11 (October 1985): 251-260   ((3, 4, 6, 7))

BARTÓK, BÉLA, 1881-1945   (Hungarian composer)

B-84   [[CHRISTENSEN, Bodil Kragh: *Béla Bartók: En selektiv diskografi.* [Thesis, Royal Danish School of Librarianship, 1972]]]

B-85   [[[Discography] in LENOIR, Yves Roger: *Vie et oeuvre de Béla Bartók aux Étas-Unis d'Amerique (1940-1945)* [Dissertation, University of Louvain, 1976] 204, 226, 160 pp.]]

B-86   Orientation discographique in CITRON, Pierre: *Bartók.* Paris: [Seuil], 1976: 182-186   ((--))

B-87   [[[Discography] in KRÓO, György: *Bartók-kalauz.* Budapest: Zeneműkiadó, 1980: 261-266]]

B-88   Discographie in his *Musique de la vie.* Paris: Stock, 1981: 221-[222]   ((7))

B-89   Diszkográfia in TALLIÁN, Tibor: *Bartók Béla.* Budapest: Gondolat, 1981: 338-340   ((7))

B-90   [[SZEPESI, Zsuzanna: A Bartók discography; records published in Hungary, 1971-1980 in *Studies in Musicologie*, XX/4 (1981): 493-499]]

B-91   Discographie in *Diapason*, No. 258 (February 1981): 29-31   ((3, 5))

B-92   HALBREICH, Harry: Centénaire de Béla Bartók: discographie critique in *Harmonie hi-fi conseil*, VII (March 1981): [38]-54   ((3))

B-93 NOBLE, Jeremy: Bartók recordings [early, piano and stage works] in *High Fidelity/Musical America*, XXXI/3 (March 1981): 43-46, 53-54; Vocal, chamber, and orchestral works in XXXI/5 (May 1981): 46-48, 65-73 ((--))

B-94 Pianist ... Bartók discography in *Record Geijutsu*, No. 368 (May 1981): 17-19 ((7))

B-95 [MODUGNO, Maurizio.]: Discografia in *Discoteca Hifi*, No. 219/220 (July-August 1981): 26-32 ((--))

CHAMBER WORKS

B-96 [Discography] in KÁRPÁTI, János: *Bartók kamarazenéje*. Budapest: Zeneműkiadó, 1976: [364] ((--))

CONCERTOS

CONCERTO, PIANO, No. 1

B-97 BARBIER, Pierre-E., et al. Le 1er concerto pour piano de Béla Bartók in *Harmonie*, No. 212 (December 1976): 42-43, 81 ((--))

PIANO WORKS

B-98 Auswahl discographie der Klavierwerke Béla Bartóks in *fono forum* (March 1981): 39 ((--))

B-99 COSSÉ, Peter: Die Klavierwerke Bartóks und die Schallplatte (Auswahl-Diskographie) in *Öesterreichische Musikzeitschrift*, XXXVI (March 1981): 192-193 ((--))

STAGE WORKS

B-100 MARINELLI, Carlo: [Discography of Wooden Prince, Miraculous Mandarin and Bluebeard's Castle] in *Musica*, No. 22 (October 1981): 238-245 ((7))

BLUEBEARD'S CASTLE (1918)

B-101 MARINELLI, Carlo: [Discography] in Roma, Teatro dell'Opera, season 1971-72: program pp. 432-436 ((5))

B-102 MARINELLI, Carlo: [Discography] in Milano, Teatro alla Scala, season 1980-81: program pp. 30-35 ((5))

B-103 Discographische Hinweise: Béla Bartók: Herzog Blaubarts Burg in *fono forum* (November 1984): 34 ((5, 7))

(THE) MIRACULOUS MANDARIN (1919)

B-104 MARINELLI, Carlo: [Discography] in Roma, Teatro dell'Opera, season 1971-72: program pp. 458-459 ((5))

B-105 MARINELLI, Carlo: [Discography] in Venezia, Teatro La Fenice, season 1977-78: program pp. 49-51 ((7))

B-106 MARINELLI, Carlo: [Discography] in Milano, Teatro alla Scala, season 1979-80: program p. 77   ((5))

B-107   MARINELLI, Carlo: [Discography] in Milano, Teatro alla Scala, season 1980-81: program pp. 60-61   ((5))

(THE) WOODEN PRINCE (1916)

B-108   MARINELLI, Carlo: [Discography] in Roma, Teatro dell'Opera, season 1971-72: program pp. 446-447   ((5))

B-109   MARINELLI, Carlo: [Discography] in Milano, Teatro alla Scala, season 1980-81: program pp. 45-47   ((5))

BASSOON

B-110   Discography of bassoon players in LANGWILL, Lyndesay G.: *The bassoon and contrabassoon.* London: Benn; New York: W. W. Norton, [1965]: 223-258   ((--))

B-111   [[Discography in JANSEN, Will: *The bassoon: its history, construction, makers, players and music.* Buren: Frits Knuf, 1978. 190 pp.]]

B-112   A discography of bassoon solos in *Instrumentalist,* XXX/9 (April 1976): 34-35   ((--))

BATTISTINI, MATTIA, 1856-1928   (Italian baritone)

B-113   KELLY, Alan, PERKINS, John F. and WARD, John: Mattia Battistini (1856-1928): a discography in *Recorded Sound,* No. 65 (January 1977): 652-656 ((3, 7))

B-114   MORAN, W. R.: Mattia Battistini (1856-1928)--a discography in PALMEGIANI, Francesco: *Mattia Battistini: il re dei baritoni.* New York: Arno Press, 1977: [201]-[216]   ((3, 6, 7))   [Includes notes on playing speeds]

B-115   A discography in SILLANPA, Tom: *An artistic profile of Mattia Battistini.* Terre Haute, Ind.: Sillanpa, 1983: 39-44   ((--))

BAX, ARNOLD, 1883-1953   (English composer)

B-116   Discography in FOREMAN, Lewis: *Bax: a composer and his times.* London; Berkeley: Scolar Press, 1983: [451]-460   ((--))

B-117   [[[Discography] in FOREMAN, Lewis: *Bax: a composer and his times.* 2d ed.   Aldershot: Scolar Press; Brookfield, VT: Gower Publ. Co., 1988:]]

B-118   Discografie in *Luister,* XIII (July 1988): 33   ((--))

BAYREUTH, Ger. (City)--Festspiele

B-119   Bayreuther Diskographie in SCHREIBER, Hermann and MONGOLD, Guido: *Werkstatt Bayreuth.* München: Knaus, 1986: [236]   ((--))   [Omits record numbers]

See also entry for

CONDUCTORS

BEAUX ARTS TRIO, USA

B-120 Discography [on Philips label]   S.l.: [Philips, 198-?]   2 leaves.
((--))

B-121 Discography for the Beaux Arts Trio (UK) in *Records & Recording*, No.
274 (July 1980): 20   ((--))

B-122 Discography in DELBANCO, Nicholas: *The Beaux Arts Trio*. New York:
Morrow, 1985: 251-254   ((--))

B-123 The Beaux Trio on compact disc [Manufacturer's list] S.l.: Philips,
1986? 1 leaf. ((--))

BECKMAN-SHCHERBINA, ELENA, 1882-1951   (Russian pianist)

B-124 METHUEN-CAMPBELL, James: Early Soviet pianists and their recordings:
a survey in *Recorded Sound*, No. 83 (January 1983): 1-16   ((--))

BEDDOE, DAN, 1863-1937   (Welsh Tenor)

B-125 LEWIS, Gareth H. Discography in *Record Collector*, XXXIII/1-2
(January 1988): 10-16   ((3, 6, 7))

BEECHAM, THOMAS, SIR, 1879-1961   (English conductor)

B-126 CHENLEY, R. B.: Sir Thomas Beecham and Berlioz: a diskography in
Berlioz Society Newsletter, No. 35 (June 1961): 8-10   ((--))

B-127 Sir Thomas Beecham Society: *Sir Thomas Beecham discography*.
Westport, CT: Greenwood Press, 1978.   77 pp.   ((1, 3, 4, 5, 6, 7))
[Reprinted from the Society's ed. of 1975]

B-128 GRAY, Michael H.: *Beecham: a centenary discography*. New York: Holmes
& Meier; London: Duckworth, 1979. 129 pp. ((1, 3, 4, 5, 6, 7))

B-129 HOEFFLER, Paul J.: The recordings of Sir Thomas Beecham in *FM Guide*,
IX/9 (1979): 24-27   ((--))

B-130 Discographie Sir Thomas Beecham in *fono forum* (May 1981): [30]-31
((--))

BEESON, JACK, 1921-   (American composer)

B-131 [[Discography in SEITZER, Janet E.: *The solo piano works of Jack
Beeson*. [DMA, Peabody Conservatory, 1986]   166 pp.]]

BEETHOVEN, LUDWIG VAN, 1770-1827   (German composer)

B-132 Discos in ODOARDO, Carmen: *Ludwig van Beethoven, bicentenario de su
nacimiento: bibliografía conmemorativa: discos, libros, partituras*.
Habana: Biblioteca Nacional José Martí, 1970: 1-19   ((--))

B-133 MARNAT, Marcel: Discographie in BOUCOURECHLIEV, André: *Beethoven*.
Paris: Seuil, [1976], c1963: 180-185   ((--))

B-134   Beethoven muvei hanglemezen in GAL, Zsuzsa: *Ludwig van Beethoven.* Budapest: Zeneműkiadó, 1977: 229-[233] ((--))

B-135   Discography in RODMAN, Selden: *The heart of Beethoven.* New York: Shorewood Pub. Co., 1977: 149-151 ((--))

B-136   BRIGGS, John: *The collector's Beethoven.* Westport, CT: Greenwood Press, 1978. 152 pp. ((--)) [Reprinted from the 1962 ed. published by Lippincot, New York]

B-137   Verzeichnis wichtiger Schall-Produktionen Beehovenscher Werke in WESSLING, Berndt W.: *Beethoven.* München: Heyne, 1978, 1982: 295-306 ((--))

B-138   Discografia Beethoveniana in RESCIGNO, Eduardo: *Beethoven.* Milano: Fabbri, 1979: 131-136 ((--))

CHAMBER WORKS

QUARTETS, STRING

B-139   BARBIER, Pierre-E.: Petit guide discographique in *Diapason-Harmonie,* No. 309 (October 1985): 101 ((--))

B-140   [[[Discography] in LONCHAMPT, Jacques: *Les quatuors à cordes de Beethoven: guide d'audition.* Paris: Fayard, 1987: 195]]

QUINTET, PIANO AND WINDS, Op. 16

B-141   [[Discography in OHLSSON, Eric Paul: *The quintets for piano, oboe, clarinet, horn and bassoon by Wolfgang Amadeus Mozart and Ludwig van Beethoven.* [DMA, Ohio State University, 1980] 130 pp.]]

SONATAS, VIOLIN

SONATA, VIOLIN AND PIANO, No. 9, Op. 47

B-142   BARBIER, Pierre-E.: Sonate "à Kreutzer"; essai de catalogue discographique in *Diapason,* No. 203 (January 1976): 17 ((5))

CHORAL WORKS

MISSA SOLEMNIS, Op. 123 (1818-1823)

B-143   Discography in FISKE, Roger: *Beethoven's Missa Solemnis.* New York: Scribner's; London: Elek, 1979: [118]-120 ((--))

STAGE WORKS

EGMONT (1810)

B-144   MARINELLI, Carlo: [Discography] in Roma, Teatro dell'Opera, season 1968: program pp. 168-170 ((5))

B-145   MARINELLI, Carlo: [Discography] in Venezia, Teatro la Fenice, season 1979-80: program pp. 551-552 ((7))

FIDELIO (1805)

B-146   MARINELLI, Carlo: [Discography] in Roma, Teatro dell'Opera, season 1970-71: program pp. 118-125   ((5))

B-147   MARINELLI, Carlo: [Discography] in Roma, Teatro dell'Opera, season 1976-77: program pp. 246-260   ((5))

B-148   WERBA, Robert: "Fidelio" auf der Schallplatte; eine kritische Diskographie der Gesamtaufnahmen in *Österreichsiche Musikzeitschrift*, XXXI/3 (March 1977): 161-164   ((--))

B-149   SEGALINI, Sergio: Discographie in *L'Avant Scène Opéra*, No. 10 (May-June 1977): 102-105; LETELLIER, Charles: [Discography of performances on 78 rpm records]   ((1, 3, 5, 7))

B-150   Discographie nach dem Katalog Bielefelder--K in PAHLEN, Kurt: *Fidelio*. München: Goldmann, 1978: 187-188   ((--)) (Opern der Welt)

B-151   MARINELLI, Carlo: Discography in Program notes for Teatro La Fenice, Venice, 1979-80 season: 422-438   ((5))

B-152   Discography in *Fidelio*. London: J. Calder; New York: Riverrun Press, 1980: 90-92   ((--))   (English National Opera guide; 4)

B-153   HOLLAND, Dietmar: Anmerkungen zur Diskographie in *Fidelio: Texte, Materialien, Kommentäre*. Reinbek bei Hamburg: Rowohlt, 1981: 214-217   ((--))   (Rororo Opernbücher)

B-154   [[[Discography] in *Stimmen, die um die Welt gingen*, No. 6 (December 1984): 5-11]]

B-155   JOELSON-STROHBACH, Harry: Diskographie der Gesamtaufnahmen in HESS, Willy: *Das Fidelio-Buch: Beethovens Oper Fidelio, ihre Geschichte und ihre drei Fassungen*. Wintherthur: Amadeus, 1986: 415-421   ((1, 7))

PIANO WORKS

DIABELLI VARIATIONS, Op. 120

B-156   OLIVIER, Philippe: 33 variations sur une valse de Diabelli, opus 120 de Beethoven: discographie critique in *Diapason*, No. 224 (January 1978): 52-53; addendum in *Diapason*, No. 226 (March 1978): 113   ((--))

SONATAS, PIANO

SONATA, PIANO, No. 31, Op. 110

B-157   PHILIPPOT, Michel-P.: L'opus 100 de Beethoven: discographie critique in *Diapason*, No. 208 (June-July 1976): 26-28   ((--))

SYMPHONIES

B-158   [Beethoven 9 Symphonies discography] in *Stereo Geijutsu*, No. 64 (July 1973): [119]-150   ((5))

B-159   The complete discography: Beethoven 9 Symphonies in *Record Geijutsu*, No. 355 (April 1980): 193-195   ((5, 7))

B-160   LEMAIRE, François-C.: Les symphonies de Beethoven: discographie des intégrales in *Harmonie-Opéra Hi-fi Conseil*, No. 15 (December 1981): 27-38   ((5))

B-161   [Beethoven 9 Symphonies discography] in *Stereo Geijutsu*, No. 191 (December 1982): 50-66   ((5, 7))

B-162   Discographie des symphonies de Beethoven [Furtwängler performances only] in *Harmonie-Panorama musique*, No. (April 1983): 59   ((1, 7))

B-163   [[[Discography, of 1927 recordings] in *Stimmen, die um die Welt gingen*, No. 5 (September 1984): 23-27]]

B-164   Discographische Hinweise: Aufnahmen der Beethoven Sinfonien zwischen 1980 und 1987 in *fono forum* (June 1987): 23, 25   ((--))

SYMPHONY, No. 1, C Major, Op. 21

B-165   [Discography] in *Stereo Geijutsu*, No. 60 (April 1973): 185   ((5))

SYMPHONY, No. 5, C Minor, Op. 67

B-166   [Discography] in *Stereo Geijutsu*, No. 132 (July 1978): 57-58   ((1, 5, 7))

SYMPHONY, No. 9, D Minor, Op. 125

B-167   [Discography] in *Stereo Geijutsu*, No. 138 (December 1978): 68-70   ((5, 7))

B-168   MARINELLI, Carlo: [Discography] in Venezia, Teatro la Fenice, Lirica, 1979-80: program pp. 555-563   ((7))

B-169   [Discography] in *Record Geijutsu*, No. 363 (December 1980): 188-191   ((1, 5, 7))

B-170   [Discography] in *Stereo Geijutsu*, No. 196 (December 1982): 50-66   ((7))

BEGALIYEV, MURAT   (Soviet composer)

B-171 Discography in *Music in the USSR* (January-March 1986): 16   ((--))

BEHR-SCHNABEL, THERESE, 1876-1959   (German soprano)

B-172 LEWIS, Paul: Therese Behr-Schnabel (1876-1959) in *Record Collector*, XXXIII/8-10 (August 1988): [214]-225   ((3, 6, 7))

BELARSKY, SIDOR   (American cantor)

B-173 COHEN, Jeffrey M.: *Bibliography & discography of music by Sidor Belarsky.* Unpublished dissertation for Cantors Institute, Seminary

College of Jewish Music, Jewish Theological Seminary of America, New York, 1986. 56 pp. ((4))

BELINSKY, ALEXANDER (Russian composer)

B-174 Discography in *Music in the USSR* (October–December 1985): 79 ((--))

BELLINCIONI, GEMMA, 1864–1950 (Italian soprano)

B-175 MORAN, W. R.: The recordings of Gemma Bellincioni (1864–1950) in STAGNO BELLINCIONI, Bianca: *Roberto Stagno e Gemma Bellincioni intimi*. New York: Arno Press, 1977: [140] ((3, 7) [Includes notes on playing speeds]

BELLINI, VINCENZO, 1801–1835 (Italian composer)

B-176 BELLINGARDI, Luigi: Discografia in ADAMO, Maria Rosaria: *Vincenzo Bellini*. Torino: ERI, 1981: 557–562 ((1, 5, 7))

B-177 Éléments de discographie in BRUNEL, Pierre: *Vincenzo Bellini*. Paris: Fayard, 1981: [392]–397 ((7))

OPERAS

BEATRICE DI TENDA (1833)

B-178 MARINELLI, Carlo: [Discography] in Palermo, Ente automono Teatro Massimo, season 1986–87: program p. 4 ((5))

(I) CAPULETI E I MONTECCHI (1830)

B-179 MARINELLI, Carlo: [Discography] in Roma, Teatro dell'Opera, season 1978–79: program pp. 144–150 ((5))

B-180 MARINELLI, Carlo: [Discography] in Palermo, Ente autonomo Teatro Masimo, anno artistico 1981–1982: program p. 13 ((7))

B-181 MARINELLI, Carlo: [Discography] in Milano, Teatro alla Scala, season 1986–87: program pp. 111–112 ((5))

NORMA (1831)

B-182 MARINELLI, Carlo: [Discography] in Roma, Teatro dell'Opera, season 1968–69: program pp. 517–519 ((5))

B-183 [[[Discography] in *Record Geijutsu* (No. 6, 1971):]]

B-184 MARINELLI, Carlo: [Discography] in Venezia, Teatro La Fenice, season lirica, 1971–72: program pp. 377–380 (())

B-185 MARINELLI, Carlo: [Discography] in Roma, Teatro dell'Opera, season 1971–72: program pp. 402–411 ((5))

B-186 TUBEUF, André: Discographie in *L'Avant Scène Opéra*, No. 29 (Sepember–October 1980): 108–111 ((1, 7))

B-187 ARNAUD, Alain: Le point sur Norma in *Diapason*, No. 255 (November 1980): 46–47 ((7))

B-188   GUANDALINI, Gina: Ma quan belle Norme, Madama Dore in *Discoteca Hi-Fi*, No. 211, (November 1980): XIII–XV (after page 64)   ((5))

(IL) PIRATA (1827)

B-189   MARINELLI, Carlo: [Discography] in Palermo, Ente autonomo Teatro Massimo, anno artistica 1985–86: program p. 3   ((7))

I PURITANI DI SCOZIA (1835)

B-190   MARINELLI, Carlo: [Discography] in Roma, Teatro dell'Opera, season 1970–71: program pp. 617–618   ((5))

B-191   MARINELLI, Carlo: [Discography] in Venezia, Teatro La Fenice, season lirica 1975–76: program pp. 226–234   ((5))

B-192   Scheda discografia in *Musica*, No. 38 (October 1985): 44   ((--))

B-193   TUBEUF, André: Discographie in *L'Avant Scéne Opèra*, No. 96 (March 1987): 106–113   ((1, 5))

QUI LA VOCE

B-194   GUANDALINI, Gina: Qui la voce, trent'anni dopo in *Musica*, No. 15 (December 1979): 298–299   ((7))

(LA) SONNAMBULA (1831)

B-195   MARINELLI, Carlo: [Discography] in Treviso, Ente Teatro Communale, Autunno Musicale Trevigiano 1978: program p. 8   ((7))

B-196   MARINELLI, Carlo: [Discography] in Bologna, Ente autonomo Teatro Comunale, Opera e Balletto, 1978–79: program pp. 35–45   ((7))

B-197   MARINELLI, Carlo: [Discography] in Palermo, Ente autonomo Teatro Massimo, anno artistico 1980–81: program p. 22   ((7))

B-198   MARINELLI, Carlo: [Discography] in Roma, Teatro dell'Opera, season 1981–82: program pp. 824–831   ((5))

B-199   MARINELLI, Carlo: [Discography] in Venezia, Teatro Malibran Teatro La Fenice, 1984 season [?]: program pp. 419–423   ((7))

B-200   MARINELLI, Carlo: [Discography] in Milano, Teatro alla Scala, season 1985–86: program pp. 91–97   ((5))

BENNETT, RICHARD RODNEY, 1936–   (English composer)

B-201 HUGHES, Eric and DAY, Timothy: Richard Rodney Bennett in *Recorded Sound*, No. 81 (January 1982): 59–77   ((1))   (Discographies of British composers; 14)

BENNETT, ROBERT RUSSELL, 1984–1981   (American composer/arranger)

B-202 Selected discography in Program notes for *Winds of change: music for wind ensemble by Robert Russell Bennett...* [Sound recording] New World Records NW 211, 1977: 3   ((--))

BENNETT, WILLIAM STERNDALE, 1875–1916   (English composer)

B-203 [[STERNDALE BENNETT, Barry: Sir William Sterndale Bennett discography (1816–1875) in *British Music Society Journal*, I (1979): 41–46]]

BENOIST, ANDRÉ, 1879–1953   (French pianist)

B-204 MALTESE, John Anthony: An André Benoist Discography in BENOIST, André: *The accompanist … and friends*. Neptune City, NJ: Paganiniana Publications, 1978: 349–370   ((--))

BENTZON, NIELS VIGGO, 1919–   (Danish composer)

B-205 Grammofonplaten med voeku af Niels Viggo Bentzons in MØLLERHOJ, Klaes: *Niels Viggo Bentzon*. Kóbenhavn: Ed. Wilhelm Hansen, 1980: 104–111   ((--))

BERBERIAN, CATHY, 1925–1983   (American soprano)

B-206 [Berberian discography] in *Record Geijutsu*, No. 276 (September 1973): 194–195   ((--))

B-207 Discografia in *Discoteca Hifi*, No. 221 (September 1981): 14–15 ((--))

BERG, ALBAN, 1885–1935   (Austrian composer)

B-208 WALKER, Arthur D.: An Alban Berg discography in *International Alban Berg Society Newsletter*, No. 3 (January 1975): 8–10   ((5))

B-209 HALBREICH, Harry: Alban Berg parmi nous: discographie critique in *Harmonie*, No. 146 (April 1979): 80–99   ((--))

B-210 A critical discography in MONSON, Karen: *Alban Berg*. Boston: Houghton Mifflin Co., 1979: [371]–373   ((--)) [Omits record numbers]

B-211 Discographische Hinweise Alban–Berg–Edition der Deutsche Grammophon in *fono forum* (May 1985): 26   ((5))

B-212 HALBREICH, Harry: Berg en mémoire in *Diapason–Harmonie* No. 307 (July–August 1985): 20–27   ((--))

CHAMBER WORKS

B-213 RIEHN, Rainer: Diskographie in *Alban Berg, Kammermusik I.* München: Edition Text u. Kritik, 1978: 76   ((--)) (Musik-Konzepte; 4)

B-214 HOLLAND, Dietmar: Auswahldiskographie in *Alban Berg. Kammermusik II.* München: Edition Text u. Kritik, 1979: 96–100   ((--)) (Musik-Konzepte; 9)

OPERAS

LULU (1934)

B-215   MARINELLI, Carlo: [Discography] in Roma, Teatro dell'Opera,
         season 1967-68: program pp. 298-300   ((5))

B-216   HOLLAND, Dietmar: Anmerkungen zur Diskographie in *Lulu; Texte,
         Materialien, Kommentäre*. Reinbek bei Hamburg: Rowohlt, 1985:
         308-311   ((5))   (Rororo Opernbücher)

WOZZECK (1925)

B-217   HOLLAND, Dietmar: Anmerkungen zur Diskographie in *Wozzeck: Texte,
         Materialien, Kommentäre*. Reinbeck bei Hamburg: Rowohlt, 1980:
         281-282   ((5))   (Rororo Opernbücher)

B-218   MARINELLI, Carlo: Discografia ragionata del Wozzeck in *Musica*,
         No. 19 (December 1980): 352-357   ((7))

B-219   GUEULLETTE, Alain: Discographie in *L'Avant Scéne Opèra*, No. 36
         (September-October 1981): 138-141   ((1, 7))

ORCHESTRAL WORKS

CONCERTO FOR VIOLIN (1935)

B-220   Discographische Hinweise: Alban Berg Violinkonzerte in *fono forum*
         (September 1985): 30   ((--))

BERGANZA, TERESA, 1934-   **(Spanish mezzo-soprano)**

B-221 Discography, Deutsche Grammophon artist information. 1980, 2 pp.
      ((--))

B-222 Discographie in SEGALINI, Sergio: *Teresa Berganza*.   Paris: Fayard,
      1982: [108]-[110]   ((5))

BERGER, ARTHUR, 1912-   **(American composer)**

B-223 Selected discography in Program notes for *Arthur Berger: Five pieces
      for piano; septet.* [Sound recording] New World Records NW 308,
      1980: [2]   ((--))

BERIO, LUCIANO, 1925-   **(Italian composer)**

B-224 ...Schallaufnahmen in DRESSEN, Norbert: *Sprache und Musik bei
      Luciano Berio.* Regensburg: Bosse, 1982: 278-279   ((5))

B-225 Discographie in STOÏANOVA, Ivanka: *Luciano Berio: chemins en
      musique.* [Paris]: Editions Richard-Masse, 1985: 487-492   ((--))

SINFONIA (1968)

B-226 Verzeichnis und Diskografie stand Januar 1977 in ALTMAN, Peter:
      Sinfonia von Luciano Berio: Eine Analytische Studie. Wien:
      Universal, 1977. 57-61   ((--))

BERKELEY, LENNOX, SIR, 1903-   **(English composer)**

B-227 HUGHES, Eric and DAY, Timothy: Sir Lennox Berkeley in *Recorded
      Sound*, No. 77 (January 1980): 63-79   ((--))   (Discographies of

British composers; 1) [Reprinted as a pamphlet, 1980]

BERLIOZ, HECTOR, 1803-1869   (French composer)

B-228   CHENLEY, R. B.: Sir Thomas Beecham and Berlioz: a diskography in *Berlioz Society Newsletter*, No. 35 (June 1961): 8-10   ((--))

B-229   Diskographie in DÖMLING, Wolfgang: *Hector Berlioz in Selbstzeugnissen und Bilddokumenten*. Reinbek bei Hamburg: Rowholt, 1977: 153-[154]   ((--))

B-230   Discographic references in *Hector Berlioz*. Paris: Bibliothèques de la Ville de Paris, 1979: 28 pp.   ((--))

B-231   VIDAL, Pierre: L'oeuvre de Berlioz: discographie critique in *Harmonie-Opéra-Hifi Conseil*, No. 23 (September 1982): 34-45   ((3))

STAGE WORKS

(LA) DAMNATION DE FAUST (1846)

B-232   CONDÉ, Gerard: La damnation de Faust par Hector Berlioz: discographie comparée in *Harmonie*, No. 139 (September 1978): 104-109   ((--))

B-233   [[Discography in *L'Avant Scène Opéra*, No. 22 [1979?]]]

B-234   CECCONI-BOTELLA, Monic: Le point sur La damnation de Faust de Berlioz in *Diapason*, No. 252 (July-August 1980): 40-41   ((5))

B-235   [[[Discographie comparée] in *Opéra International*, No. 62 (September 1983):]]

B-236   MARINELLI, Carlo: Discografie: Faust e Mefistofele nelle opere teatrali e sinfonico-vocali in *Quaderni dell'I.R.TE.M.* [Instituto di Ricerca per il Teatro Musicale] No. 3 (1986): 5-26   ((5))

(LES) TROYENS (1860/3)

B-237   MARINELLI, Carlo: [Discography] in Milano, Teatro alla Scala, season 1981-82: program pp. 119-122   ((5))

B-238   [[[Discography] in *Hector Berlioz, Les troyens*. Cambridge; New York: Cambridge University Press, 1988: (Cambridge opera handbooks)]]

ORCHESTRAL WORKS

B-239   [[Discography in NOWALIS, Sister Susan Marie: *Timbre as as structural device in Berlioz' symphonies*. [Dissertation, Case Western Reserve University, 1975] 192 pp.]]

HAROLD EN ITALIE, Op. 16 (1834)

B-240   BOUILLON, Elisabeth: Hector Berlioz: Harold en Italie: [discographie comparée] in *Harmonie*, No. 147 (May 1979): [84]-91   ((5))

B-241   Tutte le edizioni discografiche dell `Aroldo in Italia' in
         Musica, No. 46 (October 1987): 32   ((5))

SYMPHONIE FANTASTIQUE, Op. 14 (1830)

B-242   ROY, Jean: Le point sur la Symphonie fantastique d'Hector
         Berlioz in *Diapason*, No. 284 (June 1983): 38-39   ((--))

B-243   WEBER, J. F.: Berlioz--Symphonie fantastique in Clues to composer
         discography in *ARSC Journal*, XV/2-3 (1983): 56-65   ((3, 4, 5, 6,
         7))

BERMAN, LAZAR, 1930-   (Russian pianist)

B-244   MASINI, Umberto: Lazar Berman: intervista e discografia in *Musica*,
        No. 15 (December 1979): 300-304   ((7))

B-245   Discography, Deutsche Grammophon artist information, 1980, 1 pp.
        ((--))

BERNAL-RESKY, GUSTAVO   (Baritone)

B-246   [Discography] in *Record Collector*, IX/3 (March 1954): 62-63   ((--))

BERNAOLA, CARMELO, 1929-   (Spanish composer)

B-247   Discografía in IGLESIAS, Antonio: *Carmelo Bernaola*. Madrid:
        Espasa-Calpe, 1982: [153]   ((--))

BERNSTEIN, LEONARD, 1918-   (American composer/conductor)

B-248   Bernstein/Boulez discography in *Record Geijutsu*, No. 288 (September
        1974): 205-216   ((7))

B-249   Discography in GOTTLIEB, Jack: *Leonard Bernstein; a complete
        catalogue of his works*. New York: Amberson Enterprises, 1978: 35-43
        ((--))

B-250   Discography in ROBINSON, Paul: *Bernstein*. New York: Vanguard Press,
        1982: 112-148   ((7))

B-251   Schallplatten mit Werke Bernsteins in GRADENWITZ, Peter: *Leonard
        Bernstein*. Zürich: Atlantis Musikbuch-Verlag, 1984: 353-356   ((--))

STAGE WORKS

B-252   Selected discography of Leonard Bernstein's theater music in
         Program notes for *Candide*. [Sound recording] New World Records
         NW 340/341, 1982: [7]   ((--))

(THE) DYBBUK (1974)

B-253   [[Discography in PEARLMUTTER, Alan Jay: *Leonard Bernstein's
         Dybbuk: an analysis including historical, religious, and literary
         perspectives of Hasidic life and lore*. [DMA, Peabody Conservatory
         of Music, 1985]   345 pp.]]

TROUBLE IN TAHITI (1952)

B-254   MARINELLI, Carlo: [Discography] in Milano, Teatro alla Scala, season 1983-84: program p. 79   ((7))

BÉROFF, MICHEL, 1950–   (French pianist)

B-255   Discographie de Michel Béroff in *Harmonie Hi-fi conseil*, No. 8 (April 1981): 24   ((--))

BERTI, ROMEO, 1867-1954   (Italian tenor)

B-256   [Discography] in *Record Collector*, IX/3 (March 1954): 63   ((--))

BETTINELLI, BRUNO, 1913–   (Italian composer)

B-257   Discografia in SCOGNAMIGLIO, Riccardo: Bruno Bettinelli in *Discoteca Hi Fi*, No. 216 (April 1981): 28-29   ((--))

BIALAS, GÜNTER, 1907–   (German composer)

B-258   Schallplatten in *Meilensteine eines Komponistenlebens: kleine Festschr. zum 70 Geburtstag von Günter Bialas.*   Kassel; Basel; Tours; London: Bärenreiter, 1977: 121   ((--))

B-259   Diskographie in *Günter Bialas.*   Tutzing: H. Schneider, 1984: 147 ((--))   (Komponisten in Bayern; 5)

BIGGS, EDWARD POWER, 1906-1977   (American organist)

B-260   E. Power Biggs discography in *AGO*, XII/3 (March 1978): 30-31, 42 ((7))

B-261   Discography in Program notes for *A tribute to E. Power Biggs.* [Sound recording] Columbia M4X 35180, 1979: 9-31   ((5))

B-262   KAZDIN, Andrew: E. Power Biggs discography in OWEN, Barbara: *E. Power Biggs, concert organist.*   Bloomington: Indiana University Press, 1987: 220-228   ((5))   [Reprinted from the AGO discography, above]

BILLINGS, WILLIAM, 1746-1800   (American composer)

B-263   KROEGER, Karl: A discography of William Billings' music in *Sonneck Society Journal*, XIII/2 (Summer 1987): 51-53   ((--))

BINCHOIS, GILLES, ca. 1400-1460   (French composer)

B-264   WEBER, J. F.: A discography of the music of Gilles Binchois in *Fanfare*, V/2 (November-December 1981): 118-122   ((3, 5, 7))

BIRCH, MONTAGUE

See entry for

BOURNEMOUTH SYMPHONY ORCHESTRA

BIRET, IDIL   (Turkish pianist)

B-265   Discographisches Hinweise in *fono forum* (December 1986): 32   ((--))

BIRTWISTLE, HARRISON, 1934–   (English composer)

B-266 HUGHES, Eric and DAY, Timothy: Harrison Birtwistle in *Recorded Sound*, No. 78 (July 1980): 91–100 ((--)) (Discographies of British composers; 5)

B-267 Discographic notes in HALL, Michael: *Harrison Birtwistle*. London: Robson Books, 1984. 186 pp. ((--))

BIZET, GEORGES, 1838–1875 (French composer)

B-268 Discografie in RAŢIU, Ileana: *Bizet*. Bucuresti: Editura muzicala, 1974: 183–[188]   ((--))

B-269 DOISY, Marcel: L'oeuvre de Georges Bizet: discographie critique in *Harmonie-Opéra-Hifi Conseil*, No. 21 (June 1982): 24–33   ((--))

B-270 Discographie in ROY, Jean: *Bizet*. Paris: Seuil, 1983: 180–185 ((--))

OPERAS

CARMEN (1875)

B-271   MARINELLI, Carlo: [Discography] in Roma, Teatro dell'Opera, season 1969–70: program pp. 343–358 ((5))

B-272   MARINELLI, Carlo: [Discography] in Venezia, Teatro La Fenice, season lirica, 1970–71: program pp. 469–478 ((5))

B-273   MARINELLI, Carlo: [Discography] in Milano, Teatro alla Scala, season 1973–74: program pp. 74–86 ((5))

B-274   [[Discografia in *Guida illustrada a `Carmen'*. Milano: Fabbri, 1975. 94 pp.]]

B-275   FANTAPIÉ, Alain: 15 Carmen revisitées; discographie critique in *Diapason*, No. 211 (November 1976): 35–37 ((7))

B-276   THALMANN, Albert: Discographie in *Carmen: in der original-sprache*. München: W. Goldmann, 1979: 334–339 ((5)) (Opern der Welt)

B-277   MANNONI, Gérard: Discographie in *L'Avant Scéne Opèra*, No. 26 (March–April 1980): 122–129 ((1, 7))

B-278   MARINELLI, Carlo: [Discography] in Palermo, Ente automono Teatro Massimo, season 1980–81: program p. 54 ((5))

B-279   HOYLE, Martin: Discography in *Carmen*. London: J. Calder; New York: Riverrun Press, 1982: 127–128 ((--)) (English National Opera guide; 13)

B-280   Discografia in *Musica*, No. 34 (October 1984): 16 ((7))

B-281   THIELEN, Hugo: Anmerkungen zur Diskographie in *Carmen: Texte, Materialien, Kommentäre*. Reinbek bei Hamburg: Rowohlt, 1984:

303-[312] ((1, 5)) (Rororo Opernbücher)

B-282   MARINELLI, Carlo: [Discography] in Milano, Teatro all Scala, season 1984-85: pp. 140-142 ((5))

B-283   MARINELLI, Carlo: [Discography] in Roma, Teatro dell'Opera, season 1986-87: program pp. 47-62 ((5))

(LES) PECHEURS DE PERLES (1863)

B-284   MARINELLI, Carlo: [Discography] in Treviso, Ente Teatro Comunale, Autunno Musicale Trevigiano, season lirica 1975: program p. 3 ((5))

B-285   MARINELLI, Carlo: [Discography] in Bologna, Ente autonomo Teatro Comunale, Opera e Balletto, 1979-80: program pp. 43-50 ((7))

BJÖRLING, JUSSI, 1911-1960 (Swedish tenor)

B-286   ELFSTRÖM, Mats: Jussi Björling first records in *Record Research*, No. 137-138 (February-March 1976): 13 ((3, 5))

B-287   ENGLUND, Björn: Jussi Björling: discographical notes in *Talking Machine Review*, No. 59 (August 1979): 1598 ((3, 7))

B-288   PORTER, Jack and HENRYSSON, Harald: *A Jussi Bjoerling discography.* Indianapolis, Ind.: Jussi Bjoerling Memorial Archive, 1982. 192 pp. ((1, 3, 4, 5, 6, 7))

B-289   HENRYSSON, Harald and PORTER, Jack: *A Jussi Björling phonography.* Stockholm: Svenskt Musikhistoriskt arkiv, 1984. 269 pp. ((1, 3, 4, 5, 6, 7))

BLACHER, BORIS, 1903-1975 (German composer)

B-290   Discographic references in *Boris Blacher; Werkverzeichnis.* Berlin: Bote & Boch, [1967?] 24 pp. ((--))

BLACK COMPOSERS

B-291   [[DE LERMA, Dominique-René: *The collector's guide to recordings of music by Black composers.* Bloomington, IN: Denia Press, 1973. 28 pp.]]

B-292   DE LERMA, Dominique-René: *A discography of concert music by black composers.* Minneapolis: Afro-American Music Opportunities Association, 1973. 29 pp. ((4, 5))

B-293   DE LERMA, Dominique-René: *Concert music and spirituals: a selective discography.* Nashville: Fisk University Insitute for Research in Black American Music, 1981. 44 pp. ((5)) (IRBAM occasional papers; 1)

B-294   Selected discography in WHITE, Evelyn Davidson: *Choral music by Afro-American composers: a selected, annotated bibliography.* Metuchen, NJ: Scarecrow Press, 1981: 146-163 ((--))

B-295   [[DE LERMA, Dominique-René: *Black concert and recital music: a*

selective discography. Beverly Hills, CA: Theodore Front Musical
Literature, 198-?.]]

B-296 Black composers: a discography in DE LERMA, Dominique-René:
Composers beyond the pale in *Tarakan Music Letter*, IV/3 (January-
February 1983): 1, 4-5 ((--))

B-297 [[Discography] in SOUTHERN, Eileen: *The music of black Americans:
a history.* 2nd ed. New York: Norton, 1983]]

B-298 [[DE LERMA, Dominique-René: A concordance of scores and recording of
music by Black composers in *Black Music Research Journal* (1984):
60-140]]

BLACK MUSICIANS

B-299 Selected discography in DE LERMA, Dominique-René: Black conductors
and concert instrumentalists in *Tarakan Music Letter*, V/1
(September-October 1983): 1, 4-6 ((--))

BLACK SINGERS

B-300 TURNER, Patricia: *Afro-American singers: an index and preliminary
discography of long-playing recordings of opera, choral music, and
song.* Minneapolis: Turner, 1976. 240 pp. ((4))

B-301 TURNER, Patricia: *Afro-American singers: an index and preliminary
discography of long-playing recordings of opera, choral, music, and
song.* Minneapolis: Challenge Productions, 1977. 225 pp. Supplement
1980. Minneapolis: P. Turner, 1980. 44 l.; additional supplement
entitled "Afro-American singers: an index and discography of opera,
choral music, and song" in *The Black perspective in Music*, IX
(Spring 1981): 73-90 ((5))

B-302 Selected discography in DE LERMA, Dominique-René: The liberation of
the black singer: from minstrelsy to opera in *Tarakan Music Letter*,
V/2 (November-December 1983): 1, 14-16 ((--))

BLAKE, DAVID, 1936-   (English composer)

B-303 HUGHES, Eric and DAY, Timothy: Discography in *Recorded Sound*, No. 85
(January 1984): 71-74 ((--)) (Discographies of British composers;
20)

BLAUTH, BRENNO, 1931-   (Brazilian composer)

B-304 Discographic references in FERREIRA, Paulo Affonso de Moura: *Brenno
Blauth: catálogo de obras.* [Brasília]: Ministério das Relações
Exteriores, Departamento de Cooperação Cultural, Científica e
Tecnológica, 1977: [30] pp. ((--)) (Compositores brasileiros)

BLECH, LEO, 1871-1958 (German conductor)

B-305 X. Discografie in POCH, Wolfgang: *Leo Blech.* [Dissertation, Free
University of Berlin, 1985]: 246-280 ((1, 7))

BLISS, SIR ARTHUR, 1891-1975 (English composer)

B-306 GUYATT, Andrew L.: A discography of Bliss in *Le Grand Baton*, No. 36
(March 1977): 11-22   ((1, 7))

B-307 Discography in FOREMAN, Lewis: *Arthur Bliss, catalogue of the
complete works.* Sevenoaks: Novello, 1980: 127-138   ((--))

B-308 GUYATT, Andrew L.: A Bliss discography,   2d ed. in *British Music
Society Journal*, II (1980): 28-37   ((5))

B-309 Discography additions in EASTERBROOK, Giles: *Arthur Bliss:
supplement to catalogue of the complete works.* Sevenoaks, Kent:
Novello, 1982: 10-11   ((--)) [Supplement to Foreman, above]

B-310 Discography in CRAGGS, Stewart R.: *Arthur Bliss: a bio-bibliography.*
New York: Greenwood Press, 1988: 69-80   ((5))   (Bio-bibliographies
in music; 13)

BLOCH, ERNEST, 1880-1959   (Swiss-American composer)

B-311 SKOLSKY, Syd: List of recordings of music by Ernest Bloch in *The
music of Ernest Bloch: a program manual.* Prepared by the National
Jewish Music Council. [s.l.]:   The Council, 1955: 60-64   ((--))

B-312 LETHERER, Gary P.: Discography in BLOCH, Suzanne: *Ernest Bloch:
creative spirit: a program source book.*   New York: Jewish Music
Council of the National Jewish Welfare Board, 1976: 107-116   ((1))

B-313 Discography in STRASSBURG, Robert: *Ernest Bloch; voice in the
wilderness.* Los Angeles: Trident Shop, 1977: [163]-175   ((--))

B-314 [[[Discography] in KUSHNER, David: *Ernest Bloch: a guide to
research.* New York: Garland Pub., 1988]]

BLOMDAHL, CARL BIRGER, 1916-1968   (Swedish composer)

B-315 Karl-Birger Blomdahl: Diskografi/Discography in Program notes for
Aniara. [Sound recording] Caprice CAP 2016, 1985: [40]   ((--))

BLOW, JOHN, 1649-1708   (English composer)

VENUS AND ADONIS

B-316   MARINELLI, Carlo: [Discography] in Venezia, Teatro La Fenice, 1981:
Program pp. 519-520   ((7))

BOCCHERINI, LUIGI, 1743-1805   (Italian composer)

B-317 [[Discography in AMSTERDAM, Ellen I.: *The string quintets of Luigi
Boccherini.* [Dissertation, University of California at Berkeley,
1968]   177 pp.]]

BOCKELMANN, RUDOLF, 1892-1958   (German bass-baritone)

B-318 DAHMEN, Ulrich: Rudolf Bockelmann--a discography in *Record Collector*,
XXX/10-11 (October 1985): 232-238   ((1, 3, 6, 7))

B-319 [[[Discography] in *Stimmen, die um die Welt gingen*, No. 5 (September
1984):   48-54]]

BÖHM, KARL, 1894-1981   (German conductor)

B-320   [Discography] in *Stereo Geijutsu*, No. 47 (April 1972): [111]
((5, 7))

B-321   [Karl Böhm/Record] in *Stereo Geijutsu*, No. 166 (December 1980):
[37]-52 ((5, 7))

B-322   A écouter in Böhm nous a quittes in *Diapason*, No. 264 (September
1981): 44-45 ((--))

B-323   [Karl Böhm discography] in *Record Geijutsu*, No. 373 (October 1981):
66-74 ((7))

B-324   Diskographie in ENDLER, Franz: *Karl Böhm: ein Dirigentenleben*.
Hamburg: Hoffmann und Campe, 1981: 259-279 ((7))

BÖHME, KURT, 1908-   (German bass)

B-325   Schallplatten (Gesamtaufnahmen in RICHTER, Karl: *Kurt Böhme*.
Augsburg: Schroff, 1977: 230-233 ((--))

BOERO, FELIPE, 1884-1958   (Argentinian composer)

B-326   Discografia in BOERO DE IZETA, Carlota: *Felipe Boero*.   Buenos Aires:
Ediciones Culturales Argentinas, 1978: 205-206 ((--))

BÖTEL, HEINRICH, 1854-1938 (German tenor)

B-327   [[[Discography] in *Stimmen, die um die Welt gingen*, No. 1 (1983):
20]]

BOHNEN, MICHAEL, 1887-1965   (German bass-baritone)

B-328   SCHMIDT, Jürgen: The Michael Bohnen records in *Record Collector*,
XXVII/9-10 (January 1983): 197-239 ((3, 4, 6, 7))

B-329   COLIN, R. N.: Bohnen on microgroove in *Record Collector*, XXVII/11-12
(March 1983): 271-272; Appendix 1: broadcasts: 270-271 ((1))

BOIELDIEU, FRANÇOIS ADRIEN, 1775-1834   (French composer)

B-330   Schallplatten in HUBER, Karin: *François-Adrien Boieldieu: 1775 -
1975*.   Berlin: Dt. Bibliotheksverb. Arbeitsstelle für d.
Bibliothekswesen, 1975: 37-39 ((--))

BOITO, ARRIGO, 1842-1918   (Italian composer)

OPERAS

MEFISTOFELE (1868)

B-331   MARINELLI, Carlo: Discografie: Faust e Mefistofele nelle opere
teatrali e sinfonico-vocali in *Quaderni dell'I.R.TE.M.* [Instituto
di Ricerca per il Teatro Musicale] No. 3 (1986): 68-80 ((5))

BONYNGE, RICHARD, 1930-   (Australian conductor)

B-332 Discography Richard Bonynge in ADAMS, Brian: *La Stupenda, a biography of Joan Sutherland*. Melbourne: Hutchinson of Australia, 1980: 308-312   ((--))

BORODIN STRING QUARTET, USSR

B-333 Discography in *Music in the USSR* (October-December 1986): 14

BOSTON SYMPHONY ORCHESTRA

B-334 Discography, Deutsche Grammophon artist information, 1980, 4 pp. ((--))

B-335 [Discography] in *Stereo Geijutsu*, No. 178 (November 1981): 114-119 ((7))

BOULANGER, LILI, 1893-1918   (French composer)

B-336 Discographie in *Jeunesse et Orgue*, No. 42 (1981): 50   ((--))

CHORAL WORKS

FAUST ET HÉLÈNE (1913)

B-337   MARINELLI, Carlo: Discografie: Faust e Mefistofele nelle opere teatrali e sinfonico-vocali in *Quaderni dell'I.R.TE.M.* [Instituto di Ricerca per il Teatro Musicale] No. 3 (1986): 95-97   ((5))

BOULANGER, NADIA, 1887-1979   (French pedagogue/conductor/pianist)

B-338 Discographie in MONSAINGEON, Bruno: *Mademoiselle: entretiens avec Nadia Boulanger*. Luynes: Van de Velde, 1980: 138-139; English eds.: Manchester: Carcanet Press, 1985 and Boston: Northeastern University Press, 1987: discography pp. 136-137   ((--))

BOULEZ, PIERRE, 1925-   (French composer/conductor)

B-339 [[Discography in TRENKAMP, Wilma Anne: *A throw of the dice: an analysis of selected works of Pierre Boulez*. [Dissertation, Case Western Reserve University, 1973] 247 pp.]]

B-340 [Boulez discography] in *Record Geijutsu*, No. 276 (September 1973): 180-181   ((--))

B-341 Bernstein/Boulez discography in *Record Geijutsu*, No. 288 (September 1974): 205-216   ((7))

B-342 DERRIEN, Jean-Pierre and JAMEUX, Dominique: Discographie ... in *Musique en jeu*, No. 16 (November 1974): [36]-38   ((--))

B-343 PERNICK, Ben: ... a discography; as composer, as conductor in *American Record Guide* (August 1977): 8-11, 46-47 ((--))

B-344 Discographie in JAMEUX, Dominique: *Pierre Boulez*. Paris: Fayard: Fondation SACEM, 1984: [453]-470   ((--))

B-345 Diskographie in *Festschrift Pierre Boulez*. Vienna: Universal

Edition, 1985: 211-235 ((--))

B-346 Diskografi in *Pierre Boulez: komponist, dirigent, utopist.*
[Copenhagen]: Artia med støtte fra Léon Sonnings musikfond, 1985:
58-67 ((--))

BOULOGNE, JOSEPH, CHEVALIER DE

See

SAINT-GEORGE, JOSEPH BOULOGNE, CHEVALIER DE

BOULT, SIR ADRIAN CEDRIC, 1889-1983   (English conductor)

B-347 Discography in *Sir Adrian Boult, companion of honour: a tribute.*
Tunbridge Wells, Kent.: Midas Books, 1980: 80-96 ((7))

B-348 SANDERS, Alan: *Sir Adrian Boult: a discography.* Harrow, Middlesex:
General Gramophone Publications, 1981. 37 pp. ((3, 4, 6, 7))

See also

B.B.C. SYMPHONY ORCHESTRA

BOURGUE, MAURICE, 1939-   (French oboist)

B-349 Discographie in *Harmonie-Panorama musique,* No. 39 (February 1984):
12 ((--))

BOURNEMOUTH SYMPHONY ORCHESTRA

B-350 [[UPTON, Stuart: *Sir Dan Godfrey and the Bournemouth Symphony
Orchestra: a discography.* Mascotte Society, 1970: 15]]

B-351 Discography in UPTON, Stuart: *Sir Dan Godfrey & the Bournemouth
Municipal Orchestra.* West Wickham: Vintage Light Music Society,
1979: 14-17 ((3, 7)); [with] Montague Birch [and] Rudolf Schwarz:
18; Bournemouth Symphony Orchestra discography: 34 ((--))

BOYER, MARY, 1868-1951 (French soprano)

B-352 [Discography] in *Record Collector,* IX/3 (March 1954): 63 ((--))

BOZZA, EUGÈNE, 1905-   (French composer)

B-353 [[Discography in ORNELAS, Raul Sosa: *Eugène Bozza's published
compositions for solo trumpet with piano or orchestra and an
analysis of representative compositions.* [DMA, University of
Southern Mississippi, 1986] 276 pp.]]

BRAHMS, JOHANNES, 1833-1897 (German composer)

B-354 Recommended records in JACOBSON, Bernard: *The music of Johannes
Brahms.* London: Tantivy Press; Rutherford, NJ: Fairleigh Dickinson
Press, 1977: 180-218 ((--))

B-355 Discografia brahmsiana in MARTINOTTI, Sergio: *Brahms.* Milano:
Fabbri, 1980: 133-137 ((--))

B-356   [[[Discography] in DELVAILLE, Bernard: *Brahms. L'homme et son oeuvre.* Plan de la Tour: Éditions d'aujourd'hui, 1983. [Reprinted from the 1971 ed. published by Seghers, Paris]]]

B-357   [[[Discography] in MAY, Florence: *Johannes Brahms. Die Geschichte seines Lebens.* München: Matthes & Seitz, 1983]]

CONCERTOS

CONCERTOS, PIANO AND ORCHESTRA

B-358   DEPPISCH, Walter: Vergleichende Diskographie der Klavier-Konzerte von Johannes Brahms in *Brahms Studien,* II (1977): 47-48 ((--))

CONCERTO, VIOLIN & ORCHESTRA, D Major, Op. 77 (1878)

B-359   SZERSNOVICZ, Patrick: Brahms, le concerto pour violin; discographie comparée in *Harmonie,* No. 137 (May 1978): 110-115 ((--))

B-360   BARBIER, Pierre-E.: Le point sur le Concerto pour violon et orchestre de Brahms in *Diapason,* No. 283 (May 1983): 38-39 ((--))

CHORAL WORKS

(EIN) DEUTSCHES REQUIEM, Op. 45 (1868)

B-361   LACAS, Pierre-Paul: Requiem allemand de Brahms: [discographie critique] in *Diapason,* No. 224 (January 1978): 54-55 ((--))

RHAPSODIE, Op. 53 (1869)

B-362   LAWRY, Martha: Recordings of Brahms' Rhapsodie (Op. 53) in *ARSC Journal,* XI/1 (1979): 29-36 ((1, 5, 7))

PIANO WORKS

B-363   [[Discography in MILLER, Lynus Patrick: *From analysis to performance: the musical landscape of Johannes Brahms's Opus 118, No. 6.* [Dissertation, University of Michigan, 1979] 99, 53 pp.]]

SYMPHONIES

B-364   SZERSNOVICZ, Patrick: Discographie comparée: les symphonies de Brahms in *Harmonie,* No. 156 (March 1980): 132-142 ((--))

B-365   Discographie critique in *Harmonie-Opéra Hi-Fi Conseil,* No. 28 (February 1983): 39-40 ((--))

B-366   ZEISEL, Georges: Discographie in *L'Avant Scène,* No. 53 (June 1983): 114-129 ((5, 7))

SYMPHONY, No. 1, C Minor, Op. 68 (1877)

B-367   GALLOIS, Jean: La Première Symphonie de Brahms; enregistrements confrontés in *Diapason,* No. 211 (November 1976): 32-34 ((--))

BRAIN, DENNIS, 1921-1957   (English horn player)

B-368 Appendix: recordings in PETTITT, Stephen: *Dennis Brain*. London:
Hale, 1976: [175]-184   ((1, 7))

BRANT, HENRY, 1913-   (American composer)

B-369 Selected discography in Program notes for *Winds of change: music for
wind ensemble by ...Henry Brant...* [Sound recording] New World
Records NW 211, 1977: 3   ((--))

BREAM, JULIAN, 1933-   (English guitar/lute player)

B-370 Discography in PALMER, Tony: *Julian Bream, a life on the road*.
London: Macdonald, 1982; New York: F. Watts, 1983: 204-216   ((5))

BRECHT, BERTHOLD, 1898-1956   (German playwright)

B-371 [[Discography in GILBERT, Michael John T.: *Bertolt Brecht and
music--a comprehensive study*. [Dissertation, University of Wisconsin,
1985]   443 pp.]]

BRENDEL, ALFRED, 1931-   (Austrian pianist)

B-372 [Alfred Brendel records] in *Record Geijutsu*, No. 336 (September
1978): 196-206   ((7))

B-373 PAYNE, Ifan: Alfred Brendel: a discography, 1950-1976: part 1 in
American Record Guide, XLII/2 (December 1978): 8, 10-12; part 2
in *American Record Guide*, XLII/3 (January 1979): 4, 6, 40-43
((7))

B-374 Discography [on Philips label] S.l.: [Philips 198-?]   3 l. ((--))

B-375 MOLKHOV, Jean-Michel: Alfred Brendel une discographie in
Diapason-Harmonie, No. 338 (May 1988): 58-61   ((--))

BRIAN, HAVERGAL, 1876-1972   (English composer)

B-376 Havergal Brian recordings at present available in EASTAUGH,
Kenneth: *Havergal Brian: the making of a composer*. London: Harrap,
1976: 324   ((1, 4))

B-377 A note on recordings in FOREMAN, Lewis: *Havergal Brian*. [London]:
Thames Publishing, 1976: 106   ((--))

B-378 Recordings in NETTEL, Reginald: *Havergal Brian and his music*.
London: Dobson, 1976: 214-215   ((1))

B-379 Discography in *The Tigers*. Aberdeen: Abdereen Branch of the
Havergal Brian Society, 1976: 4th preliminary page   ((--))

SYMPHONIES

B-380   Appendix III: Performances and recordings in MACDONALD, Malcolm:
The symphonies of Havergal Brian. Volume Two: Symphonies 13-29.
London: Kahn & Averill, 1978: [287]-288   ((1, 7))

BRIDGE, FRANK, 1879-1941   (English composer)

B-381   BISHOP, John: Discography in PAYNE, Anthony: *The music of Frank Bridge*. London: Thames Publishing, 1976: 84-86   ((--))

B-382   FOREMAN, Lewis, HUGHES, Eric and WALKER, Malcolm: Frank Bridge (1879-1941): a discography in *Recorded Sound*, No. 66-67, (April-July 1977): 669-673   ((1, 3, 6, 7))

B-383   Selected discography in HINDMARSH, Paul: *Frank Bridge: a thematic catalogue, 1900-1941*. London: Faber Music, 1983: 172-176   ((--))

BRISTOW, GEORGE FREDERICK, 1825-1898   (American composer)

B-384   Selected discography in Program notes for *The Wind Demon and other mid-nineteenth-century piano music*. [Sound recording] New World Records NW 257, 1976: 4   ((--))

BRITTEN, BENJAMIN, 1913-1976   (English composer)

B-385   [[Discography in RHOADS, Mary R.: *Influences of Japanese Hogaku manifest in selected compositions by Peter Mennin and Benjamin Britten*. [Dissertation, Michigan State University, 1969] 397 pp.]]

B-386   Discographie in *Diapason*, No. 213 (January 1977): 29   ((--))

B-387   GAMMOND, Peter: A Britten discography: a selective listing in *Hi-Fi News & Record Review*, XXII/2 (February 1977): 82, 85   ((5))

B-388   DAVIS, Peter G.: Benjamin Britten: a discography in *Ovation*, VI/11 (December 1985): 21-26   ((--))

B-389   REED, Philip and WILSON, Paul: Benjamin Britten: the recorded repertoire in EVANS, John: *A Britten source book*. Aldeburgh, Suffolk: published for the Britten-Pears Library by the Britten Estate, 1987: [167]-187   ((1, 5, 7))

OPERAS

ALBERT HERRING (1947)

B-390   MARINELLI, Carlo: [Discography] in Milano, Teatro alla Scala, season 1979-80: program pp. 59   ((5))

DEATH IN VENICE (1973)

B-391   Discography in *Benjamin Britten: Death in Venice*. Cambridge; New York: Cambridge University Press, 1987: 45 ((--))   (Cambridge opera handbooks)

GLORIANA (1953)

B-392   HOYLE, Martin: Discography in *Peter Grimes; Gloriana*. London: J. Calder; New York: Riverrun Press, 1983: 126-127 ((--))   (English National Opera guide; 24)

(A) MIDSUMMER NIGHT'S DREAM (1960)

B-393   [[BACH, Jan Morris: *An analysis of Britten's A Midsummer night's dream.* [DMA, University of Illinois, 1971]   424 pp.]]

PETER GRIMES (1945)

B-394   PITT, Charles: Discographie in *L'Avant Scène Opéra*, No. 31 (January–February 1981): 98–100   ((7))

B-395   HOYLE, Martin: Discography in *Peter Grimes; Gloriana.* London: J. Calder; New York: Riverrun Press, 1983: 126–127   ((--))   (English National Opera Guide; 24)

B-396   WALKER, Malcolm: Discography in *Benjamin Britten, Peter Grimes.* Cambridge; New York: Cambridge University Press, 1983: 211–212 ((7))   (Cambridge opera handbooks)

(THE) RAPE OF LUCRETIA (1946)

B-397   MARINELLI, Carlo: [Discography] in Treviso, Ente Teatro Comunale, Autunno Musicale Trevigiano, season lirica 1976: program p. 4 ((5))

B-398   MARINELLI, Carlo: [Discography] in Palermo, Ente autonomo Teatro Massimo, anno artistico 1982–83: program p. 15   ((5))

TURN OF THE SCREW (1954)

B-399   MARINELLI, Carlo: [Discography] in Venezia, Teatro La Fenice, season lirica, 1971–72: program pp. 179–180   ((5))

B-400   Discography in *Benjamin Britten, The Turn of the Screw.* Cambridge; New York: Cambridge University Press, 1985: 161 ((--))   (Cambridge opera handbooks)

STAGE WORKS

(THE) PRINCE OF THE PAGODAS (1955)

B-401   MARINELLI, Carlo: [Discography] in Venezia, Teatro La Fenice, season 1979–80: program pp. 389–390   ((5))

BRONNER, MIKHAIL   (Russian composer)

B-402 Discography in *Music in the USSR* (July–September 1985): 94   ((--))

BRUCKNER, ANTON, 1824–1896   (Austrian composer)

B-403 [Bruckner records] in *Record Geijutsu*, No. 312 (September 1976): [169]–188   ((5))

B-404 Discografia in BENINATO, Giorgio: *Intorno all'opera di Anton Bruckner e disegno di una teoria di estetica musicale.* Scorzè: Stamperia artigiana La tipografica, 1978: 113–127   ((5))

B-405 Bruckners Musik auf Schallplatten in GREBE, Karl: *Anton Bruckner in Selbstzeugnissen und Bilddokumenten.* Reinbek bei Hamburg: Rowholt, 1978: 144   ((--))   [Omits record numbers]

B-406 LENOIR, Richard: Symphonies de Bruckner: les disques "Phares" in
       Diapason-Harmonie, No. 331 (October 1987): 75 ((--))

BRUGGEN, FRANS, 1934-   **(Dutch recorder player/conductor)**

B-407 [Bruggen discography] in *Record Geijutsu*, No. 276 (September 1973):
       191-192 ((--))

BRUGK, HANS MELCHIOR, 1909-   **(German composer)**

B-408 Diskographie in MESSMER, Franzpeter: *Hans Melchior Brugk*. Tutzing:
       H. Schneider, 1984: 111 ((--)) (Komponisten in Bayern; 7)

BUGLE MUSIC

B-409 [[Discography in DUDGEON, Ralph Thomas: *The keyed bugle, its
       history, literature and technique.* [Dissertation, University of
       California, San Diego, 1980] 262 pp.]]

BUNIN, STANISLAV, 1956-   **(Russian pianist)**

B-410 Discography in *Music in the USSR* (July-September 1986): 15 ((--))

BURCHULADZE, PAATA, 1937-   **(Georgian composer)**

B-411 Discography in *Music in the USSR* (April-June 1988): 19 ((--))

BURIAN, EMIL FRANTISEK, 1904-1959   (Czech composer)

B-412 [[[Discography] in KAZDA, Jaromír: *Soupis zvukových záznamú díla
       E. F. Buriana.* Praha: Hudební odbor divadelního vstvu, 1977.
       81 pp.]]

BURKHARD, WILLY, 1900-1955   (Swiss composer)

B-413 Verzeichnis der Grammophonplatten in MOHR, Ernst: *Willy Burkhard;
       Leben und Werk.* Zürich: Atlantis Verlag, 1957: 237 ((--))

BURMESTER, WILLY, 1869-1933   (German violinist)

B-414 Phonograph records of Willy Burmester in BURMESTER, Willy: *Fifty
       years as a concert violinist.* Linthicum Heights, MD: Swand
       Publications, 1975: 167 ((7)) [Originally published without
       discography by August Scherl, Berlin, 1926, as *Fünfzig Jahre
       Künstlerleben*]

BUSCH, ADOLF, 1891-1952   (German violinist)

B-415 Historische Aufnahmen mit Fritz, Adolf und Hermann Busch in *In
       Memoriam Fritz Busch.* Dahlbruch: Brüder-Busch-Gesellschaft, [1968]:
       50-51 ((--))

B-416 [Discography] in *Stereo Geijutsu*, No. 59 (March 1973): 180-181;
       No. 60 (May 1973): 182-184 ((5))

B-417 Adolf Busch on record in *Hi-Fi News & Record Review*, XXIV/5 (May
       1979): 95 ((--))

B-418 Adolf Busch, soliste et chef ... et la musique de chambre: Le quatuor Busch; Fritz Busch, chef d'orchestre in *Harmonie hi-fi conseil*, No. 9 (May 1981): 37-40 ((7))

B-419 DELALANDE, Jacques and POTTER, Tully: The Busch Brothers--a discography in *Recorded Sound*, No. 86 (July 1984): 29-90 ((1, 7))

B-420 POTTER, Tully: [Discography] in his *Adolf Busch; the life of an honest man*. Billericay, Essex: Potter, 1984: 59-135 [Includes notes on recordings by Hermann Busch] ((1, 3, 4, 6, 7))

B-421 SUGA, Hajime: Busch discography in *Record Geijutsu*, No. 441 (June 1987): 218-222; No. 442 (July 1987): 206-210; No. 443 (August 1987): 294-298; No. 444 (September 1987): 296-300; No. 445 (October 1987): 224-228; No. 446 (November 1987): 242-246; No. 447 (December 1987): 299-302; No. 448 (January 1988): 236-240; No. 449 (February 1988): 212-216; No. 450 (March 1988): 230-234; No. 451 (April 1988): 226-228 ((1, 3, 6, 7))

BUSCH, FRITZ, 1890-1951   (German conductor)

B-422 Historische Aufnahmen mit Fritz, Adolf und Herrmann Busch in *In Memoriam Fritz Busch*. Dahlbruch: Brüder-Busch-Gesellschaft, [1968]: 50-51 ((-))

B-423 DELALANDE, Jacques and POTTER, Tully: The Busch Brothers--a discography in *Recorded Sound*, No. 86 (July 1984): 29-90 ((1, 7))

BUSCH, HERMANN, 1897-1975   (German cellist)

B-424 Historische Aufnahmen mit Fritz, Adolf und Hermann Busch in *In Memoriam Fritz Busch*. Dahlbruch: Brüder-Busch-Gesellschaft, [1968]: 50-51 ((--))

B-425 DELALANDE, Jacques and POTTER, Tully: The Busch Brothers--a discography in *Recorded Sound*, No. 86 (July 1984): 29-90 ((1, 7))

BUSH, ALAN, 1900-   (English composer)

B-426 [[POULTON, Alan: [Discography] in *Time remembered, an 80th birthday symposium*. Kidderminster: Bravura Publications, 198-?]]

BUSNOIS, ANTOINE, ca. 1430-1492   (Burgundian composer)

B-427 [[Discography in HIGGINS, Paula Marie: *Antoine Busnois and musical culture in late-Fifteenth-century France and Burgundy*. [Dissertation, Princeton University, 1987] 396 pp.]]

BUSONI, FERRUCCIO, 1866-1924   (German composer/pianist)

B-428 [Diskographie] in *Diskographien herausgegeben anlässlich des 50. Todestages von Max Reger und des 100. Geburtstages von Ferruccio Busoni*. Berlin: Deutsche Musik-Phonothek, 1966: 89-108 ((4))

B-429 DYMENT, Christopher: Ferruccio Busoni phonograph recordings in *ARSC Journal*, X/2-3 (1979): 185-187 ((3, 6, 7))

B-430 Discography of recordings by Egon Petri & other pianists (pp.

347-352) [and] Busoni's recorded legacy (pp. [326]-333) in SITSKY,
Larry: *Busoni and the piano: the works the writings, and the
recordings.* Westport, CT: Greenwood Press, 1985 ((7)) [Includes
notes on Busoni's piano rolls]

See also

PETRI, EGON

OPERAS

DOKTOR FAUST (1925)

B-431   MARINELLI, Carlo: Discografie: Faust e Mefistofele nelle opere
teatrali e sinfonico-vocali in *Quaderni dell'I.R.TE.M. [Instituto
di Ricerca per il Teatro Musicale]* No. 3 (1986): 97-102 ((5))

BUSSOTTI, SYLVANO, 1931-   (Italian composer)

B-432 GARAVAGLIA, Renato: Discografia in *Discoteca*, No. 199, (October
1979): 47 ((--))

BUTSO, YURI (Russian composer)

B-433 Discography in *Music in the USSR* (July-September 1988): 7 ((--))

BUXTEHUDE, DIETRICH, 1637-1707 (Danish composer)

ORGAN WORKS

B-434   TOWE, Teri Noel: Buxtehude organ works on record in *American
Organist*, XXI/5 (May 1987): 86-87 ((--))

BYRD, WILLIAM, 1543-1623 (English composer)

B-435 TURBET, Richard: Byrd on record in *Brio*, XX/2 (1983): 41-45 ((--))

B-436 Selective critical discography in TURBET, Richard: *William Byrd, a
guide to research.* New York: Garland Pub., 1987: 283-294 ((4))

CABALLÉ, MONTSERRAT, 1933-   (Spanish soprano)

C-1   Discography [on Philips label] S.l.: [Philips, 198-?] 1 l. ((--))

CAGE, JOHN, 1912-   (American composer)

C-2   Selected discography in Program notes for *Sound forms.* [Sound
recording] New World Records NW 203, 1976: 6 ((--))

C-3   Diskographie in *John Cage.* München: Edition Text u. Kritik, 1978:
173-174 ((--)) (Musik-Konzepte; 5)

C-4   Recordings of Cage's music in *A John Cage reader.* New York: Peters,
1982: 202-207 ((--))

C-5   Discographie de John Cage in *Harmonie-Opéra-Hifi Conseil*, No. 26
(December 1982): 19-20 ((--))

C-6   HANSEN, Ivan: John Cage på plade in *Dansk Musiktidsskrift*, LVII/2
       (1982/3): 73   ((--))

C-7   Selected discography in Program notes for *Pulse; works for
       percussion and strings*. [Sound recording] New World Records
       NW 319, 1984   ((--))

C-8   Selected discography in Program notes for *Doublemusic*. [Sound
       recording] New World Records NW 330, 1985   ((--))

CALLAS, MARIA, 1923-1977   (Greek-American soprano)

C-9   Maria Callas' recordings in GALATOPOULOS, Stelios: *Callas: prima
       donna assoluta*.   London: Allan, 1976: [301]-322; Annals of Maria
       Callas' performances [includes listings of pirate records] : 325-334
       ((1, 7))

C-10   Discographic references in ARDOIN, John: *The Callas legacy*.
       London: Duckworth, 1977. 224 pp.   ((1, 4, 7))

C-11   La discografia di Maria Callas, 1949-1977 in BRAGAGLIA, Leonardo:
       L'Arte dello stupore; Omaggio a Maria Callas. Roma: Bulzoni, 1977:
       71-78   ((1, 7))

C-12   Les enregistrements de Maria Callas in LORCEY, Jacques: *Maria
       Callas*.   Paris: Editions PAC, 1977. 429 pp.   ((7))

C-13   NUSSAC, Sylvie de: Callas...[sic] éternelle in *Diapason*, No. 221
       (October 1977): 35-37   ((--))

C-14   VEGETO, Raffaele: Discografia in *Discoteca*, No. 175 (October 1977):
       [13-17]   ((1, 5, 7))

C-15   [Maria Callas discography] in *Stereo Geijutsu*, No. 123 (November
       1977): 107-122   ((1, 7))

C-16   Maria Callas discografie in KORENHOF, Paul: *Luister*, No. 302
       (November 1977): 107-122   ((1, 5, 7))

C-17   [Maria Callas discography] in *Record Geijutsu*, No. 326 (November
       1977): 266-276   ((1, 7))

C-18   TUBEUF, André: Maria Callas, 1923-1977: un héritage in *Harmonie*,
       No. 131 (November 1977): [106]-111; Discographie, 112-113   ((7))

C-19   Discography in RÉMY, Pierre Jean: *Maria Callas; a tribute*. London:
       Macdonald and Jane's; New York: St. Martins; Paris: Ed. Ramsay,
       1978: 189-192   ((1, 7)) [published by Ramsey, Paris, 1982 under
       the title Callas, une vie, with discography]

C-20   BARCLAY, Michael: Maria Callas; a critical discography, part 1 in
       American Record Guide, XLI/8 (June 1978): 7-12; Part 2 in *ARG*,
       XLI/9 (July 1978): 39-43   ((7))

C-21   GUANDALINI, Gina: Dossier Callas: Discografia (aggiornata al maggio
       1978) in *Discoteca alta fedelta*, No. 184-185, (July-August 1978):
       30-35   ((2, 7))

C-22   Discographie in SEGALINI, Sergio: *Callas: les images d'une voix*.
        Paris: F. Van De Velde, 1979: 170-171 ((3, 7))

C-23   Discography of complete operatic performances in SEGALINI, Sergio:
        Callas: portrait of a diva. London: Hutchinson, 1980: 170-171
        ((3, 7))

C-24   [Discographic references] in Cronologia di una carriera in VERGA,
        Carla: *Maria Callas*. Lugano: Edizioni Trelingue, 1980: [115]-171
        ((7))

C-25   Cronologia [with discographic references] in CHIARELLI, Cristina
        Gastel: *Maria Callas*. Venezia: Marsilio Editori, 1981: 149-195
        ((7))

C-26   Discographic references in ARDOIN, John: *The Callas legacy*. Rev. ed.
        New York: Scribner, 1982. 240 pp. ((1, 4, 7))

C-27   [Discography] in NIKOLAIDES, Vasiles: *Maria Callas*. [Athens, 1982]:
        267-276 ((7))

C-28   ARNAUD, Alain: La discographie choisie de Maria Callas in *Diapason*,
        No. 275 (September 1982): 24-27 ((5))

C-29   RAVIER, Dominique and SEGALINI, Sergio: Discographie in *L'Avant
        Scène Opéra*, No. 44 (October 1982): 170-176 ((1, 7))
        (This issue included in Pathé-EMI 2C 165 54-178/88 [Sound recording]
        1982)

C-30   Les enregistrements de Maria Callas in LORCEY, Jacques: *Maria Callas*.
        Paris: Editions PAC, 1983: 537-585 ((7))

C-31   LA ROCHELLE, Réal: Discographie et Filmo-vidéographie in *L'opéra
        POPularisé; Callas dan L'Industrie Phonographique*. [Dissertation,
        Universite de Grenoble, October 1985] 31 pp. ((1, 7))

C-32   Discographic information in "une oeuvre" in MONESTIER, Martin:
        Callas; le livre du souvenir. Paris: Sand, 1985: 217-[270]
        ((1, 7))

C-33   Discography and filmography in LA ROCHELLE, Réal: *Callas: La diva
        et le vinyle*. Montréal: Editions Tripyque, 1987: 354-382 ((1, 7))
        [Published version of his dissertation, above]

C-34   RAVIER, Dominique: The Callas discography in *Callas, as they saw
        her*. New York: Ungar Pub. Co., 1986; London: Robson Books, 1987:
        245-260 ((1, 7))

C-35   PAROVTY, Michel: Discographie--tous les enregistrements in *Diapason-
        Harmonie*, No. 329 (July-August 1987): 43-46 ((1, 7))

C-36   Discographische Hinweise in *fono forum* (September 1987): 33
        ((1, 7))

CALVÉ, EMMA, 1858-1942 (French soprano)

C-37   MORAN, W. R.: The recordings of Emma Calvé (15 Aug., 1858-6 Jan.,
        1942) in CALVÉ, Emma: *My life*. New York: Arno Press, 1977: i-viii

((1, 3, 6, 7)) [Includes notes on playing speeds] [Originally published without discography by Appleton, New York, 1922]

CAMPOS, LINA DERES DE, 1918–   **(Brazilian composer)**

C-38   Discographic references in MIGLIAVACCA, Ariede Maria: *Lina Peres de Campos: catálogo de obras.* [Brasília]: Ministério das Relações Exteriores, Departamento de Cooperação Cultural, Científica e Tecnológica, 1977. [9] pp. (Compositores brasileiros)

CANIGLIA, MARIA, 1905–1979 (Italian soprano)

C-39   GUANDALINI, Gina: Discografia di Maria Caniglia in *Discoteca HiFi*, No. 195–196 (June–July 1979): 60 ((5))

C-40   PEDEMONTE, Valeria: Discografia in Maria Caniglia, un ricordo in *Rassegna Musicale Curci*, XXXIII/2 (May 1980): 45–49 ((3))

CANTELLI, GUIDO, 1920–1956 (Italian conductor)

C-41   GRÉNIER, Jean–Marie: Les enregistrements de Guido Cantelli in *Almanach de disque*, 1957: 304 ((– –))

C-42   MASINI, Umberto: Discografia di Guido Cantelli in *Musica*, No. 1 (May–June 1977): 18–20 ((1, 7))

C-43   The recordings [and] alternative discography in LEWIS, Lawrence: *Guido Cantelli.* San Diego: A.S. Barnes; London: Tantivy Press, 1981: [163]–170 ((1, 7))

C-44   HOFTELE, Jean–Charles: Guido Cantelli, discographie suite in *Diapason–Harmonie*, No. 326 (April 1987): 113 ((– –))

CAPUANA, FRANCO, 1894–1969 (Italian conductor)

C-45   Discografia in CAGNOLI, Bruno: *L'arte musical de Franco Capuana.* Milano: Electa, 1983: 260 ((– –))

CARBON, JOHN JOSEPH (American composer)

C-46   [[Discography in CARBON, John Joseph: *Marie Laveu: a full–length Voodoo opera.* [Dissertation, Original composition, University of California, Santa Barbara, 1983] 746 pp.]]

CARDOSO, LINDEMBERGUE, 1939–   **(Brazilian composer)**

C-47   Discographic references in FERREIRA, Paulo Affonso de Moura: *Lindembergue Cardoso: catálogo de obras.* [Brasília]: Ministério das Relações Exteriores, Department de Cooperação Cultural, Científica e Tecnológica, 1976: [12] pp. (Compositores brasileiros)

CARL ROSA OPERA COMPANY, Great Britain

C-48   [[WILLIAMS, Clifford: The Carl Rosa Opera on records in *Record Collector*, XXXIII/6–7 (June 1988): 170]]

CARLOS, WENDY, 1939–   **(American composer)**

C-49   Wendy Carlos, a selected discography. [s.l.] [n.d.] 1 sheet ((--))
        [Clipping in Rodgers and Hammerstein Archives, New York Public
        Library]

CARPENTER, JOHN ALDEN, 1876-1951   (American composer)

C-50   Selected discography in Program notes for *Works of Carpenter,
        Gilbert, Weiss, Powell.* [Sound recording] New World Records
        NW 228, 1977: 5 ((--))

C-51   Selected discography in Program notes for *Sea Drift.* [Sound
        recording] New World Records NW 320, 1984 ((--))

C-52   Selected discography in Program notes for *John Alden Carpenter:
        collected piano works.* [Sound recording] New World Records NW
        328/9, 1986: [1] ((--))

CARRARA, OLGA, 1887-?   (Italian soprano)

C-53   BOTT, Michael F.: The records of Olga Carrara in *Record Collector,*
        XXX/10-11 (October 1985): 246-247 ((3, 6, 7))

CARRERAS, JOSÉ, 1946-   (Spanish tenor)

C-54   Discography [on Philips label]   S.l.: [Philips, 198-?]   2 l. ((--))

CARTER, ELLIOTT, 1908-   (American composer)

C-55   WEBER, J. F.: An Elliott Carter discography in *ARSC Journal,* VIII/1
        (1976): 33-39 ((5, 7))

C-56   Selected discography in Program notes for *Choral works of Randall
        Thompson, Elliott Carter, Seymour Shifrin.* [Sound recording] New
        World Records NW 219, 1977: 4 ((--))

C-57   WEBER, J. F.: *Carter and Schuman.* Utica, NY: Weber, 1978.   20 pp.
        ((4, 5, 7)) (Weber discography series; 19)

C-58   WHIPPLE, Harold W.: An Elliott Carter discography in *Perspectives
        of New Music,* XX/1-2 (1982-83): 181 ((5))

C-59   SHEPHARD, John: Discography in SCHIFF, David: *The music of
        Elliott Carter.* London: Eulenberg Books; New York: Da Capo Press,
        1983: 355-362 ((5))

C-60   Selected discography in Program notes for *Maryvonne le Dizes-
        Richard, violin.* [Sound recording] New World Records NW 333, 1986
        ((--))

C-61   Selected Carter discography in Program notes for *Elliott Carter:
        Piano Concerto.* [Sound recording] New World Records NW 347, 1987
        ((--))

CARUSO, ENRICO, 1873-1921   (Italian tenor)

C-62   Enrico Caruso in *Stereo Geijutsu,* No. 66 (October 1973): 182-185;
        LP's only in No. 67 (November 1973): 186-187 ((7))

C-63   SOKOL, Martin: The "Pre-Victor" recordings of Enrico Caruso in
        Antique Phonograph Monthly, V/4: 3-12 ((3, 6, 7))

C-64   FREESTONE, John: *Enrico Caruso, his recorded legacy.* Westport, CT:
        Greenwood Press, 1978. 130 pp. ((3, 4, 7)) [Reprinted from the
        1961 ed. published by T. S. Denison, Minneapolis]

C-65   CAIDIN, Jack L.: Caruso recordings, a discography in CARUSO,
        Dorothy: *Enrico Caruso, his life and death.* Westport, CT:
        Greenwood Press, 1987: 289-291 ((3, 7)) [Reprinted from the 1945
        ed. published by Simon and Schuster, New York]

C-66   BOLIG, John R.: A Caruso discography in SCOTT, Michael: *The great
        Caruso.* London: Hamish Hamilton; New York: Viking Penguin, 1988:
        265-293 ((1, 3, 6, 7))

        CARVALHO, DINORÁ DE, 1905-   **(Brazilian composer)**

C-67   Discographic references in FERREIRA, Paulo Affonso de Moura:
        Dinorá de Carvalho: catálogo de obras. [Brasília]: Ministério
        das Relações Exteriores, Departamento de Cooperação Cultural,
        Científica e Tecnológica, 1977: [30] pp. ((--)) (Compositores
        brasileiros)

        CASADESUS, JEAN-CLAUDE, 1935-   **(French conductor)**

C-68   Discographie in *Harmonie-Opéra Hi-fi Conseil*, No. 15 (December
        1981): 24 ((--))

        CASADESUS, ROBERT, 1899-1972 (French pianist)

C-69   [Casadesus discography] in *Stereo Geijutsu*, No. 56 (December 1972):
        172-175 ((--))

C-70   KIRBY, Frank Eugene: Discography in *Piano Quarterly*, No. 119
        (Fall 1982): 47-53 ((--)) [Adapted from the 1974 discography
        published in CBS Records set M 32135]

        CASALS, PABLO, 1876-1973 (Spanish cellist)

C-71   Diskographie (Auswahl) in SEEHAUS, Lothar: *Pablo Casals.* Hamburg:
        Dressler, 1980: 125 ((7))

C-72   MORIN, Philippe: Discographie chronologique in CASALS, Pablo:
        *Conversations avec Pablo Casals: souvenirs et opinions d'un
        musicien.* Paris: A. Michel, 1982: [417]-444 ((3, 6, 7))

        CASE, ANNA, 1889-1984 (American soprano)

C-73   WILE, Raymond R.: The recordings of Anna Case in *ARSC Journal*,
        X/2-3 (1979): 167-184 ((3, 5, 6, 7)) [Edison, Victor, Vitaphone
        and Columbia records]

        CASELLA, ALFREDO, 1883-1947 (Italian composer)

C-74   MARINELLI, Carlo: Alfredo Casella: Cronologia e discografia delle
        opere in La donna serpente, Ente autonomo Teatro Massimo Palermo,
        anno artistico 1981-82: program p. 18 ((7))

CASTELNUOVO–TEDESCO, MARIO, 1895–1968   (Italian composer)

C-75   [[Discography in HOLMBERG, Mark Leonard: *Thematic contours and harmonic idioms of Mario Castelnuovo-Tedesco, as exemplified in the solo concertos.* [Dissertation, Northwestern University, 1974] 400 pp.]]

C-76   Discography in ROSSI, Nick: *Catalogue of works by Mario Castelnuovo-Tedesco.* New York: International Castelnuovo–Tedesco Society, 1977: 126–137   ((1))

C-77   ROSSI, Nick: Mario Castelnuovo-Tedesco––a discography in *Fanfare*, X/3 (January–February 1987): 292–307   ((--))

CASTIGLIONI, NICCOLÒ, 1932–   (Italian composer)

C-78   Discografia in *Discoteca*, No. 192 (March 1979): 33   ((--))

CATALANI, ALFREDO, 1854–1893   (Italian composer)

LA WALLY (1892)

C-79   MARINELLI, Carlo: [Discography] in Venezia, Gran Teatro La Fenice, season 1971–72: program pp. 106–107   ((5))

CAVALLI, FRANCESCO, 1602–1676   (Italian composer)

L'ORMINDO (1644)

C-80   MARINELLI, Carlo: [Discography] in Venezia, Gran Teatro La Fenice, season 1975–76: program pp. 124–125   ((5))

CAZETTE, LOUIS, 1887–1922   (French tenor)

C-81   HALL, Lewis Morris: The recordings of Louis Cazette in *Record Collector*, XXVII/1–2 (December 1981): 20–22   ((3, 7))

CERNY, LADISLAV, 1891–1975   (Czech composer)

C-82   Diskografie in SMOLIK, Jan: *Ladislav Cerny*. Praha: Supraphon, 1977: 61–[62]   ((--))

ČESKÁ FILHARMONIE

C-83   Diskografie in *Česká Filharmonie*. Praha, 1971: 104–123   ((5))

ČESKÉ KVARTETO

C-84   [[[Discography] in VRATISLAVSKY, Jan: *České kvarteto*. Praha: Editio Supraphon, 1984: 64]]

CHABRIER, EMMANUEL, 1841–1894   (French composer)

C-85   HALBREICH, Harry: Discographic notes in Emmanuel Chabrier, un génie à redécouvrir in *Harmonie-Panorama musique*, No. 47 (November 1984): 44–53   ((--))

CHADWICK, GEORGE, 1854-1931   (American composer)

C-86   Selected discography in Program notes for *George Chadwick: Symphony No. 2.* [Sound recording] New World Records NW 339, 1986   ((--))

CHAIKOVSKY, ALEXANDER, 1946-   (Russian composer)

C-87   Discography in *Music in the USSR* (October-December 1986): 27   ((--))

CHAIKOVSKY, BORIS, 1925-   (Russian composer)

C-88   Discography in *Music in the USSR* (October-December 1985): 10   ((--))

C-89   Discography in *Music in the USSR* (January-March 1988): 7   ((--))

CHAILLY, RICCARDO, 1953-   (Italian conductor)

C-90   Discography, Deutsche Grammophon artist information, 1980, 1 p.   ((--))

CHALAYEV, SHIRVANI, 1936-   (Soviet composer)

C-91   Discography in *Music in the USSR* (July-September 1985): 82   ((--))

CHALIAPIN, FEDOR IVANOVICH, 1893-1938   (Russian bass)

C-92   LLOYD, H. Powell: Chaliapin in 'Boris Gudonov'-- discography in *Opera*, XXVII/6 (June 1976): 518-520   ((3, 6, 7))

C-93   [Gramophone recordings] in *Fedor Ivanovich Shaliapin.* Vol 3. Moskva, 1979: [343]-350   ((7))

C-94   KELLY, Alan and GURVICH, Vladimir: Discography in BOROVSKY, Victor: *Chaliapin: a critical biography.* New York: Knopf, 1988: 541-587   ((1, 3, 6, 7))

CHALMERS, THOMAS, 1884-197-?   (American baritone)

C-95   WILE, Ray: Discography in *Talking Machine Review*, No. 45 (April 1977): 947-953; No. 46 (June 1977): 1039-1044   ((3, 6, 7))

CHAMBER MUSIC--GERMANY (WEST)--HANNOVER

C-96   [Discography] in SIEVERS, Heinrich: *Kammermusik in Hannover.* Tutzing: Schneider, 1980: 193-208   ((--))

CHAMINADE, CÉCILE, 1857-1944   (French composer)

C-97   Discography in CITRON, Marcia J.: *Cécile Chaminade, a bio-bibliography.* New York: Greenwood Press, 1988: [93]-110   ((5)) (Bio-bibliographies in music; 15)

CHANLER, THEODORE, 1902-1961   (American composer)

C-98   Selected discography in Program notes for *Songs by ... Theodore Chanler ...* [Sound recording] New World Records NW 300, 1978: 4   ((--))

CHANTS (PLAIN, GREGORIAN, ETC.)

C-99   BEAUJEAN, Alfred: Diskographie in *Hi Fi Stereophonie*, IX/6 (June 1972): 520   ((--))

C-100 Recordings in BERRY, Mary: *Plainchant for everyone: an introduction to plainsong.* Croydon: Royal School of Church Music, 1979: 51-52   ((--))

C-101 Discographie in MADRIGNAC, André G.: *Le chant grégorien: histoire et pratique.* Paris: H. Champion, 1981: 139-142   ((--))

C-102 MADRIGNAC, André G. and PISTONE, Danièle: Discographie in *Revista Internazionale di Musica Sacra*, IV/2 (1983): 214-219   ((4))

C-103 Discographische Hinweise in *fono forum* (April 1988): 30   ((--))

   CHANTS (PLAIN, GREGORIAN, ETC.)

   See also

   SOLESMES, MONKS OF

   CHAPUIS, MICHEL, 1930-   (French organist)

C-104 Discographie in CHAPUIS, Michel: *Claude Duchesneau interroge Michel Chapuis.* Paris: Le Centurion, 1979: [219]-220   ((--))

   CHARPENTIER, MARC ANTOINE, ca. 1636-1704   (French composer)

C-105 Discographies in HITCHCOCK, H. Wiley: *Les oeuvres de Marc-Antoine Charpentier: catalogue raisonne = The works of Marc-Antonie Charpentier.* Paris: Picard, 1982. 419 pp.   ((5))

C-106 ALEXANDRE, Ivan A.: Discographie seléctive in *Diapason-Harmonie*, No. 342 (October 1988): 60-61   ((7))

   STAGE WORKS

   MÉDÉ (1693)

C-107   LABIE, Jean-François: Discographie in *L'Avant Scène Opéra*, No. 68 (October 1984): 125   ((--))

   CHAUSSON, ERNEST, 1855-1899   (French composer)

C-108 Discography in GROVER, Ralph Scott: *Ernest Chausson, the man and his music.* Lewisburg: Bucknell University Press, 1980: [228]-229   ((--))

   POEM, VIOLIN AND ORCHESTRA, Op. 25   (1896)

C-109   GALLOIS, Jean: Discographie in *Diapason*, No. 210 (October 1976): 36   ((--))

   CHÁVEZ, CARLOS, 1899-1978   (Mexican composer)

C-110 Discography in PARKER, Robert L.: *Carlos Chávez, Mexico's modern-day Orpheus.*   Boston, Mass.: Twayne Publishers, 1983: 152-156   ((--))

CHERUBINI, LUIGI, 1760-1842   (Italian composer)

OPERAS

MÉDÉE (1797)

C-111   MARINELLI, Carlo: [Discography] in Bologna, Teatro Comunale, season 1976-77: program p. 6   ((5))

REQUIEMS

C-112   WEBER, J. F.: A discography of the Cherubini Requiems in *Fanfare*, V/6 (July-August 1982): 102-103   ((5, 7))

CHEVALIER DE SAINT-GEORGE

See

SAINT-GEORGE, JOSEPH BOULOGNE, CHEVALIER DE

CHICAGO SYMPHONY ORCHESTRA

C-113   [Chicago Symphony discography] in *Record Geijutsu*, No. 318 (March 1977): 178-184   ((7))

C-114   MARSH, Robert Charles: Solti in Chicago: a critical discography in *Ovation* (December 1984): 26-29, 35   ((7))

CHIHARA, PAUL, 1938-   (American composer)

C-115   Selected discography in Program notes for *Works by Paul Chihara, Chou Weng-Chou, Earl Kim, Roger Reynolds.* [Sound recording] New World Records NW 237, 1977: 2   ((--))

CHOPIN, FRÉDÉRIC, 1810-1849   (French composer)

C-116   Discography in GAVOTY, Bernard: *Frédéric Chopin.*   New York: Scribner, 1977: 424-[436]   ((--))

C-117   MELVILLE, Derek: Selected recordings of Chopin's music in *Chopin: a biography with a survey of books, editions and recordings.* London: C. Bingley; Hamden, CT: Linnet Books, 1977:   92-99   ((--))

C-118   GRDUZIŃSKI, Albert: *Chopin na płatych.*   Warsawa: Towarzystwo im. Fryderyka Chopina, 1978.   54 pp.   ((--))

C-119   SCHONBERG, Harold C.: *The collector's Chopin and Schumann.* Westport, CT: Greenwood Press, 1978.   256 pp.   ((--))   [Reprinted from the 1959 ed. published by Lippincott, New York]

C-120   Discography in METHUEN-CAMPBELL, James: *Chopin playing: from the composer to the present day.* London: Gollancz;   New York: Taplinger Pub. Co., 1981: 241-267   ((5))

C-121   BRUNEL, Pierre: Frédéric Chopin l'oeuvre pour piano: discographie critique in *Harmonie Opéra Conseil*, No. 27: 27-39   ((--))

C-122   KÁNSKI, Józef: *Dyskografia Chopiniowska historyczny katalog nagran płytowch=A Chopin discography; a historical catalogue of recordings*. Krakow: Pol. wydawn. Muzyczne, 1986. 107 pp. ((4, 5, 7))

CONCERTOS, PIANO

CONCERTO, No. 1, E Minor, Op. 11 (1830)

C-123   Chopin: Le 1er concerto pour piano en mi mineur op 1 in *Diapason*, No. 241 (July-August 1979): 38-40   ((--))

PIANO WORKS

ETUDES

C-124   MANNONI, Gérard: Les 24 études de Frédéric Chopin: discographie comparée in *Harmonie*, No. 145 (March 1979): 96-110   ((--))

CHORAL MUSIC

C-125   [[Discography in BOSTIC, Ronald David: *The use of the liturgical sequence in selected twentieth-century choral compositions.* [Dissertation, Southwestern Baptist Theological Seminary, 1976] 214 pp.]]

C-126   Recommended gramophone records in JACOBS, Arthur: *Choral music: a symposium.* Middlesex; New York: Penguin Books, 1978, c1963: [427]-440   ((--))

C-127   DIELTIENS, Tony: De eigen koormuziek in de eigen discotheek in *ADEM*, XXIII/2 (1987): 70-76   ((--))

CHORAL MUSIC, FINNISH

C-128   HAAPAKOSKI, MARTTI: Selected discography of Finnish choral music in *Finnish Music Quarterly*, 1987/2: 71-74   ((5))

CHORALE DES JEUNESSES MUSICALES DE FRANCE

C-129   Discographie de la Chorale des J.M.F. in WORMS, Michel: De Delalande à Honegger: les 40 ans de la Chorale des JMF in *Harmonie-Panorama musique*, No. 29 (March 1983): 70-71   ((--))

CHOU WEN-CHUNG, 1923-   (Chinese-American composer)

C-130   Selected discography in Program notes for *Works of Paul Chihara, Chou Wen-Chung, Earl Kim, Roger Reynolds.* [Sound recording] New World Records NW 237, 1977: 2   ((--))

See also

MUSIC--ASIA

CHRISTIE, WILLIAM   (American harpsichordist/conductor)

C-131   Discographie in WALTHER, Edith: Tete d'affiche: William Christie in

Harmonie-Panorama musique, No. 46 (October 1984): 15   ((--))

CHRISTMAS MUSIC

C-132 ALEXANDRE, Ivan A.: Une discographie de Noël in *Diapason-Harmonie*,
No. 344 (December 1988): 82-83   ((--))

CHURCH MUSIC

C-133 [[Discography in TORTOLANO, William: *The mass and the twentieth-
century composer*. [DSM, University of Montréal, 1964] 164, 92 pp.]]

C-134 [[Discography in WILHITE, Charles Stanford: *Eucharistic music for
the Anglican Church in England and the United States at mid-
twentieth century (1950-1965): A sylistic study with historical
introduction*. [Dissertation, University of Iowa, 1968] 307 pp.]]

C-135 Discographie in Auswahl in RÖHRING, Klaus: *Neue Musik in der Welt
des Christentums*. München: C. Kaiser, 1975: 84-85   ((--))

CHURCH MUSIC--FRANCE

C-136 Discographie in WEBER, Edith: *La musique protestante en langue
française*. Paris: H. Champion, 1979: [181]-182   ((--))

C-137 Discographie in LABELLE, Nicole: *Les differents styles da la musique
religieuse en France: le psaume de 1539 a 1572*. Henryville:
Institute of Medieval Music, 1981-. t. 1, p. 209-216   ((--))

CHURCH MUSIC--GERMANY

C-138 Discographie sommaire in WEBER, Edith: *La musique protestante
en langue allemande*. Paris: H. Champion, 1980: [235]-237   ((--))

CHURCH MUSIC--ROMAN CATHOLIC RITE

C-139 [[SCHARNAGL, August: Einführung in die katholische Kirchenmusik in
Taschenbücher zur Musikwissenschaft, LXI. 215 pp.]]

CHURCH MUSIC--RUSSIA

C-140 [[GARDNER, Johann von: Diskographie des russischen Kirchengesangs
(8. Folge) in *Ostkirche Studien*, XIX (1970): 185-207]]

C-141 [[GARDNER, Johann von: Diskographie des russischen Kirchengesangs
(9. Folge) in *Ostkirche Studien*, XXI (1972): 153-180]]

CIANI, DINO, 1941-1974 (Italian pianist)

C-142 MASINI, Umberto: Discografia di Dino Ciani in *Musica*, No. 13 (August
1979): 166   ((7))

CICCOLINI, ALDO, 1925-   (Italian pianist)

C-143 Aldo Ciccolini, his art on Angel and Seraphim records, 1980, 1 p.
((--))

CICCOLINI, GUIDO, 1885-1963 (American baritone)

C-144 FERRARA, D. E.: Guido Ciccolini in *New Amberola Graphic*, No. 49
(Summer 1984): 11-12   ((3, 7))

C-145 FERRARA, D. E.: Recordings of Guido Ciccolini in *Record Collector*,
XXXIII/1-2 (January 1988): 20-21   ((3, 7))

CICONIA, JOHANNES, ca. 1335-1411   (Burgundian composer)

C-146 WEBER, J. F.: ... A discography of Johannes Ciconia in *Fanfare*,
IV/5 (May-June 1981): 76-77   ((5, 7))

CILEA, FRANCESCO, 1866-1950   (Italian composer)

OPERAS

ADRIANA LECOUVREUR (1902)

C-147 MARINELLI, Carlo: [Discography] in Roma, Teatro dell'Opera,
season 1965-66: program pp. 650-651   ((5))

C-148 MARINELLI, Carlo: [Discography] in Roma, Teatro dell'Opera,
season 1985: program pp. 43-49   ((5))

CIMAROSA, DOMENICO, 1749-1801   (Italian composer)

OPERAS

(IL) MATRIMONIO SEGRETO (1792)

C-149 MARINELLI, Carlo: [Discography] in Milano, Teatro alla Scala,
season 1979: program pp. 62-63   ((5))

C-150 MARINELLI, Carlo: [Discography] in Palermo, Ente automono
Teatro Massimo, season 1981-82: program p. 6   ((5))

CINCINNATI SYMPHONY ORCHESTRA

C-151 MEYERS, Betty and FELLERS, Frederick P.: *Discographies of
commercial recordings of The Cleveland Orchestra (1924-1977)
and The Cincinnati Symphony Orchestra (1917-1977)*. Westport, CT:
Greenwood Press, 1978: pp. [159]-211   ((3, 4, 5, 6, 7))

CITY OF BIRMINGHAM SYMPHONY ORCHESTRA

C-152 The records in JENKINS, Lyndon and SMITH, Beresford K.: *The
Birmingham 78's 1925-1947*. Birmingham: City of Birmingham Symphony
Orchestra, 1983: [9]-30   ((3, 4, 6, 7))

CIVIL, PABLO, 1899-1987   (Spanish tenor)

C-153 [[DZAZOPULOS, E. Juan: Pablo Civil (1899-1987) in *Record Collector*,
XXXIII/6-7 (June 1988): 174]]

CLARINET

C-154 Discography in BRYMER, Jack: *Clarinet*. London: Macdonald and
Jane's, 1976; New York: Schirmer Books, 1977: 249-[253]

C-155 [[Discography in ROSE, Clyde Robert: *A selected, annotated bibliography of writings on the clarinet.* [Dissertation, Indiana University, 1978]]

C-156 Discography in BRYMER, Jack: *Clarinet.* Rev. ed. London Macdonald and Jane's, 1979: 249-253 ((--))

C-157 PARIS, Alain: Discographie in BRYMER, Jack: *Clarinet.* Paris: Hetier, 1980: 249 ((--))

CLARINET MUSIC

C-158 [[Discography in STIER, John Charles: *a recorded anthology of twentieth-century music for unaccompanied clarinet: 1919-1959.* [DMA, University of Maryland, 1982] 65 pp.]]

CLAVICHORD MUSIC

C-159 Renaissance du piano forte in *Hifi Stéreo* (May 1978): 62-66 ((--))

See also

KEYBOARD MUSIC

CLEVELAND ORCHESTRA

C-160 FELLERS, Frederick P. and MEYERS, Betty: *Discographies of commercial recordings of The Cleveland Orchestra (1924-1977) and The Cincinnati Symphony Orchestra (1917-1977)* Westport, CT: Greenwood Press, 1978: pp. 1-158 ((3, 4, 5, 6, 7))

CLIBURN, VAN, 1934-   (American pianist)

C-161 REICH, Howard: Selected discography in *Chicago Tribune* (March 24, 1988), sec. 5, p. 10 ((--))

COATES, ALBERT, 1882-1953 (English conductor)

C-162 STROFF, Stephen M.: Albert Coates discography in *Le Grand Baton*, No. 45 (March 1980): 15-27 ((7))

C-163 HAMILTON, David: [Letter to the Editor] in *Le Grand Baton*, No. 48 (December 1980): 12-13 ((3, 6))

C-164 [[STROFF, Stephen M.: Albert Coates in *Classic Wax* (November 1981):]]

COATES, ERIC, 1886-1957 (English composer

C-165 UPTON, Stuart: *Eric Coates; a biographical discography.* London: Vintage Light Music Society, 1980. 22 pp. ((1))

C-166 LYON, J.: Additional recordings of Eric Coates' compositions by all performers on 78s: supplement to Eric Coates discography compiled by Stuart Upton in *Vintage Light Music*, No. 26 (Spring 1981): [unnumbered page inserted in issue] ((--))

COLE, MAURICE, 1902–   **(English pianist)**

C–167 PAIN, Derek: Discography in *Talking Machine Review*, No. 70 (December 1985): 1963–1964 ((5))

COLERIDGE–TAYLOR, SAMUEL, 1875–1912   **(English composer)**

C–168 Appendix D: a discography of Samuel Coleridge–Taylor in TORTOLANO, William: *Samuel Coleridge–Taylor: Anglo–Black composer, 1875–1912*. Metuchen, NJ: Scarecrow Press, 1977: 211–214 ((––))

COLGRASS, MICHAEL, 1932–   **(American composer)**

C–169 Selected discography in *Michael Colgress*. [Sound recording] New World Records NW 318, 1983: [2] ((––))

COLLEGIUM AUREUM, West Germany

C–170 Quelques enregistrements du Collegium Aureum ... in *Diapason*, No. 210 (October 1976): 24 ((––))

COMPOSERS, AMERICAN

C–171 DETTMER, Roger: [Discography of U.S. composers] in *Fanfare*, VI/1 (September–October 1982): 92–96, 506–507 ((––))

COMPOSERS, ARMENIAN

C–172 Discographies in *Music in the USSR* (January–March 1986): 8–11 ((––))

COMPOSERS, BELGIAN

C–173 VOLBORTH–DANYS, Diana von: *CeBeDeM et ses compositeurs affiliés: biographies, catalogues, discographie* ... Bruxelles: Centre belge de documentation musicale, 1977–1980. Discographie ... (30.6.1976) [for composers A–L]: pp. 199–211 in the 1977 volume; Discographie ... (31.12.1978) [for composers M–Z] pp. 233–244 in the 1980 volume ((––))

COMPOSERS, BLACK

See

BLACK COMPOSERS

COMPOSERS, BRITISH

C–174 STANDFORD, Patrick: Living British composers on record 1975 in *Composer*, No. 56 (Winter 1975–1976): 19–23; Living British composers on record in *Composer*, No. 58 (Summer 1976): 7; Living British composers on record 1978 in *Composer*, No. 63 (Spring 1978): 15–19 ((––))

C–175 KEENER, Andrew: Record documentation (of British composers new to records) in *British Music Yearbook 1982*. London: Adam & Charles Black, 1982: 39–42 ((––))

C-176 KEENER, Andrew: Record documentation (of British composers new to records) in *British Music Yearbook, 1983*. London: Classical Music, 1982: 84-90 ((--))

COMPOSERS, CANADIAN

C-177 ROBINSON, Jim: Canadian classical composers: discography in *Record Collectors Journal*, II/1 (January 1976): 10; (February 1978): 11-12 ((--))

C-178 Discography in BRADLEY, Ian L.: *Twentieth Century Canadian composers*. Volume one. Agincourt, Ont.: GLC Publications Ltd., 1977: 221-222; Discography in Volume two. (Agincourt, Ont., GLC, 1982): 280-281 ((--))

COMPOSERS, CZECHOSLOVAKIAN

C-179 Discography in YOELL, John H.: Czech composers now in *Fanfare*, VIII/4 (March-April 1985): 148-153 ((--))

COMPOSERS, FINNISH

C-180 Levytyksia in *Miten savellykseni ovat syntyneet: 12 suomalaista savltajaa kertoo*. Helsinki: Ovtava, 1976: [159]-163 ((--))

COMPOSERS, FRENCH

C-181 Discographie du Groupe des six in COCTEAU, Jean: *Le coq et l'arlequin*. Paris: Stock, 1979: 135-[162] ((--))

C-182 Discographie internationale in *Musiciens de France: la génération des grands symphonistes* (No. 324-326 of La Revue Musicale, 1979): [199]-204 ((5)) [Considers Lekeu, Koechlin, Magnard, Ropartz, and composers of organ symphonies]

COMPOSERS, GEORGIAN

C-183 Discography in *Music in the USSR* (July-September 1985): 28-30 ((--))

COMPOSERS, HUNGARIAN

C-184 Discographies in *Contemporary Hungarian composers*. Budapest: Editio musica, 1979. 217 pp. ((--))

COMPOSERS, LATIN AMERICAN

C-185 Discographic references in *Compositores de América/Composers of the Americas*. Washington: Organization of America States, 1955-1977. 17 v. ((--))

C-186 DASH, Nan: South of the border--music by Latin American composers in *Tarakan Music Letter*, III/4 (March-April 1982): 12-13 ((--))

COMPOSERS, MEXICAN

C-187 Discographies in *Música mexicana contemporánea*. México: Fondo de Cultura Económica, 1982. 241 pp. ((--))

COMPOSERS, NORTHERN EUROPEAN

C-188 [[BUCHET, Bergljot Krohn: *Nomus beställningsvuk 1970-76*.
Stockholm: Nämnden för Norsk musiksambarbete, 1977. 40 pp.]]

C-189 Discographies in RAPOPORT, Paul: *Opus Est: Six European composers
from Northern Europe*. London: Kahn and Averill, 1978; New York:
Taplinger, 1979. 200 pp. ((--))

COMPOSERS, SOUTH AFRICAN

C-190 Recordings in HENNING, Cosmo Grenville: *Four South African
composers*. Pretoria: Institute for Languages, Literature and
Arts, Human Sciences Research Council, 1975. 45 pp. ((--))
[Recordings by Herbert Du Plessis and John Joubert]

COMPOSERS, SPANISH

C-191 Discographies in *14 compositores españoles de hoy*. [Oviedo]:
Arte-musicología, Servicio de Publiciones, Universidad de Oviedo,
1982. 478 pp. ((--))

COMPOSERS, SWISS

C-192 VITTESS, L.: Schweizer Diskographie/Discographie suisse in
Schweizerische Musikzeitung, CXXII/1 (1982): 44-46 ((--))

C-193 Discographies in *Schweizer Komponisten unserer Zeit/Compositeurs
Suisses de notre Temps*. Winterhur: Amadeus, 1983. 234 pp. ((--))

See also entries under **MUSIC--GEOGRAPHICAL SUBHEADING**

COMPUTER MUSIC

C-194 Discographic notes in MELBY, Carol: *Computer music compositions
of the United States, 1976*. 2 ed. Urbana, IL: [Melby], 1976:
28 pp. ((--))

C-195 [[[Discography] in *Composers and the computer*. Los Altos, CA: W.
Kaufmann, 1985:]]

CONCERTGEBOUWORKEST, AMSTERDAM

C-196 [Amsterdam Concertgebouw discography] in *Record Geijutsu*, No. 318
(March 1977): 170-178 ((7))

CONCERTOS, PIANO

C-197 [[Discography in HANSON, John Robert: *Macroform in selected
twentieth-century piano concertos*. [Dissertation, University of
Rochester, 1969] 398 pp.]]

C-198 [[Discography in SMITH, Steven Herbert: *The piano concerto after
Bartók: a survey for performers of the piano concerto literature
with emphasis on the postwar era, 1945-1970*. [DMA, University of
Rochester, 1977] 507 pp.]]

C-199 [[Discography in HO, Allan Benedict: *The late-Romantic piano

concerto finale: a stylistic and structural analysis. [Dissertation,
University of Kentucky, 1985]   496 pp.]]

CONDUCTING

C-200 Discografia in ZURLETTI, Michelangelo: *La direzione d'orchestra:
grandi direttori di ieri e di oggi.* [Italy]: Ricordi; Florence:
Giunti Matrello, 1985: [335]-338   ((--))   [Omits record numbers]

CONDUCTORS

C-201 Diskographie in VOSS, Egon: *Die Dirigenten der Bayreuther
Festspiele.* Regensberg: Bosse, 1976: 118-136   ((1, 7))

C-202 Recordings in HART, Philip: *Conductors: a new generation.* New York:
Scribner, 1979: 267-295   ((5))

C-203 Selected discography in MAY, Robin: *Behind the baton.* London:
Muller, 1981: 144-150   ((--))

C-204 Discographies in HOLMES, John L.: *Conductors on record.* Westport,
CT: Greenwood Press, 1982.   734 pp.   ((--))

C-205 Recordings in HART, Philip: *Conductors: a new generation.* Rev. ed.
New York: Scribner, 1983, 1988: 276-313   ((--))

C-206 Discographies in HOLMES, John L.: *Conductors; a record collectors
guide.* London: Gollancz, 1988.   320 pp.   ((--))

CONDUCTORS--CZECHOSLOVAKIA

C-207 Dlouhohrajici desky Supraphon in BURGHAUSER, Jarmil: *Slavni cesti
dirigent.* Praha: Statni hudebni vydavtelstvi, 1963: 143-155   ((--))

C-208 [[[Discographies] in ČÍŽIK, Vladimír: *Slovenskí dirigenti a
zbormajstri.* Bratislava: Opus, 1986.   325 pp.]]

CONDUCTORS--UNITED STATES

C-209 Selected discography in DETTMER, Roger: The state of U.S. conductors
in *Fanfare,* VI/1 (September-October 1982): 92-96, 506-507   ((--))

CONLON, JAMES, 1950-   (American conductor)

C-210 Discographische Hinweise in *fono forum* (August 1986): 34   ((--))

CONSORTIUM CLASSICUM, West Germany

C-211 Aktueller discographische Hinweise in *fono forum* (August 1986):
23   ((--))

CONTANT, ALEXIS, 1858-1918   (Canadian composer)

C-212 Sound recordings in WILLIS, Stephen C.: *Alexis Contant; catalogue.*
Ottawa: National Library of Canada, 1982: 47-56   ((1, 7))

COPLAND, AARON, 1900-   (American composer)

C-213 Selected discography in Program notes for *Aaron Copland: works for piano 1926-1948*. [Sound recording] New World NW 280, 1976: 4 ((--))

C-214 The simple gift of genius: The music of Aaron Copland on record in *Tarakan Music Letter*, III/1 (September-October 1981): 14 ((--))

C-215 Selected discography in Program notes for *Robert Davidovici, violin*. [Sound recording] New World Records NW 334, 1987 ((--))

C-216 Discography in SKOWRONSKI, JoAnn: *Aaron Copland: a bio-bibliography*. Westport, CT: Greenwood Press, 1985: [29]-69 ((5)) (Bio-bibliographies in music; 2)

COPERARIO, JOHN, ca. 1570-1627 (English composer)

C-217 WEBER, J. F.: Discography of John Coperario in *Fanfare*, II/4 (March-April 1979): 50-51 ((5, 7))

CORBOZ, MICHEL, 1934– (Swiss conductor)

C-218 Discographie de Michel Corboz in *Harmonie* (October 1980): 22 ((--))

C-219 Discographie de Michel Corboz et de l'Ensemble vocale de Lausanne in *Michel Corboz; ou la Passion de la musique*. Lausanne: Ed. de l'aire, 1981: 135-138 ((7))

CORIGLIANO, JOHN, 1938– (American composer)

C-220 Selected discography in Program notes for *John Corigliano: Concerto for clarinet and orchestra*. [Sound recording] New World Records NW 309, 1981: 4 ((--))

C-221 [[Discography in POLLEY, Jo Ann Marie: *An analysis of John Corigliano's "Concerto for Clarinet and Orchestra"*. [DMA, Michigan State University, 1983] 124 pp.]]

C-222 Selected discography in Program notes for *Henry Herford*. [Sound recording] New World Records NW 327, 1985 ((--))

CORRÊA, SÉRGIO OLIVEIRA DE VASCONCELLOS, 1931– (Brazilian composer)

C-223 Discographic references in FERREIRA, Paulo Affonso de Moura: *Sérgio Oliveira de Vascellos Corrêa: catálogo de obras*. [Brasília]: Ministério das Relações Exteriores, Departamento de Cooperação Cultural, Científica e Tecnológica, 1976: [21] pp. ((--)) (Compositores brasileiros)

CORSINI, IGNACIO, 1891-1967 (Italian tenor)

C-224 Discografia in CORSINI, Ignacio: *Ignacio Corsini, mi padre*. Buenos Aires: Todo Es Historia, 1979: 69-94 ((3, 6, 7))

CORTOT, ALFRED, 1877-1962 (French pianist)

C-225 CARTWRIGHT, Jim: Alfred Cortot's American recordings--Victor Talking Machine Company in Immortal Performances 1977 List Number 1 [Dealer's list] Austin, TX: Immortal Performances, 1977: [30]-[36]

((3, 6, 7))   (Immortal Performances discographic data; [3])

C-226 Discographie [LP reissues only] in GAVOTY, Bernard: *Alfred Cortot.*
Paris: Editions Buchet/Chastel, 1977: [311]-316   ((--))

C-227 Discographie d'Alfred Cortot in ROY, Jean: Pour saluer Alfred
Cortot, 1977-1962 in *Diapason*, No. 220 (September 1977): 30-31
((--))

C-228 TIMBRELL, Charles: Alfred Cortot discography in *Piano Quarterly*,
No. 127 (Fall 1984): 29-31   ((5))

C-229 TIMBRELL, Charles: La discografia di Cortot in *Musica*, No. 44 (March
1987): 36-38   ((7))

CORUL MADRIGAL, Romania

C-230 Discografie in COSMA, Viorel: *Corul Madrigal al Conservatorului.*
Bucureşti, 1971: [105]-[109]   ((--))

COTRUBAS, ILEANA, 1939-   **(Rumanian soprano)**

C-231 Diskographische Hinweise in *fono forum* (September 1978): 910-912,
914   ((--))

C-232 Discographie d'Ileana Cotrubas in *Harmonie Opéra Conseil*, No. 28: 15
((--))

COUNTERTENORS

C-233 Discography in GILES, Peter: *The counter tenor.*   London: Muller,
1982: 205-208   ((--))

COUPERIN, FRANÇOIS, 1668-1733   (French composer)

C-234 Discographie sommaire in BEAUSSANT, Philippe: *Couperin.* Paris:
Fayard, 1980: 577-579   ((--))

C-235 Discographie in PLACE, Adélaide de: François Couperin: l'oeuvre de
clavecin in *Harmonie-Panorama musique*, No. 43 (June 1984): 38-42
((--))

COWELL, HENRY, 1897-1965   (American composer)

C-236 Selected discography in Program notes for *Works by Arthur Shepard,
Henry Cowell, Roy Harris.* [Sound recording] New World Records NW
218, 1977: 4   ((--))

C-237 Selected discography in Program notes for *Exultation.* [Sound
recording] New World Records NW 304, 1979: [3]   ((--))

C-238 Selected discography in Program notes for *Pulse: works for
percussion and strings.* [Sound recording] New World Records
NW 319, 1984   ((--))

COWIE, EDWARD, 1943-   **(English composer)**

C-239 HUGHES, Eric and DAY, Timothy: Edward Cowie in *Recorded Sound*, No.

79 (January 1981): 125-127   ((--))   (Discographies of British
composers; 11)

CRABBÉ, ARMAND, 1883-1947   (Belgian baritone)

C-240 DENNIS, J.: Armand Crabbé [discography] in *Record Collector*,
XXIV/5-6 (July 1978): 121-130   ((3, 4, 6, 7))

CRAWFORD-SEEGER, RUTH, 1901-1953   (American composer)

C-241 Selected discography in Program notes for *Pulse*. [Sound recording]
New World Records NW 319, 1984   ((--))

C-242 Discography in GAUME, Matilda: *Ruth Crawford Seeger: memoirs,
memories, music*. Metuchen, NJ: Scarecrow Press, 1986: 245-246
((5))   (Composers of North America; 3)

CRESPIN, RÉGINE, 1943-   (French soprano)

C-243 Discographie in CRESPIN, Régine: *La vie et l'amour d'une femme*.
Paris: Fayard, 1982: 313-[316]   ((--))

CROIZA, CLAIRE, 1882-1946   (French mezzo-soprano)

C-244 Discographie in *Hommage à Claire Croiza*. Paris: Bibliothèque
nationale, 1984: [41]-[47]   ((7))

CROOKS, RICHARD, 1900-1972   (American tenor)

C-245 MORGAN, Charles I.: Richard Crooks discography in *Record Collector*,
XXXI/11-12 (November 1986): 258-279; additions and corrections in
XXXII/9-10 (September 1987): 238   ((1, 3, 6, 7))

CROSSE, GORDON, 1937-   (English composer)

C-246 HUGHES, Eric and DAY, Timothy: Gordon Crosse in *Recorded Sound*, No.
80 (July 1981): 133-141   ((1))   (Discographies of British composers;
12)

CRUMB, GEORGE, 1929-   (American composer)

C-247 [[Discography in ROUSE, Christopher Chapman, III: *The music of
George Crumb: stylistic metamorphosis as reflected in the Lorca
cycle*. [DMA, Cornell University, 1977] 188 pp.]]

C-248 [[Discography in SHUFFETT, Robert Vernon: *The music, 1971-1975, of
George Crumb: a style analysis*. [DMA, Peabody Conservatory of Music,
1979] 571 pp.]]

C-249 Discography in *George Crumb, profile of a composer*. New York: C.
F. Peters, 1985: 85-86   ((--))

C-250 Selected discography in Program notes for *A haunted landscape*.
[Sound recording] New World Records NW 326, 1985   ((--))

CUÉNOD, HUGUES, 1902-   (French tenor)

C-251 Discographie in SPYCKET, Jérôme: *Un Diable de musicien: Hugues*

Cuénod. Lausanne: Editions Payot, 1979: 226-229   ((--))

CULP, JULIA, 1880-1970   (Dutch contralto)

C-252   [[[Discography] in *Stimmen, die um die Welt gingen,* No. 4 (June 1984): 26-34]]

C-253   [WILLIAMS, Clifford]: Discography in *Record Collector,* XXXI/4-5 (May 1986): 96-110; additions and corrections in XXXI/6-7 (July 1986): 168; additions & corrections in XXXII/6-7 (June 1987): 157 ((3, 4, 6, 7))   [Includes notes on playing speeds]

CURITIBA, HENRIQUE DE, 1934-   (Brazilian composer)

C-254   Discographic references in MIGLIAVACCA, Ariede Maria: *Henrique de Curitiba: catálogo de obras.* [Brasília]: Ministério das Relações Exteriores, Departamento de Cooperação Cultural, Científica e Tecnológica, 1977: [14] pp.   ((--))   (Compositores brasileiros)

CUTNER, SOLOMON, 1902-1988   (English pianist)

C-255   GRAY, Michael H.: A Solomon discography in *ARSC Journal,* X/2-3 (1979): 188-209   ((3, 4, 6, 7))

CZIFFRA, GYÖRGY, 1921-   (Bulgarian painist)

C-256   FANTAPIÉ, Alain: Quelques enregistrements de Cziffra pour EMI La Voix de son Maitre in *Diapason,* No. 212 (December 1976): 32   ((--))

C-257   CAMACHO-CASTILLO, Mildred: A selected Cziffra discography in *High Fidelity,* XXXIV/10 (October 1984): 82   ((--))

DAETWYLER, JEAN, 1907-   (Swiss composer)

D-1   Discographie in DAETWYLER, Jean: *Croches et anicroches en pays valaisan.* Sierre: Monographie, SA, 1984: 237   ((--))

DAHL, INGOLF, 1912-1970   (American composer)

D-2   [[Discography in BERDAHL, James Nilson: *Ingolf Dahl: his life and works.* [Dissertation, University of Miami, 1975]   275 pp.]]

D-3   Selected discography in Program notes for *Chamber music of ... Ingolf Dahl.* [Sound recording] New World Records NW 281, 1976: 2 ((--))

DALBERG, FREDERICK, 1908-1988   (English bass)

D-4   [[Discographic references in TURNER, Wayne: Frederick Dalberg, 1908-1988 in *Record Collector,* XXXIII/8-10 (August 1988): 250-252]]

DALBERTO, MICHEL, 1955-   (French pianist)

D-5   Sa discographie in *Diapason-Harmonie,* No. 334 (January 1988): 40 ((--))

DALLAPICCOLA, LUIGI, 1904-1975   (Italian composer)

D-6   Discografia in *Luigi Dallapiccola: saggi, testimonianze, carteggio, biografia e bibliografia.* Milano: Edizioni Suvini Zerboni, 1975: 169-171 ((--))

D-7   Schallplatten in KÄMPER, Dietrich: *Gefangenschaft und Freiheit.* Köln: Gitarre + Laute Verlag, 1984: 195-198 ((--))

D-8   Discografia di Luigi Dallapiccola in *Musica,* No. 40 (March 1986): 42 ((--))

See also

PIANO MUSIC

DAMBIS, PAULS, 1936–   (Latvian composer)

D-9   [Discography] in *Music in the USSR* (April–June 1985): 7 ((--))

DANIEL–LESUR, 1908–   (French composer)

D-10   Discographie in *Daniel–Lesur.* Paris: Choudens, 1973: 75-78 ((--))

DARA, ENZO, 1938–   (Italian bass)

D-11   Discografia in *Musica,* No. 36 (March 1985): 20 ((--))

DARGAVEL, BRUCE, 1905-1985   (Welsh bass–baritone)

D-12   Bruce Dargavel discography in *Record Collector,* XXXII/11-12 (November 1987): 253-255 ((1, 7))

DARGOMIZHKY, ALEXANDER, 1813-1869   (Russian composer)

(THE) STONE GUEST (1872)

D-13   MARINELLI, Carlo: [Discography] in Milano, Teatro alla Scala, season 1982-83: program pp. 23-24 ((5))

DAVIDOVICH, BELLA, 1928–   (Russian pianist)

D-14   Discography [on Philips label] S.l.: [Philips, 198-?] 1 leaf. ((--))

DAVIDOVSKY, MARIO, 1934–   (American composer)

D-15   Selected discography in Program notes for *Parnassus.* [Sound recording] New World Records NW 306, 1980: [2] ((--))

DAVIES, FANNY, 1861-1934   (English pianist)

D-16   SAUL, Patrick and ELLIS, Chris: Fanny Davies: the recordings: 1, Discs in *Recorded Sound,* No. 70-71 (April-July 1978): 779-780 ((3, 7))

D-17   STONEHILL, Gerald: Fanny Davies: the recordings: 2, Piano rolls in *Recorded Sound,* No. 70-71 (April-July 1978): 780 ((--))

D-18   SUGA, Hajime: Davies ... [discography] in *LP Techno,* October 1980:

81   ((3))

DAVIES, PETER MAXWELL, 1934–   (English composer)

D-19   HUGHES, Eric and DAY, Timothy: Peter Maxwell Davies in *Recorded
       Sound,* No. 77 (January 1980): 81–93 ((--)) (Discographies of
       British composers; 2) [Also published as a pamphlet, 16 pp., 1980]

D-20   [[Discography in JACOB, Jeffrey Lynn: *Peter Maxwell Davies' Vesalii
       Icones: Origins and analysis.* [DMA, Peabody Conservatory of Music,
       1980] 132 pp.]]

D-21   List of works and recordings in GRIFFITHS, Paul: *Peter Maxwell
       Davies.* London: Robson Books, 1982: 179–190 ((--))

DAVIS, SIR COLIN, 1927–   (English conductor)

D-22   Discography [on Philips label] S.l.: [Philips, 198-?] 7 l. ((--))

DEBUSSY, CLAUDE, 1862–1918 (French composer)

D-23   MARNAT, Marcel: Discographie in BARRAQUÉ, Jean: *Debussy.* Paris:
       Seuil, 1977: 183–191 ((--))

D-24   RIEHN, Rainer: Verzeichnis der von Debussy eingespielten Aufnahmen
       Claude Debussy. München: Edition Text u. Kritik, 1977: 134 ((--))
       (Musik-Konzepte; 1)

D-25   Diskographie in HIRSBRUNNER, Theo: *Debussy und seine Zeit.*
       [Bern?]: Laaber, 1981: 251–254 ((--))

D-26   Discography in WENK, Arthur B.: *Claude Debussy and twentieth-century
       music.* Boston: Twayne Publishers, 1983: 158–159 ((--))

D-27   ROUSSILLE, Jean Paul: Discographie seléctive in GOUBAULT, Christian:
       Claude Debussy. Paris: H. Champion, 1986: 253–259 ((7))

OPERAS

PELLÉAS ET MÉLISANDE (1902)

D-28   MARINELLI, Carlo: [Discography] in Milano, Teatro alla Scala,
       season 1972–73: program pp. 412–414 ((5))

D-29   MARINELLI, Carlo: [Discography] in Venezia, Gran Teatro La
       Fenice, season 1973–74: program pp. 157–160 ((5))

D-30   POUGET, François: Discographie: Pelléas et le 78 in *L'Avant Scène
       Opéra,* No. 9 (March–April 1977): 108–110 ((1, 3, 5, 6, 7))

D-31   [[[Discography] in *Claude Debussy, Pelléas et Mélisande.* München:
       Bayerische Staatsoper, 1979: 84]]

D-32   ROY, Jean: Le point sur Pelléas et Mélisande de Claude Debussy
       in *Diapason,* No. 259 (March 1981): 42–43 ((--))

D-33   Discography in *Pelléas & Mélisande.* London: J. Calder; New York:
       Riverrun Press, 1982: 96 ((--)) (English National Opera guide; 9)

D-34   MARINELLI, Carlo: [Discography] in Roma, Teatro dell'Opera.
        season 1983-84: program pp. 72-78 ((5))

D-35   MARINELLI, Carlo: [Discography] in Milano, Teatro alla Scala,
        season 1985-86: program pp. 91-95 ((5))

D-36   [[[Discography] in NICHOLS, Roger: *Claude Debussy, Pelléas et
        Mélisande*. Cambridge; New York: Cambridge University Press, 1988:
        (Cambridge opera handbooks)]]

   ORCHESTRAL WORKS

   JEUX (1912)

D-37   MARINELLI, Carlo: [Discography] in Roma, Teatro dell'Opera,
        season 1966-67: program pp. 73-75 ((5))

   (LE) MARTYRE DE SAINT-SEBASTIEN (1911)

D-38   MARINELLI, Carlo: [Discography] in Milano, Teatro alla Scala,
        season 1985-86: program pp. 44-45 ((5))

   (LA) MER (1904)

D-39   [[Discography in ROLF, Marie: *La Mer: a critical analysis in the
        light of early sketches and editions*. [Dissertation, Univerity
        of Rochester, 1976] 357 pp.]]

D-40   SZERSNOVICZ, Patrick: La mer de Claude Debussy [discographie
        comparée] in *Harmonie*, No. 144 (February 1979): 84-89
        ((--))

   SONGS

D-41   [[[Discography] in COBB, Margaret G.: *Poetic Debussy: a
        collection of his song texts and selected letters*. Boston:
        Northeastern University Press, 1982: -]]

   DEL CAMPO, SOFIA, 1884-1964 (Chilean soprano)

D-42   MORAN, W. R.: The recordings of Sofia del Campo in *Record
       Collector*, XXIV/3-4 (March 1978): 90-92, 95 ((3, 6, 7))

   DE CLERY, MAURICE, 1873-?   (Belgian tenor)

D-43   [Discography] in *Record Collector*, IX/3 (March 1954): 63-64 ((--))

   DE LARA, ADELINA, 1872-1961 (English pianist)

D-44   Adelina de Lara: discography of published records in *Recorded Sound*,
       No. 78 (July 1980): 51-54 ((1))

   DELIBES, LÉO, 1836-1891 (French composer)

   BALLETS

   COPPÉLIA (1870)

D-45   MARINELLI, Carlo: [Discography] in Roma, Teatro dell'Opera, season 1969-70: program p. 430 ((5))

D-46   MARINELLI, Carlo: [Discography] in Milano, Teatro alla Scala, season 1973: program p. 113 ((5))

D-47   MARINELLI, Carlo: [Discography] in Milano, Teatro alla Scala, season 1985-86: program pp. 32-33 ((5))

OPERAS

LAKMÉ (1883)

D-48   MARINELLI, Carlo: [Discography] in Bologna, Teatro Comunale, season 1980-81: program pp. 43-50 ((5))

DELIUS, FREDERICK, 1862-1934 (English composer)

D-49   [[THOMSEN, Inger: *Frederick Delius: et udvalg af indspilninger udkommet efter 1960.* [Thesis, Royal Danish School of Librarianship, 1973]]]

D-50   [Delius discography] in Program notes for *The Music of Delius* [Sound recording] Toshiba-EMI Angel EAC 60060/4, 1977: 18-19 ((5, 7))

D-51   LLOYD, Stephen: A select discography in *Delius, 1862-1934.* [London]: Delius Trust, 1984: [7-8] ((--))

D-52   Discographische Hinweise: Frederick Delius in *fono forum* (December 1984): 38-39 ((--))

DELLER, ALFRED, 1912-1979 (English countertenor)

D-53   Discographie d'Alfred Deller in *Harmonie*, No. 150 (September 1979): 119 ((--))

D-54   HOWLETT, Alan: Alfred Deller: complete discography in HARDWICK, Michael and HARDWICK, Mollie: *Alfred Deller, a singularity of voice.* London; New York: Proteus, 1980: 193-197 ((--))

DELLO JOIO, NORMAN, 1913-1988 (American composer)

D-55   Selected discography in Program notes for *Songs by ... Norman Dello Joio ....* [Sound recording] New World Records NW 300, 1978: [4] ((--))

D-56   Discography in BUMGARDNER, Thomas A.: *Norman Dello Joio.* Boston: Twayne Publishers, 1986: 171-173 ((5)) (Twayne's music series)

DE LUCIA, FERNANDO, 1860-1925 (Italian tenor)

D-57   HENSTOCK, Michael E.: Discography in *Record Collector*, XXX/5-6 (June 1985): 101-139; XXX/7-9 (August 1985): 149-212; Additions & corrections in XXXIII/8-10 (August 1988): 231-236 ((3, 6, 7)) [Includes notes on unissued records]

DEL MONACO, MARIO, 1915-1982 (Italian tenor)

D-58 Discographie in SEGOND, André: *Mario Del Monaco, ou, Un ténor de légende.* Lyon: J. M. Laffont, 1981: 243-254 ((1, 5))

DEMESSIEUX, JEANNE, 1921-1968 (French organist)

D-59 Catalogue discographique in COLLENEY, Christiane: *Jeanne Demessieux: une vie de luttes et de gloire.* Avignon: Presses universelles, 1977: 235-237 ((--)))

DEMUS, JÖRG, 1928– (Austrian pianist)

D-60 RISALITI, Riccardo: Discografia di Joerg Demus su strumenti antichi in DEMUS, Jörg: Jörg Demus e i pianoforti d'epoca in *Musica,* No. 18 (September 1980): 274-276 ((--))

DENISOV, EDISON, 1929– (Russian composer)

D-61 Discography in *Music in the USSR* (January-March 1988): 21 ((--))

DE REZKE, JEAN, 1850-1925 (Polish tenor)

D-62 TAYLOR, G. W.: The recorded legacy of Jean de Reszke in *Record Collector,* XXXIII/1-2 (January 1988): 22-25 ((3, 7))

D-63 ASPINAL, Michael: Jean de Reszke, live!--The Mapleson cylinders in *Record Collector,* XXXIII/6-7 (June 1988): 151-160; pt. 2 in XXXIII/8-10 (August 1988): 236-246 ((1, 7))

DERMOTA, ANTON, 1910– (Austrian tenor)

D-64 SCHMIDT, Jürgen E.: Diskographie in DERMOTA, Anton: *Tausendundein Abend: mein Sängerleben.* Wein; Berlin: Neff, 1978: 343-[352] ((5, 7))

D-65 SCHMIDT, Jürgen E.: Diskographie in *Musik und Dichtung: Anton Dermota zum 70. Geburtstag: eine Festschrift.* Wien: Institut für Österreichische Musikdokumentation ..., 1980: 60-69 ((7))

DERVAUX, PIERRE, 1917– (French conductor)

D-66 Discographie de Pierre Dervaux in *Harmonie hi-fi conseil,* No. 5 (January 1981): 28-33 ((--))

DE SABATA, VICTOR, 1892-1967 (Italian conductor)

D-67 Phonographie Victor de Sabata in *fono forum* (December 1977): 1312 ((7))

D-68 BELLINGARDI, Luigi: Discografia in CELLI, Teodoro: *L'arte di Victor de Sabata.* Torino: ERI, 1978: 164-168 ((1, 7))

DESTINN, EMMY, 1878-1930 (Czech soprano)

D-69 Diskografie in POSPÍŠIL, Miroslav: *Veliké srdce: Ema Destinnová.* Praha: Editio Supraphon, 1980: 234-248 ((3, 6, 7))

DETROIT SYMPHONY ORCHESTRA

D-70   KOLDYS, Mark: Paul Paray conducts the Detroit Symphony Orchestra: a discography in *American Record Guide*, XLIII/4 (February 1980): 12 ((1, 5, 7))

DEUTEKOM, CHRISTINA, 1931–   (Dutch soprano)

D-71   [[STROFF, Stephen: Discography in *Goldmine* (May 25, 1984):]]

DE VALMAR, MR.   (Tenor)

D-72   [Discography] in *Record Collector*, IX/3 (March 1954): 71 ((--))

DE VITO, GIOCONDA, 1907–   (Italian violinist)

D-73   Discografia in *Musica*, No. 43 (March 1987): 49 ((7))

DE VITRY, PHILIPPE, 1291–1361 (French composer)

D-74   WEBER, J. F.: A discography of the music of Philippe de Vitry in *Fanfare*, V/3 (January–February 1982): 36–37 ((5, 7))

DE WAART, EDO

See

WAART, EDO DE

DIAMOND, DAVID, 1915–   (American composer)

D-75   Selected discography in *Diamond, David: Symphony No. 4.* [Sound recording] New World Records NW 258, 1976: 4 ((--))

D-76   Discography in KIMBERLING, Victoria J.: *David Diamond, a bio-bibliography.* Metuchen, NJ: Scarecrow Press, 1987: 161–163 ((5))

DICHTER, MISHA, 1945–   (American pianist)

D-77   Discography [on Philips label] S.l.: [Philips, 198–?] 1 leaf. ((--))

DIEMER, EMMA, 1927–   (American composer)

D-78   [[Discography in BROWN, Cynthia Clark: *Emma Lou Diemer: composer, performer, educator, church musician.* [DMA, Southern Baptist Theological Seminary, 1985] 267 pp.]]

D-79   [[Discography in OUTLAND, Joyanne Jones: *Emma Lou Diemer: solo and chamber works for piano through 1986.* [Dissertation, Ball State University, 1986] 293 pp.]]

DIEREN, BERNARD VAN, 1884–1936 (English composer)

D-80   [[WILLIAMS, Robert: Bernard van Dieren discography (1887–1936) in *British Music Society Journal*, I (1979): 53–63]]

DMITRIYEV, ALEXANDER (Russian composer)

D-81   Discography in *Music in the USSR* (January–March 1988): 23; (July–
September 1988): 67 ((––))

DOBROWEN, ISSAY, 1894–1953   (Russian conductor)

D-82   KURTZBERG, Robert: Issay Dobrowen discography in *Le Grand Baton*,
No. 59 (October 1988): 12–21   ((3, 7))

DODGSON, STEPHEN, 1924–   (English composer)

D-83   HUGHES, Eric: Recordings of music by Stephen Dodgson in *Recorded
Sound*, No. 68 (October 1977): 737–738   ((7))

DOGA, YEVGENI DMITRIYEVCH, 1937–   (Russian composer)

D-84   [Discography] in *Music in the USSR* (October–December 1985): 95 ((––))

DOHNANYI, CHRISTOPH VON, 1929–   (German conductor)

D-85   [[BADAL, James: Discography in *Goldmine* (June 8, 1984):]]

DOKSHITSER, TIMOTEI, 1921–   (Russian trumpeter)

D-86   Discography in *Music in the USSR* (April–June 1988): 68   ((––))

DOMANINSKA, LIBUSE, 1924–   (Czech soprano)

D-87   [[[Discography] in JIRASKOVA, Jirina: *Libuse Domanínská*.
Praha: Supraphon, 1983: 47–49]]

DOMINGO, PLACIDO, 1937–   (Spanish tenor)

D-88   Discography, Deutsche Grammophon artist information, 1980, 2 pp. ((––))

D-89   Discography in his *My first forty [sic] years*. New York: Knopf, 1983:
237–241   ((5))

DONATONI, FRANCO, 1927–   (Italian composer)

D-90   SZERSNOVICZ, Patrick: Franco Donatoni – Catalogue des oeuvres Discographie in *Musique en jeu*, No. 20 (September 1975): [24]–27   ((––))

D-91   Discografia in *Discoteca*, No. 193 (April 1979): 20   ((––))

D-92   Discografia in CRESTI, Renzo: *Franco Donatoni*. Milano: Edizioni
Suvini Zerboni, 1982: 109–110   ((––))

DONIZETTI, GAETANO, 1797–1848   (Italian composer)

D-93   Diskographie in STEINER-ISENMANN, Robert: *Gaetano Donizetti: sein
Leben und seine Opern*. Bern: Hallwag, 1982: 523–532   ((5))

D-94   Discografia donizettiana in *Gaetano Donizetti*. Milano: Nuovo
edizioni, 1983: 275–278   ((––))

OPERAS

ANNA BOLENA (1830)

D-95   MARINELLI, Carlo: [Discography] in Roma, Teatro dell'Opera,
        season 1976-77: program pp. 297-303 ((5))

D-96   MARINELLI, Carlo: [Discography] in Bologna, Teatro Comunale,
        season 1978-79: program pp. 40-45 ((5))

D-97   MARINELLI, Carlo: [Discography] in Roma, Teatro dell'Opera,
        season 1978-79: program pp. 608-615 ((5))

D-98   MARINELLI, Carlo: [Discography] in Milano, Teatro alla Scala,
        season 1981-82: program pp. 86-89 ((5))

(IL) CAMPANELLO DEL NOTTE (1836)

D-99   MARINELLI, Carlo: [Discography] in Treviso, Ente Teatro
        Comunale, season 1976-77: program p. 2 ((5))

DON PASQUALE (1843)

D-100   MARINELLI, Carlo: [Discography] in Milano, Teatro alla Scala,
        season 1972-73: program pp. 412-414 ((5))

D-101   MARINELLI, Carlo: [Discography] in Roma, Teatro dell'Opera,
        season 1978-79: program pp. 396-400 ((5))

D-102   MARINELLI, Carlo: [Discography] in Treviso, Ente Teatro
        Comunale, season 1979: program p. 7 ((5))

D-103   MARINELLI, Carlo: [Discography] in Milano, Teatro alla Scala,
        season 1983-84: program pp. 84-88 ((5))

D-104   MARINELLI, Carlo: [Discography] in Palermo, Ente automono
        Teatro Massimo, season 1984-85: program pp. 34-36 ((5))

D-105   MARINELLI, Carlo: [Discography] in Roma, Teatro dell'Opera,
        season 1984-85: program pp. 40-47 ((5))

D-106   MARINELLI, Carlo: [Discography] in Milano, Teatro alla Scala,
        season 1984-85: program p. 80 ((5))

D-107   CABOURG, Jean and VOISIN, Georges: Discographie in *L'Avant
        Scène Opéra*, No. 108 (August-September 1988): 94-104 ((1, 5))

L'ELISIR D'AMORE (1832)

D-108   MARINELLI, Carlo: [Discography] in Venezia, Gran Teatro
        La Fenice, season 1976-77: program pp. 125-130 ((5))

D-109   MARINELLI, Carlo: [Discography] in Milano, Teatro alla Scala,
        season 1979: program pp. 65-70 ((5))

D-110   MARINELLI, Carlo: [Discography] in Venezia, Gran Teatro La
        Fenice, season 1983: program pp. 355-360 ((5))

D-111   MARINELLI, Carlo: [Discography] in Roma, Teatro dell'Opera,
        season 1985-86: program pp. 52-58 ((5))

D-112   CABOURG, Jean: Discographie and VOISIN, Georges: Airs séparés in

L'Avant Scène Opéra, No. 95 (February 1987): 90–100 ((1, 7))

(LA) FAVORITE (1840)

D-113   MARINELLI, Carlo: [Discography] in Roma, Teatro dell'Opera, season 1970–71: program pp. 217–220 ((5))

D-114   [[[Discography] in *Record Geijutsu* (No. 9, 1971):]]

D-115   MARINELLI, Carlo: [Discography] in Milano, Teatro alla Scala, season 1973–74: program pp. 47–53 ((5))

(LA) FILLE DU RÉGIMENT (1841)

D-116   MARINELLI, Carlo: [Discography] in Roma, Teatro dell'Opera, season 1967–68: program p. 218 ((5))

LUCIA DI LAMMERMOOR (1835)

D-117   MARINELLI, Carlo: [Discography] in Venezia, Gran Teatro La Fenice, season 1972–73: program pp. 179–190 ((5))

D-118   HALFT, Franz Werner: Lucia di Lammermoor: ein Vergleich von 21 Gesamtaufnahmen aus funf Jahrehnten: Teil II in *fono forum* (October 1977): 1008–1010, 1012, 1014–1016, 1018–1019 ((--))

D-119   MARINELLI, Carlo: [Discography] in Palermo, Ente automono Teatro Massimo, season 1982–83: program p. 47 ((5))

D-120   MARINELLI, Carlo: [Discography] in Milano, Teatro alla Scala, season 1982–83: program pp. 69–75 ((5))

D-121   Discografia in GUANDALINI, Gina: Appunti sulla Lucia in disco in *Musica*, No. 28 (March 1983): 62–63 ((5))

D-122   MARINELLI, Carlo: Discographie and VOISIN, Georges: Airs séparés in *L'Avant Scène Opéra*, No. 55 (September 1983): 110–[127] ((1, 7))

LUCREZIA BORGIA (1833)

D-123   MARINELLI, Carlo: [Discography] in Roma, Teatro dell'Opera, season 1967–68: program pp. 786–788 ((5))

D-124   MARINELLI, Carlo: [Discography] in Roma, Teatro dell'Opera, season 1979–80: program pp. 850–852 ((5))

D-125   MARINELLI, Carlo: [Discography] in Venezia, Gran Teatro La Fenice, season 1983: program pp. 124–125 ((5))

D-126   [[[Comparative discography] in *Opéra International*, No. 68 (March 1984):]]

ROBERTO DEVEREUX (1837)

D-127   MARINELLI, Carlo: [Discography] in Venezia, Gran Teatro La Fenice, season 1971–72: program pp. 278–279 ((5))

DORÁTI, ANTAL, 1906-1988   (Hungarian conductor)

D-128 Discography [on Philips label]   S.l.: [Philips, 198-?]   4 l.   ((--))

DORGAN, VLADIMIR   (Ukrainian composer)

D-129 [Discography] in *Music in the USSR* (April-June 1985): 95   ((--))

DOUBLE BASS

D-130 Schallplatten in PLANYAVSKY, Alfred: *Geschichte des Kontrabasses.*
Tutzing: H. Schneider, 1984: 852-878   ((--))

DOUBLE-BASS MUSIC

D-131 Discography in PRAEKEL, David: The double bass on record in *Hi-fi
News and Record Review*, XXVI/1 (January 1981): 71-73   ((--))

D'OYLY CARTE OPERA COMPANY, London

D-132 TRAUBNER, Richard: A retrospective of the D'Oyly Carte in
American Record Guide, XLIV/6 (April 1981): 35-40   ((--))

D-133 WOLFSON, John: *Savoyards on record.* Chichester, West Sussex:
Packard, 1985. 96 pp. ((3, 5, 6, 7))

See also

SULLIVAN, SIR ARTHUR

DRESDEN. MUSIKALISCHE KAPELLE DER SACHSISCHEN STAATS-
THEATER

D-134 Dresden Staatskapelle selected discography in *Hi-Fi News & Record
Review*, XXII/11 (November 1977): 145, 147   ((--))

DRESDEN PHILHARMONIC ORCHESTRA

D-135 Schallplattenaufnahmen mit der Dresdener Philharmonic bei Eterna
1970-1985 (stand 30.6.1985; Auswahl) in HÄRTWIG, Dieter: *Die Dresden
Philharmonic.* Leipzig: Bibliographisches Institut, 1985: 102-107
((--))

DRUCKMAN, JACOB, 1928-   (American composer)

D-136 Selected discography in Program notes for *Works by Jacob Druckman.*
[Sound recording] New World Records NW 318, 1983: [2]   ((--))

D-137 Selected discography in Program notes for *Jacob Druckman: Prism.*
[Sound recording] New World Records NW 335, 1986   ((--))

DRZEWIECKI, ZBIGNIEW, 1890-1971   (Polish composer)

D-138 Dyskográfia in DRZEWIECKI, Zbigniew: *Wspomnienia muzyka.*
Kraków: Polskie Wydawn. Muzyczne, 1971: 185   ((--))

DUFAY, GUILLAUME, before 1400-1474   (Flemish composer)

D-139 WEBER, J. F.: Discography of the music of Guillaume Dufay
[part 1] in his The beginning of the Renaissance in *Fanfare*,
III/3 (January–February 1980): 16–18, 20–22, 24–25; Part 2 in
Fanfare, III/4 (March–April 1980): 22–24, 26, 28, 30–31
((5, 7))

DUKAS, PAUL, 1865–1935   (French composer)

D-140 Discographie in HELBÉ, Jacques: *Paul Dukas: 1865–1935*. Paris:
Editions P.M.P., 1975: 86   ((--))

DUMAY, AUGUSTIN, 1949–   (French violinist)

D-141 Sa discographie in *Diapason-Harmonie*, No. 342 (October 1988): 47
((--))

DUMORTIER, ANDRÉ   (French pianist)

D-142 Discographie in *Discorama*, No. 5 (May 1960): 12   ((--))

DU PLESSIS, HUBERT,

See

COMPOSERS--SOUTH AFRICA

DU PRÉ, JACQUELINE, 1945–1987   (English cellist)

D-143 Discography in *Jacqueline de Pré: impressions*.   New York: Vanguard
Press, 1983: [139]–141   ((--))

DUPRÉ, MARCEL, 1886–1971   (French organist/composer)

D-144 [Discography] in MURRAY, Michael: *Marcel Dupré, the work of a master
organist*.   Boston: Northeastern University Press, 1985: 232–238
((1))

D-145 COLLENEY, Christiane: Discographie in *Marcel Dupré 1886–1971, ou, La
cause de l'orgue*. Special number of *Jeunesse et orgue*, No. 65–67
(1986): 78   ((--))

DURAND, GEORGES   (French tenor)

D-146 [Discography] in *Record Collector*, IX/3 (March 1954): 64   ((--))

DURUFLÉ, MAURICE, 1902–1986   (French composer)

D-147 [[Discography in MCINTOSH, John Stuart: *The organ music of Maurice
Duruflé*. [DMA, University of Rochester, 1973]   180 pp.]]

DUSSEK, JAN LADISLAW, 1760–1812   (Czech composer)

D-148 DOSCHER, David: Discography in CRAW, Howard Allen: *A Biography
thematic catalogue of the works of Johann Ladislaus Dussek (1760–
1812)* [Dissertation, University of Southern California, 1964]

DUTILLEUX, HENRI, 1916–   (French composer)

D-149 A écouter in *Diapason*, No. 239 (May 1979): 50   ((--))

D-150 BROWN, Royal S.: A Dutilleux discography in *Fanfare*, VI/1
(September-October 1982): 214-215   ((--))

D-151 Discographie in *Harmonie-Panorama musique*, No. 48 (December 1984):
26   ((--))

D-152 Discographie in HUMBERT, Daniel: *Henri Dutilleux: l'oeuvre et le
style musical.* Paris: Champion; Genève: Slatkine, 1985: [247]
((--))

DUTOIT, CHARLES, 1936-   **(Swiss conductor)**

D-153 Discographie de Charles Dutoit in *Harmonie-Opéra-Hifi Conseil*, No.
21 (June 1982): 23   ((--))

D-154 Discographie in NICHOLSON, Georges: *Charles Dutoit: le maître
de l'orchestre.* Montréal: Éditions de l'homme; Lausanne: P. M.
Favre, 1986: 227-234   ((--))

D-155 Discographische Hinweise in *fono forum* (November 1987): 22-[23]
((--))

DVOŘÁK, ANTONÍN, 1841-1904   (Czech composer)

CONCERTO, VIOLONCELLO, OP. 104, B MINOR

D-156 BARBIER, Pierre-E.: Le point sur le Concerto pour violoncelle
(en si mineur) de Dvořák in *Diapason*, No. 250 (May 1980): 42-43
((5))

Ensemble vocal et instrumental "Les Arts Florissants"

See

(LES) ARTS FLORISSANTS, Paris

EAMES, EMMA, 1865-1952   (American soprano)

E-1   MORAN, W. R.: Recordings of Emma Eames (13 Aug., 1865-13 Jan., 1952)
A discography in EAMES, Emma: *Some memories and reflections.*
New York: Arno Press, 1977: [313]-[320] ((1, 3, 6, 7)) [Includes
notes on playing speeds; originally published without discography
by Appleton & Co., New York and London, 1927]

EASTMAN SCHOOL OF MUSIC, USA

E-2   An Eastman discography; from the first American opera to the Eastman
Marimba Band in *Eastman Notes* (September 1976): 2, 6-8   ((--))

E-3   Eastman discography; faculty soloists, ensembles in *Rochester Review*
(Spring 1977): 32-34   ((--))

E-4   Eastman discography; composers, ensembles in *Rochester Review*
(Summer 1977): 28   ((--))

E-5   SANTUCCIO, John: An Eastman discography in *Eastman Notes*, XVII/3

(June 1984): 4-16 ((--))

EASTON, FLORENCE, 1882-1955   (English soprano)

E-6   Additions and corrections to discography in *Record Collector*,
XXI/9-10 (January 1974) in XXVII/3-4 (March 1982): 84-95 ((--))

ÉGLISE SAINT-NICHOLAS, BRUSSELS--ORGAN

E-7   Discographie in FÉLIX, Jean Pierre: *Histoire des orgues de l'église
Saint-Nicolas a Bruxelles.* Brussels: Félix, 1977: leaf 95 ((1, 7))

EGMOND, MAX VAN, 1936-   (Dutch bass-baritone)

E-8   Discografie in MULLER, Juul: *Max van Egmond, toonaangevend
kunstenaar.* Zutphen: Thieme, 1984: 422-431 ((--))

EHMANN, WILHELM, 1904-   (German conductor)

E-9   Diskographie in EHMANN, Wilhelm: *Voce et tuba: ges. u. Aufsätze,
1934-1974.* Basel; Tours; London: Bärenreiter, 1976: 621-631 ((7))

EINEM, GOTTFRIED VON, 1918-   (German composer)

E-10   Diskographie in SAATTHEN, Friedrich: *Einem Chronik.* Wien; Köln;
Graz: Hermann Böhlars Nachf., 1982: 369-370 ((--))

EISLER, HANNS, 1898-1962 (German composer)

E-11   Hanns Eisler--Diskografie in *Hanns Eisler: Musik im Klassenkampf.*
Berlin: Universum-Buchdienst, 1975: 194-196 ((--))

E-12   Diskographie in *Hanns Eisler--Kompostionen für den Film.* Berlin:
Freunden der Deutschen Kinemathek, 1982: 78 ((--))

E-13   Discographic notes in GRABS, Manfred: *Hanns Eisler: Komposistionen,
Schriften, Literatur: ein Handbuch.* Leipzig: VEB Deutscher Verlag
für Musik, 1984. 415 pp. ((5, 7))

E-14   Werkverzeichnis/Schallplatten in HENNENBERG, Fritz: *Hanns Eisler.*
Leipzig: Bibliographisches Institut, 1986: 106-108 ((--))

EKIMOVSKY, VICTOR, 1947-   (Russian composer)

E-15   [Discography] in *Music in the USSR* (October-December 1986): 96
((--))

ELECTRONIC MUSIC

E-16   [[Discography in HENRY, Otto Walker: *The evolution of idiomatic and
psychoacoustical resources as a basis for unity in electronic music.*
[Dissertation, Tulane University, 1970] 278 pp.]]

E-17   FRANK, Peter: A discography of electronic music on recordings in
BMI--The Many Worlds of Music (Summer 1970): [14]-22 ((--))

E-18   Discography in DRAKE, Russell: *How to make electronic music.*
Pleasantville, NY: Educational Audio Visual, 1975: 102-103 ((--))

E-19   Discographie in CHION, Michel and REIBEL, Guy: *Les musiques electroacoustiques.* Aix-en-Provence: INA-GRM; Edisud, 1976: 326-336 ((--))

E-20   Discography in DRAKE, Russell: *How to make electronic music.* New York: Harmony House, 1978: 102-103 ((--))

E-21   Discography in GRIFFITHS, Paul: *A guide to electronic music.* London: Thames & Hudson, 1978: 95-116 ((--))

E-22   KONDRACKI, Miroslaw: *Internationale Diskographie elektronischer Musik.* Mainz; London; New York; Tokyo: Schott, 1979. 174 pp. ((4, 5))

E-23   Selected discography in WELLS, Thomas B.: *The technique of electronic music.* New York: Schirmer Books, 1981; London: Collier-Macmillan, 1981: 294-295 ((--))

E-24   [[[Discography] in JACKSON, Hanley: *Synthesis, analog and digital: a comprehensive guide to the electronic music studio.* Manhattan, KS: L&M Publishers, 1982: 1. [194]-196]]

E-25   Discografie in WEILAND, Frits C.: *Elektronische muziek.* Utrecht: Bohn, Scheltema & Holkema, 1982: 224-230 ((--))

E-26   [[[Discography] in NAUMANN, Joel: *Analog electronic music techniques: in tape, electronic, and voltage-controlled synthesizer studios.* New York: Longman, 1984:]]

E-27   Ancient instruments and rare recordings in HOLMES, Thomas B.: *Electronic and experimental music.* New York: Scribner's, 1985: 228-233 ((--))

E-28   Discography in MANNING, Peter: *Electronic and computer music.* Oxford: Clarendon Press; New York: Oxford University Press, 1985: [266]-278 ((--))

E-29   Discography in SCHWARTZ, Elliott: *Electronic music: a listener's guide.* New York: Da Capo Press, 1986: 293-298 ((--)) [Reprinted from the 1975 ed. published by Praeger, New York]

ELGAR, SIR EDWARD, 1857-1934   (English composer)

E-30   KNOWLES, John: *Elgar's interpreters on record: an Elgar discography.* Malvern: The Elgar Society, 1977: 68 pp. ((5, 7)); Additions & corrections in Elgar Society Journal, I/1 (January 1979): 29-31 ((5))

E-31   KNOWLES, John: *Elgar's interpreters on record: an Elgar discography.* 2d ed. London: Thames Pub. Co., 1985. 133 pp. ((4, 5, 7))

DREAM OF GERONTIUS (1900)

E-32   MARCHINGTON, Bryan: Edison Bell and "The Dream of Gerontius" in *Hillandale News*, No. 32 (August 1966): 12-13 ((3))

ENGELMANN, HANS ULRICH, 1921–   (German composer)

E-33   Discographie in *Commedia humana; Hans Ulrich Engelmann und sein Werk.* Wiesbaden: Breitkopf und Härtel, 1985: 137 ((--))

ENGLERT, GIUSEPPE GIORGIO, 1927–   (Italian composer)

E-34   Discographie in *Giuseppe G. Englert.* Zürich: Pro Helvetia, 1980: 73 ((--))

ENGLISH CHAMBER ORCHESTRA, London

E-35   The ECO--A current discography in WOODHOUSE, Anthony: *The English Chamber Orchestra: a pictorial review: twentieth anniversary, 1980-81.* London: Bruton Hay, 1980: 151-153 ((--))

ENGLISH SINGERS

E-36   BLACKER, George: Disco-ing ... The English Singers – and Roycroft – revisited! in *Record Research,* No. 211/212 (February 1985): 4-5, 11 ((3, 6))

ENSEMBLE OF BOLSHOI THEATRE ORCHESTRA SOLOISTS, Moscow

E-37   Discography in *Music in the USSR* (April-June 1985): 95 ((--))

EPHRIKIAN, ANGELO, 1913–   (Italian conductor)

E-38   Discographie d'Angelo Ephrikian in TRAVERS, Roger-Claude: Entretien avec Angelo Ephrikian in *Diapason,* No. 225 (February 1978): 48-49 ((--))

ERB, KARL, 1877-1958   (German tenor)

E-39   GRUNDHEBER, Jürgen: Karl Erb discography in *Record Collector,* XXIV/3-4 (March 1978): 72-86 ((3, 4, 5))

ERDMANN, DIETRICH, 1917–   (German composer)

E-40   [[[Discography] in BRUDE, Wolfgang: *Musica multicolore-- Dietrich Erdmann, Werk und Vita.* Wiesbaden: Breitkopf und Härtel, 1987: 32-39]]

ERROLLE, RALPH, 1890-1973   (American tenor)

E-41   FERRARA, D. E.: Neglected Edison disc artists in *New Amberola Graphic,* No. 51 (Winter 1985): 11-12 ((3, 7))

E-42   The Edison records of Ralph Errolle in *Record Collector,* XXXII/8-10 (September 1987): 222 ((3, 7)) [Includes unissued records]

ERSHOV, IVAN VASILEVICH, 1867-1943   (Russian singer)

E-43   Diskografiia I.V. Ershova in GOZENPUD, A.: *van Ershov: zhizn i stsenicheskaia deiatelnost: issledovanie.* Leningrad: "Sov. kompozitor", Leningradskoe otd-nie, 1986: 297-298 ((3, 7))

ESHPAI, ANDREI, 1926–   (Soviet composer)

E-44   Discography in *Music in the USSR* (July–September 1986): 68   ((--))

ESTES, SIMON, 1938–   (American bass–baritone)

E-45   Discographische Hinweise: Simon Estes in *fono forum* (May 1986): 33 ((--))

EVANS, GERAINT, SIR, 1922–   (Welsh baritone)

E-46   Discography in EVANS, Geraint: *Sir Geraint Evans, a knight at the opera*. London: M. Joseph, 1984: 266–268 ((5))

EVANS, GREEK, 1889–1967   (American baritone)

E-47   The records of Greek Evans in *Record Collector*, XXX/10–11 (October 1985): 250; additions & corrections in XXXI/1–3 (February 1986): 72 ((--))

EVETT, ROBERT, 1922–1975   (American composer)

E-48   Selected discography in Program notes for *Exultation*. [Sound recording] New World Records NW 304, 1979: [3] ((--))

EYREAMS, CÉCILE, 1874–?   (Soprano)

E-49   [Discography] in *Record Collector*, IX/3 (March 1954): 64   ((--))

FAGOAGA, ISIDORO, 1895–1976 (Spanish tenor)

F-1   BOTT, Michael F.: The recordings of Isidoro Fagoaga in *Record Collector*, XXX/3–4 (April 1985): 74; additions & corrections in XXII/1–2 (January 1987): 31 ((3, 6, 7))

FALCINELLI, ROLANDE, 1920–   (French organist)

F-2   Disques in *Rolande Falcinelli et la classe d'orgue du Conservatoire*. Paris: Association des amis de l'Orgue, 1981: [55]–56 ((--))

FALIK, YURI, 1936–   (Russian composer)

F-3   Discography in *Music in the USSR* (July–September 1985): 93 ((--))

FALLA, MANUEL DE, 1876–1946 (Spanish composer)

F-4   Discographie sélective in *Diapason*, No. 212 (December 1976): 30 ((--))

F-5   Discographie critique in CAMPODONICO, Luis: *Falla*. Paris: Seuil, 1980: 182–183 ((--))

F-6   GAUTHIER, André: Manuel de Falla: discographie critique in *Harmonie*, No. 155 (February 1980): [52]–61 ((--))

F-7   [[[Discographies] in CHASE, Gilbert and BUDWIG, Andrew: *Manual de Falla: a bibliography and research guide*. New York: Garland Pub., 1988. 145 pp. (Garland composer resource manuals; 4)]]

STAGE WORKS

(EL) RETABLO DE MAESE PEDRO (1923)

F-8   MARINELLI, Carlo: [Discography] in Venezia, Gran Teatro La
      Fenice, season 1983: program pp. 369-372 ((5))

PIANO WORKS

F-9   Discografía pianística de Manuel de Falla in IGLESIAS, Antonio:
      Manuel de Falla: su obra para piano. Madrid: Alpuerto, [1983]:
      281-285 ((--))

FARKAS, FERENC, 1905-   (Hungarian composer)

F-10 Discographie in *Inventaire du fonds musical Ferenc Farkas: catalogue
      des oeuvres.* Lausanne: BCU, 1979: 46-47 ((--))

FARRENC, LOUISE, 1804-1875   (French composer)

F-11 Discography in FRIEDLAND, Bea: *Louise Farrenc, 1804-1875:
      composer, performer, scholar.* Ann Arbor: UMI Research Press, 1980:
      181 ((--))

FAURÉ, GABRIEL-URBAIN, 1845-1924   (French composer)

F-12 NECTOUX, Jean-Michel: *Gabriel Fauré: 1900-1977.* Paris:
      Bibliothèque nationale, Departement de la phonothèque nationale et
      de l'audiovisuel, 1979.   262 pp.   ((1, 3, 4, 6, 7))
      (Phonographies; 1)

F-13 SMOLIAN, Steve: Discography in VUILLERMOZ, Émile: *Gabriel Fauré.*
      New York: Da Capo Press, 1983: [173]-259 ((5)) [Reprinted from the
      1969 ed. published by Chilton Books, New York]

F-14 Catalogue des oeuvres et discographie in NECTOUX, Jean-Michel:
      Fauré. 2nd. ed.   Paris: Seuil, 1986: 180-[186] ((--))

REQUIEM (1887)

F-15 BRAS, Jean-Yves: Le Requiem de Fauré (discographie comparée) in
      Diapason-Harmonie, No. 308 (September 1985): 93-94 ((--))

FEDOSEYEV, VLADIMIR, 1932-   (Russian conductor)

F-16 USSR Radio and Television Full Symphony Orchestra under Fedoseyev in
      Music in the USSR (April-June 1987): 4 ((--))

FEINBERG, SAMUEL, 1890-1962   (Russian pianist)

F-17 METHUEN-CAMPBELL, James: Early Soviet pianists and their
      recordings: a survey in *Recorded Sound*, No. 83 (January 1983):
      1-16 ((--))

FEREMANS, JAN-JOZEF FRANCISCA, 1907-1964   (Belgian composer)

F-18 Werken op plaat Vastgelegd in *Gaston Feremans herdacht.* Antwerp:
      Gaston Feremans-Huldecomite, 1966: 178-179 ((--))

FERNANDEZ, OSCAR LORENZO, 1897-1948 (Brazilian composer)

F-19 Discographic references in FRANÇA, Eurico Nogueira: *Lorenzo Fernandez; compositor brasileiro.* Rio, 1950: [95]-[96] ((--))

FERRARI, LUC, 1929-   (Italian composer)

TAUTOLOGOS II

F-20 MARINELLI, Carlo: [Discography] in Roma, Teatro dell'Opera, season 1968-69: program p. 604 ((5))

FERRAS, CHRISTIAN, 1933-1982 (French violinist)

F-21 BESSON, François: [Discography] in *Diapason*, No. 276 (October 1982): 61 ((--))

FERRIER, KATHLEEN, 1912-1953 (English contralto)

F-22 Fortegnelse over opptals av Kathleen Ferrier in RAMBERG, Ruth: *Kathleen Ferrier: fra 14 år gammel yrkeskvinne til sanger av verdensformat.* [Oslo: s.n.], 1974: 188-[191] ((7))

F-23 Discografia di Kathleen Ferrier in *Musica*, No. 10 (December 1978): 238 ((7))

FEUERMANN, EMANUEL, 1902-1942 (Austrian cellist)

F-24 CALLAND, Fred and ITZKOFF, Seymour W.: Discography of Feuermann recordings in ITZKOFF, Seymour W.: *Emanuel Feuermann, virtuoso.* University, Ala.: University of Alabama Press, 1979: 235-245 ((1, 3, 6, 7))

F-25 SAMUELS, Jon: A complete discography of the recordings of Emmanuel Feuermann in *ARSC Journal*, XII/1-2 (1980): 33-77; XII/3 (1980): 196-239 ((1, 3, 4, 6, 7))

FICARELLI, MARIO, 1937-   (Brazilian composer)

F-26 Discographic references in FERREIRA, Paulo Affonso de Moura: *Mario Ficarelli: catálogo de obras.* [Brasília]: Ministério das Relações Exteriores, Departamento de Cooperação Cultural, Científica e Tecnológica, 1977: [14] pp. ((--)) (Compositores brasileiros)

FIEDLER, ARTHUR, 1894-1979 (American conductor)

F-27 Discography in MOORE, Robin: *Fiedler, the colorful Mr. Pops: the man and his music.* New York: Da Capo Press, 1980: [293]-363 ((3, 6, 7)) [Reprinted from the 1968 ed. published by Little, Brown]

F-28 [[[Discography] in ALEXANDER, Jesse J.: *Arthur Fiedler, his concert years at Stanford.* [United States]: Jesse Alexander, [1983?]:]]

FILS, JOHANN ANTON, 1733-1760 (German composer)

F-29 Diskographie in *Johann Anton Fils (1733-1760)* Tutzing: H. Schneider, 1983: 53 ((--))

FINE, IRVING, 1914-1962   (American composer)

F-30   Selected discography in Program notes for *Songs by ... Irving Fine* ... [Sound recording] New World Records NW 300, 1978: [4] ((--))

FINNEY, ROSS LEE, 1906-   (American composer)

F-31   Selected discography in Program notes for *Winds of change: music for wind ensemble by ... Ross Lee Finney* ... [Sound recording] New World Records NW 211, 1977: 3 ((--))

F-32   [[Discography in APPLE, Linda Key: *The solo piano music of Ross Lee Finney.* [Dissertation, Peabody Conservatory, 1986] 242 pp.]]

FINZI, GERALD, 1901-1956   (English composer)

F-33   Discography in *Records & Recording*, No. 268 (January 1980): 33 ((--))

F-34   MCVEAGH, Diana Mary: A Finzi discography in *Tempo*, No. 136 (March 1981): 19-22   ((--))

FISCHER, ANNIE, 1914-   (Hungarian pianist)

F-35   Annie Fischer--Petite discographie in *Discorama*, No. 4 (March-April 1960): 13   ((--))

FISCHER, EDWIN, 1886-1960   (Swiss pianist/conductor)

F-36   [SELVINI, Michele]: Disco-natrografia in *Musica*, No. 19 (December 1980): 370-371   ((7))

F-37   SMITHSON, Roger: *The recordings of Edwin Fischer.* London: Smithson, 1983. [12 pp.]   ((1, 7))

F-38   BADORES, Gonzalo: Edwin Fischer cien años in *Ritmo*, No. 572 (1986 especial fin de año): 71-73   ((7))

FISCHER-DIESKAU, DIETRICH, 1925-   (German baritone)

F-39   [Fischer-Dieskau discography] in *Record Geijutsu*, No. 276 (September 1973): 193-194   ((--))

F-40   The "best of the best" of Fischer-Dieskau recordings in HOFFMAN, Keith: A voice for the ages: the recordings of Dietrich Fischer-Dieskau in *Tarakan Music Letter*, II/1 (September-October 1980): 1, 8   ((--))

F-41   Discography, Deutsche Grammophon artist information, 1980, 5 pp. ((--))

F-42   WRIGHT, Maurice R.: Discography in WHITTON, Kenneth S.: *Dietrich Fischer-Dieskau, mastersinger.* New York: Holmes & Meier, 1981: [311]-342   ((7))

FITELBERG, GREGOR, 1879-1953   (Polish composer/conductor/violinist)

F-43   Dyskografia/Recordings in BIAS, Iwona: *Katalog tematyczny dziet Grzegorza Fitelgerga.* Katowice: [s.n.], 1979: 63-64   ((--))

FLAGSTAD, KIRSTEN, 1895-1962   (Norwegian soprano)

F-44   SANNER, Howard: *Kirsten Flagstad discography.* [MA Thesis, University of Maryland, 1981] 244 leaves. ((1, 3, 4, 7))

F-45   "A ecouter" in BOURGEOIS, Jacques: La mémoire des voix: Kirsten Flagstad in *Diapason,* No. 281 (March 1983): 28 ((5))

FLEISHER, LEON, 1928-   (American pianist/conductor)

F-46   MOLKHOV, Jean-Michel: Discographie; les grands deux époques de Leon Fleisher in *Diapason-Harmonie,* No. 325 (March 1987): 119-120 ((--))

FLETA, MIGUEL, 1893-1938   (Spanish tenor)

F-47   Discografía de Miguel Fleta in SAIZ VALDIVIELSO, Alfonso Carlos: *Miguel Fleta: memoria de una voz.* Madrid: Albia-Grupo, 1986: 332-338 ((3, 6, 7))

FLONZALEY QUARTET, USA

F-48   REUTLINGER, Dale: The Flonzaley Quartet: discography in *Grand Baton,* XIV/2 (No. 37, June 1977): 12-13   ((1, 3))

F-49   SAMUELS, Jon: A complete discography of the Flonzaley Quartet in *ARSC Journal,* XIX/1 (1987): 28-62   ((3, 4, 5, 6, 7))

FLUTE

F-50   [[[Discography] in JONES, William John: *The literature of the transverse flute in the seventeenth and eighteenth centuries.* [Disertation, Northwestern University, 1952] Vol. 2: leaves [512]-516]]

F-51   [[ROBERTS, Alice: *Discography of the flute.* [MLS Thesis, Kent State University, 1972] 72 pp.]]

F-52   Selected discography in GALWAY, James: *Flute.* London: Macdonald; New York: Schirmer Books, 1982: 238   ((--))

FLUTE MUSIC

F-53   Pour un discothèque idéale de la flute in RAMPAL, Jean Pierre: *La Flute.* Paris: Denoel, 1978: 44-45   ((--))

F-54   HIGBEE, Dale: The Baroque flute (transverso) on records in *National Flute Association Newsletter,* II/4 (August 1977): 10, 20   ((--))

F-55   HIGBEE, Dale S.: Baroque flute discography in *Early Music,* VII/2 (April 1979): 250-253   ((--))

F-56   Discographie in GARTNER, Jochen: *The vibrato, with particular consideration given to the situation of the flutist.* Regensberg:

G. Bosse, 1981: 161-163   ((--))

F-57   Diskografie in *Concerning the flute: ten articles about flute literature, flute playing, flute making, and flutists.* Amsterdam: Broekmans & van Poppel, 1984: 23-27   ((--))

FLUTE-PLAYERS--FRANCE

F-58   Discographies in DORGEUILLE, Claude: *L'école française de flûte, 1890-1950.* Paris: Editions Coderg; Tours: Libr. Ars Musicae, 1983. 72 pp.   ((--))

FOERSTER, JOSEF BOHUSLAV, 1859-1951   (Czech composer)

F-59   [[BARTOŠ, Jaroslav: Diskografie J. B. Foerstra in *Tempo*, XIX (1946-1947): 119-121]]

FOOTE, ARTHUR, 1853-1937   (American composer)

F-60   Discography in CIPOLLA, Wilma Reid: *A catalogue of the works of Arthur Foote, 1853-1937.* Detroit: College Music Society, 1980: 132-138; piano rolls pp. 138-139   ((--))

See also

KEYBOARD MUSIC

FORSELL, JOHN, 1868-1941   (Swedish baritone)

F-61   LILIEDAHL, Karleric: *John Forsell.* Stockholm: Kungliga Biblioteket, 1977. 26 l.   ((3, 6, 7))   (Nationalfonotekets diskografier; 510)

FORTEPIANO MUSIC

F-62   BASART, Ann P.: *The sound of the fortepiano, a discography of recording on early pianos.* Berkeley, CA: Fallen Leaf Press, 1985. 472 pp.   ((4))

FORTNER, WOLFGANG, 1907-1987   (German composer)

F-63   Discographische Hinweise: Wolfgang Fortner in *fono forum* (October 1982): 35   ((--))

FOSS, LUKAS, 1922-   (American composer)

F-64   Selected discography in Program notes for *Chamber music of ... Lukas Foss ...* [Sound recording] New World Records NW 281, 1977.   ((--))

F-65   Selected discography in Program notes for *Double music.* [Sound recording] New World Records NW 330, 1985   ((--))

FOSTER, LAWRENCE, 1941-   (American conductor)

F-66   Discographie in *Harmonie-Panorama musique*, No. 49 (January 1985): 16   ((--))

FOURNIER, PIERRE, 1906-1986   (French cellist)

F-67   Pierre Fournier a enregistré chez D.G.G. in *Harmonie*, No. 345
(February 1968): 44   ((--))

FRANCA, NEUSA, 1920–   **(Brazilian composer)**

F-68   Discographic references in MIGLIAVACCA, Ariede Maria: *Neusa
Franca: catálogo de obras.* [Brasília]: Ministério das Relações
Exteriores, Departamento de Cooperação Cultural, Científica e
Tecnológica, 1977: [20] pp.   ((--))   (Compositores brasileiros)

FRANCK, CÉSAR, 1822–1890   **(Belgian composer)**

F-69   [[[Discography] in GALLOIS, Jean: *Franck.* Paris: Seuil, 1980]]

ORGAN WORKS

F-70   NOISETTE DE CRAUZAT, Claude: Discographie comparée: l'oeuvre
d'orgue de Cesar Franck in *Harmonie* (No. 127, May 1977): 106-111
((--))

FRANÇOIS, SAMSON, 1924–1970   (French pianist)

F-71   À écouter [et] A rééditer in LOMPECH, Alain: Il y a dix ans: Samson
François in *Diapason*, No. 254 (October 1980): 60-61   ((--))

F-72   BESSON, François: Samson François: discographie critique complète
in *Harmonie Hi-fi Conseil*, No. 3 (November 1980): 31-39
((1, 7))

F-73   Discographie in SPYCKET, Jérôme: *Scarbo: le roman de Samson
François.* Luynes: Van de Velde; Lausanne: Payot, 1985: 230-233
((7))

FRANZ, PAUL, 1876–1950   (French tenor)

F-74   RICHARD, Jean-Roger: Discographie in *Almanach du disque*, 1951:
248-249   ((7))

FREMSTAD, OLIVE, 1871–1951   (American soprano)

F-75   MORAN, W. R.: The recordings of Olive Fremstad (16 Feb., 1868-21
Apr., 1951) in CUSHING, Mary Watkins: *The rainbow bridge.*
New York: Arno Press, 1977: i-iv   ((3, 6, 7))   [Originally published
without discography by Putnam, New York, 1954]

FRENCH HORN MUSIC

F-76   HERNON, Michael: *French horn discography.* Westport, CT: Greenwood
Press, 1986. 293 pp.   ((4))   (Greenwood Press discographies; 24)

FRESCOBALDI, GIROLAMO, 1583–1643   (Italian composer)

F-77   Discography in HAMMOND, Frederick: *Girolamo Frescobaldi: a guide to
research.* New York: Garland Pub., 1987: 349-364   ((4))

FRICSAY, FERENC, 1914–1963   (Hungarian conductor)

F-78   WINTHER, Soren: *Ferenc Fricsay discografi.* Slagese: Slagese

Centralbibliotek. 1974.   11 pp.   ((--))

F-79   FALINCELLI, Sylviane: Discographie des oeuvres du XXe in *Diapason*, No. 211 (November 1976): 24   ((5))

FRÖHLICH, FRIEDRICH THEODOR, 1803-1836   (Swiss composer)

F-80   Discographie in SARBACH, Pierre: *Friedrich Theodor Fröhlich (1803-1936)* Winterthur: Musikhug AG, 1984: 190   ((--))

FUENLLANA, MIGUEL DE, early 16th century-after 1568 (Spanish composer)

F-81   [[Discography in JOHNSON, Rebecca Tate: *Analysis, guitar transcription and performance practices of the twelve songs from Miguel de Fuenllana's Orphenica lyra derived from polyphonic Villancios by Juan Vasquez.* [DMA, University of Southern Mississippi, 1981] 235 pp.]]

FURTWÄNGLER, WILHELM, 1886-1954   (German conductor)

F-82   [Furtwängler discography] in *Record Geijutsu*, No. 291 (December 1974): 259-263   ((--))

F-83   MCCRAW, Harry W.: Furtwängler abroad: a critical discography of his non-German recordings in *Le Grand Baton*, No. 39 (December 1977): 14-19   ((7))

F-84   The Music Discount Centre: *Furtwängler discography, April 1978.* [Dealer's list], reprinted in *The Wilhelm Furtwängler Society Newsletter*, No. 15 (August-September 1978): 4 pp.   ((--))

F-85   [Furtwängler discography] in *Record Geijutsu*, No. 345 (June 1979): 192-201   ((5, 7))

F-86   Discography in PIRIE, Peter: *Furtwängler and the art of conducting.* London: Duckworth, 1980: 131-144   ((--))

F-87   Furtwängler memorial discography from Deutsche Grammophon "Das Vermaechtnis" series in Furtwängler Memorial Discs Issued / by Wilhelm Furtwängler in *The Wilhelm Furtwängler Society Newsletter*, No. 22 (June-July 1980): Supplement: 1 p.   ((--))

F-88   NAKAMURA, Masayuki: Addition to a previous discography of Wilhelm Furtwängler in Buenos Aires (Newsletter No. 21) in *The Wilhelm Furtwängler Society Newsletter*, No. 22 (June-July 1980): 1 ((7))

F-89   Les symphonies de Bruckner par Furtwängler in LEMAIRE, François-C.: Bruckner de Furtwängler à G. Wand in *Hifi Musique*, No. 283-284 (Summer-September 1980): 21-22   ((--))

F-90   DE KAY, Kenneth: Recordings of the Furtwängler repertoire: Part I, The later years, 1947-1954. Wilhelm Furtwängler Society. Supplement to Newsletter No. 23 (October 1980), 2 p.

F-91   DE KAY, Kenneth: Recordings of the Furtwängler repertoire in *Kastlemusik Monthly Bulletin*, V/10 (October 1980): 6-7   ((--))

F-92   Furtwängler Edition in FURTWÄNGLER, Elisabeth: Furtwängler e il
disco in *Musica*, No. 20 (March 1981): 28-30 ((--))

F-93   [Furtwängler discography] in *Record Geijutsu*, No. 406 (July 1984):
256-260; No. 407 (August 1984): 264-268; No. 408 (September 1984):
238-242; No. 409 (October 1984): 259-262; No. 410 (November 1984):
272-276; No. 411 (December 1984): 268-272; No. 412 (January 1985):
266-270; No. 413 (February 1985): 197-200; No. 414 (March 1985):
194-198; No. 415 (April 1985): 196-200; No. 416 (May 1985): 182-184
((3, 5, 6, 7))

F-94   HUNT, John: The Furtwängler sound in SQUIRE, John and HUNT, John:
Furtwängler and Great Britain. [s.l.]: Wilhelm Furtwängler Society,
1985: [79]-128 ((1, 7))

F-95   Discography in *Diapason-Harmonie*, No. 303 (March 1985): 26 ((--))

F-96   [[MITCHELL, Charles P. Wilhelm Furtwängler, early orchestral
recordings (1926-1945) in *Goldmine* (October 25, 1985):]]

F-97   GEFFEN, Gérard: *Furtwängler; une biographie par le disque*.
Paris: Belfond, 1986 229 pp. ((1, 4, 7))

F-98   HUNT, John: Der Furtwängler Klang; eine Discographie in MATZNER,
Joachim: *Furtwängler; Analyse, Dokument, Protokoll*. Köln:
Atlantis, 1986: 175-211 ((1, 3, 6, 7))

F-99   MATZNER, Joachim: Wilhelm Furtwängler Hundert in *fono forum*
(January 1986): 36-41 ((-))

GALEFFI, CARLO, 1882-1961   (Italian baritone)

G-1   Discografia in CELLETTI, Rodolfo: *Carlo Galeffi e la Scala*.
Milano: Teatro alla Scala; Milano: Electa, 1977: 96-97 ((3))

GALLI-CURCI, AMELITA, 1882-1963   (Italian soprano)

G-2   LP collections of Galli-Curci in LE MASSENA, C. E.: *Galli-Curci's
life of song*. Beverly Hills, CA: Monitor Book Co., 1978: 267-273
((3, 6, 7)) [Includes unissued records]

G-3   CARTWRIGHT, Jim: Amelita Galli-Curci in Immortal Performances 1981
[Dealer's list] Austin, TX: Immortal Performances, 1981: [17 pp.]
((1, 3, 6, 7)) (Immortal Performances discographic data; 8)
[Includes unissued records]

G-4   SUGA, Hajime: Amelita Galli-Curci in *LP Techno*, November 1982:
85-94 ((3, 7))

GARDEN, MARY, 1874-1967   (Scottish soprano)

G-5   BARNES, Harold: Mary Garden (1874-1967): discography in *Recorded
Sound*, No. 76 (October 1979): 113-116 ((3, 4, 6, 7))

GARDNER, SAMUEL, 1892-1984   (American violinist)

G-6   LEWIS, John Sam: The violinists: Sam Gardner in *Record Research*

(May 1985): 11-12   ((3, 6))

GARDINER, HENRY BALFOUR, 1877-1950   (English composer)

G-7   Discography in LLOYD, Stephen: *H. Balfour Gardiner.* Cambridge; New York: Cambridge University Press, 1984: 257-260   ((1, 7))

GARDINER, JOHN ELIOT, 1943-   (English conductor)

G-8   Discographie de John Eliot Gardiner in *Harmonie Hi-Fi Conseil*, No. 11 (July-August 1981): 36   ((--))

G-9   Discography in *Diapason*, No. 287 (October 1983): 41-42   ((--))

GASLINI, GIORGIO, 1947-1985   (Italian composer)

G-10   Discografia di Girogio Gaslini in GASLINI, Giorgio: *Giorgio Gaslini: vita, lotte, opere di un protagonista della musica contemporanea.* Padova: F. Muzzio, 1986: [188]-197   ((--))

GATTI, GABRIELLA, 1908-   (Italian soprano)

G-11   HALL-LEWIS, Morris and TIBERI, Maurizio: Gabriella Gatti in *Record Collector*, XXXI/8-10 (September 1986): 194-199; additions & corrections in XXXII/6-7 (June 1987): 167-168   ((3, 6, 7))

GAVAZZENI, GIANANDREA, 1909-   (Italian conductor)

G-12   Discografia di Gianandrea Gavazzeni in *Musica*, No. 30 (October 1983): 257, 259   ((3, 7))

GAVRILIN, VALERI ALEXANDROVICH, 1939-   (Russian composer)

G-13   [Discography] in *Music in the USSR* (October-December 1985): 79   ((--))

G-14   Discography in *Music in the USSR* (July-September 1987): 87   ((--))

GAVRILOV, ANDREI, 1956-   (Russian pianist)

G-15   Discographische Hinweise in *fono forum* (January 1985): 34   ((5, 7))

G-16   Discographische Hinweise in *fono forum* (April 1986): 22   ((--))

GEDDA, NICOLAI, 1925-   (Swedish tenor)

G-17   Inspelningar in GEDDA, Nicolai: *Gavan ar inte gratis.* Stockholm: Bonnier, 1977: 219-[224]   ((7))

G-18   [Discography] in *Opfer 1988; Jahrbuch der Zeitschrift Opernwelt.* Zürich: Füssli & Friedrich Verlag, 1988: 27-32   ((--))

GENCER, LEYLA, 1924-   (Turkish soprano)

G-19   Discografia di Leyla Gencer in GUANDALINI, Gina: Ore 11: lezioni di Gencer in *Musica*, No. 14 (October 1979): 241-242   ((5))

G-20   Discografia in CELLA, Franca: *Leyla Gencer: romanzo vero di una primadonna.* Venezia: CGS, 1986: 525–531   ((1, 7))

GENZMER, HARALD, 1909–   (German composer)

G-21   Diskographie in *Harald Genzmer.* Tutzing: H. Schneider, 1983:
       112–114   ((--))   (Komponisten in Bayern; 1)

GERGIYEV, VALERY   (Russian composer)

G-22   Discography in *Music in the USSR* (July–September 1987): 17   ((--))

GERHARD, ROBERTO, 1896–1970   (Spanish–English composer)

G-23   HUGHES, Eric and DAY, Timothy: Roberto Gerhard in *Recorded
       Sound*, No. 78 (July 1980): 101–110   ((1))   (Discographies of British
       composers; 6)

GERHARDT, ELENA, 1883–1961   (German mezzo–soprano)

G-24   KELLY, Alan and COSENS, Ian: Elena Gerhardt – a discography in
       Record Collector, XXXII/8–10 (September 1987): 183–213; additions &
       corrections in XXXIII/1–2 (January 1988): 37   ((1, 3, 6, 7))
       [Includes notes on unissued records and playing speeds]

GERLIN, RUGGERO, 1899–   (French harpischordist)

G-25   DREYFUS, Huguette: Ruggero Gerlin à écouter in *Diapason*, No. 286
       (September 1983): 9   ((--))

GERMAN, SIR EDWARD, 1862–1936   (English composer)

G-26   UPTON, Stuart: The original recordings of Sir Edward German in
       Vintage Light Music, No. 13 (Winter 1978): 7   ((3, 7))

GERSHWIN, GEORGE, 1898–1937   (American composer)

G-27   JABLONSKI, Edward: Gershwin at 80: observations, discographical and
       otherwise ... in *American Record Guide*, XLI/11 (September 1978):
       6–12, 58   ((--))

G-28   Discography in SCHWARTZ, Charles: *Gershwin, his life and music.* New
       York: Da Capo Press, 1979: 354–365   ((--)) [Reprinted from the 1973
       ed. published by Bobbs–Merrill]

G-29   Discographie sélective in LACOMBE, Alain: *George Gershwin.* Paris:
       F. van de Velde, 1980: 185–200   ((--))

G-30   Discographie commentée in LIPMANN, Eric: *L'Amérique de George
       Gershwin.* Paris: Messine: Diffusion Vilo, [1981]: [167]–215   ((--))

G-31   [Selected discography] in Concert stage, Broadway stage: The music
       of George Gershwin and Kurt Weill in *Tarakan Music Letter*, III/4
       (March–April 1982): 3   ((--))

G-32   Selected discography in JABLONSKI, Edward: *Gershwin.* Garden City,
       NY: Doubleday, 1987: 402–415   ((--))

STAGE WORKS

PORGY AND BESS (1935)

G-33   KAMINSKI, Piotr: Discographie in *L'Avant Scéne Opéra*, No. 103
(August–September 1987): 106–109 ((5))

GHASNE, ALEXIS, 1868–?   **(French baritone)**

G-34   [Discography] in *Record Collector*, IX/3 (March 1954): 64   ((−−))

GHIAUROV, NICOLAI, 1929–   **(Bulgarian bass)**

G-35   Discographie in GRENECHE, Philippe: *Nicolai Ghiaurov*. [Paris, 1982]:
59–62   ((−−))

G-36   Discographie in *Nikolai Ghiaurhov*. Sofia, 1985: [265]–267   ((−−))

GIBSON, SIR ALEXANDER, 1926–   **(Scottish conductor)**

G-37   FORD, Christopher: Discography in *Records and Recording*,
No. 242 (November 1977): 16–17   ((−−))

G-38   Alexander Gibson discography in *British Music Yearbook: a survey
and directory of statistics and reference articles*. London: Adam &
Charles Black, 1979: 13–16   ((7))

GIDEON, MIRIAM, 1906–   **(American composer)**

G-39   Selected discography in Program notes for *Works of American
composers*. [Sound recording] New World Records NW 317, 1984   ((−−))

GIESEKING, WALTER, 1895–1956   (German pianist)

G-40   GRÉNIER, Jean-Marie: Quelques-uns des merveilleux enregistrements
de Walter Gieseking in *Almanach du disque*, 1956: 306   ((−−))

GIGLI, BENIAMINO, 1890–1957   (Italian tenor)

G-41   STANNARD, John: Gigli's acoustic legacy in *Hillandale News*, No. 92
(October 1976): 28–29 [the Milan H.M.V. recordings, 1918–1919 only]
((3, 7))

G-42   RICALDONE, Mark: A Gigli discography in GIGLI, Beniamino: *The
memoirs of Benamino Gigli*. New York: Arno Press, 1977: 236–270
((3, 4, 7)) [Reprinted from the 1957 edition published by Cassell,
London]

G-43   STANNARD, John: Gigli's acoustic legacy: part 2 in *Hillandale News*,
No. 94 (February 1977): 96–98 [New York recordings, 1921–1924]
((3, 7))

G-44   Discografia in GIGLI, Rina: *Beniamino Gigli mio padre*. [Parma]:
Azzali, 1986: 245–257   ((1, 7))

GILBERT, HENRY FRANKLIN, 1868–1928   (American composer)

G-45   [[Discography LONGYEAR, Katherine Eide: *Henry F. Gilbert, his life
and works*. [Dissertation, University of Rochester, 1968] 281 pp.]]

G-46   Selected discography in Program notes for *Carpenter, Gilbert, Weiss, Powell.* [Sound recording] New World Records NW 228, 1976: 4 ((--))

GILELS, EMIL, 1916-1985   (Russian pianist)

G-47   [Gilels discography] in *Stereo Geijutsu,* No. 47 (April 1972): 150-153   ((--))

G-48   SCHWARZ, Falk: Discography in *Recorded Sound,* No. 80 (July 1981): 14-58   ((7))   [Also issued as a booklet by BIRS, 1981. 76 pp.]

G-49   SCHWARZ, Falk: La discografia in *Musica,* No. 31 (December 1983): 391-392, 394-398   ((7))

G-50   Discography in *Music in the USSR* (April-June 1985): 16   ((--))

GILLES, JEAN, 1668-1705   (French composer)

G-51   [[Discography in HAJDU, John H.: *The life and works of Jean Gilles (1668-1705)* [Dissertation, University of Colorado, 1973]   417 pp.]]

G-52   Discographie in PRADA, Michael: *Jean Gilles (1668-1705) L'homme et l'oeuvre.* Béziers: Société musicologie de languedoc Béziers, 1985: 255   ((--))

GIMÉNEZ, RAUL, 1951-   (Argentinian tenor)

G-53   Discographical references in BEBB, Richard: Raúl Giménez in *Record Collector,* XXXIII/3-5 (March 1988): 121-124   ((--))

GINASTERA, ALBERTO, 1916-1983   (Argentine composer)

G-54   FOREMAN, Lewis: Ginastera: a discography in *Tempo,* No. 118 (September 1976): [17]-22   ((--))

G-55   Diskographie in *Alberto Ginastera.* Bonn: Boosey & Hawkes, 1984: 116-119   ((--))   [Adapted from the previous entry]

GINZBURG, GRIGORY, 1904-1961   (Russian pianist)

G-56   METHUEN-CAMPBELL, James: Early Soviet pianists and their recordings: a survey in *Recorded Sound,* No. 83 (January 1983): 1-16   ((--))

GIORDANO, UMBERTO, 1867-1948   (Italian composer)

OPERAS

ANDREA CHÉNIER (1896)

G-57   MARINELLI, Carlo: [Discography] in Milano, Teatro alla Scala, season 1982-83: program p. 95   ((5))

G-58   MARINELLI, Carlo: [Discography] in Milano, Teatro alla Scala, season 1984-85: program p. 109   ((5))

FEDORA (1898)

G-59   MARINELLI, Carlo: [Discography] in Roma, Teatro dell'Opera, season 1967-68: program pp. 334-335 ((5))

GIULINI, CARLO MARIA, 1914-   (Italian conductor)

G-60   STONE, Ralph: A Carlo Maria Giulini discography in *Le Grand Baton*, No. 38 (September 1977): 16-20 ((--))

G-61   Discography, Deutsche Grammophon artist information, 1980, 1 p. ((--)

G-62   MARTIN, Serge: Carlo Maria Giulini: discographie complète in *Harmonie hi-fi conseil*, No. 6 (February 1981): [40]-53 ((5))

G-63   Les enregistrements de Giulini qui s'imposent in *Diapason*, No. 283 (May 1983): 28 ((--))

GIUZELEV, NIKOLA, 1936-   (Bulgarian bass)

G-64   [Discography] in ABADZHIEV, Aleksandur: *Nikola Giuzelev*. Sofia: Musika, 1979: 89 ((--))

GLASGOW ORPHEUS CHOIR

G-65   [[[Discography] in ROBERTSON, Sir Hugh Stevenson: *Orpheus with his lute: a Glasgow Orpheus Choir anthology*. London: Pergamon, 1963: 325-327]]

GLASS, PHILIP, 1936-   (American composer)

G-66   Selected discography in Program notes for *Cadenzas & variations*. [Sound recordings] New World Records NW 313, 1981 ((--))

G-67   Discography in GLASS, Philip: *Music by Philip Glass*. New York: Harper & Row, 1987: 216-217 ((--))

GLAZUNOV, ALEXANDER, 1865-1936 (Russian composer)

STAGE WORKS

RAYMONDA (1897)

G-68   MARINELLI, Carlo: [Discography] in Roma, Teatro dell'Opera, season 1981-82: program pp. 1044-1045 ((5))

GLINKA A CAPPELLA CHOIR, Leningrad

G-69   Discography in *Music in the USSR* (July-September 1986): 13 ((--))

GLOBOKAR, VINKO, 1934-   (Yugoslav composer)

G-70   [Globokar discography] in *Record Geijutsu*, No. 276 (September 1973): 192 ((--))

GLUCK, CHRISTOPH WILLIBALD, 1714-1787 (German composer)

G-71   Discographische Hinweise in *fono forum* (November 1987): 34 ((--))

OPERAS

ALCESTE (1776)

G-72   MARINELLI, Carlo: [Discography] in Roma, Teatro dell'Opera, season 1967-68: program pp. 439-440 ((5))

G-73   MARINELLI, Carlo: [Discography] in Milano, Teatro alla Scala, season 1986-87: program pp. 84-85 ((5))

G-74   TUBEUF, André: Discographie in *L'Avant Scène Opéra*, No. 73 (March 1987): 98-102 ((1, 7))

IPHIGENIE EN TAURIDE (1779)

G-75   Gesamtaufnahmen auf Schallplatte in *Iphigenie auf Tauris*. München:

Bayerische Staatsoper, 1979: 78 ((5))

G-76   TUBEUF, André: Discographie in *L'Avant Scène Opéra*, No. 62 (April 1984): 94-99 ((7))

G-77   MARINELLI, Carlo: [Discography] in Roma, Teatro dell'Opera, season 1985-86: program pp. 50-54 ((5))

ORFEO ED EURIDICE (1762)

G-78   MARINELLI, Carlo: [Discography] in Roma, Teatro dell'Opera, season 1967-68: program pp. 100-106 ((5))

G-79   POUGET, François: Discographie in *L'Avant Scène Opéra*, No. 5 (September-October 1976): 83-84 ((5))

G-80   MARINELLI, Carlo: [Discography] in Bologna, Teatro Comunale, season 1977-78: program pp. 34-45 ((5))

G-81   [[Discography in *L'Avant Scène Opéra*, No. 23 [1979]]]

G-82   WALKER, Malcolm: Discography in *C. W. von Gluck, Orfeo*. Cambridge; New York: Cambridge University Press, 1981: 137-139 ((5)) (Cambridge opera handbooks)

G-83   MARINELLI, Carlo: [Discography] in Verona, Teatro Filharmonico, season 1985: program pp. 15-17 ((5))

GLYNDEBOURNE OPERA, Great Britain

G-84   The Glyndebourne recordings in HUGHES, Spike: *Glyndebourne: a history of the Festival opera founded in 1934 by Audrey and John Christie*. Newton-Abbot: David & Charles, 1982: 336-338 ((--))

GOBBI, TITO, 1913-1984 (Italian baritone)

G-85   STEANE, John: Discography in GOBBI, Tito: *My life*. London: Macdonald and Jane's, 1979: 201-210; Garden City, NY: Doubleday, 1980: 203-220 ((1, 3, 6, 7))

G-86   Discografia di Tito Gobbi in CHIADÒ, Michele: Tito Gobbi in *Musica*,

No. 33 (June 1984): 59-61   ((2, 5))

G-87 [[STROFF, Stephen: Discography in *Goldmine* (April 27, 1984):]]

GODFREY, SIR DAN, 1868-1938   (English conductor)

G-88 UPTON, Stuart: *Sir Dan Godfrey and the Bournemouth Municipal Orchestra: a discography.* West Wickham: Vintage Light Music Society, 1970: 12; addenda in *Commodore* (Autumn 1972): 7   ((--))

GODOWSKY, LEOPOLD, 1880-1938   (Russian pianist)

G-89 SUGA, Hajime: Leopold Godowsky Records in *LP Techno,* November 1980: 81-83   ((3))

G-90 CRIMP, Bryan: Leopold Godowsky: a discography of his English Columbia Recordings in program notes for *Godowsky: the pianists' pianist.* [Sound recording] CDARP 7011/APR 7011, 1988: 7-11   ((3, 6, 7))

GOEHR, ALEXANDER, 1932-   (English composer)

G-91 HUGHES, Eric and DAY, Timothy: Alexander Goehr in *Recorded Sound,* No. 77 (January 1980): 95-103   ((--)) (Discographies of British composers; 3) [Also issued as a pamphlet by BIRS, 1980]

GOGORZA, EMILIO EDUARDO DE, 1874-1949   (Italian baritone)

G-92 LORENZ, Kenneth M.: Emilio De Gogorza (1874-1949)--The early years: 1898-1906 in *Kastlemusik Monthly Bulletin,* III/12 (E-49; December 1978): 12-14   ((3, 7))

GOLDENWEIZER, ALEXANDER, 1875-1961   (Russian pianist)

G-93 METHUEN-CAMPBELL, James: Soviet pianists and their recordings: a survey in *Recorded Sound,* No. 83 (January 1983): 1-16   ((--))

GOLDMAN, RICHARD FRANKO, 1910-1980   (American conductor)

G-94 [[Discography in LESTER, Noel K.: *Richard Franko Goldman: his life and works.* [DMA, Peabody Conservatory, 1984] 338 pp.]]

GOLDSTEIN, BORIS EMMANUILOVICH, 1921-   (Russian violinist)

G-95 Diskographie in SOROKER, Jakov: *Boris Goldstein: das Leben eines Geigers.* Jerusalem: J. Sorocker, 1983: 118-122   ((--))

GOLOVANOV, NIKOLAI, 1891-1953   (Russian conductor)

G-96 [Discography] in *N.S. Golovanov: literaturnoe, nasledie ...* Moskva: Vses. izd-vo Sov. kompozitor, 1982: 258-[273]   ((7))

GOLSCHMANN, VLADIMIR, 1893-1972   (Russian conductor)

G-97 TITZLER, John W.: Vladimir Golschmann (1893-1972): a discography in *Le Grand Baton,* No. 44 (September-December 1977): 59-65   ((--))

GOMES, ANTONIO CARLOS, 1836-1896   (Brazilian composer)

OPERAS

(IL) GUARANY (1870)

G-98   LÉON, Jacques Alain: A discography of "Il Guarany" in *Record Collector*, XIII/7-9 (August 1960): 137-139 ((--))

GOMEZ, GRACIANO, 1895-1980   (Cuban composer)

G-99   Obras existentes en la discoteca del instituto cubano de radio y television (ICRT) in MUGUERCIA MUGUERCIA, Alberto: *Sobre Graciano Gómez y su música*. La Habana: Departmento de Información y Documentación de la Cultura, 1983: 35-38 ((--))

GOMÓŁKA, MIKOLAJ, ca. 1535-?   (Polish composer)

G-100   Dyskografia in PERZ, Miroslaw: *Mikołaj Gomółka: monografia*. Krakow: Polskie Wydawn. Muzyczne, 1981: 327 ((--))

GOODMAN, ISADOR, 1909-1982   (South African composer)

G-101   Isador Goodman discography in GOODMAN, Virginia: *Isador Goodman, a life in music*. Sydney: Collins, 1983: 209-211 ((--))

GOOSSENS, FREDERIC, 1927-   (American composer)

G-102   Selected discography in Program notes for *Exultation*. [Sound recording] New World Records NW 304, 1979: [3] ((--))

GOTHENBURG SYMPHONY ORCHESTRA, Sweden

G-103   Diskografi Göteborgs Symphoniker in *The Gothenberg Symphony Orchestra*. [Sound recording] BIS 301/303, 1985. [12 pp.] ((1, 3, 6, 7))

GOTTSCHALK, LOUIS MOREAU, 1829-1869   (American composer)

G-104   Recordings in DOYLE, John G.: *Louis Moreau Gottschalk, 1829-1869: a bibliographical study and catalog of works*. Detroit: Published for the College Music Society by Information Coordinators, 1982: 345-363 ((4))

G-105   Discography in KORF, William E.: *The orchestral music of Louis Moreau Gottschalk*. Henryville: Institute of Mediaeval Music, 1983: 162 ((--))

GOULD, GLENN, 1932-1982   (Canadian pianist)

G-106   [Gould discography] in *Record Geijutsu*, No. 276 (September 1973): 187-188 ((--))

G-107   Discography in PAYZANT, Geoffrey: *Glenn Gould, music & mind*. Toronto: Van Nostrand, 1978: 177-183; adapted and published as Glenn Gould--discography in *Piano Quarterly*, No. 115 (Fall 1981): 26-28 ((--))

G-108   [Glenn Gould discography] in *Stereo Geijutsu*, No. 171 (April 1981):

110-113   ((7))

G-109   MCLEAN, Eric: Discography/Discographie in *Musicanada*, No. 46
(June 1981): 2   ((--))

G-110   Vollständige Discographie Glenn Gould in *fono forum* (June 1981):
26-27   ((5))

G-111   PAYZANT, Geoffrey: Glenn Gould--discography in *Piano Quarterly*, No.
115 (Fall 1981): 26-28   ((--))

G-112   MEYER, Martin: Discografia di Glenn Gould in *Musica*, No. 23
(November 1981): 378-379   ((5))

G-113   Les principaux disques de Gould in *Diapason*, No. 277 (November
1981): 10   ((--))

G-114   Glenn Gould discography in *Discophiliac*, I/7-8 (November 1982?):
16   ((5))

G-115   [Gould ... Discography] in *Record Geijutsu*, No. 387 (December 1982):
189-194   ((5, 7))

G-116   Discography in *Glenn Gould*. Toronto: Doubleday Canada; Garden
City, NY: Doubleday, 1983: 311-317   ((5, 7))

G-117   Discography in COTT, Jonathan: *Conversations with Glenn Gould.*
Boston: Little, Brown, 1984: [139]-150 [Includes private tapes
and radio and television programs] [Adapted from the discography in
Piano Quarterly, No. 115 (Fall 1981), pp. 26-28, with additions
by Ruth Pincoe, CBS Records]   ((1, 5, 7))

G-118   STRICKLAND, Edward: The legacy of Glenn Gould in *Fanfare*, VIII/1
(September-October 1984): 136-146   ((-))

G-119   [Discography] in WERA, Matheis: *Glenn Gould, die Unheilige am
Klavier.* München: Scaneg, 1987: 123-137   ((--))

G-120   MOTHY, A.: La discographie complète in *Diapason-Harmonie*, No.
331 (October 1987): 58-61   ((--))

GOULD, MORTON, 1913-   (American composer)

G-121   Morton Gould--a selected discography of his works in *Music &
Musicians* (February 1987): 17   ((--))

G-122   Morton Gould on record: a selective discography in *Podium*, No. 18
(Spring-Summer 1987): 22-24   ((--))

GOUNOD, CHARLES, 1818-1893   (French composer)

OPERAS

FAUST (1859)

G-123   MARINELLI, Carlo: [Discography] in Roma, Teatro dell'Opera,
season 1971-72: program pp. 234-238   ((5))

G-124   MANNONI, Gérard: Faust--discographie comparée in *L'Avant Scène Opéra*, No. 2 (March-April 1976): 90-93 ((--))

G-125   [[Diskographie in *Charles Gounod, Faust ("Margarethe"): Oper in fünf Akten* ... München: Bayerische Staatsoper, 1980. 72, [27] pp.]]

G-126   MARINELLI, Carlo: Discografie: Faust e Mefistofele nelle opere teatrali e sinfonico-vocali in *Quaderni dell'I.R.TE.M.* [Instituto di Ricerca per il Teatro Musicale] No. 3 (1986): 43-65 ((5))

G-127   Discografia in *Musica*, No. 48 (February-March 1988): 25 ((1))

ROMÉO ET JULIETTE (1867)

G-128   DUTRONC, Jean-Louis: Discographie in *L'Avant Scène Opéra*, No. 41 (May-June 1982): 84-86 ((1, 7))

GRAINGER, PERCY, 1882-1961   (Australian composer)

G-129   Discography: performances by Grainger in BIRD, John: *Percy Grainger*. London: Elek, 1976: 292-303 ((3, 6, 7)) [Includes unissued recordings]

G-130   BIRD, John: Current discography in *The Percy Grainger companion*. London: Thames, 1981: 237-240 ((--))

G-131   Discography in SIMON, Robert: *Percy Grainger: the pictorial biography*. Troy, NY: Whitston Pub. Co., 1983: 129-133 ((--))

G-132   OULD, Barry Peter: Grainger: a discography in *Grainger Journal*, IX/1 (1987): 40-52 ((--))

GRANADOS, ENRIQUE, 1867-1916   (Spanish composer)

G-133   Granados' songs recorded by Conchita Badia in Granados: a personal portrait in *Recorded Sound*, No. 77 (January 1980): 57-62 ((--))

GRANDI, MARGHERITA, 1894-   (Australian soprano)

G-134   BOTT, Michael: The recordings of Margherita Grandi in *Record Collector*, XXV/3-4 (June 1979): 70-72 ((1, 3, 7)) Addenda in Record Collector, XXVII/7-8 (August 1982): 181-183 ((--))

GRAVEURE, LOUIS, 1888-1965 (English tenor)

G-135   STONE, Bob: Discography in *New Amberola Graphic*, No. 9 (Spring 1974): 3-4 ((5))

GREENE, HARRY PLUNKETT, 1865-1936   (Irish bass-baritone)

G-136   OAKES, Graham: Plunkett Greene: discography in *Record Collector*, XXXI/6-7 (July 1986): 125-126; additions and corrections in XXXI/8-10 (September 1986): 231-232 ((3, 7))

GRETCHANINOV, ALEXANDER, 1864-1956 (Russian composer)

G-137   [Discography] in *Aleksandr Grechaninov*. Moskva, Sov. Kompozitor,

1978: 98-[101]   ((--))

GRIEG, EDVARD, 1843-1907   (Norwegian composer)

CONCERTO, PIANO, A Minor, Op. 16

G-138   DOISY, Marcel: Dans l'intimité des chefs-d'oeuvre: le concerto
de Grieg in *Revue des Disques et Haute-Fidelité*, No. 257 (October
1977): 527-529   ((--)

GRIFFES, CHARLES TOMLINSON, 1884-1920   (American composer)

G-139   Selected discography in Program notes for *Charles Tomlinson Griffes*.
[Sound recording] New World Records NW 273, 1976: 5-6   ((--))

G-140   Discography in ANDERSON, Donna K.: *Charles T. Griffes: an
annotated bibliography-discography*. Detroit: Published for College
Music Society by Information Coordinators, 1977: [175]-206   ((--))

G-141   Selected discography in Program notes for *William Parker recital*.
[Sound recording] New World Records NW 305, 1980: [4]   ((--))

G-142   Discography of piano works in Program notes for *Charles
Tomlinson Griffes: collected works for piano*. [Sound recording]
New World Records NW 310/1, 1981   ((--))

GRINBERG, MARIA, 1908-ca. 1979   (Russian pianist)

G-143   METHUEN-CAMPBELL, James: Early Soviet pianists and their recordings:
a survey in *Recorded Sound*, No. 83 (January 1983): 1-16   ((--))

GRINBLATS, ROMVALD, 1930-   (Russian composer)

G-144   [Discography] in *Music in the USSR* (April-June 1985): 93   ((--))

GROUPE DE RECHERCHES MUSICALES, Paris

G-145   GEZELS, Jacqueline: Discographie in *Revue Musicale*, No. 394-397
(1986): [305]-312   ((5))

GRUBB, SAVI RAJ, 1926-   (Indian record producer)

G-146   Discography in GRUBB, Savi Raj: *Music makers on record*. London:
H. Hamilton, 1986: 227-238   ((--))

GRUBEROVA, EDITA, 1946-   (Czech soprano)

G-147   Discographische Hinweise in *fono forum* (October 1987): 22   ((--))

GUARNERI STRING QUARTET, USA

G-148   DILLON, Patrick: Discography in BLUM, David: *The art of quartet
playing: the Guarneri Quartet in conversation with David Blum*.   New
York: Knopf, 1986: 233-237   ((--))

GUARNIERI, ANTONIO, 1880-1952   (Italian composer)

G-149   CONTINI, Marco and SELVINI, Michele: Discografia in *Musica*,

No. 20 (March 1981): 26   ((3))

GUARNIERI, CAMARGO, 1907–   (Brazilian comoposer)

G–150 Discographic references in MIGLIAVACCA, Ariede Maria: *Camargo Guarnieri: catálogo de obras*. [Brasília]: Ministério das Relações Exteriores, Departamento de Cooperação Cultural, Científica e Tecnológica, 1977: [75] pp.   ((––))   (Compositores brasileiros)

GUBAIDULINA, SOPHIA ASGATOVNA, 1931–   (Russian composer)

G–151 Discography in *Music in the USSR* (April–June 1985): 88   ((––))

GUBARENKO, VITALY, 1934–   (Ukrainian composer)

G–152 Discography in *Music in the USSR* (January–March 1987): 23   ((––))

GUITAR MUSIC

G–153 PURCELL, Ronald C.: *Classic guitar, lute and vihuela discography*. Melville, NY: Belwin–Mills Pub. Corp., 1976.   116 pp.   ((4))

G–154 [[CASTRO–MENDIVIL, L. F.: *A guide to the recorded music for the classical guitar*.   Modesto, CA: Castro–Mendivil (P.O. Box 105, Modesto CA 95353)   77 pp.]]

G–155 Discography in WADE, Graham: *Traditions of the classical guitar*. London: Calder, 1980: [231]–255   ((––))

G–156 [[[Discography] in WAGER–SCHNEIDER, John: *The contemporary guitar*. Berkeley: University of California Press, 1981:]]

G–157 Diskographie in SCHMITZ, Alexander: *Das Gitarrenbuch*. [Frankfurt am Main]: W. Kruger, 1982: 511–539   ((––))

G–158 [[BADA, Susanne: Wohl und Weh mit Zupf und Zopf. Gittaren–Transkriptionen: ein discographischen Rückblick in *Girrate & Laute*, VII/4 (1986): 20–24]]

GUITAR MUSIC––MEXICO

G–159 Guitar discography in OTERO, Corazón: *Manuel M. Ponce and the guitar*. Shatesbury: Musical New Services, 1983: 82   ((––))

GUITAR MUSIC––SPAIN

G–160 [[Discography in PENNINGTON, Neil Douglas: *The development of baroque guitar music in Spain, including a commentary on and transcription of Santiago de Murcia's passacalles y obras*. [Dissertation, University of Maryland, 1979]   393, 352 pp.]]

GULDA, FRIEDRICH, 1930–   (Austrian pianist)

G–161 [Gulda discography] in *Record Geijutsu*, No. 276 (September 1973): 188–189   ((––))

GULLI, FRANCO, 1926–   (Italian violinist)

G-162 Discografia [Franco Gulli] in *Musica*, No. 37 (June 1985): 37   ((--))

GUSTAVSON, EVA, 1917–   **(Norwegian mezzo–soprano)**

G-163 Eva Gustavson Norsk rikskringkastings Lydopptak in *Eva Gustavson; fra Dovrehallen til Toscanini*. Oslo: Dreyer, 1983: [227]–[228] ((--))

GUTMAN, NATALIYA, 1942–   **(Russian composer)**

G-164 [Discography] in *Music in the USSR* (April–June 1985): 77   ((--))

GUTNIKOV, BORIS, 1931–   **(Russian violinist)**

G-165 Discography in *Music in the USSR* (October–December 1986): [82] ((--))

HÁBA, ALOIS, 1893–1973   (Czech composer)

H-1   Discographic notes in VYSLOUŽIL, Jiří: *Alois Hába, zivot a dílo*. Prague: Panton, 1974: 357–377   ((--))

HACQUART, CAROLUS, 1640?–1701   (Dutch composer)

H-2   [[Discography in ANDRIESSEN, Pieter: *Carolus Hacquart (1640?–1701). Een biographische bijdrage. Het godsdienstig en instrumentaal werk.* [Dissertation, University of Louvain, 1969] 223 pp.]]

HADLEY, HENRY, 1871–1931   (American composer)

H-3   Selected discography in Program notes for *Scherzo diabolique*. [Sound recording] New World Records NW 320, 1984   ((--))

HAGEN STRING QUARTET, West Germany

H-4   Discographische Hinweise Hagen Quartett in *fono forum* (July 1986): 26   ((--))

HAITINK, BERNARD, 1929–   **(Dutch conductor)**

H-5   Bernard Haitink; eine Auswahl aus der Diskografie in *fono forum* (November 1976): 1094   ((--))

H-6   Discography [on Philips label] S.l.: [Philips, 198-?]   7 l.   ((--))

HALÉVY, JACQUES, 1799–1862   (French composer)

OPERAS

(LA) JUIVE (1835)

H-7   CABOURG, Jean and VOISIN, Georges: Discographie in *L'Avant Scéne Opéra*, No. 100 (July 1987): 112–[117]   ((5))

HALFFTER, CRISTÓBAL, 1930–   **(Spanish composer)**

H-8   Discografia in CASARES, Emilio: *Cristóbal Halffter*. Oviedo: Departmento de Arte–Musicología, Servicio de Publicaciones,

Universidad de Oviedo, 1980: 200   ((--))

HALFFTER, RODOLFO, 1900–   **(Spanish composer)**

H-9   Discografía in ALCARAZ, José: *La música de Rodolfo Hallfter*.
        México City: Dirección General de Difusión UNAM, Departmento de
        Música, 1977: 58–61 ((--)) (Cuadernos de música; Nueva serie; 4)

HALLE ORCHESTRA, Manchester

H-10   Hallé recordings since 1944 in KENNEDY, Michael: *Hallé, 1858–1976:
        a brief survey of the orchestra's history, travels, and
        achievements*. Manchester: Hallé Concerts Society, 1977: 60–784
        ((--))

H-11   UPTON, Stuart: Sir Hamilton Harty and the Hallé Orchestra in
        Vintage Light Music, No. 27 (Summer 1981): 6–8 ((3))

HALLER, HERMANN, 1914–   **(Swiss composer)**

H-12   Discographie in *Hermann Haller, geboren am 9. Juni 1914:
        Werkverzeichnis=Liste des oeuvres*. Zürich: Schweizerisches
        Musik–Archiv, 1981: 9 ((--))

HAMILTON, IAIN, 1922–   **(Scottish composer)**

H-13   HUGHES, Eric and DAY, Timothy: Iain Hamilton in *Recorded Sound*,
        No. 85 (January 1984): 79–87 ((1, 7)) (Discographies of British
        composers; 22)

HANDEL, GEORGE FRIDERIC, 1685–1759   (German–English composer)

H-14   Discographie sélective in GALLOIS, Jean: *Haendel*. Paris: Seuil,
        1980: 186–188 ((--))

H-15   Discographie in LABIE, Jean–François: *George Frédéric Haendel*.
        Paris: R. Laffont, 1980: [834]–845 ((--))

H-16   [[GOSSMAN, Otto: Händel–Diskographie I: Opern und Schauspielmusiken
        in *Göttinger Händel–Beiträge* I (1984): 211–218]]

H-17   MARINELLI, Carlo: Haendel: proposte per un ascolto in Ente
        autonomo Teatro Massimo, Palermo, Quarderni 1985: 21–35 ((--))

H-18   Discografia essenziale in MAZZOLA NANGERONI, Gabriella: *Invito
        all'ascolto di Georg Friedrich Haendel*. Milano: Mursia, 1985:
        [292]–303 ((--))

H-19   Skladby Georga Friedricka Handela na dlouhohrajicick deskach in
        PECMAN, Rudolf: *George Friedrich Handel*. Praha: Supraphon,
        1985: 375–[376] ((--))

H-20   Discography in FERNANDEZ, Dominique: Bach, Haendel et l'opéra
        italien in *Diapason–Harmonie*, No. 303 (March 1985): 50–54 ((--))

H-21   CHIEN, George: Teldec's 300th–birthday bash in *Fanfare*, VIII/4
        (March–April 1985): 110–114 ((--))

H-22   [[GOSSMAN, Otto: Händel-Diskographie II: Die Oratorio, Serenaten
und Odeon in *Göttinger Händel-Beiträge* II (1986):   267-283]]

OPERAS

H-23   Discographische Hinweise: Händels Opern auf Schallplatte in *fono
forum* (February 1985): 23   ((--))

H-24   A note on recordings in MEYNELL, Hugo Anthony: *The art of Handel's
operas.* Toronto; Lewiston, NY: E. Mellen Press, 1986:   263-264
((--))

ALCINA (1735)

H-25   MARINELLI, Carlo: [Discography] in Milano, Teatro alla Scala,
season 1984-85: program p. 53   ((5))

H-26   MARINELLI, Carlo: [Discography] in Palermo, Ente automono
Teatro Massimo, season 1984-85: program p. 5   ((5))

ARIODANTE (1735)

H-27   MARINELLI, Carlo: [Discography] in Milano, Teatro alla Scala,
season 1980-81: program pp. 54-55   ((5))

GIULIO CESARE (1724)

H-28   MARINELLI, Carlo: [Discography] in Roma, Teatro dell'Opera,
season 1984-85: program pp. 34-35   ((5))

H-29   FLINOIS, Pierre: Discographie in *L'Avant Scène Opéra*, No. 97
(April 1987): 98-101   ((1, 5))

RINALDO (1711)

H-30   GALLOIS, Jean: Discographie in *L'Avant Scène Opéra*, No. 72
(February 1985): 92-93   ((1, 7))

ORATORIOS

MESSIAH (1742)

H-31   À écouter in LABIE, Jean-François: Le point sur le Messie de
Haendel in *Diapason*, No. 256 (December 1980): 40-41   ((5))

H-32   TOWE, Teri Noel: Messiah: reduplication without redundancy.
Editions and recordings past and present in *High Fidelity*
(January 1983): 59-62, 90-91; (February 1983): discography
p. 51 ((--)) [Reprinted in the *American Organist*, XIX (February
1985): 74-90]

ORCHESTRAL WORKS

WATER MUSIC

H-33   [Discography, including Royal Fireworks Music] in *Stereo
Geijutsu*, No. 191 (August 1982): 56-61   ((7))

VOCAL WORKS

H-34   WEBER, J. F. A tercentenary feast of Handel vocal music in
        Fanfare, VIII/4 (March–April 1985): 215–217 ((5, 7))

HANSON, HOWARD, 1896–1981 (American composer)

H-35   BROWN, Nathan E.: The recordings of Howard Hanson in *Le Grand
        Baton*, No. 49 (March 1981): 4–9 ((--))

HARBISON, JOHN, 1938–   (American composer)

H-36   Selected discography in Program notes for *John Harbison: Symphony
        No. 1*. [Sound recording] New World Records NW 331, 1985 ((--))

HARNONCOURT, NIKOLAS, 1929–   (Austrian cellist and conductor)

H-37   Discografia in *Musica*, No. 37 (June 1985): 40–42 ((--))

HARP MUSIC

H-38   With strings attached: a basic repertoire of music for the harp in
        Tarakan Music Letter, III/5 (May–June 1982): 11–15 ((--))

H-39   FERRARA, Dennis E.: The harp in the recording studio in
        American Harp Journal, X/4 (Winter 1986): 14–19 ((3, 6, 7))
        [Primarily recording pioneers; includes unissued recordings]

HARPISCHORD MUSIC

H-40   PALMER, Larry: Discography [harpischord in the orchestra] in
        Diapason, LXVII/4 (March 1976): 19 ((--))

H-41   [[Discography in THORP, Keith Andrew: *The Twentieth-century
        harpsichord: approaches to composition and performance as evidenced
        by the contemporary repertoire*. [Dissertation, University of
        Illinois at Urbana-Champaign, 1981] 311 pp.]]

H-42   Des disques de base in BEDIN, Veronique: Le clavecin: de l'écoute
        à pratique in *Harmonie-Panorama musique*, No. 29 (March 1983): 69
        ((--))

        See also

        KEYBOARD MUSIC

        HARRIS, ROY, 1898–1979 (American composer)

H-43   Harris's works on records in *American Music Lover*, III/11 (March
        1938): 410 ((--))

H-44   Discographic references in SLOMINSKY, Nicholas: Roy Harris in
        Musical Quarterly, XXXIII/1 (January 1947): 37 ((--))

H-45   HALL, David: Roy Harris: the music on records in *Stereo Review*,
        XXII/12 (December 1968): 73 ((1))

H-46   Selected discography in Program notes for *Music by Arthur Shepherd*,

Henry Cowell, Roy Harris. [Sound recording] New World Records NW 218, 1977: 4 ((--))

H-47   Current critical discography in GIBBS, L. Chesley: The Roy Harris revival in *American Record Guide* (May 1979): 8-10, 12-13; (June 1979): 4-6, 8, 57-59 ((--))

H-48   CURTIS, William D.: Roy Harris (1898-1979), a discography in *ARSC Journal,* XIII/3 (1981): 60-79 ((1, 3, 4, 5, 6, 7))

HARRISON, BEATRICE, 1892-1935 (English cellist)

H-49   Discography in HARRISON, Beatrice: *Cello and the nightingales: the autobiography of Beatrice Harrison.* London: J. Murray, 1985: 168-172 ((--))

HARRISON, LOU, 1917-   (American composer)

H-50   Selected discography in Program notes for *Chamber music by ... Lou Harrison ...* [Sound recording] New World Records NW 281, 1977. ((--))

H-51   Selected discography in Program notes for *Pulse.* [Sound recording] New World Records NW 319, 1984 ((--))

H-52   [[Discography in BAKER, Don Russell: *The percussion ensemble music of Lou Harrison: 1939-1942.* [DMA, University of Illinois, Urbana-Champaign, 1985] 253 pp.]]

H-53   Selected discography in Program notes for *Double Music.* [Sound recording] New World Records NW 330, 1985 ((--))

HARTMANN, KARL AMADEUS, 1905-1963 (German composer)

H-54   Schallplatten in MCCREDIE, Andrew D.: *Karl Amadeus Hartmann: sein Leben u. Werk.* Wilhelmshaven: Heinrichshofen, 1980: 205-208 ((--))

HARTY, SIR HAMILTON, 1879-1941 (Irish conductor and composer)

H-55   HOLMES, Bill: Sir Hamilton Harty: his recorded legacy in *Le Grand Baton,* No. 42 (December 1978): 15-22 ((--))

H-56   Sir Hamilton Harty on LP: an annotated discography in NISS, Charles: The age of the 78: "A fine musician!" in *Le Grand Baton,* No. 42 (December 1978): 23-26 ((--))

H-57   EHRLICH, Cyril: Discography in *Hamilton Harty: his life and music.* Belfast: Blackstaff Press, 1979; New York: Da Capo Press, 1980: 133-140 ((--))

H-58   UPTON, Stuart: Sir Hamilton Harty and the Halle Orchestra in *Vintage Light Music,* No. 27 (Summer 1981): 6-8 ((3))

HARVEY, JONATHAN, 1939-   (English composer)

H-59   HUGHES, Eric and DAY, Timothy: Jonathan Harvey in *Recorded Sound,* No. 84 (July 1983): 83-87 ((1, 7)) (Discographies of British composers; 19)

HASKIL, CLARA, 1895–1960   (Rumanian pianist)

H-60   Petite discographie in *Discorama*, No. 4 (March–April 1960): 11
((--))

H-61   Clara Haskil--the published records in *Recorded Sound*, No. 63–64
(July–October 1976): 623–624   ((--))

H-62   Clara Haskil--private recordings in *Recorded Sound*, No. 63/64
(July–October 1976): 625   ((1, 7))

H-63   BORIE, Alexandre: Clara Haskil: tous ses disques in *Harmonie*,
No. 244 (November 1979): 90–91   ((5))

H-64   SPYCKET, Jérôme: Clara Haskil: discographie critique complète
etabile in *Harmonie*, (October 1980): 34–37   ((--))

H-65   [Clara Haskil discography] in *Record Geijutsu*, No. 452 (May 1988):
234–238; No. 453 (June 1988): 246–250; No. 454 (July 1988): 240–244;
No. 455 (August 1988): 240–244; No. 456 (September 1988): 240–244;
No. 457 (October 1988): 246–250; No. 458 (November 1988): 244–248
((1, 3, 7))

HAUER, JOSEF MATTHIAS, 1883–1959   (Austrian composer)

H-66   Schallplate, Tonbandbeispiele in *Josef Matthias Hauer zum 100.
Geburtstag am 19. März 1983*. Wien: Historisches Museum der Stadt
Wien, 1983: 72   ((--))

HAYDN, JOSEPH, 1732–1809   (Austrian composer)

H-67   BURKE, C. G.: *The collector's Haydn*. Westport, CT: Greenwood
Press, 1978.   316 pp.   ((--))   [Reprinted from the 1959 ed. published
by Lippincott, New York]

H-68   [Haydn discography] in *Record Geijutsu*, No. 348 (September 1979):
194–201   ((5, 7))

H-69   Diszkografia in SOMFAI, Laszlo: *Joseph Haydn zongoraszonatai*.
Budapest: Zeneműkiado, 1979: 301–302   ((--))

CHORAL WORKS

MASSES

H-70   WEBER, J. F.: Discography of the masses of Franz Joseph Haydn
in *Fanfare*, VI/1 (September–October 1982): 76, 78, 80, 82–84,
504, 505   ((3))

(THE) SEASONS (1801)

H-71   NYS, Carl de: Discocraphie [i.e., Discographie] in *Diapason*,
No. 207 (May 1976): 22   ((--))

INSTRUMENTAL WORKS

(THE) SEVEN LAST WORDS OF CHRIST (1787)

H-72   BARBIER, Pierre-E.: Les sept dernières paroles du Christ en croix, de Joseph Haydn: discographie critique in *Dispason*, No. 227 (April 1978): 46-47   ((5))

H-73   WEBER, J. F.: ... a discography of Haydn's Last Seven Words in *Fanfare*, XI/1 (1987): 92-94   ((5, 7))

OPERAS

ORLANDO PALADINO (1782)

H-74   NYS, Carl de, VIGNAL, Marc, HALBREICH, Harry and GAUTHIER, André: Discographie in *L'Avant Scène Opéra*, No. 42 (July-August 1982): 106-108   ((--))

SONATAS, PIANO

H-75   [[[Discography] in TAGGERT, James L.: *Franz Joseph Haydn's keyboard sonatas: an untapped gold mine*. Lewiston, NY: E. Mellen Press, 1988:]]

SYMPHONIES

H-76   DEARLING, Robert: Recommended recordings in HODGSON, Antony: *The music of Joseph Haydn, the symphonies*. London: Tantivy Press; Rutherford, NJ: Fairleigh Dickinson University Press, 1976: 162-[204]   ((--))

HEIFETZ, JASCHA, 1902-1987   (Russian-American violinist)

H-77   Violinist of the century: a profile of Jascha Heifetz in *Tarakan Music Letter*, III/4 (March-April 1982): 5, 11   ((--))

H-78   MALTESE, John: Rare jewels in *STRAD*, No. 1157 (September 1986): 329-336 ((1, 7))   [Heifetz's non-commercial recordings]

H-79   FUTTER, Julian and WESCHLER-VERED, Artur: Discography in WESCHLER-VERED, Artur: *Jascha Heifetz*. New York: Schirmer Books, 1986: 203-[228]   ((1, 7))

HEILLER, ANTON, 1923-1979   (Austrian composer/organist)

H-80   [[Discography in GANT, Robert Edward: *The organ works of Anton Heiller*. [DMA, University of Rochester, 1975] 182 pp.]]

HEINZE, BERNARD, 1894-1982   (Australian conductor)

H-81   Records made by Sir Bernard Heinze in RADIC, Thérèse: *Bernard Heinze: a biography*. South Melbourne: Macmillan Co. of Australia, 1986: 207-209   ((1, 7))

HEINRICH, JULIA, 1880-1919   (American soprano)

H-82   FERRARA, D. E.: Neglected Edison disc artists in *New Amberola Graphic*, No. 45 (Summer 1983): 8-9   ((3, 7))   [Includes unissued records]

H-83   FERRARA, D. E.: The Edison recordings of Julia Heinrich in *Record Collector*, XXXII/1-2 (January 1987): 32 ((3, 7))

HELFFER, CLAUDE, 1922–   (French pianist)

H-84   Discographie de Claude Helffer in *Harmonie hi-fi conseil*, No. 6 (February 1981): 32 ((--))

HEMPEL, FRIEDA, 1885-1955 (German soprano)

H-85   [[[Discography] in *Stimmen die um die Welt Gingen*, No. 11 (March 1986): 51-55]]

HENDL, WALTER, 1917–   (American conductor)

H-86   [[Walter Hendl on record in *Podium*, No. 13 (Spring-Summer 1984): 25-26]]

HENDLER, MAXIMILIAN, 1939–   (Austrian composer)

H-87   Diskographie in ILINČIĆ, Johann: *Neue Musik in der Steiermark: Maximilian Hendler.* Graz: Leykam, 1986: [135] ((--))

HENDRICKS, BARBARA, 1948–   (American soprano)

H-88   Discographie in WALTER, Edith: Tête d'affiche: Barbara Hendricks in *Harmonie-Panorama musique*, No. 44 (July-August 1984): 15 ((--))

H-89   LOUIS, Remy: Discographie in *Diapason-Harmonie*, No. 336 (March 1988): 44 ((1))

HENRY, PIERRE, 1927–   (French composer)

H-90   [Pierre Henry]: à écouter in *Diapason*, No. 239 (May 1979): 51 ((--))

H-91   Discographie sommaire in CHION, Michel: *Pierre Henry.* [Paris]: Fayard/Fondation SACEM, 1980: [213]-214 ((--))

HENSCH, WILHELM, 1860-1908 (German bass)

H-92   NORTON-WELSH, Christopher: Wilhelm Hensch in *Record Collector*, XXXIII/6-7 (June 1988): [134]-150 ((4, 5))

HENSCHEL, SIR GEORGE, 1850-1934 (British baritone/conductor)

H-93   Sir George Henschel discography in *Recorded Sound*, No. 62 (April 1976): 536-537 ((3, 6, 7))

HENSELT, ADOLPH VON, 1814-1889 (German composer)

H-94   [[Discography in GRAHAM, Daniel Martin: *An analytical study of twenty-four etudes by Adolph von Henselt.* [DMA, Peabody Conservatory of Music, 1979] 127 pp.]]

HENZE, HANS WERNER, 1926–   (German composer)

H-95   Bibliographie Hans Werner Henze in *Musik und Bildung*, X/2
        (February 1978): 111-114   ((--))

H-96   Nota discografica in *Henze*.   Torino: EDT-/Musica, 1986: 428-432
        ((--))

H-97   [[[Discography] in PETERSEN, Peter: *Hans Werner Henze, ein
        politischer Musiker: zwölf Vorlesungen*. Hamburg: Argument, 1988:
        279-282]]

        HERBERT, VICTOR, 1859-1924   (American composer)

H-98   WARNER, Larry: The original and authentic sounds of Victor Herbert
        in *Kastlemusik Monthly Bulletin*, V/12 (December 1980): 1, 5   ((7))

        HERREWEGHE, PHILLIPE   (French conductor)

H-99   Discographie: La Chapelle Royale, Philippe Herreweghe (cond.) in
        Program notes for Harmonia Mundi, France, HMC 901167 [Sound
        recording], 1985: p. 16   ((--))

        HERRMANN, BERNARD, 1911-1975   (American composer)

H-100   Discography in JOHNSON, Edward: *Bernard Herrmann, Hollywood's
        music-dramatist*. Rickmansworth: Triad Press, 1977: 43-56
        ((1, 5, 7))

H-101   [[PROX, Lothar: Bernard Herrmann. Eine Monographie Skizze in
        Filmmusik Information, I (February 1979): 4-9]]

        HERRMANN, HUGO, 1896-1967   (German composer)

H-102   [[Discography in HARRINGTON, Helmi Hanni Strahl: *Hugo
        Herrmann and his contributions to the contemporary German Lied*.
        [Dissertation, University of Texas, 1978] 2 v.]]

        HERTZ, ALFRED, 1872-1942   (German conductor)

H-103   CARTWRIGHT, Jim: Alfred Hertz recordings in Immortal Peformances
        1979: List Number 1 [Dealer's List] Austin, TX: Immortal
        Performances, 1979: [79]-[87]   ((1, 3, 6, 7))   (Immortal
        Performances discographic data; 7)

        HERVÉ, FLORIMOND RONGER, 1825-1892   (French composer)

        OPERAS

        LE PETIT FAUST (1869)

H-104   MARINELLI, Carlo: Discografie: Faust e Mefistofele nelle
        opere teatrali e sinfonico-vocali in *Quaderni dell'I.R.TE.M.*
        [Instituto di Ricerca per il Teatro Musicale] No. 3 (1986): 65-68
        ((5))

        HESPOS, HANS-JOACHIM, 1938-   (German composer)

H-105   Schallplatten (records) in *Hespos*. Regensberg: G. Bosse, 1982:
        [12]   ((5))

HESS, DAME MYRA, 1890–1965   (English pianist)

H-106 BROWN, Nathan E.: Myra Hess discography in MCKENNA, Marian C.:
       Myra Hess: a portrait. London: Hamilton, 1976: [281]–290
       ((1, 3, 6, 7))

HEWARD, LESLIE, 1897–1943   (English conductor)

H-107 HOLMES, Bill: Leslie Heward discography in *Le Grand Baton*, No. 48
       (December 1980): 17–21   ((--))

HEYNIS, AAFJE, 1924–   (Dutch contralto)

H-108 Petite discographie in *Discorama*, No. 5 (May 1960): 22   ((--))

HILDEGARD OF BINGEN, 1098–1179   (German composer)

H-109 WEBER, J. F.: Discography in *Fanfare*, VIII/6 (July–August 1985):
       191   ((7))

H-110 WEBER, J. F.: The recordings of Hildegard of Bingen in *Quodlibet;
       Newsletter of the International Society of Hildegard von Bingen
       Studies*, II/1 (Fall–Winter 1986): 7–8   ((7))

HILL, ALFRED, 1870–1960   (Australian composer)

H-111 A select list of records in THOMSON, John Mansfield: *A distant
       music: the life and times of Alfred Hill, 1870–1960.* Auckland,
       Melbourne: Oxford University Press, 1980: 227–228   ((1, 7))

HINDEMITH, PAUL, 1895–1963   (German composer)

H-112 [[HERZBERG, Karin: *Paul Hindemith som udóvende kunstner. En
       diskografi.* [Thesis, Royal Danish School of Librarianship, 1972]]]

H-113 [[Discography in PAULDING, James E.: *Paul Hindemith (1895–1963):
       a study of his life and works.* [Dissertation, University of Iowa,
       1974] 485 pp.]]

H-114 Diskographie in HINDEMITH, Paul: *Briefe.* Frankfurt am Main:
       Fischer Taschenbuch Verlag, 1982: 262–263   ((--))

H-115 Diskographie in SCHUBERT, Giselher: *Paul Hindemith in Selbst-
       zeugnissen und Bilddokumenten.* Reinbek bei Hamburg: Rowohlt, 1981:
       150–151   ((--))

CHORAL WORKS

MESSE (1963)

H-116   [Schallplatte] in RÖSSLER, Franz-Georg: *Paul Hindemith;
         Messe (1963)* München: Wilhelm Fink, 1986: 67   ((--))

ORCHESTRAL WORKS

(THE) FOUR TEMPERMENTS--THEME AND VARIATIONS FOR PIANO AND
STRING ORCHESTRA (1940)

H-117 MARINELLI, Carlo: [Discography] in Roma, Teatro dell'Opera, season 1970-71: program pp. 515-516 ((5))

HINDERAS, NATALIE, 1927-1987 (American pianist)

H-118 [[DE LERMA, Dominique-René : The Hinderas discography in *Sonorities in Black Music*, III (1980): 13-19]]

HISLOP, JOSEPH, 1884-1977 (Scottish tenor)

H-119 Addenda [to discography in *Record Collector* XXIII/9-10] in *Record Collector*, XXV/1-2 (March 1979): 36-42 ((3, 6, 7))

HLOBIL, EMIL, 1901- (Czech composer)

H-120 Seznam gramofonových nahrávek in BERGER, Jiří: *Emil Hlobil; hudební putování stoletim.* Praha: Panton, 1984: 285-288 ((--))

HODDINOTT, ALUN, 1929- (Welsh composer)

H-121 Appendix II: gramophone recordings in DEANE, Basil: *Alun Hoddinott.* Cardiff: University of Wales Press for Welsh Arts Council, 1978: 73 ((--))

H-122 Discography in *Records & Recording*, No. 272 (May 1980): 25-26 ((--))

HOFMANN, JOSEF, 1876-1957 (Polish pianist)

H-123 [[Discography in HUSARIK, Stephen: *Josef Hofmann (1876-1957), the composer and pianist, with an analysis of available reproductions of his performances.* [Dissertation, University of Iowa, 1983] 468 pp.]]

HOFFMANN, PETER, 1944- (German tenor)

H-124 Diskographie in MÜLLER, Marieluise: *Peter Hoffmann: Singen ist wie Fliegen.* Bonn: Keil Verlag, 1983: 224-225 ((5))

HOGWOOD, CHRISTOPHER, 1941- (English harpsichordist/conductor)

H-125 GRÜNEWALD, Helge: Discographische Hinweise, Christopher Hogwood in *fono forum* (December 1985): 32-34 ((--))

H-126 Discografia in *Musica*, No. 49 (April-May 1988): 26-27 ((--))

HOIBY, LEE, 1926- (American composer)

H-127 Selected discography in Program notes for *William Parker recital.* [Sound recording] New World Records NW 305, 1980: [4] ((--))

HOLLANDER CAVALCANTI, NESTOR DE, 1949- (Brazilian composer)

H-128 Discographic notes in MIGLIAVACCA, Ariede Maria: *Nestor de Hollander Cavalcanti: catálogo de obras.* [Brasília]: Ministério das Relações Exteriores, Departamento de Cooperação Cultural, Científica e Tecnológica, 1979: [15] pp. ((--)) (Compositores brasileiros)

HOLLIGER, HEINZ, 1939–   (Swiss oboist)

H-129 [Discography] in *Record Geijutsu*, No. 276 (September 1973): 192–193
((--))

H-130 Discography [on Philips label]. S.l. [Philips, 198–?] 2 l. ((--))

HOLLOWAY, ROBIN, 1943–   (English composer)

H-131 HUGHES, Eric and DAY, Timothy: Robin Holloway in *Recorded Sound*,
No. 79 (January 1981): 117–119 ((1)) (Discographies of British
composers; 9)

HOLLYWOOD STRING QUARTET, USA

H-132 GRAY, Michael H.: The Hollywood String Quartet: a discography in
ARSC Journal, XIV/2 (1982): 37–42 ((3, 7))

H-133 MOLKHOV, Jean-Michel, BENNETT, John and JAMBLIENNE, A. de.:
Discographie--Le Hollywood String Quartet in *Diapason-Harmonie*,
No. 321 (November 1986): 120–121 ((7))

HONEGGER, ARTHUR, 1892–1955 (French composer)

H-134 GRÉNIER, Jean-Marie: Les grands enregistrements de l'oeuvre
d'Arthur Honegger in *Almanach du disque*, 1956: [236]–241 ((--))

H-135 LE CALVÉ, Jacques: Discographie critique (Janvier 1978) in
LANDOWSKI, Marcel: *Honegger*. Paris: Seuil, 1978: 181–187
((--))

H-136 [[[Discography] in SZÖLLÖSY, András: *Honegger*. Budapest: Gondolat,
1980: 287–300]]

SYMPHONIES

H-137   Discographie in MAILLARD, Jean and NAHOUM, Jacques: *Les symphonies
d'Arthur Honegger*. Paris: Alphonse Leduc, 1974: 116–117 ((7))

HORENSTEIN, JASCHA, 1898–1973 (Russian conductor)

H-138 BROWN, Nathan E. and HORENSTEIN, Peter: Horenstein conducts:
airchecks, in-hall tapes in *Le Grand Baton*, No. 35 (June 1976):
2–7 ((1, 7))

H-139 SELVINI, Michele: Discografia di Jascha Horenstein in *Musica*,
No. 14 (October 1979): 246–248   ((--))

HORNE, MARILYN, 1934–   (American mezzo-soprano)

H-140 Discography in HORNE, Marilyn: *Marilyn Horne, my life*. New York:
Atheneum, 1983: 241–245 ((5))

HOROWITZ, VLADIMIR, 1903–   (Russian-American pianist)

H-141 [Horowitz discography] in *Record Geijutsu*, No. 313 (October 1976):
260–262 ((7))

H-142 ALDER, Caine: The unknown recordings of Vladimir Horowitz in *High Fidelity* (January 1978): 69-74 ((1, 7))

H-143 Horowitz on record in *Tarakan Music Letter*, IV/1 (September-October 1982): 4 ((--))

H-144 MCALEAR, Robert: Discography in PLASKIN, Glenn: *Horowitz, the biography of Vladimir Horowitz*. New York: Morrow, 1983: 503-[568] ((3, 6, 7))

H-145 1927-1982: Sa discographie complète (Vladimir Horowitz) in *Diapason-Harmonie*, No. 309 (October 1985): 47-49 ((--))

HORTUS MUSICUS, USSR

H-146 [Discography] in *Music in the USSR* (October-December 1986): 11 ((--))

HOTTER, HANS, 1909-   (German bass-baritone)

H-147 Discography in TURING, Penelope: *Hans Hotter: man and artist*. London: J. Calder; New York: Riverrun Press, 1983: 263-274 ((7))

H-148 [[[Discography] in TURING, Penelope: *Hans Hotter: ein Sängerporträt*. Wien: Neff, 1983.   236 pp.]]

H-149 Discography in BOURGEOIS, Jacques: Hans Hotter, interprete du surhumain in *Diapason*, No. 287 (October 1983): 27 ((--))

HOUSTON SYMPHONY ORCHESTRA

H-150 Auswahl--Diskographie in *fono forum* (August 1976): 724 ((--))

HOWELLS, HERBERT, 1892-1983 (English composer)

H-151 [[Discography in HODGSON, Peter John: *The music of Herbert Howells*. [Dissertation, University of Colorado, 1970]   345 pp.]]

H-152 HUGHES, Eric and DAY, Timothy: Herbert Howells in *Recorded Sound*, No. 79 (January 1981): 79-97 ((1, 7)) (Discographies of British composers; 7)

HUBER, KLAUS, 1924-   (Swiss composer)

H-153 Discographie in *Klaus Huber; geboren am 30. November 1924*. Zürich: Schweizerisches Musik-Archiv, 1980: 14-15 ((--))

HUBERMAN, BRONISLAW, 1882-1947 (Polish violinist)

H-154 WENDEL, Wolfgang: "-die Sonne schien durch die Wolken": Bronislaw Hubermann: eine Diskografie (II) in *fono forum* (July 1977): 642-644 ((-)) [Prose discography, includes "Auswahl-diskografie", p. 644]

H-155 Discography in Bronislaw Huberman Archive: *Bronislaw Huberman archive catalog*. Tzni Avai: Museum of Tel Aviv, Yafo Dept. of Culture, Youth and Sport, 1977: 22-27 ((--))

HÜSCH, GERHARD, 1901-1984 (German baritone)

H-156 [[[Discography] in *Stimmen die um die Welt gingen*, No. 13 (September 1986): 3-19]]

H-157 Selected discography in *Stimmen die um Welt gingen*, No. 21 (September 1988): 64-65 ((--))

HUMMEL, BERTHOLD, 1925-   (German composer)

H-158 [[Discography in CRUMMER, Larry D.: *The solo organ works of Berthold Hummel*. [Dissertation, Indiana University, 1983] 170 pp.]]

HUMMEL, JOHANN NEPOMUK, 1778-1837   (German composer)

H-159 [[Discography in BARNUM, Marion Phyllis: *J. N. Hummel and his treatise on piano playing*. [DMA, University of Iowa, 1971] 153 pp.]]

CHAMBER WORKS

H-160   [[[Discography] in ZIMMERSCHIED, Dieter: *Die Kammermusik Johann Nepomuk Hummels*. [Dissertation, University of Mainz, 1967]   554 pp.]]

HUMPERDINCK, ENGELBERT, 1854-1921   (German composer)

OPERAS

HÄNSEL UND GRETEL (1893)

H-161   FLINOIS, Pierre: Discographie in *L'Avant Scéne Opèra*, No. 104 (December 1987): 100-103 ((5))

HUSA, KAREL, 1921-   (American composer)

H-162 [[Discography in MCLAURIN, Donald Malcolm: *The life and works of Karel Husa with emphasis on the significance of his contribution to the wind band*. [Dissertation, Florida State University, 1985] 241 pp.]]

IBERT, JACQUES, 1890-1962   (French composer)

I-1   Références discographiques (33 t et 45 t) in *Jacques Ibert*. [Publisher's catalog] Paris: Alphonse Leduc, 197-?: 27-30 ((--))

IGUMNOV, KONSTANTIN, 1873-1948   (Russian pianist)

I-2   METHUEN-CAMPBELL, James: Early Soviet pianists and their recordings: a survey in *Recorded Sound*, No. 83 (January 1983): 1-16 ((--))

INGHELBRECHT, DÉSIRÉ ÉMILE, 1880-1965   (French conductor)

I-3   Discographie in INGHELBRECHT, Germaine: *D. E. Inghelbrecht et son temps*. Neuchâtel: Éditions de la Baconnière, 1978: 183-184 ((--))

IRELAND, JOHN, 1879-1962   (English composer)

I-4   Gramophone records available for purchase during 1979 in SEARLE, Muriel V.: *John Ireland, the man and his music*. Tunbridge Wells:

Midas Books, 1979: 158-161   ((--))

ISAKADZE, LIANA, 1944–   **(Russian violinist)**

I-5   Discography in *Music in the USSR* (July–September 1987): 24   ((--))

ISOIR, ANDRÉ, 1935–   **(French organist)**

I-6   GALLOIS, Jean: Quelques enregistrements d'André Isoir in *Diapason*, No. 209 (September 1976): 19   ((--))

ISRAELYAN, MARTUN, 1938–   **(Armenian composer)**

I-7   [Discography] in *Music in the USSR* (October–December 1985): 81 ((--))

IURLOV, ALEXANDER ALEXANDROVICH   **(Russian conductor)**

I-8   [Discography] in *Alexsandr Iurlov: stati i vospominaniia: materialy*. Moskva: Sov. Kompozitor, 1983: 191-193   ((--))

IVALDI, CHRISTIAN, 1938–   **(French pianist)**

I-9   Discographie de Christian Ivaldi; Discographie du duo Noël Lee/ Christian Ivaldi in *Harmonie hi-fi conseil*, No. 4 (December 1980): 26 ((5))

IVES, CHARLES, 1874-1954   (American composer)

I-10   LOWE, Steven: Ives on record in *FM Guide* (New York Area), (October 1974): 38-44   ((--))

I-11   WARREN, Richard, Jr.: *Charles E. Ives: discography*. Westport, CT: Greenwood Press, 1978.   124 pp. ((1, 3, 4, 6, 7)) [Reprinted from the 1972 ed. published by Yale University Press]

I-12   HALL, David: A list of the recorded compositions of Charles Edward Ives in COWELL, Henry: *Charles Ives and his music*. New York: Da Capo Press, 1983: 228-243   ((--)) [Original ed. published by Oxford University Press, 1969, c1955]

I-13   Discografia in IVES, Charles: *Ensayos ante una sonata*. México: Universidad Nacional Autónoma de México, 1982: 153-158   ((7))

I-14   [[[Discography] in BLOCK, Geoffrey Holden: *Charles Ives, a bio-bibliography*. New York: Greenwood Press, 1988. (Bio-bibliographies in music; 14)]]

IVOGÜN, MARIA, 1891-1987   (Hungarian soprano)

I-15   Discographische Hinweise: Maria Ivogün in GOHL, Hans: Maria Ivogün: Einst unumstrittene Autoritat ihres Fachs in *fono forum* (November 1981): 44-46   ((--))

I-16   FRANKENSTEIN, Alfred: Maria Ivogün (1891-1987) in *Record Collector*, XXXIII/3-5 (March 1988): 118   ((--))

JABÔR, NAJLA   (Brazilian composer)

J-1   Discographic notes in FERREIRA, Paulo Affonso de Moura: *Najla Jabôr: catálogo de obras*. [Brasília]: Ministério das Relações Exteriores, Departamento de Cooperação Cultural, Científica e Tecnológica, 1977: [27] pp. ((--)) (Compositores brasileiros)

JACOBS, PAUL, 1930-1983   (American pianist)

J-2   Discography [on Nonesuch label]. S.l. [Nonesuch Records, 1984?] 1 leaf. ((--))

JACOBS, RENÉ, 1946-   (Belgian countertenor)

J-3   LEBRUN, Camille: Discographie in *Diapason-Harmonie*, No. 326 (April 1987): 40-43 ((--))

JANÁČEK, LEOŠ, 1854-1928   (Czech composer)

J-4   [[ŠEDA, Jaroslav: *Janáček hovrovi k dnesku*. Praha: Supraphon, 1950. 12 pp.]]

J-5   [Discographic references] in SEDA, Jaroslav: *Leoš Janáček*. 3d ed. Praha: Orbis, 1960: 69-[80] ((--))

J-6   PROCHÁZKA, Jaroslav: Diskografie Leose Janácka in *Opus Musicum*, VII/7-8 (1976): 212-213 ((--))

J-7   [Discographic references] in STEDRON, Bohumír: *Leos Janácek: k jeho lidskému a umeleckému profilu*. Praha: Panton, 1976: 196-226 ((--))

J-8   CURTIS, William D.: *Leoš Janáček*. Utica, NY: J. F. Weber, 1978. 65 pp. ((3, 4, 5, 6, 7)) (Weber discography series; 18)

J-9   HOLLAND, Dietmar: Diskographie in *Leos Janácek*. München: Edition Text u. Kritik, 1979: [112]-113 ((--)) (Musik-Konzepte; 7)

J-10   Discographie in ERISMANN, Guy: *Janáček, ou, La passion de la vérité*. Paris: Seuil, 1980: 345-[350] ((5))

J-11   Werkverzeichnis und Diskographie in HONOLKA, Kurt: *Leoš Janáček: sein Leben, sein Werk, seine Zeit*. Stuttgart: Belser, 1982: [299]-311 ((--))

VOCAL WORKS

DIARY OF A YOUNG MAN WHO DISAPPEARED (1919)

J-12   MARINELLI, Carlo: [Discography] in Venezia, Gran Teatro La Fenice, season 1981: program pp. 330-334 ((5))

RIKALDA FOR VOICES AND CHAMBER ENSEMBLE (1925)

J-13   MARINELLI, Carlo: [Discography] in Venezia, Gran Teatro La Fenice, season 1981: program pp. 335-336 ((5))

OPERAS

(THE) CUNNING LITTLE VIXEN (1924)

J-14   BARBIER, Pierre-E.: Discographie in *L'Avant Scène Opéra*, No. 84
(February 1986): 104-106 ((1, 5))

FROM THE HOUSE OF THE DEAD (1930)

J-15   MARINELLI, Carlo: [Discography] in Venezia, Teatro La Fenice,
season 1972-73: program pp. 217-219 ((5))

J-16   LISCHKE, André: Discographie in *L'Avant Scène Opéra*, No. 107
(March 1988): 88-91 ((5, 7))

JENUFA (1904)

J-17   MARINELLI, Carlo: [Discography] in Milano, Teatro alla Scala,
season 1973-74: program pp. 34-35 ((5))

J-18   LISCHKE, André: Discographie in *L'Avant Scène Opéra*, No. 102
(October 1987): 102-107 ((1, 5, 7))

KÁTYA KABANOVÁ (1921)

J-19   WALKER, Malcolm: Discography in *Leoš Janáček, Káta Kabanová*.
Cambridge; New York: Cambridge University Press, 1982: 228 ((5))
(Cambridge opera handbooks)

JANOWITZ, GUNDULA, 1937-   (German soprano)

J-20   Discography, Deutsche Grammophon artist information, 1980. 2 pp.
((--))

JENNY, ALBERT, 1912-   (Swiss composer)

J-21   Discographie in *Albert Jenny: Werkverzeichnis*. Zürich:
Schweizerisches Musik-Archiv, 1985: [83]-84 ((--))

JOACHIM, JOSEPH, 1831-1907 (German violinist/composer)

J-22   LEWIS, John Sam: A whisper from the past: Joseph Joachim in *Record
Research*, No. 185/6 (October 1981): 10 ((--))

JOACHIM, OTTO, 1910-   (Canadian composer)

J-23   [[[Discography] in PLAMONDON, Christine and MARCOUX, Micheline
Coulombe: *Otto Joachim*. Montréal: Centre de musique canadienne,
1980]]

JOBIN, RAOUL, 1906-1974 (Canadian tenor)

J-24   Discographie de Raoul Jobin in MAHEU, René: *Raoul Jobin*. Paris:
P. Belfond, 1983: 231-[234] ((5))

JOCHUM, EUGEN, 1902-1987 (German conductor)

J-25   SCHAUMKELL, Claus-Dieter: Discographische Hinweise in *fono forum*
(June 1986): 22-23 ((--))

JOHANSEN, GUNNAR, 1906–   **(American pianist)**

J-26   Liszt--the works for piano performed by Gunnar Johansen in *Fanfare*, VI/4 (March–April 1983): 100–109 ((4))

JOHNSON, EDWARD, 1878–1959 (Canadian tenor)

J-27   MCPHERSON, J. B. and MORAN, W. R. : The recordings of Edward Johnson in MERCER, Ruby: *The tenor of his time: Edward Johnson of the Met.* Toronto: Clarke, Irwin, 1976: 317–[322] ((1, 3, 6, 7)) [Includes notes on playing speeds]

JOHNSTON, BEN, 1926–   **(American composer)**

J-28   Discography in VON GUNDEN, Heidi: *The music of Ben Johnston.* Metuchen, NJ: Scarecrow Press, 1986: [193]–194 ((1))

JONES, GWENYETH, 1936–   **(Welsh soprano)**

J-29   [Discography] in *Stereo Geijutsu*, No. 48 (May 1972): 158–161 ((--))

J-30   [Discography] in *Record Geijutsu*, No. 276 (September 1973): 195 ((--))

J-31   [[[Discography] in MUTAFIAN, Claude: *Gwyneth Jones.* Paris: Opéra International, 1980. 63 pp.]]

JORDAN, ARMIN, 1932–   **(Swiss conductor)**

J-32   Discographie in WALTER, Edith: Armin Jordan, l'orchestre et le théâtre en Suisse: entretien avec Edith Walter in *Harmonie–Opéra Hi-Fi Conseil*, No. 17 (February 1982): 44 ((--))

JOSQUIN, DES PREZ, ca. 1440–1521 (French composer)

J-33   ZUBER, Barbara: Auswahldiskographie in *Josquin des Prés.* München: Edition Text + Kritik, [1982]: [119]–127 ((5)) (Musik-Konzepte; 26/27)

J-34   Discography in CHARLES, Sydney Robinson: *Josquin des Prez: a guide to research.* New York: Garland Publishing, 1983: 127–153 ((4))

J-35   [[WIND, Thiemo: Josquin des Prez: een discografie in *TOM*, I/2 (1986): 52–54]]

JOUBERT, JOHN, 1927–   **(South African composer)**

See entry for

COMPOSERS--SOUTH AFRICA

JUILLIARD STRING QUARTET, USA

J-36   [Discography] in *Record Geijutsu*, No. 276 (September 1973): [197] ((--))

KABAIVANSKA, RAINA, 1934–   **(Bulgarian soprano)**

K-1   GUANDALINI, Gina: Discografia in *Musica*, No. 19 (December 1980): 346-347   ((7))

K-2   [[[Discography] in *Opéra International*, December 1983]]

KAGAN, OLEG   (Russian violinist)

K-3   Discography in *Music in the USSR* (October-December 1987): 84   ((--))

KAGEL, MAURICIO, 1931-   (Argentinian composer)

K-4   Schallplatten in KLÜPPERHOLZ, Werner: *Mauricio Kagel; 1970-1980*. Köln: DuMont Buchverlag, 1981: 279   ((--))

KAKHIDZE, JANSUG   (Georgian composer)

K-5   [Discography] in *Music in the USSR* (October-December 1986): 92 ((--))

KÁLIK, VÁCLAV, 1891-1951   (Czech composer)

K-6   Seznam gramofonových desek se skladbam: Válcala Kálika in VRATISLAVSKY, Jan: *Václav Kálik; život a dílo*. Brno: Krajské Nak. v ostravě, 1961: 158-159   ((--))

KAMINSKI, HEINRICH, 1886-1946   (German composer)

K-7   Diskographie in *Heinrich Kaminski*. Tutzing: H. Schneider, 1986: 179-182   ((--))   (Komponisten in Bayern; 11)

KANCHELI, GIYA, 1935-   (Georgian composer)

K-8   Discography in *Music in the USSR* (October-December 1985): 89   ((--))

KARAJAN, HERBERT VON, 1908-   (Austrian conductor)

K-9   Karajan Record List in *Record Geijutsu* (March 1966): 180-181   ((--))

K-10   [Discography] in *Record Geijutsu*, No. 276 (September 1973): 181-184 ((--))

K-11   SURTEES, Bruce: Discography in ROBINSON, Paul: *Karajan*. London: Macdonald & Jane's, 1976; Toronto: Lester and Orpen, 1976: 125-152 ((7))

K-12   [Karajan record discography] in *Record Geijutsu*, No. 315, (December 1976): 194-200   ((5, 7))

K-13   Discography [in notes for] *The Art of Herbert von Karajan*. [Sound recording] Angel [Japan] sets EAC 37001/19 and 37020/38, 1978: 7-8 ((7))

K-14   Diskographie in HAUSSERMAN, Ernst: *Herbert von Karajan*. München; Wien; Zürich; Innsbruck: Molden, 1978: 295-310   ((--))

K-15   Diskographie in LÖBL, Karl: *Das Wunder Karajan*. München: Heyne, 1978: 168-191   ((--))

K-16   Discographie in LORCEY, Jacques: *Herbert von Karajan.* Paris: PAC, 1978: 195-255 ((5))

K-17   WILLIAMS, Anthony: *Herbert von Karajan--a discography.* Harrow: General Gramophone Publications, 1978. 39 pp. ((3, 7)) [Includes unpublished records]

K-18   Karajan et l'opéra au disque in TUBEUF, André: Karajan: trente ans de disque lyrique: I, L'avant-Salzbourg in *Diapason,* No. 251 (June 1980): 37-38 ((5))

K-19   Karajan et l'opéra au disque in TUBEUF, André: Karajan: trente ans de disque lyrique: II, Salzbourg in *Diapason,* No. 252 (July-August 1980): 38-39 ((5))

K-20   HUNT, John: *From Adam to Webern: the recordings of Herbert von Karajan.* London: Hunt, 1987: 6-137 ((7))

K-21   [Discography] in *Opfer 1988; Jahrbuch der Zeitschrift Opernwelt.* Zürich: Orell Füssili & Friedrich Verlag, 1988: 45-47 ((--))

KARAYEV, FARADZH, 1943-   **(Russian composer)**

K-22   Discography in *Music in the USSR* (October-December 1987): 19   ((--))

KARAYEV, KARA, 1918-   **(Russian composer)**

K-23   Discography in *Music in the USSR* (July-September 1988): 14   ((--))

KARLOWICZ, MIECZYSLAW,, 1876-1909   (Polish composer)

K-24   MICHAŁOWSKI, Korneł: Dyskografia Mieczyslawa Karolwicza in *Ruch Muzyczny,* XX/25 (1976): 7-8 ((5))

KARR, GARY, 1941-   (American double-bassist)

K-25   Selected discography in *Ovation,* IX/2 (March 1988): 12-14+   ((--))

KATSARIS, CYPRIEN, 1951-   (Greek pianist)

K-26   Diskographie Cyprien Katsaris in COSSÉ, Peter: Enthusiasmus für ausfefallene Projekte in *fono forum* (November 1980): 26-35   ((--))

K-27   Discographische Hinweise in *fono forum* (May 1987): 22   ((--))

KATZ, ARNOLD   (Russian composer)

K-28   [Discography] in *Music in the USSR* (April-June 1986): 14   ((--))

KAUNZINGER, GUNTHER   (German organist)

K-29   Discographische Hinweise in *fono forum* (March 1985): 34-35   ((--))

KAY, ULYSSES, 1917-   (American composer)

K-30   [[Discography in HAYES, Laurence Melton: *The music of Ulysses Kay, 1939-1963* [Dissertation, University of Wisconsin, 1971]   342 pp.]]

KAZAKOV, YURI   (Banyan player)

K-31   Discography in *Music in the USSR* (July–September 1987): 81   ((--))

KEILBERTH, JOSEPH, 1908–1968   (German conductor)

K-32   Discographische Hinweise: Joseph Keilberth in *fono forum* (Janaury 1983): 70   ((--))

KELTERBORN, RUDOLF, 1931–   (Swiss composer)

K-33   Schallplatten in LARESE, Dino and GOEBELS, Franzpeter: *Rudolf Kelterborn; eine Lebensskizze, Der Komponist.* Amriswil: Bücherei, 1970: 48–49   ((--))

K-34   Discographie in *Rudolf Kelterborn; geboren am 3. September 1931.* Zürich: Schweizerisches Musik–Archiv 1980: [16]–18   ((--))

KEMPE, RUDOLF, 1910–1976   (German conductor)

K-35   Rudolf Kempe; Auswahl--Diskografie in *fono forum* (August 1976): 720   ((--)

K-36   [Rudolf Kempe discography] in *Record Geijutsu*, No. 311 (August 1976): 229–221   ((--))

K-37   Diskographie in KEMPE–OETTINGER, Cordula: *Rudolf Kempe: Bilder e. Lebens.* München: List, 1977: 162–167   ((--))

K-38   BLYTH, Charles and FORD, Denham: Discography in *Rudolf Kempe; pictures of a life.* London: Springwood Book, 1979: 162–179   ((5))

K-39   BLYTH, Charles: A Rudolf Kempe discography in *Le Grand Baton*, No. 40 (March–June 1979): 8–27   ((1, 7))

KERÉKJARTO, DUCI DE, 1898–1962   (Hungarian violinist)

K-40   LEWIS, John Sam: Discography in *Record Research*, No. 183/4 (July 1981): 12–13   ((3, 6))

KERN, ADELE, 1901–1980   (German soprano)

K-41   SCHMIDT, Jürgen E.: A Kern discography in *Record Collector*, XXVII/3–4 (March 1982): 62–67; addenda in XXX/3–4 (April 1985): 83 ((3))

KERTÉSZ, ISTVAN, 1929–1973   (Hungarian conductor)

K-42   Discography in *Record Geijutsu*, No. 275 (August 1973):   268–269 ((--))

KEYBOARD MUSIC

K-43   Selected discography in Program notes for *Fugues, fantasias and variations.* [Sound recording] New World Records NW 280, 1976: 4 ((--))

K-44   [[[CORDARA, Franco: Discography] in LESCHIUTTA, Sigfrido:

Appunti per una bibliografia sui clavicembalo, clavicordo e fortepiano. Collana di studi musicali 21 (Padua: Zanibon, 1983) 130 pp.]]

KHACHATURIAN, ARAM, 1903–1978   (Russian composer)

K-45   [Discography] in PERSON, David: *A. Hačaturjan.* Mozkva: Sov. kompozitor, 1978: 97–[101] ((−−))

K-46   [Discography] in ARUTYUNOV, D. A.: *A. Khachaturian i muzyka Sovetskogo Vostoka.* Moskva: "Muzya", 1983: 391–[392] ((−−))

KHARAJANYAN, RAFFI   (Russian pianist)

K-47   Discography in *Music in the USSR* (October–December 1987): 17 ((−−)) [Member of piano duet Novik and Kharajanyan]

KHOLMINOV, ALEXANDER NIKOLAYEVICH, 1925–   (Russian composer)

K-48   Discography in *Music in the USSR* (July–September 1985): 23 ((−−))

K-49   Discography in *Music in the USSR* (July–September 1986): 93 ((−−))

KHRENNIKOV, TIHKON, 1913–   (Russian composer)

K-50   [Discography] in PERSON, David: *T. H. Khrennikov.* Moskva: Sov. kompozitor, 1973: 67–70 ((−−))

K-51   [Discography] in LEVTONOVA, O.: *Simfonii i kontserty T.Khrennikova.* Moskva: Sov. kompozitor, 1979: 199–[200] ((−−))

K-52   Discography [operas and ballets] in *Music in the USSR* (April–June 1985): 86 ((−−))

K-53   Discography [operas and ballets] in *Music in the USSR* (October–December 1985): 24 ((−−))

K-54   [Discography] in *Music in the USSR* (January–March 1986): 16 ((−−))

KIEFER, BRUNO, 1923–   (Brazilian composer)

K-55   Discographic notes in FERREIRA, Paulo Affonso de Moura: *Bruno Kiefer: catálogo de obras.* [Brasília]: Ministério das Relações Exteriores, Departamento de Cooperação Cultural, Científica e Tecnológica, 1975: [14] pp. ((−−)) (Compositores brasileiros)

KIEPURA, JAN, 1902–1966   (Polish tenor)

K-56   Nagrania plytowe Jana Kiepury in WALDORFF, Jerzy: *Jan Kiepura.* Wyd. 2 popr. Kraków: Polski Wydaw. Muzyczne, 1976: 88–93 ((5))

KIKTA, VALARY, 1941–   (Russian composer)

K-57   Discography in *Music in the USSR* (January–March 1987): 89 ((−−))

KIM, EARL, 1920–   (American composer)

K-58   Selected discography in Program notes for *Works of Paul Chihara,*

Chou Wen-Chung, Earl Kim, Roger Reynolds. [Sound recording] New World Records NW 237, 1977: 2 ((--))

KINCAID, WILLIAM, 1895-1967 (American flutist)

K-59   SOLUM, John: William Kincaid, A discography of solo and chamber music in *National Flute Association Inc. Newsletter*, VIII/4 (Summer 1983): 16 ((--))

KIRCHNER, LEON, 1919-   (American composer)

PIANO WORKS

K-60   [[Discography in TRUEL, Nelita: *A style analysis of the published solo piano works of Leon Kirchner.* [DMA, Peabody Conservatory, 1976] 300 pp.]]

KIRKPATRICK, RALPH, 1911-1984 (American harpsichordist)

K-61   Discography, Deutsche Grammophon artist information, 1980. 1 p. ((--))

KIRSTEN, DOROTHY, 1917-   (American soprano)

K-62   BOWKER, Stanley A.: Discography in KIRSTEN, Dorothy: *A time to sing.* Garden City, NY: Doubleday, 1982: [235]-239 ((1, 5))

KLAVIERTRIO PEKINEL, West Germany

K-63   Discographische Hinweise: Klaviertrio Pekinel in *fono forum* (September 1987): 22 ((--))

KLEIBER, CARLOS, 1930-   (Austrian conductor)

K-64   FLOWERS, William: Carlos Kleiber, a legend at 50 in *Le Grand Baton*, No. 52 (March 1982): 14 ((--))

KLEIBER, ERICH, 1890-1956 (Austrian conductor)

K-65   SUGA, Hajime: Erich Kleiber in *LP Techno* (June 1979): 92-95; (August 1979): 96-99, 108 ((3))

KLEMPERER, OTTO, 1885-1973 (German conductor)

K-66   [Otto Klemperer discography] in *Deltio Kritikes Diskographias*, No. 10-13 (July 1973-July 1974): 231-234 ((--))

K-67   Otto Klemperer [discography] in *Stereo Geijutsu*, No. 69 (January 1974): 213-219 ((5))

K-68   [[[Discography] in BOROS, Attila: *Klemperer Magyarorszagon.* Budapest: Zenemukiado, 1973: 71]]

K-69   VINCENTINI, Mario: Klemperer e il disco in *Discoteca*, No. 167 (February 1977): 18-22 ((--))

K-70   GRAY, Michael H.: Discography: commercial recordings by Otto Klemperer in HEYWORTH, Peter: *Otto Klemperer, his life and times.* Cambridge; New York: Cambridge University Press, 1983: 444-452 ((3, 6, 7))

KNAPPERTSBUSCH, HANS, 1888-1965 (German conductor)

K-71 SUGA, Hajime: Knappertsbusch discography in *Record Geijutsu,* No. 437 (February 1987): 186-190; No. 438 (March 1987): 204-208; No. 439 (April 1987): 210-214; No. 440 (May 1987): 224-228 ((3, 6, 7))

KNÜPFER, PAUL, 1865-1920 (German bass)

K-72 SCHMIDT, Jürgen E. Discographie in *Stimmen die um Welt gingen,* No. 19 (March 1988): 1-23 ((3, 7))

KNUSHEVITSKY, SVIATOSLAV, 1908-1963 (Russian cellist)

K-73 [Discography] in GAIDAMOVICH, Tatiana Alexseevna: *Sviatoslav Knushevitskii: monografisheskii ocherk.* Moskva: Sov. kompozitor, 1985: 91-93 ((--))

KODÁLY, ZOLTÁN, 1882-1967 (Hungarian composer)

K-74 Discographie in AMANN, Jean-Pierre: *Zoltán Kodály.* Lausanne: Editions de l'Aire, 1983: 116-120 ((5))

KOECHLIN, CHARLES, 1867-1950 (French composer)

K-75 Discographische Hinweise: Musik von Charles Koechlin in *fono forum* (March 1985): 30 ((--))

See also entry for

COMPOSERS, FRENCH

KÖHLER, SIEGFRIED, 1927-1984 (German composer)

K-76 Discographic notes in SCHÖNFELDER, Gerd: *Siegfried Köhler.* Leipzig: Deutscher Verlag für Musik, 1984: 65-70 ((--))

KOKARI, GIDO, 1921- (Latvian composer)

K-77 Koru ireaksti Firmas "Melodija" skanvplates in VERNERS, Arturs: *Kordirigenti Imants un Gido Kolkari.* Riga: Liesma, 1981: 174-[179] ((--))

KOKKONEN, JOONAS, 1921- (Finnish composer)

K-78 Discography in his *Viimeiset kiusaukset.* Savonlinna: Savonlinnan Oopperajuhlien Kannatusyhdistys, 1978: [108] ((--))

K-79 Joonas Kokkonen levytettyja teoksia in KOKKONEN, Joonas: *Joonas Kokkonen ja Timo Makinen keskustelevat musiikista ja elemasta.* [Savonlinna]: Savonlinnanooppera juhilen kannatusyhdistys: Savonlinnan kirjap, 1979: 169-170 ((--))

KOLLO, RENÉ, 1937- (German tenor)

K-80   Diskographie in FÁBIÁN, Imre: *Imre Fábián im Gesprach mit René
        Kollo.* Zürich: O. Füssli, 1982: 163–[172]   ((--))

K-81   STRACKE, Hans Richard: Tenor im Zenit, René Kollo in *fono forum*
        (September 1985): 20–22, 26–27   ((--))

KORNGOLD, ERICH WOLFGANG, 1897–1957   (Austrian composer)

K-82   Selected discography in CARROLL, Brendan G.: *Erich Wolfgang
        Korngold, 1897-1957.* Paisley, Scotland: Wilfion Books, 1984: 37–39
        ((--))

K-83   YOELL, John H.: Korngold and Zemlinsky: a selected discography
        (33 1/3 rpm) in *Fanfare*, VIII/2 (November–December 1984): 129–133
        ((--))

K-84   [[WILMUT, Roger and AISTLEITNER, Peter: Erich Wolfgang Korngold
        diskographie in *Stimmen die um die Welt Gingen*, No. 14 (December
        1986): 24–51]]

KOSHETZ, NINA, 1894–1965   (Russian soprano)

K-85   Discographical references in CRANE, Allan Crean: Mainly Koshetz in
        Record Collector, XXXIII/3–5 (March 1988): 119–120   ((--))

KRAPP, EDGAR, 1947–   (German organist)

K-86   Discographie in *fono forum* (April 1982): 22–23   ((--))

KRAUS, ALFREDO, 1927–   (Spanish tenor)

K-87   Discografia in *Musica*, No. 40 (March 1986): 28   ((5))

KRAUSS, CLEMENS, 1893–1954   (Austrian conductor)

K-88   SUGA, Hajime: Clemens Krauss SP record discography in *LP
        Techno*, April 1980: 104–108; [addendum in LP Techno]

K-89   WEHRUNG, Brendan: Recordings of Clemens Krauss in *Le Grand
        Baton*, No. 58 (November 1986): 17–42   ((--))

KREBBERS, HERMAN, 1923–   (Dutch violinist)

K-90   Discographie in VAN VERRE, Tony: *Herman Krebbers.* Amsterdam:
        Meulenhoff Nederland, 1981: [135–136]   ((--))

KREISLER, FRITZ, 1875–1962   (Austrian–American violinist)

K-91   [Discography] in IAMPOLSKIĬ, Izrail Markovich: *Frits Kreisler.*
        Moskva: Muzyka, 1975: 149–[159]   ((--))

K-92   Discography in LOCHNER, Louis P.: *Fritz Kreisler.* St. Clair
        Shores, Mich.: Scholarly Press, 1977: 417–428   ((--)) [Reprinted
        from the 1950 ed. published by MacMillan, New York]

K-93   Scheda discografia in *Musica*, No. 34 (October 1984): 58   ((--))

K-94   WEN, Eric: Kreisler discography in *STRAD* (January 1987): 61–67

((3, 6, 7))

KREJCI, ISA, 1904–   (Czech conductor)

K-95   Grammofonové snímky in HOLZKNECHT, Václav: *Isa Krejcí*. Praha: Panton, 1976: 237–239   ((--))

KREMER, GIDON, 1947–   (Russian violinist)

K-96   Diskographie in LEWINSKI, Wolf-Eberhard von: *Gidon Kremer: Interviews, Tatsachen, Meinungen*. München: Goldmann, 1982: 145–[153]   ((7))

K-97   [Gideon Kremer recordings] [Pamphlet] [Hamburg]: Deutsche Grammophon, 1988. 1 l.   ((--))

K-98   MOLKHOV, Jean-Michel: Gidon Kremer une discographie in *Diapason-Harmonie*, No. 337 (April 1988): 59–61   ((7))

KRENEK, ERNST, 1900–   (Austrian composer)

K-99   SZMOLYAN, Walter: Ernst Krenek--Diskographie in *Österreichische Musikzeitschrift*, XXXV (September 1980): 510–512   ((--))

K-100 Schallplatten in ZENCK-MAURER, Claudia: *Ernst Krenek, ein Komponist im Exil*. Wien: Lafite, 1980: 324   ((--))

JONNY SPIELT AUF (1927)

K-101   MARINELLI, Carlo: [Discography] in Palermo, Ente automono Teatro Massimo, season 1986–87: program p. 2   ((5))

See also

PIANO MUSIC

KREUZBERGER STREICHQUARTETT, West Germany

K-102 Discographische Hinweise: Kreuzberger Streichquartett in *fono forum* (February 1982): 28   ((--))

KŘIČKA, JAROSLAV, 1882–1969   (Czech composer)

K-103 Skladby na gramofonových deskách in DOSTÁL, Jiří: *Jaroslav Křička*. Praha: Hudební matice umelécké Besedy (899), 1944: 179–180   ((--))

KRIPS, JOSEF, 1902–1974   (Austrian conductor)

K-104 Discographie in MARTIN, Odíle: Krips retrouvé in *Harmonie-Panorama musique*, No. 42 (May 1984): 22   ((--))

K-105 Discographie Josef Krips in *fono forum* (February 1981): 20–21   ((--))

KUBELIK, JAN, 1880–1940   (Czech violinist)

K-106 Diskografie in VRATISLAVSKY, Jan: *Jan Kubelik*. Praha:

Supraphon, 1978: 74-76 ((--))

KUBELIK, RAFAEL, 1914-   (Czech conductor)

K-107 Discography, Deutsche Grammophon artist information, 1980. 4 pp.
       ((--))

KULIYEV, JAVANSHIR, 1950-   (Azerbaijani composer)

K-108 Discography in *Music in the USSR* (July-September 1985): 95 ((--))

KURENKO, MARIA, 1890-1980 (Russian soprano)

K-109 KNIGHT, Arthur E.: The records in *Record Collector*, VIII
       (October 1953): 224-226 ((--))

KURZ, SELMA, 1874-1933 (Silesian soprano)

K-110 KELLY, Alan: Selma Kurz: a discography in *Recorded Sound*, No.
       73 (January 1979): 2-6 ((3, 7))

KVARTET IMENI N.V. LYSENKO, USSR

K-111 [Discography] in BOROVYK, Mykola: *Kvartet imeni Lysenko*. Kiev:
       "Muz. Ukraina", 1980: 80-82 ((--))

LABELS, RECORD

*This section contains discographies of record manufacturers
and record labels. In several instances, entries in this
section will also appear under other subject headings
in the Bibliography.*

ACCENT Label

L-1   [Discography] in *Record Geijutsu*, No. 371 (August 1981): 254 ((--))

AMERICAN GRAMOPHONE SOCIETY Label

L-2   MECINSKI, Henry R.: The mauve and gold series of the American
       Gramophone Society in *Record Collector*, VIII/6 (June 1953): 132-135
       ((--))

ARTIST DIRECT Label

L-3   Liszt--the works for piano performed by Gunnar Johansen in *Fanfare*,
       VI/4 (March-April 1983): 100-109   ((4))

ASSOCIATION PHONIQUE DES GRANDS ARTISTES Label

L-4   GIRARD, Victor: Association Phonique des Grands Artistes (APGA)
       in *Record Collector*, IX/3 (March 1954): 61-73 ((--))

BERLINER Label

L-5   PERKINS, John F. and KELLY, Alan: Gramophone Company "Berliner"
       matrix numbers, 1898-1900 in *Record Collector*, XXVII/7-8 (August
       1982): 177-180 ((3, 7))

BIRS HISTORIC MASTERS SERIES

L-6   BIRS Historic Masters in *Recorded Sound*, No. 42-43 (April-July 1971): 776-778 ((3)) [Reprinted from *Gramophone*, April 1971]

COLUMBIA Label (France)

L-7   MONNERAYE, Marc, L'HOST, H. and ROIG, G.: Datation des matrices Columbia à partir de janvier 1935 [10" CL series only] in *Sonorités*, No. 13 (July 1985): 13-14 ((7))

COLUMBIA Label (United States)

L-8   MOORE, Jerrold N. and WITTEN, Laurence G.: Columbia Grand Opera Records of 1903 in *Record Collector*, XV/3-4 (May 1963): 68-71 ((3, 6, 7))

COLUMBIA GRAPHOPHONE Label (England)

L-9   GRAY, John: LX series of 12-inch light blue 78 rpm records: a numerical list in *BIRS Bulletin*, No. 11-12 (Spring 1959): 11-31; corrections in No. 15-16 (Spring 1960) ((--))

L-10   HUGHES, Eric: The Columbia (British) LB series of 10-inch light blue 78 rpm records; a numerical list in *BIRS Bulletin*, No. 15-16 (Spring 1960): 8-14 ((--))

L-11   SMITH, Michael and COSENS, Ian: *Columbia Graphophone Company, ltd. English celebrity issues: D and LB series, L and LX series, X and PB series, 7000 and PX series, ROX and SCX series, YB series.* Lingfield, Surrey: Oakwood Press, 1970; Westport, CT: Greenwood Press, 1978. ((3, 4, 6)) (Voices of the past; 8)

L-12   POULTON, Alan J.: *A label discography of long-playing records, series 1 [C, CX, S, SX series, 1952-1962].* [Blandford, Eng.] Oakwood Press, 1975. 90 pp. (Voices of the past; LP1)

DEUTSCHE GRAMMOPHON GESELLSCHAFT m. b. H Label

L-13   BENNETT, John R.: *A catalogue of the vocal recordings from the 1898-1925 German catalogues of the Gramophone Company Limited, Deutsche Grammophon A.-G.* Westport, CT: Greenwood Press, 1978. 404 pp. ((5)) (Voices of the past; 7) [Reprinted from the 1967 ed. published by Oakwood Press]

L-14   [[Deutsche Grammophon part 2 in *Stimmen, die um die Welt gingen*, No. 4 (June 1984): 22-25]]

EDISON Label

L-15   ANNAND, H. H.: *Numerical catalogue of all British blue amberol Edison cylinder records, 1912-1915.* [Hillington, Middlesex, 1960] 1 v. ((4))

L-16   CARTER, Sydney H.: *The complete catalogue of the Edison blue amberol records.* Worthing, Eng., 1963-64. 2 v. ((--))

L-17   CARTER, Sydney H.: *Edison Blue Amberol cylinder records: the complete catalogue of the Edison Blue Amberol records, arr. in numerical order.* Worthing, Eng., 1963-64. 3 v. ((4))

L-18   CARTER, Sydney H.: *Edison amberol cylinder records.* Worthing, Eng., 1963-65. 3 v. ((--))

L-19   CARTER, Sydney H.: *The complete catalogue of the Edison two minute wax cylinder records ... 1888 [to 1912]* Worthing, Eng., 1964-65. 7 v. ((--))

L-20   GRAY, S.: Edison Diamond discs in *Record Collector*, XV/11-12 (May 1964): [243]-285; Addenda in XVI/9-10 (January 1966): 220-225 ((3, 7))

L-21   BETZ, Peter C.: *Edison Concert cylinder records: a catalogue of the series issued 1899-1901.* Bournemouth: City of London Phonograph & Gramophone Society, 1968. [20] pp. ((--))

L-22   MORBY, Paul: Brown wax and Blue Amberol--and the McCormack cylinders in *Record Collector*, XVIII/1-2 (October 1968): 5-42   ((3, 6))

L-23   KOENIGSBERG, Allen: *Edison cylinder records, 1889-1912, with an illustrated history of the phonograph.* New York: Stellar Productions, 1969. 159 pp.; 2d ed. APM Press, 1987. 170 pp. ((4, 5, 7))

L-24   [[KARLIN, Frederick: *Edison diamond discs, 1912-1929* [Santa Monica, CA: Bona Fide Pub. Co., 1972] 1 v.]]

L-25   Edison wax Amberol records in *New Amberola Graphic*, No. 5 (Spring 1973): [9-11]; No. 6 (Summer 1973): [11]; No. 8 (Winter 1974): [9-11]; No. 9 (Spring 1974): [13]; No. 10 (Summer 1974): [7-9]; No. 11 (Fall 1974): [13]; No. 12 (Winter 1975): [11]; No. 13 (Spring 1975): [9-13]; No. 14 (Summer 1975): [13]; No. 17 (Spring 1976): [14a]; No. 18 (Summer 1976): [14a]; No. 19 (Fall 1976): [14a]; No. 20 (Winter 1977): [15]; No. 21 (Spring 1977): [13]   ((--))

L-26   WILE, Raymond: Edison disc masters in *Talking Machine Review International*, No. 5 (August 1970): 141-143; No. 11 (August 1971): 72-74; No. 12 (October 1971): 97-100; No. 13 (December 1971): 125-128; No. 14 (February 1972): 153-156; No. 16 (June 1972): 220-223; No. 17 (August 1972): 11-18; No. 18 (October 1972): 45-46; No. 22 (June 1973): [183]-186; No. 23 (August 1973): 234-235; No. 25 (December 1973): 26-28; No. 28 (April 1974): 134-137; No. 30 (October 1974): 205-207; No. 31 (December 1974): 257-258; No. 38 (February 1976): 592-595; No. 39 (April 1976): 658-660; No. 42 (October 1976): 796, 813-815; No. 44 (February 1977): 941-943; No. 54-55 (October-December 1978): 1432-1433 ((3, 6, 7))

L-27   WILE, Raymond R.: *Edison disc artists & records, 1910-1929.* Brooklyn, NY: APM Press, 1975. 177 pp. ((4, 5, 7))

L-28   CARTER, Sydney: *Blue Amberol cylinders: a catalogue.* London: Talking Machine Review, 1978. 130 p. ((4))

L-29   WILE, Raymond R.: *Edison disc recordings.* Philadelphia:

Eastern National Park and Monument Association, 1978.   427 pp.
((3, 5, 6))

EDISON BELL Label

L-30   CARTER, Sydney H.: *The complete catalogue of the Edison-Bell
gold moulded two and four minute cylinder records, 1902 to 1913*.
Worthing, Eng., 1965.   2 v.   ((--))

L-31   CARTER, Sydney H.: *Edison Bell cylinders: a listing*.
Bournemouth: Talking Machine Review, [197-?]   1 v.   ((5))

EJS Label

L-32   SHAMAN, William: The EJS project in *Record Collector*, XXXII/6-7
(June 1987): 139-146; XXXII/8-10 (September 1987): 231-235;
XXXIII/1-2 (January 1988): 26-31; XXXIII/6-7 (June 1988): 161-164
((1, 3, 7))

ELECTROLA Label (Germany)

L-33   [[[History] in *Stimmen, die um die Welt gingen*, No. 10 (December
1985): 25-41]]

EVERLASTING INDESTRUCTIBLE Label

L-34   ANNAND, H. H.: *The complete catalogue of the United States
Everlasting Indestructible cylinders, 1905-1913*. Bournemouth: City
of London Phonograph & Gramophone Society, 1966.   [38] pp.   ((--))

L-35   ANNAND, H. H.: *The catalogue of the United States Everlasting
Indestructible cylinders, 1908-1913*. 2nd ed.   Bournemouth: The
Talking Machine Review International, 1973.   [36 pp.]   ((4))

FONOTIPIA Label

L-36   BENNETT, J.: *Dischi Fonotipia [Numerical catalogue] A golden
treasury*. Ipswich, Suffolk, Eng.: J. Dennis for the Record
Collector Shop, 1953. 88 pp. ((3))   Supplement in Record Collector,
XVIII/1-2 (October 1968): 44-45   ((--))

L-37   BENNETT, John R.: *Supplement to "Dischi fonotipia"*. Lingfield,
Surrey: Oakwood Press, 1957. 72 pp.   ((3, 4, 7)) (Voices of the
past; 3)

L-38   WITTEN, Laurence: The Paris Fonotipias in *Record Collector*,
XII/1-2 (January-February 1958); XII/3 (March 1958): 61-64   ((--))

GRAMOPHONE AND TYPEWRITER COMPANY Label

L-39   HEVINGHAM-ROOT, L.: The London Red G.& T.'s of 1902 in *Record
Collector*, XIII/1/2 (March-April 1960): 2-[47]; HURST, P. G.:
The London Red G. & T.'s in XIII/3 (May 1960): 67-69   ((3))

L-40   WARD, John: The Gramophone & Typewriter Company Matrix series
in *Record Collector*, XV/3-4: 72-80; XV/7-8: 169-170   ((3))

L-41   DENNIS, J.: G&T off the beaten track [Russian records] in *Record

Collector, XVIII/11-12 (December 1969): 275-278 ((--))

L-42   SHAMAN, William: Discography of the Vatican G&T's in *Record
        Collector,* XXVIII/7-8 (December 1983): 169-191; addendum in
        XXX/11-12 (December 1985): 287-293 ((3, 4, 6, 7))

GRAMOPHONE COMPANY Labels

L-43   BENNETT, John R.: *A catalogue of vocal recordings from the
        English catalogues of the Gramophone Company, 1893-1899; the
        Gramophone Company Limited, 1899-1900; the Gramophone & Typewriter
        Company Limited 1901-1907; and the Gramophone Company Limited,
        1907-1925.* Lingfield, Surrey: Oakwood Press, 1956; Westport, CT:
        Greenwood Press, 1978. 238 pp. ((3, 4, 5, 7)) (Voices of the past;
        1)

L-44   BENNETT, John R.: *Vocal recordings, 1893-1925. Italian
        catalogue.* Lingfield, Surrey: Oakwood Press, 1956; Westport, CT:
        Greenwood Press, 1978. 147 pp. ((3, 4, 6, 7)) (Voices of the
        past; 2)

L-45   BENNETT, John R. and HUGHES, Eric: *The international red
        label catalogue of `DB' & `DA': His master's voice recordings, 1924-1956.
        Bk. 1, `DB' (12 inch).* Lingfield, Surrey: Oakwood Press, [195?];
        Westport, CT: Greenwood Press, 1978. 400 pp. ((3, 4, 6))
        (Voices of the past; 4)

L-46   SMITH, M.: *The catalogue of `D' & `E': His master's voice
        recordings: straight couplings: "D," 1-1212, "E," 1-610; automatic
        couplings: "D,", 7000-7872, "E,", 7000-7008.* Lingfield, Surrey:
        Oakwood Press, [195?]; Westport, CT: Greenwood Press, 1978.
        xviii, 131 pp. ((4)) (Voices of the past; 5)

L-47   BENNETT, John R. and HUGHES, Eric: *The international red
        label catalogue of `DB' & `DA': His master's voice recordings,
        1924-1956. Bk. 2, `DA'* Lingfield, Surrey: Oakwood Press,
        [1964]; Westport, CT: Greenwood Press, 1978. 233 pp.
        ((3, 4, 5, 6)) (Voices of the past; 6)

L-48   ROSENBERG, Herbert: *The Danish His Master's Voice; "DA and "DB"
        series, 1936-1952.* Copenhagen: Nationaldiskoteket, 1965. 35 l.
        ((3, 4, 6, 7))

L-49   Nationaldiskoteket: *The Scandinavian His Master's Voice M-series.*
        Copenhagen, 1966. 47 pp. ((3, 4, 6, 7)) (Nationaldiskoteket
        discographies; 202)

L-50   BENNETT, John R. and WIMMER, Wilhelm: *A catalogue of vocal
        recordings from the 1898-1925 German catalogues of the Gramophone
        Company Limited, Deutsche Grammophon A.-G..* Lingfield, Surrey:
        Oakwood Press, 1967; Westport, CT: Greenwood Press, 1978. 404 pp.
        ((3, 4, 7)) (Voices of the past; 7)

L-51   Nationaldiskoteket: *The Danish His Master's Voice "DA" and "DB"
        series.* 2d ed. Copenhagen: Nationaldiskoteket, 1967. 29 l.
        (Nationaldiskoteket discographies; 203)

L-52   BENNETT, John R.: *A catalogue of vocal recordings from the*

*1898-1925 French catalogues of the Gramophone Company Limited,
Compagnie française du gramophone*. Lingfield, Surrey: Oakwood
Press, 1971; Westport, CT: Greenwood Press, 1978. 304 pp.
((3, 4, 5)) (Voices of the past; 9)

L-53   LILIEDAHL, Karleric: *The Gramophone Company*. Trelleborg,
Sweden: Liliedahl, 1973. 188 pp. ((3, 4, 6, 7))

L-54   Nationaldiskoteket: *The Scandinavian His Master's Voice V-series,
1920-1932*. København: Nationaldiskoteket, 1973. 59 pp.
((3, 4, 6, 7)) (Nationaldiskoteket discographies; 208)

L-55   SMITH, Michael and ANDREWS, Frank: *His master's voice recordings,
plum label "C" series (12 inch)*. [Blandford]: Oakwood Press, 1974.
274 pp. ((3, 4, 6, 7)) (Voices of the past; 10)

L-56   POULTON, Alan J.: *A label discography of long-playing records,
series 2 [HMV ALP/BLP/CLP/DLP, 1952-62]* [Dorset, Eng.: Oakwood
Press, 1975. 90 pp. ((4, 5)) (Voices of the past; LP2)

L-57   POULTON, Alan J.: *A label discography of long-playing records,
series 3 [HMV Plum Label; HMV/Columbia GROC Labels; Golden Treasury
Label; HMV Concert Classics Label]* [Dorset, Eng.]: Oakwood Press,
1975. 88 pp. ((4, 5)) (Voices of the past; LP3)

L-58   BENNETT, John Reginald: *A catalogue of vocal recordings from
the Russian catalogues of the Gramophone Company Limited*. Dorset:
Oakwood Press, 1977. 220 pp. ((3, 4)) (Voices of the past; 11)

L-59   Catalogue of early Viennese Gramophone recordings in *Recorded Sound*,
No. 69 (January 1978): 759-761 ((7))

L-60   HMV-Victor Recreation series [re-recordings of acoustic masters
with new orchestral accompaniments] in *Talking Machine Review*,
No. 51 (April 1978): 1296-1299 ((3, 6, 7))

L-61   KELLY, Alan: Gramophone Company (UK) matrix listing, 1905-1920
in *Hillandale News*, No. 133 (August 1983): 234 ((7))

L-62   KELLY, Alan: *His Master's Voice/La voce del Padrone; the
Italian catalogue; a complete numerical catalogue of Italian
gramophone recordings made from 1898 to 1929 in Italy and else-
where by The Gramophone Company Ltd*. New York: Greenwood Press,
1988. 462 pp. ((3, 4, 6, 7)) (Greenwood Press discographies; 30)

GSS RECORDINGS COMPANY Label

L-63   Discography in *Fanfare*, VIII/2 (November-December 1984): 106-108
((--))

HOMOCORD Label (Germany)

L-64   [[[History] in *Stimmen, die um die Welt gingen*, No. 6 (December
1984): 13-15]]

MELODIYA Label

L-65   BENNETT, John R.: *Melodiya: a Soviet Russian L.P. discography*.

Westport, CT: Greenwood Press, 1981.   832 pp.   ((4, 5))
(Greenwood Press discographies; 6)

MUSIC MINUS ONE Label

L-66   Music Minus One + 5: profile of a unique record company in *Tarakan Music Letter*, II/4 (March-April 1981): 4, 7   ((--))

NATIONAL MUSIC LOVERS Label

L-67   COTTER, Dave: Opera song series in *New Amberola Graphic*, No. 18 (Summer 1978): 8-9   ((--))

NEOPHONE Label

L-68   ANDREWS, F.: Discography in *Talking Machine Review*, No. 54-55 (October-December 1978): 1397-1400   ((3))

NEW ALBION Label

L-69   Discographische Hinweise in *fono forum* (October 1987): 27   ((--))

NEW MUSIC QUARTERLY RECORDS Label

L-70   HALL, David: New Music Quarterly Recordings - a discography in *ARSC Journal*, XVI/1-2 (1984): 10-27   ((3, 4, 5, 6, 7))

ODEON Label (Germany)

L-71   [[[Matrix numbers and recording dates] in *Stimmen, die um die Welt gingen*, No. 4 (June 1984):]]

L-72   [[[History] in *Stimmen, die um die Welt gingen*, No. 8 (June 1985): 7-76]]

PATHÉ Label (France)

L-73   ROIG, Gérard: Datation des matrices Pathé serie CPT, 1ère partie (mars 1934-décembre 1952) in *Sonorités*, No. 11 (September 1984): 31-33   ((3, 7))

PATHÉ SALABERT Label (France)

L-74   ROIG, Gérard and NEVERS, Daniel and MONNERAYE, Marc: Pathé Salabert: Des compléments d'information in *Sonorités*, No. 10 (May 1984): 5-7   ((3, 7))

PHONOTYPE RECORDS Label

L-75   DENNIS, J. F. E.: Phonotype records in *Record Collector*, VIII/9 (September 1953): [193]-206   ((--))

POLYDOR Label (France)

L-76   ROIG, Gérard, L'HOST, Hervé and MONNERAYE, Marc: Datation des matrices Polydor in *Sonorités*, No. 12 (January 1985): 23-24 ((3, 7))

SONORA Label

L-77   ENGLUND, Björn: *Sonora IV.* Stockholm: Kungliga biblioteket,
1968: 1. 23-27 ((3, 4, 6 7)) [Classical series, K-9500's]
(Nationalfonotekets diskografier; 8)

TELEFUNKEN Label (Germany)

L-78   [[[Series list] in *Stimmen, die um die Welt gingen*, No. 2 (December
1983): 28-29]]

TRI-ERGON Label (Germany)

L-79   [[[History] in *Stimmen, die um die Welt gingen* (March 1985):
55-58]]

ULTRAPHON Label (Germany)

L-80   [[[Series list] in *Stimmen, die un die Welt gingen*, No. 2 (December
1983): 28-29]]

ULTRAPHON Label (Sweden)

L-81   ELFSTRÖM, Mats and ENGLUND, Björn: *Ultraphon.* [Stockholm]:
Kungliga Biblioteket, 1968. 14 pp. ((3, 4, 7)) (Nationalfonotekets
diskografier; 3)

VICTOR Label

L-82   SMOLIAN, Steven: Complete numerical listing of RCA Victor "Red Seal"
albums in *American Record Guide,* XXX/9 (May 1964): 892-895;
XXX/10 (June 1964): 1002-1004; XXX/11 (July 1964): 1056-1058;
XXXI/1 (September 1964): 82-84; XXXI/2 (October 1964): 165-167;
XXXI/3 (November 1964): 271-273; XXXI/6 (February 1965): 582-583;
XXXI/8 (April 1965): 763-765 ((--))

L-83   LÉON, Jacques Alain: *Catálogo numérico dos discos vocais Victor
Sêlo Vermêlho. Numerical catalogue of Red-Seal Victor vocal records.
Part 1 [numbers 500-9999]:* Printed by Batista, Brazil, 1964. 177
pp.; *Part 2: [Numbers 10000 to 18546]* Printed by Batista,
Brazil, 1968. 86 pp. ((4))

L-84   BRYANT, William R. and FAGAN, Ted: Victor Talking Machine
60000 series in *New Amberola Graphic,* No. 7 (Fall 1973): 3-10;
Index in No. 10 (Summer 1974): 5-6 ((3, 4, 6, 7))

L-85   BRYANT, William R. AND FAGAN, Ted: Victor Talking Machine
70000 series in *New Amberola Graphic,* No. 9 (Spring 1974): 5-[10];
Index in No. 10 (Summer 1974): 5-6 ((3, 4, 6, 7))

L-86   HMV-Victor Recreation series [re-recordings of acoustic masters with
electrically recorded orchestral accompaniments] in *Talking Machine
Review,* No. 51 (April 1978): 1296-1299 ((3, 6, 7))

L-87   FAGAN, Ted: Pre-LP recordings of RCA at 33 1/3 rpm. through
1931 to 1934 in *ARSC Journal,* XIII/1 (1981): 20-42; XIV/3 (1982):
41-61; XV/1 (1983): 25-68 ((3, 4, 6, 7))

L-88   FAGAN, Ted and MORAN, William R.: *The encyclopedic discography of Victor recordings. Pre-Matrix series.* Westport, CT: Greenwood Press, 1983. 393 pp. ((3, 4, 6, 7))

L-89   FAGAN, Ted and MORAN, William R.: *The encyclopedic discography of Victor recordings. Matrix series 1 through 4999: the Victor Talking Machine Company, 24 April 1903 to 7 January 1908.* Westport, CT: Greenwood Press, 1986. 648 pp. ((3, 4, 6, 7))

VOX Label (Germany)

L-90   [[[History] in *Stimmen, die um die Welt gingen,* No. 5 (September 1984): 28-31]]

WORLD'S GREATEST MUSIC Label

L-91   GRAY, Michael: The World's Greatest Music records in *Le Grand Baton,* No. 4 (December 1974): 33-38 ((7))

L-92   GRAY, Michael H.: The "World's Greatest Music" and "World's Greatest Opera" labels in *ARSC Journal,* VII/1-2 (1975): 34-55 ((3, 6, 7))

ZONOFONE Labels

L-93   WOLF, Albert: Celebrity Zonofono discs [Italy] in *Record Collector,* II/10 (October 1947): 7-8 ((--))

L-94   Zonophone 5-inch (12.5 cm) discs [Germany] in *Talking Machine Review,* No. 32 (February 1975): 299-309 ((3))

See also

PHONOCYLINDERS

LABÈQUE, KATIA/LABÈQUE, MARIELLE (French pianists)

L-95   Discographie in *Harmonie-Panorama musique,* No. 42 (May 1984): 15-19 ((--))

LACERDA, OSVALDO, 1927–   (Brazilian composer)

L-96   Discographic notes in FERREIRA, Paulo Affonso de Moura: *Osvaldo Lacerda: catálogo de obras.* [Brasília]: Ministério das Relações Exteriores, Departamento de Cooperação Cultural, Científica e Tecnológica, 1976: [33] pp. ((--)) (Compositores brasileiros)

LAFONT, JULIEN (Bass-baritone)

L-97   [Discography] in *Record Collector,* IX/3 (March 1954): 65 ((--))

LAHUSEN, CHRISTIAN, 1886-1975 (German composer)

L-98   Discographie in WEINECK, Isolde Maria: *Christian Lahusen.* [Dissertation] Wesfählischen: Wilhelms-universität, 1978: [366]-371 ((--))

LALO, ÉDOUARD, 1823-1892 (French composer)

OPERAS

LE ROI D'YS (1888)

L-99   DUTRONC, Jean-Louis: Cinq voix pour une intégral and CABOURG, Jean and VOISIN, Georges: Le roi d'ys et le 78 tours in *L'Avant Scène Opéra*, No. 65 (July 1984): 72-74   ((7))

ORCHESTRAL WORKS

SYMPHONIE ESPAGNOLE (1873)

L-100   TELLART, Roger: La Symphonie espagnole d'Édouard Lalo, ou L'Espagne venue du Nord in *Diapason*, No. 222 (November 1977): 48-50   ((--))

LAMARE, BERTHE, 1880-?   (French soprano)

L-101 [Discography] in *Record Collector*, IX/3 (March 1954): 65   ((--))

LANDOWSKI, MARCEL, 1915-   (French composer)

L-102 Discographie des oeuvres de Marcel Landowski in *Marcel Landowski, musicien de l'espérance*. Paris: La Revue musicale, No. 372-374, 1984: [159]-161   ((--))

LANGLAIS, JEAN, 1907-   (French organist)

L-103 JACQUET, Marie Louise: Enregistrements sur disques des oeuvres d'orgue récentes de Jean Langlais in *Jeunesse et orgue*, No. 36/37 (Spring-Summer 1978): 91   ((--))

L-104 THOMERSON, Kathleen Armstrong: The organ music of Jean Langlais: discography of solo organ works and improvisations in *Diapason*, LXXIII (February 1982): 18-20   ((--))

L-105 Discography in THOMERSON, Kathleen: *Jean Langlais: a bio-bibliography*. New York: Greenwood Press, 1988: [57]-96   ((5, 7))   (Bio-bibliographies in music; 10)

LANKOW, EDWARD, 1883-1940   (American bass)

L-106 BOTT, Michael F.: Edward Lankow, discography in *Record Collector*, XXV/3-4 (June 1979): 95   ((3, 6, 7))

LANZA, MARIO, 1921-1959   (American tenor)

L-107 Discography in STRAIT, Raymond: *Lanza, his tragic life*. Englewood Cliff, NJ: Prentice-Hall, 1980: 173-175   ((--))

L-108 *Mario Lanza discography*. Banbury: British Mario Lanza Society, 1980. 52 pp.   ((4))

LARIN, ALEXEI   (Russian composer)

L-109 [Discography] in *Music in the USSR* (October-December 1984): 94   ((--))

LaSALLE STRING QUARTET, USA

L-110 [Discography] in *Record Geijutsu*, No. 276 (September 1973): 196
((--))

L-111 Discography, Deutsche Grammophon artist information, 1980. 1 p.
((--))

L-112 Discografia in *Musica*, No. 42 (October 1986): 46 ((--))

LASSALLE, JEAN-LOUIS, 1847-1909 (French baritone)

L-113 ROUSSILLON, Georges: Discographie in *Sonorités*, No. 4 (March
1982): 38-39 ((3, 7))

LAURENTI, MARIO, 1890-1922 (Italian baritone)

L-114 The Edison recordings of Mario Laurenti in FERRARA, Dennis E.:
Mario Laurenti, a record collector's baritone (Neglected Edison
Diamond Discs artists) in *New Amberola Graphic*, No. 44 (Spring
1983): 9-11 ((3, 7))

L-115 FERRARA, Dennis E.: Discography in *Record Collector*, XXXII/6-7
(June 1987): 147-150; additions & corrections in XXXII/8-10
(September 1987): 238 ((7)) [Includes unissued records]

LAURI-VOLPI, GIACOMO, 1892-1959 (Italian tenor)

L-116 PEDEMONTE, Valeria: Lauri-Volpi per sempre in *Discoteca hi fi*,
No. 204 (March 1980): 32-35 ((7))

L-117 Discografia di Giacomo Lauri-Volpi in BRAGAGLIA, Leonardo: *La voce
solitaria: cinquanta personaggi per Giacomo Lauri-Volpi*. Roma:
Bulzoni, 1982: 242-253 ((5, 7))

L-118 SERBANDINI, Silvio: Discografia in LAURI-VOLPI, Giacomo: *A viso
aperto*. Bologna: Bongiovanni, 1982-1983: v. 2: 251-266 ((3, 6, 7))

LAUTE-BRUN, ANTOINETTE, 1876-?   (French soprano)

L-119 [Discography] in *Record Collector*, IX/3 (March 1954): 65 ((--))

LAWRENCE, MARJORIE, 1909-1979 (Australian soprano)

L-120 HOGARTH, Will and SEE, R. T.: Marjorie Lawrence discography
in *Record Collector*, XXXII/1-2 (January 1987): 7-18; additions &
corrections in XXXIII/11-12 (November 1988): 300-303 ((1, 3, 6, 7))

LAZARENO, MANUEL, 1909-1975 (Spanish composer)

L-121 Works of Manuel Lazareno in *Recorded Sound*, No. 73 (January 1979):
8-9 ((7))

LAZZARI, CAROLINA, 1891-1946 (American mezzo-soprano)

L-122 STONE, Robert B.: Neglected Edison Diamond Disc artists: Carolina
Lazzari in *New Amberola Graphic*, No. 36 (Spring 1981): 8-9 ((7))

L-123 Discography--Carolina Lazzari in *Record Collector*, XXXII/3-5
(April 1987): 112   ((3, 7))   [Includes unissued records]

LEDENPOV, ROMANA   (Russian composer)

L-124 [Discography] in *Music in the USSR* (April-June 1986): 22   ((--))

LEE, NOEL, 1924-   (American pianist)

L-125 Discographie de Noël Lee; Discographie du duo Noël Lee/Christian
Ivaldi in *Harmonie Hi-fi Conseil*, No. 4 (December 1980): 26   ((5))

LEGGE, WALTER, 1906-1979   (English record producer)

L-126 SANDERS, Alan: A selected discography in SCHWARZKOPF, Elisabeth:
On and off the record: a memoir of Walter Legge. London: Faber
and Faber, 1982; New York: Scribners, 1982: 243-288   ((7))

L-127 SANDERS, Alan: *Walter Legge: a discography*. Westport, CT: Greenwood
Press, 1984. 452 pp.   ((3, 4, 6, 7))

LEHÁR, FERENC, 1870-1948   (Austrian composer)

OPERAS

(DIE) LUSTIGE WITWE (1905)

L-128   LAMB, Andrew M.: Die lustige Witwe, Part 1 in *Opera*, XXII/2
(February 1981): 128-137; with WALKER, Malcolm: LP discography
p. 136; Part 2, XXII/3 (March 1981): 243-247   ((--))   (Opera on
the gramophone; 50)

L-129   TASSART, Maurice: Discographie in *L'Avant Scène Opéra*, No.
45 (November 1982): 118-121   ((7))

LEHEL, GYÖRGY, 1926-   (Hungarian conductor)

L-130 György Lehel diszkográfia in BOROS, Attila: *Muzsika és mikrofon:
a Rádiózenekar négy évtizede*. Budapest: Zenemukiado, 1985:
185-[201]   ((--))

LEHMANN, HANS ULRICH, 1937-   (Swiss composer)

L-131 Discographie in *Hans Ulrich Lehmann, geboren am 4. Mai 1937:
Werkverzeichnis*. Zürich: Schweizerisches Musik-Archiv, 1981:
9   ((--))

LEHMANN, LILLI, 1848-1929   (German soprano)

L-132 DENNIS, J.: Lilli Lehmann; discography [and] STRATTON, John:
The Lilli Lehmann recordings in *Record Collector*, XXVI/9-10 (May
1981): 199-214; additions & corrections in XXVII/3-4 (March 1982):
94   ((--))

LEHMANN, LOTTE, 1888-1976   (German soprano)

L-133 [[[Discography] in *Stimmen, die um die Welt gingen* (March 1985):

2-54]]

L-134 HICKLING, Gary: Lotte Lehmann discography in GLASS, Beaumont:
       Lotte Lehmann, her life in opera and song. Santa Barbara, CA:
       Capra Press, 1988: 303-322 ((1, 3, 4, 6, 7))

   LEIDER, FRIDA, 1888-1975 (German soprano)

L-135 BURROS, Harold: Frida Leider discography in LEIDER, Frida:
       Playing my part. New York: Da Capo Press, 1978: 211-214
       ((1, 3, 5, 6, 7)) [Reprinted from the original ed. published by
       Calder & Boyars, 1966]

L-136 [[[Discography] in *Stimmen, die um die Welt gingen,* No. 3 (March
       1984): 6-19]]

   LEKEU, GUILLAUME, 1870-1894 (Belgian composer)

   See entry for

   COMPOSERS, FRENCH

   LEMESHEV, SERGEI IAKOVLEVICH, 1902-1977 (Russian tenor)

L-137 [Discography and bibliography] in *S. IA. Lemeshev: iz
       biograficheskikh zapisok, stat'i, besedy, pis'ma, vospomiananiĩa
       o S.IA. Lemesheve.* Moskva: "Sov. kompozitor", 1987: 371-[384]
       ((7))

   LENINGRAD PHILHARMONIC ORCHESTRA

L-138 Discography of the Leningrand Philharmonic Symphony Orchestra under
       Yevgeni Mravinsky in *Music in the USSR* (January-March 1988): 13
       ((--))

   LEONCAVALLO, RUGGIERO, 1857-1919 (Italian composer)

   OPERAS

   PAGLIACCI (1892)

L-139   MARINELLI, Carlo: [Discography] in Roma, Teatro dell'Opera,
         season 1971-72: program pp. 509-517 ((5))

L-140   MARINELLI, Carlo: [Discography] in Treviso, Ente Teatro
         Comunale, season 1978: program pp. 18 ((5))

L-141   MARINELLI, Carlo: [Discography] in Milano, Teatro alla Scala,
         season 1980-81: program pp. 116-117 ((5))

L-142   CABOURG, Jean: Discographies comparées [with Mascagni,
         Cavalleria Rusticana] in *L'Avant Scène Opéra,* No. 50 (March
         1983): 130-143 ((1, 7))

L-143   MARINELLI, Carlo: [Discography] in Milano, Teatro alla Scala,
         season 1983-84: program pp. 59-60 ((5))

L-144   MARINELLI, Carlo: [Discography] in Milano, Teatro alla Scala,

season 1986-87: program pp. 111-113   ((5))

LEPPARD, RAYMOND, 1927-   **(English conductor)**

L-145 Discography [on Philips label] S.l.: [Philips, 198-?] 2 l.   ((--))

LEVINAS, MICHAEL, 1949-   **(French composer/pianist)**

L-146 Discographie in *Harmonie-Panorama musique*, No. 47 (November 1984): 23   ((--))

LEVITZKI, MISCHA, 1898-1941   (Russian pianist)

L-147 SUGA, Hajime: Mischa Levitski in *LP Techno*, September 1982: 76-79   ((3))

LEWIS, MARY, 1900-1941   (American soprano)

L-148 MORAN, W. R.. and DOUGAN, Michael B.: The recordings of Mary Lewis in *Record Collector*, XXIII/7-8 (December 1976): 184-[189], 191 ((1, 3, 6, 7)) [Includes notes on playing speeds]

LHÉVINNE, JOSEF, 1874-1944   (Russian pianist)

L-149 Discography in WALLACE, Robert K.: *A century of music-making: the lives of Josef & Rosina Lhevinne.* Bloomington, Indiana University Press, 1976: 337-340   ((1, 7))

LIEBERSON, PETER, 1946-   **(American composer)**

L-150 Selected discography in Program notes for *Peter Lieberson Bagatelles.* [Sound recording] New World Records NW 344, 1987   ((--))

LIGETI, GYÖRGY, 1923-   **(Hungarian composer)**

L-151 Discographic references in NORDWALL, Ove: *Det omöjligas konst; Anteckningar kring György Ligetis musik.* Stockholm: Nordtedt, 1966: 89-97   ((--))

L-152 Discographic references in NORDWALL, Ove: *Ligeti-dokument.* Stockholm: Norstedt, 1968: 297-309   ((--))

L-153 Discographic references in NORDWALL, Ove: *György Ligeti; eine Monographie.* Mainz: Schott, 1971: 202-219   ((--))

L-154 Werke von Ligeti auf Schallplatten in *Musik und Bildung*, VII (1975): 525   ((--))

L-155 György Ligeti; discografi mars 1978 in *Musik Revy*, XXXIII/3 (1978): 92-93   ((--))

L-156 List of works and recordings in GRIFFITHS, Paul: *György Ligeti.* London: Robson Books, 1983: 116-122   ((--))

L-157 Discographie in MICHEL, Pierre: *György Ligeti, compositeur d'aujourd'hui.* [Paris]: Minerve: Alternative Diffusion, 1985: 245-[247]   ((--))

L-158 Nota discografica in VARI, Autori: *Ligeti*. Torino: E.D.T., 1985: 259-262 ((--))

L-159 [[[Discography] in NORDWALL, Ove: *Ligeti-dokument*. Stockholm: Nordstedt, 1988: 297-309]]

L-160 Discographische Hinweise: György Ligeti in *fono forum* (June 1988): 30 ((--))

LIPATTI, DINU, 1917-1950   (Rumanian pianist)

L-161 MASINI, Umberto: Discografia completa in *Discoteca*, No. 166 (December 1976): 33-34 ((1, 7))

L-162 Diskografie Dinu Lipatti in MEYER, Martin: Wirklichkeit und Legende: ein Porträt des Pianisten Dinu Lipatti, 1917-1950 in *fono forum* (June 1978): 606-609 ((7))

L-163 Discografia di Dinu Lipatti in *Musica*, No. 51 (August-September 1988): 52-53 ((7))

LISITSIAN, PAVEL GERASIMOVICH, 1911-   (Russian baritone)

L-164 LINNELL, Norman: Discography ... in *Record Collector*, XXVIII/5-6 (October 1983): 106-119 ((4))

LISZT, FRANZ, 1811-1886   (Hungarian composer)

L-165 [[[Discography] in WESSLING, Berndt W.: *Franz Liszt*. München: Heyne, 1979: 253-255]]

L-166 ARNOLD, Ben and HO, Allan B.: Liszt research and recordings in *Journal of the American Liszt Society*, XV (June 1984): 118-138; XVI (December 1984): 35-52; XVII (1985): 24-38; XVIII (1985): 36-46; XX (1986): 4-29 ((4))

L-167 [Discography] in HAMBURGER, Klára: *Liszt kalauz*. Budapest: Zeneműkiadó, 1986: 419-420 ((--))

L-168 Discographische Hinweise in *fono forum* (October 1986): 30, 32, 34 ((--))

CHORAL WORKS

L-169   L'abbe Liszt au disque in *Diapason*, No. 277 (November 1982): 38 ((--))

EIN FAUST-SYMPHONIE, G. 108 (1854)

L-170   MARINELLI, Carlo: Discografie: Faust e Mefistofele nelle opere teatrali e sinfonico-vocali in *Quaderni dell'I.R.TE.M.* [Instituto di Ricerca per il Teatro Musicale] No. 3 (1986): 30-43 ((5))

CONCERTOS, PIANO

CONCERTO, PIANO AND ORCHESTRA, No. 1, E-Flat, G. 124

L-171   BEROFF, Michel and FRÉIRE, Nelson: Liszt: le Première

concerto (discographie) in *Diapason–Harmonie*, No. 313
(February 1986): 90–93 ((--))

PIANO WORKS

L-172   FAGAN, Keith: Selective piano discography in *Piano Quarterly*,
No. 89 (Spring 1975): 51–56 ((--))

L-173   Liszt--the works for piano performed by Gunnar Johansen in
Fanfare, VI/4 (March–April 1983): 100–109 ((4))

RHAPSODIES HONGROISES

L-174   Discography in COSSÉ, Peter: Aufforderung zur Freiheit: Franz
Liszts "Ungarische Rapsodien" und ihre Interpreten in *fono forum*
(September 1980): 32–40 ((--))

LLOYD, DAVID, 1913–1969 (Welsh tenor)

L-175   JONES, W. D. and MORGAN, Charles I.: David Lloyd discography in
Record Collector, XXXI/6–7 (July 1986): 130–138; additions &
corrections in XXXI/8–10 (September 1986): 230 ((3, 6, 7))

LLOYD WEBBER, ANDREW, 1948–   (English composer)

L-176   Discography in MCKNIGHT, Gerald: *Andrew Lloyd Webber*. London:
Granada, 1984; New York: St. Martins, 1984: [265]–[273] ((5))

LLOYD WEBBER, JULIAN, 1951–   (English cellist)

L-177   Discography in LLOYD WEBBER, Julian: *Travels with my cello*.
London: Pavilion, 1984: 121–123 ((--))

LOBANOV, VASILY (Russian pianist)

L-178   Discography in *Music in the USSR* (April–June 1988): 21 ((--))

LOCATELLI, PIETRO, 1695–1764 (Italian composer)

L-179   [[Discography in CALMEYER, John Hendrick: *The life, times and
works of Antonio Pietro Locatelli*. [Dissertation, University of
North Carolina, 1969]   465 pp.]]

LODÉON, FRÉDERIC (French cellist)

L-180   Discographie de Fréderic Lodéon in *Harmonie–Opéra–Hifi Conseil*,
No. 24 (October 1982): 25 ((--))

LOEFFLER, CHARLES MARTIN, 1861–1935 (American composer)

L-181   Selected discography in Program notes for *Music of Charles Martin
Loeffler*. [Sound recording] New World Records NW 332, 1985 ((--))

LONDON SINFONIETTA

L-182   [[[Discography] in *The complete instrumental and chamber music
of Roberto Gerhard*. London: Sinfonietta Productions, 1973: 138–139]]

LONDON STRING QUARTET

L-183 [Discography] in UPTON, Stuart: *Sir Dan Godfrey & the Bournemouth Symphony Orchestra*. London: Vintage Light Music Society, 1979: 32 ((--))

LORENGAR, PILAR, 1928–   (Spanish soprano)

L-184 Pilar Lorengar auf Schallplatten in *Pilar Lorengar: ein Portrait*. Berlin: Stapp, 1985: 146–151 ((--)) [Omits record numbers]

LORENZ, MAX, 1901–1975 (German tenor)

L-185 [Discography] in *Max Lorenz*. [Hamburg: Sammlung Jürgen Schäfer, 1973]: 6–14 ((1, 7))

L-186 HACKENBERG, Hubert: Discographie in HERRMANN, Walter: *Max Lorenz*. Wien: Österr. Bundesverl., 1976: 41–[47] ((7))

L-187 [[[Discography] in *Stimmen, die um die Welt gingen*, No. 10 (December 1985): 17–23; No. 15 (March 1987): 48–51]]

LOS ANGELES PHILHARMONIC ORCHESTRA

See entry for

MEHTA, ZUBIN

LOTHAR, MARK, 1902–1985 (German composer)

L-188 Diskographie in *Mark Lothar*. Tutzing: H. Schneider, 1986: 159 ((--)) (Komponisten in Bayern; 10)

LUBIN, GERMAINE, 1890–1979 (French soprano)

L-189 LUBIN, Jacques, MARTY, Daniel and MONNERAYE, Marc: Germaine Lubin in *Sonorités*, No. 15 (July 1986): 43–47 ((3, 6, 7)) [Includes unissued records]

LUENING, OTTO, 1900–   (American composer)

L-190 Discography in LEUNING, Otto: *The Odyssey of an American composer: the autobiography of Otto Luening*. New York: Scribner, 1980: [593]–594 ((--))

LULLY, JEAN–BAPTISTE, 1632–1687 (French composer)

OPERAS

ATYS (1676)

L-191   TELLART, Roger: Discographie in *L'Avant Scène Opéra*, No. 94 (January 1987): 104–105 ((--))

LUNDBORG, ERIK, 1948–   (American composer)

L-192 Selected discography in Program notes for *Parnassus*. [Sound recording] New World Records NW 306, 1978: [2] ((--))

LUPU, RADU, 1945–   (Rumanian pianist)

L–193 [Discography] in *Record Geijutsu*, No. 276 (September 1973): 188
((−−))

LUTOSŁAWSKI, WITOLD, 1913–   (Polish composer)

L–194 Discographic references in JAROCIŃSKI, Stefan: *Witold Lutosławski; materiały do monografii.* Kraków: Polskie Wydawn. Muzyczne, 1967. 91 pp. ((−−))

L–195 Discographic references in NORDWALL, Ove: *Lutosławski.* Stockholm: Edition Wilhelm Hansen, 1968: 127–134 ((−−))

L–196 Discographic notes in KACZYŃSKI, Tadeusz: *Rozmowy z Witoldem Lutosłoawkim.* Kraków: Pol. Wydawn. Muz., 1972. 253 pp. ((−−))

L–197 Werkverzeichnis Uraffführungen/Schallplatten in KACZYNSKI, Tadeusz: *Gespräch mit Witold Lutosławski.* Leipzig: P. Reclam, 1976: 231–[238] ((−−))

L–198 Discographie in COUCHOUD, Jean Paul: *La musique polonaise et Witold Lutosławski.* Paris: Stock Plus, 1981: 225–[228] ((−−))

L–199 Discography in STUCKY, Steven: *Lutosławski and his music.* Cambridge; New York: Cambridge University Press, 1981: 213–218 ((−−))

L–200 Discographie in *Diapason–Harmonie*, No. 341 (September 1988): 68–69 ((−−))

LYUBIMOV, ANATOLY, 1941–   (Russian composer)

L–201 [Discography] in *Music in the USSR* (January–March 1986): 27 ((−−))

MCCABE, JOHN, 1939–   (English composer)

M–1 HUGHES, Eric and DAY, Timothy: John McCabe in *Recorded Sound*, No. 82 (July 82): 77–85 ((1, 7)) (Discographies of British composers; 16)

MACEDA, JOSE

See

MUSIC––ASIA

MACONCHY, ELIZABETH, 1907–   (English composer)

M–2 ALEXANDER, John: Elizabeth Maconchy––a discography in *Music & Musicians* (March 1987): 34 ((−−))

MCCORMACK, JOHN, 1884–1945   (Irish tenor)

M–3 FAWCETT-JOHNSTON, Brian: John Count McCormack––complete pre-1910 discography in *Record Collector*, XXIX/1–3 (June 1984): 33–68; XXIX/4–6 (August 1984): 77–106; additions & corrections in

XXXIII/1-2 (January 1988): 38-40   ((3, 4, 6, 7))

M-4   WORTH, Paul W. and CARTWRIGHT, Jim: *John McCormack: a comprehensive discography.* Westport, CT: Greenwood Press, 1986. 185 pp. ((1, 3, 4, 6, 7))   (Greenwood Press discographies; 21)

MCEACHERN, MALCOLM, 1883-1945   (Australian bass)

M-5   MORGAN, Charles I.: Malcolm McEachern discography in *Record Collector*, XXVII/7-8 (August 1982): 155-163   ((3, 6, 7))

MCPHEE, COLIN, 1910-1980   (American composer)

M-6   [[Discography in OJA, Carol J.: *Colin McPhee (1900-1964): a composer in two worlds.* [Dissertation, City University of New York, 1985] 504 pp.]]

MA, YO YO, 1955-   (Chinese cellist)

M-7   Discographisiche Hinweise in *fono forum* (October 1986): 22   ((--))

MAAZEL, LORIN, 1930-   (American conductor)

M-8   Quelques enregistrements de Lorin Maazel in BRAS, Jean-Yves: Lorin Maazel à la recherche permanente du raffinement in *Diapason*, No. 223 (December 1977): 14-17   ((--))

M-9   Discography, Deutsche Gramophon artist information, 1980. 1 p. ((--))

M-10   WERNER-JENSEN, Arnold: Auswahl-Diskographie Lorin Maazel in *Neue Zeitschrift für Musik* (June-July 1982): 47   ((--))

MACHAUT, GUILLAUME DE, ca. 1300-1377   (French composer)

M-11   WEBER, J. F.: A discography of the music of Guillaume Machaut in *Fanfare*, III/1 (September-October 1979): 12-16, 206-210   ((5, 7))

MACKERRAS, CHARLES, 1927-   (Australian conductor)

M-12   WALKER, Malcolm: Discography in PHELAN, Nancy: *Charles Mackerras: a musician's musician.* London: Gollancz, 1987: [337]-353 ((7))

MADERNA, BRUNO, 1920-1973   (Italian composer and conductor)

HYPERION

M-13   MARINELLI, Carlo: [Discography] in Venezia, Gran Teatro La Fenice, season 1977-78: program p. 84   ((5))

MAGELSDORFF, ALBERT   (Trombonist)

M-14   [[Albert Magelsdorff discography in *International Trombone Association Newsletter*, VI/2 (1978): 9]]

MAGNARD, ALBÉRIC, 1865-1914   (French composer)

See entry for

COMPOSERS, FRENCH

MAHAR, MR.   (Tenor)

M-15   [Discography] in *Record Collector*, IX/3 (March 1954): 65   ((--))

MAHLE, ERNEST, 1929-   (Brazilian composer)

M-16   Discographic references in FERREIRA, Paulo Affonso de Moura: *Ernst Mahle: catálogo de obras.* [Brasília]: Ministério das Relações Exteriores, Departamento de Cooperação Cultural, Científica e Tecnológica, 1976: [30] pp.   ((--))   (Compositores brasileiros)

MAHLER, GUSTAV, 1860-1911   (Austrian composer)

M-17   Orientación discográfica in VIGNAL, Marc: *Mi tiempo llegará.* [Madrid]: M. Castellote, [1974?]: [195]-198   ((--))

M-18   Discografia de Mahler in SOPEÑA IBANEZ, Federico: *Estudios sobre Mahler.* Madrid: Servicio de Publicaciones del Ministerio de Educación y Ciencia, 1976: [105]-112   ((--))

M-19   Discographie in WESSLING, Berndt W.: *Gustav Mahler: Prophet der neuen Musik.* München: Heyne, 1980: 286-296   ((--))

M-20   A selective discography in SECKERSON, Edward: *Mahler, his life and times.* Tunbridge Wells, Kent: Midas Books, 1982: 144-146   ((--))

M-21   FÜLÖP, Peter: The discography of Gustav Mahler's work in *Studia Musicologica Academiae Scientiarum Hungaricae*, (XXVI 1984): 220-418   ((3, 4, 5, 6, 7))

M-22   Recommended records in JAMES, Burnett: *The music of Gustav Mahler.* Rutherford, NJ: Fairleigh Dickinson University Press; London: Associated University Presses, 1985: 203-226   ((--))

SYMPHONIES

M-23   VINCENTINI, Mario: Le sinfonie de Mahler: aggiornamento discografico in *Discoteca Hi-Fi*, No. 192 (March 1979): 90-91   ((5))

M-24   HALBREICH, Harry: Les symphonies de Gustav Mahler: discographie critique in *Harmonie-Opéra-Hifi Conseil*, No. 20 (May 1982): 40-51   ((--))

M-25   SMOLEY, Lewis M. *The symphonies of Gustav Mahler: a critical discography.* Westport, CT: Greenwood Press, 1986.   191 pp.   ((4))   (Greenwood Press discographies; 23)

SYMPHONY, No. 1, D Major

M-26   TELLART, Roger: Discographie in *Diapason*, No. 206 (April 1976): 22   ((--))

M-27   Discographie Gustav Mahler: 1. sinfonie in *fono forum* (January

1988): 32 ((5, 7))

SYMPHONY, No. 8, E-Flat, "Symphony of a Thousand"

M-28   MARINELLI, Carlo: Discografie: Faust e Mefistofele nelle opere teatrali e sinfonico-vocali in *Quaderni dell'I.R.TE.M.* [Instituto di Ricerca per il Teatro Musicale] No. 3 (1986): 80-95 ((5))

MAJO, ERNEST, 1916-   (German composer)

M-29   Diskographie in SUPPAN, Wolfgang: *Komponieren für Amateure: Ernest Majo und die Entwicklung der Blasorchesterkomposition.* Tutzing: H. Schneider, 1987: 219-223 ((--))

MALKO, NICOLAI, 1883-1961   (Russian conductor)

M-30   WEHRUNG, Brendan: Recordings by Nicolai Malko in *Le Grand Baton*, No. 51 (September-December 1981): 32, 37-43 ((4, 5))

MANSURYAN, TIGRAN, 1939-   (Armenian composer)

M-31   Discography in *Music in the USSR* (July-September 1987): 19 ((--))

MANZ, PAUL, 1919-   (American composer)

M-32   GEBAUER, Victor Earl: Recordings in *Church Music*, (1979): 41 ((--))

MANZONI, GIACOMO, 1932-   (Italian composer)

M-33   Discografia in *Discoteca Hifi*, No. 194 (May 1979): 21 ((--))

MAPLESON, LIONEL, 1865-1937   (American librarian and violinist)

M-34   STRATTON, John: The Mapleson cylinders in *Record Collector*, XIV/3-4: 70-77 ((3, 7))

M-35   ROBERTSON, David: The Mapleson collection in *Hillandale News* [Reprint of numbers 1-12, 1960-1967]: 11-12, 15, 16 ((--))

M-36   HALL, David: The Mapleson Cylinder project in *ARSC Journal*, XIII/3 (1981): 5-13; A Provisional Mapleson chronology: 14-20 ((7))

M-37   HALL, David: The Mapleson Cylinder Project: repertoire, performers and recording dates in *Recorded Sound*, No. 83 (January 1983): 21-55 ((3, 4, 7))

M-38   [HAMILTON, David]: [Discographic notations] in *The Mapleson Cylinders: complete edition, 1900-1904.* [Sound recording] Rodgers & Hammerstein Archives, New York Public Library, 1985: program notes pp. 68-69 ((3, 7))

See also

METROPOLITAN OPERA, NEW YORK

MARAIS, MARIN, 1656-1728   (French composer)

M-39   [[Discography in BOWLES, Garrett H.: *The computer-produced thematic catalogue: An index to the Pièces de violes of Marin Marais*. [Dissertation, Stanford University, 1978]   180, 267 pp.]]

MARCHESI, BLANCHE, 1863-1940   (French soprano)

M-40   MORAN, W. R.: The recordings of Blanche Marchesi (4 Apr., 1883-15 Dec., 1940) in MARCHESI, Blanche: *Singer's pilgrimage*. New York: Arno Press, 1977: [305]-307]   ((3, 6, 7))   [Originally published without discography by Small, Maynard, Boston, 1923]

MARÉCHAL, MAURICE, 1892-   (French cellist)

M-41   [Discography] in GINSBURG, D. C.: *Maurice Maréchal*. Moskva, 1972: 172-[174]   ((--))

MARK PELARSKY PERCUSSION ENSEMBLE, USSR

M-42   [Discography] in *Music in the USSR* (October-December 1985): 19   ((--))

MARKEVITCH, IGOR, 1912-1983   (Russian conductor)

M-43   MASINI, Umberto: Discografia di Igor Markevitch in *Musica*, No. 13 (August 1979): 168-171   ((5))

M-44   GRAEFF, Alexander: Diskographie in *Igor Markevitch*. Bonn: Boosey & Hawkes, 1982: 101-110   ((7))

MARLBORO MUSIC FESTIVAL, USA

M-45   Music from Marlboro discography in *American Record Guide*, XLIII (May 1980): 9   ((--))

MARRINER, NEVILLE, 1924-   (English conductor)

M-46   [Discography] in *Record Geijutsu*, No. 276 (September 1973): 184-185   ((--))

M-47   Discography [on Philips label]. S.l.: [Philips, 198-?] 4 l.   ((--))

MARTIN, FRANK, 1890-1974   (Swiss composer)

M-48   Diskographie in KLEIN, Rudolf: *Frank Martin; sein Leben und Werk*. Wien: Österreichische Musikzeitschrift, 1960: [75]   ((--))

M-49   KING, Charles: A discography of the music of Frank Martin in *ARSC Journal*, XIV/3 (1982): 20-40   ((4, 7))

M-50   KING, Charles: Discographie seléctive in *Frank Martin*. 2nd ed. Lausanne: Société Frank Martin, 1984: 159-162   ((5))

VOCAL WORKS

M-51   [[Discography in HODGES, Craig Harris: *A performer's manual to the solo vocal works of Frank Martin (1890-1974)* [DMA, Southern Baptist Theological Seminary, 1983]   299 pp.]]

MARTIN, RICCARDO, 1874-1952   (American tenor)

M-52   MORAN, W. R. and BOTT, M. F.: Riccardo Martin discography in
       Record Collector, XXVI/1-2 (May 1980): 4-42   ((3, 6, 7))

MARTINELLI, GIOVANNI, 1885-1969   (Italian tenor)

M-53   COLLINS, William J.: The recordings in *Record Collector*, XXV/7-9
       (October 1979): 170-204; XXV/10-12 (February 1980): 253-255;
       [DENNIS, J.]: Martinelli--Addenda & corrigenda in *Record Collector*,
       XXVI/9-10 (May 1981): 237-239   ((1, 3, 4, 6, 7))

MARTINI, MARGUERITE, 1868-?   (Soprano)

M-54   [Discography] in *Record Collector*, IX/3 (March 1954): 65   ((--))

MARTINO, DONALD, 1931-   (American composer)

M-55   Selected discography in Program notes for *Donald Martino: Seven
       pious pieces*. [Sound recording] New World Records NW 210, 1977:
       4   ((--))

M-56   Selected discography in Program notes for *Randall Hopkinson recital*.
       [Sound recording] New World Records NW 320, 1984   ((--))

MARTINON, JEAN, 1910-1976   (French conductor)

M-57   Jean Martinon: the Chicago Symphony years: a chronological discography
       of their RCA Victor recordings in *The Podium*, I/2 (1977): 7, 29
       ((1, 7))

MARTINŮ, BOHUSLAV, 1890-1959   (Czech composer)

M-58   [[Discography in PETTAWAY, B. Keith: *The solo and chamber
       compositions for flute by Bohuslav Martinů*. [DMA, University of
       Southern Mississippi, 1980] 154 pp.]]

MARTIRANO, SALVATORE, 1927-   (American composer)

M-59   Selected discography in Program notes for *Salvatore Martirano: Mass*
       [Sound recording] New World Records 210, 1977: 4   ((--))

MARTON, EVA, 1943-   (Hungarian soprano)

M-60   Discografia in *Musica*, No. 41 (June 1986): 23   ((--))

MARTUCCI, GIUSEPPE, 1856-1909   (Italian composer)

M-61   A Martucci discography [in program notes for] *Arturo Toscanini
       conducts the music of Giuseppe Martucci* [Sound recording]
       Arturo Toscanini Society ATS 1071-1074, 1974: p. 4   ((--))

MARX, KARL, 1897-   (German composer)

M-62   Diskographie in *Karl Marx*. Tutzing: H. Schneider, 1984: 151-152
       ((--)) (Komponisten in Bayern; 3)

MASCAGNI, PIETRO, 1863-1945   (Italian composer)

OPERAS

CAVALLERIA RUSTICANA (1890)

M-63   MARINELLI, Carlo: [Discography] in Roma, Teatro dell'Opera, season 1971-72: program pp. 480-490   ((5))

M-64   MARINELLI, Carlo: [Discography] in Treviso, Ente Teatro Comunale, season 1978: program p. 19   ((5))

M-65   MARINELLI, Carlo: [Discography] in Venezia, Gran Teatro La Fenice, season 1979-80: program pp. 83-105   ((5))

M-66   MARINELLI, Carlo: [Discography] in Milano, Teatro alla Scala, season 1980-81: program pp. 70-71   ((5))

M-67   CABOURG, Jean: Discographie comparées [with I Pagliacci] in *L'Avant Scène Opéra*, No. 50 (March 1983): 130-143   ((1, 7))

M-68   MARINELLI, Carlo: [Discography] in Roma, Teatro dell'Opera, season 1985-86: program pp. 82-95   ((5))

MASINI, GALLIANO, 1896-1986   (Italian tenor)

M-69   Discografia essenziale in CALVETTI, Mauro, et al.: Galliano Masini in *Musica*, No. 31 (December 1983): 437   ((--))

MASON, DANIEL GREGORY, 1873-1953   (American composer)

M-70   [[Discography in KAPEC, David Neal: *The three symphonies of Daniel Gregory Mason: style-critical and theoretical analyses.* [Dissertation, University of Florida, 1982]   168 pp.]]

MASSENET, JULES, 1842-1912   (French composer)

OPERAS

DON QUICHOTTE (1910)

M-71   CABOURG, Jean: Discographie in *L'Avant Scène Opéra*, No. 93 (December 1986): 96-101   ((5))

HÉRODIADE (1881)

M-72   MARINELLI, Carlo: [Discography] in Roma, Teatro dell'Opera, season 1985-86: program pp. 50-51   ((5))

MANON (1885)

M-73   MARINELLI, Carlo: [Discography] in Roma, Teatro dell'Opera, season 1980-81: program pp. 1144-1151   ((5))

M-74   GUANDALINI, Gina: Le Manon de Massenet in *Musica*, No. 23 (November 1981): 370   ((3, 5))

M-75   MARINELLI, Carlo: [Discography] in Venezia, Gran Teatro La Fenice, season 1981-82: program pp. 77-81   ((5))

M-76   Discography in *Manon*. London: J. Calder; New York: Riverrun
       Press, 1984: 111   ((--))   (English National Opera guide; 25)

THAÏS (1894)

M-77   MARINELLI, Carlo: [Discography] in Roma, Teatro dell'Opera,
       season 1977-78: program pp. 444-448   ((5))

M-78   DUTRONC, Jean-Louis: Discographie in *L'Avant Scène Opéra*,
       No. 109 (May 1988): 96-100   ((1, 7))

WERTHER (1892)

M-79   MARINELLI, Carlo: [Discography] in Roma, Teatro dell'Opera,
       season 1969-70: program pp. 590-594   ((5))

M-80   LORD HAREWOOD: Werther in *Opera*, XXVIII/3 (March 1977):
       222-229; XXVIII/4 (April 1977): 332-339   ((-))   (Opera on the
       gramophone; 41)

M-81   MARINELLI, Carlo: [Discography] in Milano, Teatro alla Scala,
       season 1979-80: program pp. 68-71   ((5))

M-82   DUTRONC, Jean-Louis: Discographie and CABOURG, Jean and VOISIN,
       Georges: Werther et le 78 tours in *L'Avant Scène Opéra*, No. 61
       (March 1984): 104-111   ((7))

M-83   MARINELLI, Carlo: [Discography] in Palermo, Ente automono
       Teatro Massimo, season 1984-85 : program p. 6   ((5))

MASUR, KURT, 1927-   (German conductor)

M-84   Schallplattenverzeichnis (Auswahl) in HÄRTWIG, Dieter: *Kurt Masur*.
       Leipzig: Deutscher Verlag für Musik, VEB, 1976: 59-[63]   ((--))

MATACIC, LOVRO VON, 1899-1985   (Yugoslav conductor)

M-85   MODUGNO, Maurizio: Discografia di Lovro von Matacic in *Musica*,
       No. 8-9 (October 1978): 151   ((7))

MATHIAS, WILLIAM, 1934-   (Welsh composer)

M-86   FORBES, Elliot: List of recordings in *American Choral Review*,
       XXI/4 (1979): 32   ((--))

M-87   MILLER, Karl F.: A brief Mathias discography in *American Record
       Guide*, XLI/9 (July 1978): [13], 43   ((--))

MATTHUS, SIEGFRIED, 1934-   (German composer)

M-88   Discographic notes in DÖHERT, Hellmut: *Siegfried Matthus: für sie
       Porträtiert*. Leipzig: VEB Deutscher Verlag für Musik, 1979: 58-62
       ((--))

MATZENAUER, MARGARET, 1881-1963   (Hungarian mezzo-soprano)

M-89   WILE, Raymond: The Edison recordings of Margaret Matzenauer in

Record Research, No. 30 (October 1960): [9]   ((3, 6, 7))

M-90   MILLER, Philip Lieson: Discography in *Record Collector,* XXII/1-2 (January 1976): 28-47   ((1, 3, 6, 7))   [Includes notes on playing speeds]

MAW, NICHOLAS, 1935–   **(English composer)**

M-91   HUGHES, Eric and DAY, Timothy: Nicholas Maw in *Recorded Sound,* No. 81 (January 1982): 79-86; additions & corrections in No. 82 (July 1982): 76   ((1))   (Discographies of British composers; 15)

MEDICA, TOMMASO   (Italian baritone)

M-92   [Discography] in *Record Collector,* IX/3 (March 1954): 65-66   ((--))

MEDTNER, NIKOLAI, 1880–1951   (Russian composer)

M-93   Medtner recordings in *Recorded Sound,* No. 70-71 (April–July 1978): 794-805   ((1, 3, 4, 6, 7))

M-94   [Discography] in ZETEL, I.: *N.K. Metner--pianist.*   Moskva: Muzyka, 1981: [230]   ((--))

MEHTA, ZUBIN, 1936–   **(Indian conductor)**

M-95   [Discography] in *Record Geijutsu,* No. 276 (September 1973): 183   ((--))

M-96   A discography of Zubin Mehta with the Los Angeles Philharmonic in Program notes for *Nielsen: Symphony No. 4* [Sound recording] London CS 6848, 1974   ((--))

M-97   MARTIN, Serge: Zubin Mehta: une discographie in *Diapason-Harmonie,* No. 341 (September 1988): 58-60   ((--))

MEISTERSINGER

M-98   Schallplatten in HAHN, Reinhard: *Meistergesang.* Leipzig: VEB Bibliographisches Institut, 1985: 99   ((--))

MELBA, DAME NELLIE, 1861–1931   (Australian soprano)

M-99   CARTWRIGHT, Jim: Dame Nellie Melba in Immortal Performances List of New Unplayed LPs [Dealer's list] Austin, TX: Immortal Performances, 1977: [27]-39]   ((3, 6, 7))   (Immortal Performances discographic data; 4)

M-100 HOGARTH, Will: Nellie Melba discography in *Record Collector,* XXVII/3-4 (March 1982): 72-87   ((3, 4, 6, 7))   [Includes notes on unissued records]

M-101 MORAN, William R.: Discography: the Melba recordings in *Nellie Melba, a contemporary review.* Westport, CT: Greenwood Press, 1984: [447]-472   ((3, 4, 6, 7))

M-102 HOGARTH, William: Discography in RADIC, Thérèse: *Melba: the voice of Australia.*   Saint Louis, MO: MMB Music, 1986: [194]-198

((1, 3, 6, 7))   [Reprinted from the March 1982 discography in *Record Collector*]

MELBY, JOHN, 1941–   (American composer)

M–103 Selected discography in Program notes for *Maryvonne le Dizes-Richard, violin*. [Sound recording] New World Records NW 333, 1986 ((––))

MELCHISSEDEC, LÉON, 1843–1925   (French baritone)

M–104 [Discography] in *Record Collector*, IX/3 (March 1954): 65   ((––))

MELIKOV, ARIF, 1931–   (Azerbaijani composer)

M–105 Discography in *Music in the USSR* (October–December 1986): 18   ((––))

MELIS, CARMEN, 1885–1967   (Italian soprano)

M–106 Discographie de Carmen Melis in SEGOND, André: *Renata Tebaldi*. Lyon: Laffont, 1981: 253–254   ((?))

M–107 Discografia in GADOTTI, Adonide: *Carmen Melis: un grande soprano del "verismo"*. Roma: Bardi, 1985: 239–244   ((3, 7))

MELOS QUARTET   (West Germany)

M–108 Discography, Deutsche Grammophon artist information, 1980.   1 p. ((––))

MENDELSSOHN, FANNY HENSEL, 1805–1847   (German composer)

M–109 [[Discography in QUIN, Carol Lynelle: *Fanny Mendelssohn Hensel: her contributions to nineteenth-century musical life*. [Dissertation, University of Kentucky, 1981]   307 pp.]]

MENDELSSOHN, FELIX, 1809–1847   (German composer)

M–110 [[Discography in STONER, Thomas Alan: *Mendelssohn's published songs*. [Dissertation, University of Maryland, 1972]   428 pp.]]

MENDES, GILBERTO, 1922–   (Brazilian composer)

M–111 Discographic references in FERREIRA, Paulo Affonso de Moura: *Gilberto Mendes: catálogo de obras*. [Brasília]: Ministério das Relações Exteriores, Departamento de Cooperação Cultural, Científica e Tecnológica, 1976: [22] pp.   ((––)) (Compositores brasileiros)

MENGELBERG, WILLEM, 1871–1951   (Dutch conductor)

M–112 DØSSING, Bo: *Willem Mengelberg: a discography*.   2d rev. ed. [Sneslev, Denmark]: The Author, 1976.   24 pp.   ((4, 7))

M–113 ZEISEL, Georges: Les 233 enregistrements de Willem Mengelberg in *Diapason*, No. 229 (June 1978): 48–54   ((1, 7))

M–114 SUGA, Hajime: Willem Mengelberg SP discography in *LP Techno*,

September 1979: 96-99   ((7))

M-115   Willem Mengelberg-Discography in *Record Geijutsu*, No. 422 (November 1985): 222-226; No. 423 (December 1985): 215-218; No. 424 (January 1986): 220-224; No. 425 (February 1986): 182-186; No. 426 (March 1986): 216-220; Corrections in No. 427 (April 1986): 220 ((3, 6, 7))

M-116   [[*L'Héritage sonore de Willem Mengelberg*. Aulnay-sous-Bois: Société Willem Mengelberg, 1987 [18 rue Marcel Sembat, 93600 Aulney-soudl Bois ((4))]]

MENNIN, PETER, 1923-1983   (American composer)

M-117   [[Discography in RHOADS, Mary R.: *Influences of Japanese Hogaku manifest in selected compositions by Peter Mennin and Benjamin Britten*. [Dissertation, Michigan State University, 1969] 397 pp.]]

MENOTTI, GIAN CARLO, 1911-   (Italian composer)

M-118   TIEDTKE, Mark: Discography in ARDOIN, John: *The stages of Menotti*. Garden City, NY: Doubleday, 1985: 248-249   ((--))

OPERAS

AMAHL AND THE NIGHT VISITORS (1951)

M-119   MARINELLI, Carlo: [Discography] in Roma, Teatro dell'Opera, season 1971-72: program pp. 307   ((5))

AMELIA AL BALLO (1937)

M-120   MARINELLI, Carlo: [Discography] in Roma, Teatro dell'Opera, season 1966-67: program p. 607   ((5))

(THE) CONSUL (1950)

M-121   MARINELLI, Carlo: [Discography] in Palermo, Ente automono Teatro Massimo, season 1983-84: program p. 2   ((5))

MENUHIN, SIR YEHUDI, 1919-   (Anglo-American violinist)

M-122   Diskographie der in Deutschland erhältlichen Schallplatten-Aufnahmen in *Yehudi Menuhin und das Berliner Philharmonische Orchester*. Berlin: Das Orchester, 1979: 74-77   ((--))

MENZINSKY, MODEST   (Galacian tenor)

M-123   SAWYCKY, Roman: Discography in *Record Collector*, XXIV/9-10 (October 1978): 216-233; additions & corrections in XXV/3-4: 82 ((3, 7))

MERIKANTO, AARE, 1893-1958   (Finnish composer)

M-124   Levyluettelo in HEIKINHEIMO, Seppo: *Aaare Merikanto: säveltäjänkohtalo itsenäisessä Suomessa*. Porvoo: Söderström, 1985: 567   ((--))

MESSIAEN, OLIVIER, 1908–   (French composer)

M–125 [[Discography in DAVIDSON, Audrey Jean Ekdahl: *Olivier Messiaen's Tristan trilogy: time and transcendence.* [Dissertation, University of Minnesota, 1975] 285, 155 pp.]]

M–126 HALBREICH, Harry: Messiaen, 70 ans en 33 tours, discographie critique in *Harmonie*, No. 142 (December 1978): 62–73 ((--))

M–127 Orientation discographique in PÉRIER, Alain: *Messiaen.* Paris: Seuil, 1979: 178–185 ((--))

M–128 Discographie in HALBREICH, Harry: *Olivier Messiaen.* Paris: Fayard: Fondation SACEM, 1980: 527–528 ((--))

M–129 RIEHN, Rainer: Schallplattenaufnahmen in *Olivier Messiaen.* München: Ed. Text und Kritik, 1982: [126] ((--)) (Musik–Konzepte; 28)

M–130 Discography in BELL, Carla Huston: *Olivier Messiaen.* Boston: Twayne Publishers, 1984: 151–155 ((--)) (Twayne's music series)

M–131 Discographie in MESSIAEN, Olivier: *Musique et couleur: nouveaux entretiens avec Claude Samuel.* Paris: Belfond, 1986: 293–302 ((--))

M–132 Messiaen: discographie complète in *Diapason*, No. 344 (December 1988): 78–79 ((--)) [Adapted from Samuel, above]

ORGAN WORKS

M–133   [[Discography in ADAMS, Beverly Decker: *The organ compositions of Olivier Messiaen.* [Dissertation, University of Utah, 1969] 153 pp.]]

M–134   [[Discography in HOLLOWAY, Clyde: *The organ works of Olivier Messiaen and their importance in his oeuvre.* [Dissertation, Union Theological Seminary, 1974] 470 pp.]]

PIANO WORKS

M–135   Discographie in REVERDY, Michèle: *L'oeuvre pour piano d'Olivier Messiaen.* Paris: A. Leduc, 1978: 99 ((--))

MESTRES–QUADRENY, JOSEP MARIA, 1929–   (Spanish composer)

M–136 Discografia in GASSER, Luis: *La música contemporanea a traves de la obra de Josep Ma. Mestres-Quadreny.* [Oviedo]: Universitdad de Oviedo, Servicio de Publicaciones, 1983: 251–252 ((--))

METROPOLITAN OPERA, NEW YORK, N.Y.

M–137 FELLERS, Frederick P.: *The Metropolitan Opera on record: a discography of the commercial recordings.* Westport, CT: Greenwood Press, 1984. 101 pp. ((3, 4, 5, 6, 7)) (Greenwood Press discographies; 9)

See also

MAPLESON, LIONEL

METTERNICH, JOSEF, 1915–   (Austrian baritone)

M-138 WALTER, Günter: Josef Metternich in *Stimmen die um Welt gingen*,
No. 20 (June 1988): 28–42 ((3, 7))

MEULMANS, ARTHUR, 1884–1966 (Belgian composer)

M-139 Discographie in *Aan Meester Arthur Meulmans*. Antwerpen: Arthur
Meulemens Fonds, 1964: 168 ((––))

MEYER, ERNST HERMANN, 1905–   (German composer)

M-140 Musik von Ernst Hermann Meyer auf Schallplatten in *Musik und
Gesellschaft*, XXX/12 (December 1980): 725–727
((––))

MEYER, MARCELLE, 1897?–1958 (French pianist)

M-141 MORIN, Philippe: Discographie in *Diapason–Harmonie*, No. 320
(October 1986): 121–123 ((5, 7))

MEYER, SABINE (German clarinetist)

M-142 Discographische Hinweise in *fono forum* (January 1986): 29
((––))

MEYERBEER, GIACOMO, 1791–1864 (German composer)

M-143 Schallplatten in *Giacomo Meyerbeer, ein Leben in Briefen*.
Wilhelmshaven: Heinrichshofen, 1983: 265 ((––))

M-144 Discographie in WESSLING, Berndt W.: *Meyerbeer: Wagners Beute,
Heines Geisel*. Dusseldorf: Droste, 1984: 300–302 ((––))

M-145 Discographie in SEGALINI, Sergio: *Meyerbeer: diable ou prophète?*
Paris: BEBA, 1985: 147–154 ((1, 7))

OPERAS

ROBERT LE DIABLE (1836)

M-146   CABOURG, Jean and VOISIN, Georges: Discographie in *L'Avant Scène
Opéra*, No. 76 (June 1985): 98–100 ((1, 7))

MIAKOVSKY, NIKOLAI, 1881–1950 (Russian composer)

M-147 [[Discography in FOREMAN, George Calvin: *The symphonies of Nikolai
Yakovlevich Miakovsky*. [Dissertation, University of Kansas, 1981]
246, 217 pp.]]

MIDDLETON, ARTHUR (American singer)

M-148 WILE, Ray: From the Edison vaults: the Edison recordings of
Arthur Middleton in *New Amberola Graphic*, No. 37 (Summer 1981):
10–13 ((––))

MIDGLEY, WALTER, 1914–1980 (English tenor)

M-149   MORGAN, Charles I.: Walter Midgley discography in *Record Collector*,
XXX/12-13 (December 1985): 272-274   ((3, 6, 7))

MIEG, PETER, 1906-   (Swiss composer)

M-150   Vollstandige Diskographie in DASTER, Ulrich, et al.: *Peter Mieg:
eine Monographie*.   Aarau: Sauerlander, 1976: 52-53   ((--))

MIGNONE, FRANCISCO, 1897-1980   (Brazilian composer)

M-151   Discographic references in *Francisco Mignone: catálogo de obras*.
[Brasília]: Ministério das Relações Exteriores, Departamento de
Cooperação Cultural, Científica e Tecnológica, 1978: [61] pp.
((--))   (Compositores brasileiros)

MIGOT, GEORGES, 1891-1976   (French composer)

M-152   Discographie in PINCHARD, Max: *Connaissance de Georges Migot,
musicien français*. Paris: Les Éditions Ouvrières, 1959: 133   ((--))

M-153   Discographie in *Catalogue des oeuvres musicales de Georges Migot*.
Strasbourg: Institut de musicologie, 1977: 106-108   ((--))

M-154   Recordings readily available in *Georges Migot: the man and his work*.
Strasbourg: Amis de l'oeuvre et de la pensée de Georges Migot,
Institut de musicologie, 1982: 18   ((--))

MILHAUD, DARIUS, 1892-1974   (French composer)

M-155   [[[Discography] in *Darius Milhaud*. Paris: Salabert, 1980.]]

M-156   BLOCH, Francine: Discographie in COLLAER, Paul: *Darius Milhaud*.
Genève: Slatkine, 1982: 579-598   ((--))

M-157   Discographie in MILHAUD, Madeleine: *Catalogue des oeuvres de Darius
Milhaud*.   Genève: Slatkine, 1982: 579-598   ((--))

M-158   [[Discography in MACKENZIE, Nancy Mayland: *Selected clarinet solo
and chamber music of Darius Milhaud*. [Dissertation, University of
Wisconsin, 1984]   353 pp.]]

M-159   BLOCH, Francine: Discographie des oeuvres de Darius Milhaud in
MILHAUD, Darius: *Ma vie heureuse*. Paris: P. Belfond, 1987:
[317]-[339]   ((5))

OPERAS

(LE) PAUVRE MATELOT (1927)

M-160   MARINELLI, Carlo: [Discography] in Treviso, Ente Teatro
Comunale, season 1977-78: program p. 2   ((5))

MILLER, FRANK, 1912-1986   (American cellist)

M-161   Frank Miller on records; a discography in *Podium*, No. 17 (Spring-
Summer 1987): 17   ((--))

MILNES, SHERRILL, 1935-   (American baritone)

M-162 Discography, Deutsche Grammophon artist information, 1980. 1 p.
      ((--))

MILWAUKEE SYMPHONY ORCHESTRA

M-163 Radio Doctors & Records: Discography of works performed during season
      in *Milwaukee Orchestra twentieth anniversary commemorative book:
      1978-1979*. Milwaukee: The Orchestra, 1978: 91-93 ((--))

MINKUS, ALOIS, 1826-1917 (Russian composer)

DON QUIXOTE (1869)

M-164   MARINELLI, Carlo: [Discography] in Roma, Teatro dell'Opera,
         season 1978-79: program p. 216 ((5))

M-165   MARINELLI, Carlo: [Discography] in Milano, Teatro alla Scala,
         season 1986-87: program p. 36 ((5))

MINNEAPOLIS SYMPHONY ORCHESTRA

See entry for

ORMANDY, EUGENE

MINNESOTA ORCHESTRA

M-166 Minnesota Orchestra discography. [S.n., 1982] 1 leaf ((--))
      [From Rodgers and Hammerstein Archives, New York Public Library]

MINTZ, SHLOMO, 1957-   (Israeli violinist)

M-167 Shlomo Mintz [recordings] [Pamphlet] [Hamburg]: Deutsche Grammophon,
      1988. 1 leaf. ((--))

MITTLER, FRANZ, 1893-1970 (Austrian composer)

M-168 [[Discography in BATTIPAGLIA, Diana Mittler: *Franz Mittler:
      composer, pedagogue and practical musician.* [DMA, University of
      Rochester, 1974] 100 pp.]]

MOESCHINGER, ALBERT, 1897-1985 (Swiss composer)

M-169 Discographie in GLAUS, Vreni: *Albert Moeschinger: geboren am 10.
      Januar 1897: Werkverzeichnis=liste des oeuvres.* Zürich: Schweizer-
      isches Musik-Archiv, 1982: 23 ((--))

MOLIKOV, ARIF (Azerbaijani composer)

M-170 [Discography] in *Music in the USSR* (October-December 1986): 18
      ((--))

MOLODOBASANOV, KALY, 1929-   (Russian composer)

M-171 Discography in *Music in the USSR* (July-September 1987): 74 ((--))

MOMPOU Y DENCAUSSE, FEDERICO, 1893-1987 (Spanish composer)

M-172 Discografia de Federico Mompou in IGLESIAS, Antonio: *Federico Mompou: (su obra para piano).* Madrid: Alpuerto, 1976: 359-365 ((--))

M-173 Discografia de Federico Mompou in IGLESIAS, Antonio: *Federico Mompou.* Madrid: Dirección general del patrimonio artístico y cultural, 1977: 77-84 ((--))

M-174 [Mompou discography] in *Record Geijutsu,* No. 402 (March 1984): 239 ((--))

M-175 Discografia in JANÉS, Clara: *Federico Mompou: vida, textos, documentos.* Madrid: Fundación Banco Exterior, [1987?]: 487-488 ((--))

MONIGHETTI, IVAN, 1948–   (Russian cellist)

M-176 Discography in *Music in the USSR* (January–March 1987): 75   ((--))

MONIUSZKO, STANISŁAW, 1819–1872   (Polish composer)

M-177 MICHAŁOWSKI, Korneł: List of recordings in PROSNAK, Jan: *Moniuszko.* Cracow: Polskie Wydawn. Muzyczne, 1980: 184–[205] ((5))

MONTEUX, PIERRE, 1875–1964   (French conductor)

M-178 CORSETTI, Pierre-Paul: Les 150 disques de Pierre Monteux in *Diapason,* No. 258 (February 1981): 15–18   ((5))

MONTEVERDI, CLAUDIO, 1567–1643   (Italian composer)

M-179 Discografia in PAOLI, Domenico de: *Monteverdi.* Milano: Rusconi, 1979: 553–571   ((5))

M-180 Diskographie in LEOPOLD, Silke: *Claudio Monteverdi und seine Zeit.* [Laaber]: Laaber-Verlag, 1982: 343–360   ((5))

M-181 Diskographie in HARNONCOURT, Nikolaus: *Der musikalische Dialog: Gedanken zu Monteverdi, Bach und Mozart.* Salzburg: Residenz Verlag, 1984: 290–304   ((--))

M-182 Diskografie in ŠTĔDROŇ, Miloš: *Claudio Monteverdi: génius opery.* Praha: Editio Supraphon, 1985: 209–210   ((--))

STAGE WORKS

(IL) BALLO DELLE INGRATE

M-183   MARINELLI, Carlo: [Discography] in Roma, Teatro dell'Opera, season 1969-70: program pp. 170–172   ((5))

M-184   MARINELLI, Carlo: [Discography] in Venezia, Gran Teatro La Fenice, season 1981: program pp. 513–517   ((5))

OPERAS

M-185   WEBER, J. F.: A discography of the Monteverdi operas in *Fanfare*,
         V/4 (March–April 1982): 202–203   ((5, 7))

L'INCORONAZIONE DI POPPEA (1642)

M-186   MARINELLI, Carlo: [Discography] in Treviso, Ente Teatro
         Comunale, season 1975: program p. 5   ((5))

M-187   MARINELLI, Carlo: [Discography] in Venezia, Gran Teatro La
         Fenice, season 1976–77: program pp. 503–507   ((5))

ORFEO (1607)

M-188   WALKER, Malcolm: Discography in WHENHAM, John: *Claudio
         Monteverdi, Orfeo*. Cambridge; New York: Cambridge University
         Press, 1985: 203–204   ((7))   (Cambridge opera handbooks)

M-189   Orfeo et le disque in *Diapason*, No. 307 (July–August 1985):
         76–78   ((--))

VESPRO DELLA BEATA VERGINE (1610)

M-190   WEBER, J. F.: Discography in *Fanfare*, V/5 (May–June 1981):
         108–109   ((7))

MONTSALVATGE, XAVIER, 1911–   (Catalan composer)

M-191 Discografia in FRANCO, Enrique: *[Xavier de Montsalvatge]* Madrid:
      Servicio de Publicaciones del Ministerio de Educación y Ciencia,
      1975: 155–156   ((--))

MORTENSEN, FINN, 1922–1983   (Norwegian composer)

M-192 Discografi in *Mortensen 60 ...* [Oslo]: Cappelen, 1982: 35–[38]
      ((--)

MORTON, RACHEL, 1889–1982   (American soprano)

M-193 MORAN, W. R.: The recordings of Rachel Morton in *Record Collector*,
      XXIX/9–12 (December 1984): 283–284   ((3, 6, 7))

MOSCOW CHAMBER OPERA

M-194 Discography in *Music in the USSR* (October–December 1987): 74
      ((--))

MOSKVITINA, EMILIA   (Russian harpist)

M-195 Discography in *Music in the USSR* (January–March 1988): 95   ((--))

MOSS, LAWRENCE K., 1927–   (American composer)

M-196 [[Discography in KELLEY, Danny Roy: *The solo piano works of
      Lawrence K. Moss*. [DMA, Peabody Conservatory, 1985]   147 pp.]]

MOZART, WOLFGANG AMADEUS, 1756–1791   (Austrian composer)

M-197 VITTOZ, Jean: Discographie anthologique in *Almanach du disque*,

1956: [41]-48   ((--))

M-198 Schallplattenverzeichnis in HENNENBERG, Fritz: *Wolfgang Amadeus Mozart.* 2 ed. Leipzig: Reclam, 1976: 298-[323]   ((--))

M-199 Kunitachi Ongaku Daigaku: Toshokan: *Mozart's disc.* Tachikawa, Japan: Kunitachi Music College Library, 1977. 168 pp. ((4)) (Discography series; 4)

M-200 [Discography] in *Stereo Geijutsu*, No. 140 (January 1979): ?; No. 141 (February 1979): 115-122   ((5, 7))

M-201 Discography in KENYON, Max: *Mozart in Salzburg: a study and guide.* Westport, CT: Hyperion Press, 1979: [213]-214   ((--)) [Reprinted from the 1953 ed. published by Putnam, New York]

M-202 Discografia mozartiana in RESCIGNO, Eduardo: *Mozart.* Milano: Fabbri, 1979: 132-137   ((--))

M-203 Diskographie in HARNONCOURT, Nikolaus: *Der musikalische Dialog: Gedanken zu Monteverdi, Bach und Mozart.* Salzburg: Residenz Verlag, 1984: 290-304   ((--))

CHAMBER WORKS

QUINTETS, STRINGS

M-204   RISSIN, David: Les quintettes de Mozart: discographie comparée in *Harmonie*, No. 151 (October 1979): 116-125   ((--))

QUINTET, PIANO AND WINDS, E-FLAT, K. 452

M-205   [[Discography in OHLSSON, Eric Paul: *The quintets for piano, oboe, clarinet, horn and bassoon by Wolfgang Amadeus Mozart and Ludwig van Beethoven.* [DMA, Ohio State University, 1980]   130 pp.]]

CONCERTOS

M-206   Discografia in DELLA CROCE, Luigi: *I concerti di Mozart: guida all'ascolto.* Milano: A. Mondadori, 1983: 259-262   ((--))

CONCERTOS, HORN

M-207   Discography in *fono forum* (April 1977): 316   ((--))

OPERAS

BASTIEN UND BASTIENNE, K. 50

M-208   MARINELLI, Carlo: [Discography] in Venezia, Gran Teatro La Fenice, season 1976-77: program pp. 21-24   ((5))

(LA) CLEMENZA DI TITO, K. 621 (1791)

M-209   MARINELLI, Carlo: [Discography] in Palermo, Ente automono Teatro Massimo, season 1980-81: program p. 17   ((5))

M-210   MARINELLI, Carlo: [Discography] in Venezia, Gran Teatro La

Fenice, season 1986: program pp. 621-623 ((5))

M-211   LECLERCQ, Fernand: Discographie in *L'Avant Scène Opéra*, No. 99 (June 1987): 118-121 ((1, 5))

COSÌ FAN TUTTE, K. 588 (1790)

M-212   MARINELLI, Carlo: [Discography] in Roma, Teatro dell'Opera, season 1970-71: program pp. 178-182 ((5))

M-213   MARINELLI, Carlo: [Discography] in Venezia, Gran Teatro La Fenice, season 1973-74: program pp. 271-279 ((5))

M-214   [[[Discography] in *Wolfgang Amadeus Mozart: Così fan tutte ...* München: Die Staatsoper, 1978: 75]]

M-215   LEIVINTER, Roger: Discographie in *L'Avant Scène Opéra*, No. 16/17 (May-June 1978): 146-149 ((1, 5))

M-216   MARINELLI, Carlo: [Discography] in Roma, Teatro dell'Opera, season 1978-79: program pp. 319-328 ((5))

M-217   MARINELLI, Carlo: [Discography] in Milano, Teatro alla Scala, season 1982-83: program p. 41 ((5))

M-218   HOYLE, Martin: Discography in *Così fan tutte*. London: J. Calder: New York: Riverrun Press, 1983: 126-127 ((--)) (English National Opera guide; 22)

M-219   MARINELLI, Carlo: [Discography] in Venezia, Gran Teatro La Fenice, season 1983: program pp. 783-789 ((5))

M-220   THALMANN, Albert: Diskographie in *Così fan tutte*. München: Goldmann, 1983: 396-399 ((1, 7)) (Opern der Welt)

M-221   WERBA, Robert: Die Gesamtaufnahmen von "Così fan Tutte" in *Österreichische Musikzeitschrift*, XXXVIII/10 (October 1983): 598-602 ((5))

M-222   GERHARTZ, Leo Karl: Anmerkungen zur Diskographie in *Così fan tutte: Texte, Materialien, Kommentäre*. Reinbek bei Hamburg: Rowohlt, 1984: 311-312 ((1, 7)) (Rororo Opernbücher)

M-223   TUBEUF, André: Così fan tutte; 50 ans apres in *Diapason-Harmonie*, No. 310 (November 1985): 101-106 ((5))

DON GIOVANNI, K. 527 (1787)

M-224   MARINELLI, Carlo: [Discography] in Roma, Teatro dell'Opera, season 1969-70: program pp. 137-146 ((5))

M-225   MARINELLI, Carlo: [Discography] in Venezia, Gran Teatro La Fenice, season 1971-72: program pp. 32-44 ((5))

M-226   MARINELLI, Carlo: [Discography] in Treviso, Ente Teatro Comunale, season 1977-78: program pp. 25 ((5))

M-227   FLINOIS, Pierre: Don Juan: discographie comparée in *Harmonie*,

No. 152 (November 1979): [40]–49   ((5))

M-228   TUBEUF, André: Don Giovanni au disque in *Diapason*, No. 244
(November 1979): 54–56   ((5))

M-229   [[Discography in *L'Avant Scène Opéra*, No. 24 [1979]]]

M-230   CSAMPAI, Attila: Anmerkungen zur Diskographie in *Don Giovanni:
Texte, Materialien, Kommentäre*. Reinbek bei Hamburg: Rowohlt,
1981, 1984: 279–280   ((1, 5))   (Rororo Opernbücher)

M-231   THALMANN, Albert: Diskographie in *Don Giovanni* ... München:
W. Goldmann; [Mainz]: B. Schott's Sohne, 1981, 1984: 395–399
((1, 5))   (Opern der Welt)

M-232   WALKER, Malcolm: Discography in RUSHTON, Julian: *W. A. Mozart,
Don Giovanni*. Cambridge; New York: Cambridge University Press,
1981: 159–161   ((5))   (Cambridge opera handbooks)

M-233   Le edizioni complete del "Don Giovanni" in microsolco in *Musica*,
No. 16 (March 1981): 40   ((5))

M-234   DUAULT, Alain: Aix-en-Provence: Don Giovanni in *Harmonie Hi-Fi
Conseil*, No. 11 (July–August 1981): 43–46   ((3, 5))

M-235   HOYLE, Martin: Discography in *Don Giovanni*. London: J. Calder;
New York: Riverrun Press, 1983: 110–111   ((--))   (English
National Opera guide; 18)

M-236   MARINELLI, Carlo: [Discography] in Roma, Teatro dell'Opera,
season 1984-85: program pp. 84–100   ((5))

M-237   FLINOIS, Pierre: Discographie comparée in *Diapason-Harmonie*,
No. 317 (June 1986): 97–100   ((--))

M-238   CABOURG, Jean: Discographie and WILLIART, Jean-Paul and
VOISIN, Georges: Airs séparés in *L'Avant Scène Opéra*, No. 93
(December 1986): 96–101   ((7))

M-239   TREU, Paul and WERBA, Robert: Discographie der Gesamtaufnahmen
in *Wege zu Mozart*. Wien: Hölder-Pinchler-Tempsky, 1987–   v. 1,
pp. 186–189   ((1, 7))

M-240   Le edizioni complete del "Don Giovanni" in microsolco e in
compact disc in *Musica*, No. 46 (October 1987): 48
((7))

(DIE) ENTFÜHRUNG AUS DEM SERAIL, K. 384 (1782)

M-241   MARINELLI, Carlo: [Discography] in Roma, Teatro dell'Opera,
season 1968-69: program pp. 62–66   ((5))

M-242   MARINELLI, Carlo: [Discography] in Venezia, Gran Teatro La
Fenice, season 1970-71: program pp. 402–404   ((5))

M-243   THALMANN, Albert: Diskographie in *Die Entführung aus dem Serail*.
München: Goldmann; [Mainz]: Schott, 1980: 252–254   ((1, 5))
(Opern der Welt)

M-244   MARINELLI, Carlo: [Discography] in Bologna, Teatro Comunale, season 1980-81: program pp. 46-54 ((5))

M-245   MARINELLI, Carlo: [Discography] in Venezia, Gran Teatro La Fenice, season 1982: program pp. 219-226 ((5))

M-246   CSAMPAI, Attila: Anmerkungen zur Diskographie in PAHLEN, Kurt: *Die Entführung aus dem Serail*. Reinbeck bei Hamburg: Rowohlt, 1983: 214-215 ((5)) (Rororo Opernbücher)

M-247   MARINELLI, Carlo: [Discography] in Palermo, Ente automono Teatro Massimo, season 1983-84: program pp. 10 ((5))

M-248   GUEULLETTE, Alain: Discographie and VOISIN, Georges and CABOURG, Jean: 78's in *L'Avant Scène Opéra*, No. 59 (January 1984): 112-117; ((1, 7))

M-249   Discography in BAUMAN, Thomas: *W. A. Mozart, Die Entführung aus dem Serail*. Cambridge; New York: Cambridge University Press, 1987: 135-137 (Cambridge opera handbooks)

IDOMENEO, K. 366 (1781)

M-250   MANN, William: Idomeneo in *Opera*, XXIX/3 (March 1978): 247-256; with WALKER, Malcolm: Idomeneo--LP discography: 256 ((--)) (Opera on the gramophone; 43)

M-251   HEIN, Ulrich: "Idomeneo"--Diskographie in *Wolfgang Amadeus Mozart, Idomeneo* ... München; Zürich: Piper, 1981: 236-247 ((7))

M-252   MARINELLI, Carlo: [Discography] in Venezia, Gran Teatro La Fenice, season 1981: program pp. 297-303 ((5))

M-253   Discography "Idomeneo" in *fono forum* (May 1981): [42] ((--))

M-254   MARINELLI, Carlo: [Discography] in Palermo, Ente automono Teatro Massimo, season 1982-83: program pp. 29 ((5))

M-255   MARINELLI, Carlo: [Discography] in Roma, Teatro dell'Opera, season 1982-83: program pp. 397-406 ((5))

M-256   MARINELLI, Carlo: [Discography] in Milano, Teatro alla Scala, season 1983-84: program pp. 70-74 ((5))

M-257   [[[Discography] in *Opéra International*, No. 70 (May 1984):]]

M-258   KAMINSKI, Piotr: Discographie in *L'Avant Scène Opéra*, No. 89 (July 1986): 124-132 ((1, 5))

LUCIO SILLA, K. 135 (1772)

M-259   MARINELLI, Carlo: [Discography] in Milano, Teatro alla Scala, season 1983-84: program pp. 78-80 ((5))

MITRIDATE, RÈ DI PONTO K. 87

M-260   FLINOIS, Pierre: Discographie in *L'Avant Scène Opéra*, No. 54

(July 1983): 82-84   ((1, 7))

(LE) NOZZE DI FIGARO, K. 492 (1786)

M-261   MARINELLI, Carlo: [Discography] in Milano, Teatro alla Scala, season 1973-74: program pp. 49-63   ((5))

M-262   MARINELLI, Carlo: [Discography] in Roma, Teatro dell'Opera, season 1976-77: program pp. 404-421   ((5))

M-263   MANNONI, Gérard: Mozart: Les noces dé Figaro: discographie comparée in *Harmonie*, No. 132 (December 1977): 118-125   ((--))

M-264   DE NYS, Carl: Le point sur les noces de Figaro ou les avatars discographiques de la "folle journee" in *Diapason*, No. 229 (June 1978): 88-89   ((--))

M-265   [[Discography in *L'Avant Scène Opéra*, No. 21 [1978?]]]

M-266   SELVINI, Michele: Le edizioni complete de "Le nozze di Figaro" in microsolco in *Musica*, No. 15 (December 1979): 319   ((5))

M-267   MARINELLI, Carlo: [Discography] in Milano, Teatro alla Scala, season 1980-81: program pp. 113-114   ((5))

M-268   MARINELLI, Carlo: [Discography] in Milano, Teatro alla Scala, season 1981-82: program pp. 113-114   ((5))

M-269   THALMANN, Albert: Diskographie in *Figaros Hochzeit: in der originalsprache.* München: Goldmann, 1982: 297-300   ((1, 7)) (Opern der Welt)

M-270   HOYLE, Martin: Discography in *Le nozze di Figaro.* London: J. Calder; New York: Riverrun Press, 1983: 126-127   ((--)) (English National Opera guide; 17)

M-271   [[MARINELLI, Carlo: [Discography] in Roma, Teatro dell'Opera, season 1987: program pp. --   ((5))]]

M-272   WALKER, Malcolm: Discography] in CARTER, Tim: *W.A. Mozart, Le nozze di Figaro.* Cambridge; New York: Cambridge University Press, 1987: 168-173   ((1, 7)) (Cambridge opera handbooks)]

(IL) RÈ PASTORE, K. 208

M-273   MARINELLI, Carlo: [Discography] in Milano, Teatro alla Scala, season 1979-80: program pp. 44-45   ((5))

(DIE) ZAUBERFLÖTE, K. 620 (1791)

M-274   MARINELLI, Carlo: [Discography] in Roma, Teatro dell'Opera, season 1967: program pp. 729-734   ((5))

M-275   MONNIER, Fréderico: Pour une discographie critique in *L'Avant Scène Opéra*, No. 1 (January-February 1976): 124-126   ((5))

M-276   Le edizioni complete del "Flauto magico" in microsolco in CONTINI, Marco, and SELVINI, Michele: I grandi interpreti del

Flauto magico in 78 giri in *Musica*, No. 1 (May–June 1977): 27–29 ((7))

M-277   Discographie nach dem Bielefelder Katalog-K in PAHLEN, Kurt: *Die Zauberflöte*. München: Goldmann, 1978: 247–249 ((--)) (Opern der Welt)

M-278   MARINELLI, Carlo: [Discography] in Venezia, Gran Teatro La Fenice, season 1979–80: program pp. 510–515 ((5))

M-279   Discography in *The Magic Flute*. London: J. Calder; New York: Riverrun Press, 1980: 124–127 ((--)) (English National Opera guide; 3)

M-280   ORANGE: Le flute enchantée in *Harmonie Hi-Fi Conseil*, No. 11 (July–August 1981): 38–39 ((3, 5))

M-281   MARINELLI, Carlo: [Discography] in Palermo, Ente automono Teatro Massimo, season 1981–82: program p. 55   ((5))

M-282   CSAMPAI, Attila: Anmerkungen zur Diskographie in *Wolfgang Amadeus Mozart, die Zauberflöte: Texte, Materialien, Kommentäre*. Reinbek bei Hamburg: Rowohlt, 1982: 276–[280] ((1, 5)) (Rororo Opernbücher)

M-283   Discografia in BARRETO, Roberto Menna: *A magica transacional de "A flauta mágica"* São Paulo: Summus Editorial, 1984: 147 ((7))

M-284   MARINELLI, Carlo: [Discography] in Milano, Teatro alla Scala, season 1984–85: program pp. 210–122 ((5))

M-285   MARINELLI, Carlo: [Discography] in Milano, Teatro alla Scala, season 1986–87: program pp. 123–125 ((5))

M-286   KAMINSKI, Piotr: Discographie in *L'Avant Scéne Opèra*, No. 101 (September 1987): 138–151 ((1, 5))

REQUIEM, K. 626

M-287   WEBER, J. F.: A discography of the Mozart Requiem in *Fanfare*, VII/1 (September–October 1983): 221–224 ((3, 5, 7))

SYMPHONIES

M-288   Discografia in DELLA CROCE, Luigi: *Le 75 sinfonie de Mozart: guida e analisi critica*. Torino: EDA, 1977: 300–303 ((--))

M-289   [Discography] in DEARLING, Robert: *The music of Wolfgang Amadeus Mozart, the symphonies*. Rutherford, NJ: Fairleigh Dickinson University Press, 1982: 173–[194] ((--))

MRAVINSKY, YEVGENY, 1902–1988   (Russian conductor)

M-290   [Discography] in FOMIN, V.: *Evgenii Aleksandrovich Mravinskii*. Moskva: Muzyka, 1983: 188–[190] ((--))

M-291   Discography of the Leningrad Philharmonic Symphony Orchestra under Yevgeni Mravinsky in *Music in the USSR* (January–March 1988): 13

((--))

MUCK, KARL, 1859-1940   (German conductor)

M-292 CARTWRIGHT, Jim and DYMENT, Christopher: Karl Muck; a discography
in *ARSC Journal*, IX/1 (1977): 69-77   ((3, 6, 7))

M-293 SUGA, Hajime: Karl Muck in *LP Techno*, November 1978: 80-81   ((7))

MUKHAMEJANOV, TOLEGEN   (Kazhak composer)

M-294 Discography in *Music in the USSR* (April-June 1987): 5   ((--))

MULE, MARCEL, 1901-   (French saxophonist)

M-295 A discography of Marcel Mule in ROUSSEAU, Eugène: *Marcel Mule, his
life and the saxophone*. Shell Lake, Wis.: Étoile, 1982: 144-149
((--))

MUNCH, CHARLES, 1891-1968   (French conductor)

M-296 OLIVIER, Philippe: *Charles Munch: une biographie par le disque*.
Paris: P. Belfond, 1987. 209 pp.   ((7))

M-297 Discographische Hinweise in *fono forum* (March 1988): 33   ((--)))

MURATORE, LUCIEN, 1878-1954   (French tenor)

M-298 [Discography] in *Record Collector*, IX/3 (March 1954): 66-67   ((--))

MUSGRAVE, THEA, 1928-   (Scottish composer)

M-299 Discography in HIXON, Donald L.: *Thea Musgrave, a bio-bibliography*.
Westport, CT: Greenwood Press, 1984: [49]-51   ((7))
(Bio-bibliographies in music; 1)

MUSIC

M-300 [[NIELSEN, Bjarne: *Klassisk musik: Orkestermusik/Kammermusik skrevet
før 1928. En diskografi*. [Thesis, Royal Danish School of Librarianship, 1971]]]

M-301 [[NIELSEN, P. Holm: *Klassisk musik: Vokalmusic/Kammermusik skrevet
efter 1828. Et udvalg af de bedste indspilninger*. [Thesis, Royal
Danish School of Librarianship, 1971]]]

> *NOTE: In the entries that follow, headings about music are
> arranged in three groups: those about a country or region,
> those concerning a particular historical period or epoch, and
> those treating a specific style.*

MUSIC--GEOGRAPHIC STUDIES

MUSIC, AMERICAN

M-302   MOSES, Julian Morton: *The record collector's guide: American
celebrity discs*. New York: Concert bureau, College of the city of

New York, 1936. 44 pp. ((--))

M-303   MOSES, Julian Morton: *Collectors' guide to American recordings,*
         1895-1925. New York: American Record Collectors' Exchange, 1949;
         New York: Dover Publications, 1977. 199 pp. ((4, 7))

M-304   LEBOW, Bernard: *The American record index.* New York: Elaine Music
         Shop, 1950. [Only Vol. 1, No. 1 [A-B] and Vol. 1, No. 2 [C-Delr
         issued] ((--))

M-305   American Music Center: *American music on records; a catalogue of*
         recorded American music currently available. New York, 1956.
         39 pp.; Supplement No. 1 (Summer 1958) 23 pp. ((--))

M-306   Recordings of American music in *American Composers' Concerts, and*
         Festivals of American music, 1925-1971: cumulative repertoire.
         Rochester, NY: Institute of American Music of the University of
         Rochester, 1972: 67-72 ((--)) [Omits record numbers]

M-307   [[Discography in ALBRECHT, Theodore John: *German singing societies*
         in Texas. [Dissertation, North Texas State University, 1975]
         221 pp.]]

M-308   *American music before 1865 in print and on records: a biblio-*
         discography. Brooklyn: Institute for Studies in American Music,
         Brooklyn College, New York, 1976. 113 pp. ((4)); HEINTZE, James
         R.: Supplement to music on records in *NOTES,* XXXIV/3 (March
         1978): 571-580; Second supplement to music on records in XXXVII/1
         (September 1980): 31-36 ((--))

M-309   [[[Discography] in MEAD, Rita H.: *Henry Cowell's New Music,*
         1925-1936: the Society, the music editions, and the recordings.
         Ann Arbor, Mich.: UMI Research Press, 1981: [Originally her
         Dissertation, City University of New York, 1978]]]

M-310   Music of the 20th century: Part IV, Nationalism in American music
         in *Tarakan Music Letter,* III/1 (September-October 1981): 12-13
         ((--))

M-311   OJA, Carol, ed.: *American music recordings: a discography of 20th*
         century U.S. composers. Brooklyn, N.Y.: Institute for Studies in
         American Music, 1982. 368 pp. ((4, 5))

M-312   BROOKS, William: American music on record in CHASE, Gilbert:
         America's music, from the pilgrims to the present. 3d rev. ed.
         Urbana: University of Illinois Press, 1987: [639]-646 ((--))

M-313   Discography in HAMM, Charles: *Music in the New World.* New York:
         Norton, 1987: 695-706 ((--))

MUSIC, AMERICAN--20TH CENTURY

M-314 Discography ... in TAWA, Nicholas E.: *A most wondrous bubble:*
         American art music and the American musical scene, 1950-1985. New
         York: Greenwood Press, 1987: [251]-261 ((--))

MUSIC--ARGENTINA

M-315 Argentine Dirección General de Relaciones Culturales y Difusión:
Música de compositores argentinos (grabada en disco) [Buenos Aires,
1955]   54 pp. ((--))

MUSIC--ARMENIA

M-316 SARIAN, John M.: *Record guide, Armenian musicians and composers.*
[s.l.]: Ararat Press, 1979.   49 pp.   ((4))

MUSIC--ASIA

M-317 Selected discography in FELICIANO, Francisco F.: *Four Asian
contemporary composers: the influence of tradition on their works.*
Quezon City: New Day Publishers, 1983: 143-144   ((--))

MUSIC--AUSTRIA--VIENNA--20TH CENTURY

M-318 Discographie (ausgewahlt) in GERLACH, Reinhard: *Musik und
Jugendstil der Wiener Schule, 1900-1908.* Laaber: Laaber-Verlag,
1985: [316]   ((--))

MUSIC--AUSTRALIA

M-319 Discographic references in Australia Music Centre: *Catalogue of
instrumental and chamber music.* Sydney: Australia Music Centre,
1976.   142 pp.   ((--))

M-320 Discographic references in Australia Music Centre: *Catalogue of
orchestral music.* Sydney: Australia Music Centre, 1976. 109 pp.
((--))

M-321 Discographies in *Australian composers in the twentieth century.*
Melbourne: Oxford University Press, 1978.   248 pp. ((1, 7))

M-322 [[Sound recordings] in BUZACOTT, Martin: *Music Australia: a select
list of books, sound recordings, and music scores in print.* Sydney:
Australian Music Centre, 1978.   13 pp.]]

M-323 Sound recordings in BUZACOTT, Martin: *Music Australia: a select
list of literature, music scores, and sound recordings.* 2d ed.
Sydney: Australian Music Centre, 1979: 7-13   ((--))

M-324 Sound recordings in BUZACOTT, Martin: *Music Australia, 1981:
A selected list of literature, music scores and sound recordings in
print.* Sydney: Australia Music Centre, 1981: 21-39   ((--))

MUSIC--BELGIUM

M-325 Discografie in *Muziek in België.* Brussel: A. Manteau, 1967: 161-176
((--))

M-326 Discographie--Discografie--Discography (30.6.1976) in VOLBORTH-
DANYS, Diana von: *CeBeDeM et ses compositeurs affiliés: biographies,
catalogues, discographie ...* [A-L] Bruxelles: Centre belge de
documentation musicale, 1977: 199-211; [M-Z] Discographie--Disco-
grafie--Discography (31.12.1978) Bruxelles: Centre belge de
documentation musical, 1980: 233-244   ((--))

MUSIC--CANADA

M-327 Discographies in *The 1980/81 CBC classic recordings reference book*.
Toronto: CBC, 1980: in French and English sections. ((4))

M-328 Discographies in PROCTER, George A.: *Canadian music in the
twentieth century*. Toronto: University of Toronto Press, 1980.
297 pp. ((--))

M-329 EDWARDS, Barry: A critical discography of Canadian music in
Musicanada, No. 46 (June 1981): 22-24; with Une discographie
sélective de musique canadienne (1ière parte)/a selective discography
of Canadian music (pt. 1), p. 2 of French section; pt. 2 in
Musicanada, No. 47 (December 1981): p. 2 of French section ((--))

M-330 Discographies in *Encyclopedia of music in Canada*. Toronto; Buffalo:
University of Toronto Press, 1981: 1076 pp.; French ed., Montréal:
Fides, 1981. 1142 pp. ((--))

M-331 Readings, recordings and films in MCGEE, Timothy J.: *The music
of Canada*. New York: Norton, 1985: 229-246 ((--))

MUSIC--CZECHOSLOVAKIA

M-332 Gramofonové závody, Prague: *Musicae bohemicae anthologia*. Prague,
1948. 23 pp. ((--))

M-333 Gramofonové desky in *Městská lidová knihovna. Knihovna Bedricha
Smetany: 15 let z*ivota ČSR v hudbé, divadelhích hrách a filmu ...*
Praha, 1960: 17-22 ((--))

M-334 [[Discography in CHEW, Geoffrey Alexander: *The Christmas
pastorella in Austria, Bohemia and Moravia.* [Dissertation,
University of Manchester, 1968]]]

M-335 *Vyberovy katalog ukoncene tyorby ceskych skladatelu 20. stoleti.*
Praha: Panton, 1976. 151 pp. ((4))

MUSIC--DENMARK

M-336 Skandinavisk grammophon aktieselskab: *Catalogue of Danish music on
records.* [Copenhagen, 1947]. 43 pp. ((--))

M-337 Gramophone records in *Musical Denmark*, No. 1 (March 1952): [6-8];
New recordings of Danish Music in No. 2 (November 1952): [6-7];
Other works recorded in Denmark, pp. [7-8]; Danish gramophone
records in No. 3 (March 1953): [6-8]; Gramophone records in No. 4
(November 1953): [6-7]; New Danish gramophone records in No. 5
(June 1954): [6-7]; New gramophone recordings in No. 7: [9-10];
Some new gramophone recordings in No. 8 (January 1956): [8];
[Discography] in No. 9 (1957): [10-11]; Selected recordings in No.
11 (1959): 14-15; Gramophone records in No. 12 (1960): 16-18;
Selected gramophone records in No. 13 (1962): 14-15; Selected
gramophone records in No. 15 (Spring 1964): 40-41; Selected
gramophone records in No. 17 (May 1966): 16-18; ROSENBERG,
Herbert: Danish music on records [a selection 1935-1967]: 9-23;
Danish music on gramophone records in No. 19 (June 1968): 10-[16];
Danish music on gramophone records in No. 20 (June 1969): 11-14;

Danish music on gramophone records in No. 21 (1969/70): 15-22;
Danish music on gramophone records in No. 22 (1970/71): 13-[16];
Danish music on gramophone records and tapes in No. 23 (1971/72):
15-16; Danish music on gramophone records and tapes in No. 24
(1972/3): 19-21; Danish music on gramophone records and tapes in
No. 25 (1973/4): 19-[20]; Danish music on gramophone records and
tapes in No. 26 (1974/5): 22-[24]; Danish music on gramophone
records issued from March 1st--December 31st 1975 in No. 27
(1975/6): 15-20; Danish music on gramophone records in No. 28
(1976/7): 41-[44]; Danish music on gramophone records in No. 29
(1977/8): 27-31; Danish music on gramophone records in No. 30
(1978/9): 41-47   ((--))

M-338   [[BRUN, Peter: Dansk musik fra det 19. og 20. århundrede. En
         diskografi. [Thesis, Royal Danish School of Librarianship, 1971]]]

M-339   [[DUJARDIN, Erling: Dansk scenisk musik på plade og bånd. En
         diskografi. [Thesis, Royal Danish School of Librarianship, 1973]]]

M-340   LARSEN, Freddy: Dansk musik på plade.   Ballerup: Biblioteks-
         centralen, 1978: 83 pp. ((4))

M-341   HANSEN, Ivan: Ny dansk på plade 1960-1980 komponeret af. med-
         lemmer af Dansk Komponist forening in Dansk Musiktidskrift, LV/5
         (April 1981): 253-257 ((--))

MUSIC--EUROPE

M-342   Discographic notes in COHN, Arthur: Twentieth-century music in
         Western Europe; the compositions and the recordings. Philadelphia:
         Lippincott, [1965] 510 pp. ((--))

MUSIC--FINLAND

M-343   HAAPANEN, Urpo: Catalogue of Finnish records 1946-1966.
         Helsinki: Finnish Institute of Recorded Sound, 1967. 613 pp. ((4))
         (Finnish Institute of Recorded Sound; 1)

M-344   HAAPANEN, Urpo: Suomalasiten äänilevyjen luettelo 1967 =
         Catalogue of Finnish records 1967. Helsinki: Finnish Institute of
         Recorded Sound, 1969. 142 pp. ((4)) (Finnish Institute of
         Recorded Sound; 2)

M-345   HAAPANEN, Urpo: Suomalasiten äänilevyjen luettelo 1969 =
         Catalogue of Finnish records 1968. Helsinki: Finnish Institute of
         Recorded Sound, 1969. 162 pp. ((4)) (Finnish Institute of
         Recorded Sound; 3)

M-346   HAAPANEN, Urpo: Catalogue of Finnish records 1902-1945.
         Helsinki: Finnish Institute of Recorded Sound, 1970. 262 pp. ((4))
         (Finnish Institute of Recorded Sound; 4)

M-347   HAAPANEN, Urpo: Suomalasiten äänilevyjen luettelo 1970 =
         Catalogue of Finnish records 1970. Helsinki: Finnish Institute of
         Recorded Sound, 1971. 239 pp. ((4)) (Finnish Institute of
         Recorded Sound; 6)

M-348   HAAPANEN, Urpo: Suomalasiten äänilevyjen luettelo 1971 =

Catalogue of Finnish records 1971. Helsinki: Finnish Institute of
Recorded Sound, 1972. 196 pp. ((4)) (Finnish Institute of
Recorded Sound; 7)

M-349 HAAPANEN, Urpo: *Suomalasiten äänilevyjen luettelo 1972 =*
Catalogue of Finnish records 1972. Helsinki: Finnish Institute of
Recorded Sound, 1973. 239 pp. ((4)) (Finnish Institute of
Recorded Sound; 8)

M-350 HAAPANEN, Urpo: *Suomalasiten äänilevyjen hakemisto 1902-1971 =*
Alphabetical index of Finnish records, 1902-1971. Helsinki: [Suomen
äänitearkisto]. 1973-1975. 2 v., 686 pp. ((4)) (Finnish Institute
of Recorded Sound; 9-10)

M-351 HAAPANEN, Urpo: *Suomalasiten äänilevyjen luettelo 1974-75 =*
Catalogue of Finnish records 1974-75. Helsinki: Finnish Institute
of Recorded Sound, 1976. 321 pp. ((4)) (Finnish Institute of
Recorded Sound; 12)

M-352 HAAPANEN, Urpo: *Suomalasiten äänilevyjen luettelo 1976 =*
Catalogue of Finnish records 1976. Helsinki: Finnish Institute of
Recorded Sound, 1977. 207 pp. ((4)) (Finnish Institute of
Recorded Sound; 13)

M-353 HAAPANEN, Urpo: *Suomalasiten äänilevyjen luettelo 1977 =*
Catalogue of Finnish records, 1977. Helsinki: Finnish Institute of
Recorded Sound, 1978. 268 pp. ((4)) (Finnish Institute of
Recorded Sound; 14)

M-354 HAAPANEN, Urpo: *Suomalasiten äänilevyjen luettelo 1978 =*
Catalogue of Finnish records, 1978. Helsinki: Finnish Institute of
Recorded Sound, 1979. 304 pp. ((4)) (Finnish Institute of
Recorded Sound; 15)

M-355 HAAPANEN, Urpo: *Suomalasiten äänilevyjen luettelo 1979 =*
Catalogue of Finnish records, 1979. Helsinki: Finnish Institute of
Recorded Sound, 1980. 256 pp. ((4)) (Finnish Institute of
Recorded Sound; 16)

M-356 HAAPANEN, Urpo: *Alphabetical index of Finnish records, 1972-1979.*
A-L. Helsinki: Finnish Institute of Recorded Sound, 1981. 370 pp.
((4)) (Finnish Institute of Recorded Sound; 17)

M-357 Levyluettelot in AROMÄKI, Juhani: *Elämäni on musiikki: tunnetut*
musiikkimiehet kertovat. Porvoo; Helsinki; Juva: WSOY, 1980: 371-384
((--))

M-358 HAAPANEN, Urpo: *Alphabetical index of Finnish records, 1972-1979.*
M-Ö. Helsinki: Finnish Institute of Recorded Sound, 1980. 371 pp.

M-359 HAAPANEN, Urpo: *Catalogue of Finnish records, 1980.* Helsinki:
Finnish Institute of Recorded Sound, 1981. 288 pp. ((4)) (Finnish
Institute of Recorded Sound; 18)

M-360 STRÖMMER, Rainer and HAAPANEN, Urpo: *Catalogue of Finnish*
records, 1920-1935. Finnish Institute of Recorded Sound, 1981.
484 pp. ((4)) (Finnish Institute of Recorded Sound; 19)

M-361 HAAPANEN, Urpo: *Alphabetical index of Finnish records, 1972-1979. A-Ö.* Helsinki: Finnish Institute of Recorded Sound, 1982. 886 pp. ((4)) (Finnish Institute of Recorded Sound; 20)

M-362 TUOMINEN, Kalle: *Catalogue of Finnish Records, 1981.* Helsinki: Finnish Institute of Recorded Sound, 1982. 546 pp. ((4)) (Finnish Institute of Recorded Sound; 21)

M-363 TUOMINEN, Kalle: *Catalogue of Finnish Records, 1982.* Helsinki: Finnish Institute of Recorded Sound, 1983. 573 pp. ((4)) (Finnish Institute of Recorded Sound; 22)

M-364 TUOMINEN, Kalle: *Catalogue of Finnish Records, 1984.* Helsinki: Finnish Institute of Recorded Sound, 1984. 413 pp. ((4))

M-365 TUOMINEN, Kalle: *Catalogue of Finnish Records, 1983.* Helsinki: Finnish Institute of Recorded Sound, 1985. 370 pp. ((4))

MUSIC--FRANCE

M-366 [[Discography in NAZLOGLOU, Catherine: *Le gout musical en France à travers l'art lyrique 1815-1840.* [Dissertation, Nice, 1975] 250 pp.]]

MUSIC--FRANCE--LYON

M-367 Discographie in FERRATON, Yves: *Cinquante ans de vie musique à Lyons: les Witkowski et l'Orchestre philharmonique de Lyon, 1903-1953.* Trévoux: Editions de Trévoux, 1984: 353 ((--))

MUSIC--GERMANY, FEDERAL REPUBLIC

M-368 BETZ, Anneliese: *Auftragskompositionen im Rundfunk 1946-1977.* Frankfurt am Main: Deutsches Rundfunkarchiv, 1977. 2210 pp. ((1, 4, 7)) (Bild und Tonträgerverzeichnisse; 7)

MUSIC--GERMANY, FEDERAL REPUBLIC--MANNHEIM

M-369 HÖFT, Brigitte: *Die Mannheimer Schule: Discographie.* Berlin: Deutscher Bibliothekswesen, 1976. 45 pp. ((4))

M-370 [[Mannheimer Schule ... Schallplatten ... in *Ein führer durch die Sondersammlung der Stadtbücherei Mannheim.* 3d ed. Mannheim: Stadtbücherei Mannheim Musikableilung, 1978]]

MUSIC--GREAT BRITAIN

M-371 [[Discography in JOHNSON, Paula: *Form and transformation in the music and poetry of the English Renaissance.* [Dissertation, Yale University, 1969] 256 pp.]]

M-372 Index of composers and list of gramophone records in BACHRACH, A. L., ed.: *British music of our time.* Wilmington, Del.: International Academic Pub., 1979: 235-256 ((--)) [Reprinted from the 1946 ed. published by Pelican Books]

M-373 KEENER, Andrew: Record documentation [British music or artists new to records] in *British Music Year book.* London: Adam & Charles

Black, 1982: pp. 39-42; London: Classical Music, 1983: 84-90; 1984 ed. (London: Classical Music, 1984): 99-110; 1985 ed. (London: Rhingold Publishing Ltd., 1985): 97-101   ((--))

MUSIC--GREECE

M-374 ZAKYTHINOS, Alexis D.: *Discography of Greek classical music.* Buenos Aires: A. D. Zakythinos, 1984. 68 pp. ((4, 5))

M-375 [[ZAKYTHINOS, Alexis D.: *Discography of Greek classical music.* [2d ed.] Brasilia: A. D. Zakythinos (SHIS QL4 Conjunto 1 Casa 17, Brasilia, Brazil). 91 pp.]]

MUSIC--HUNGARY

M-376 HAGLUND, Rolf: Diskografi oever Ungersk nutida music (ett urval) in *Nutida Musik*, XXIX/2 (1985-1986): 29   ((--))

MUSIC--ICELAND

M-377 *Islensk hljodritaskra=Bibliography of Islandic sound recordings.* Reykjavik: Landsbokasafn Islands, 1980-[1983 ed.= 19 pp.; 1984 ed. = 32 pp.]   ((--))

M-378 [[KJARTANNSSON, Jon R.: *Skra yfir islenzkan hljompoutur 1907-1955.* Utgefardi: Kjar, 1984. 52 pp.]]

MUSIC--ISRAEL

M-379 ELIAS, William: Israeli music on commercial records in *Israel Music Weeks, 30.11.69-31.12.69.* [Tel-Aviv]: League of Composers in Israel, [1969]: 21-23   ((--)) [Omits record numbers]

MUSIC--ITALY

M-380 Discografias in MOLLIA, Michaela: *Autobiografia della musica contemporanea.* Roma: Lerici, 1979. 351 pp. ((--))

MUSIC--JAPANESE

M-381 [[CRANDALL, David and MINEGISHI, Yuji: *Discography of Japanese music.* 57 pp.]]

M-382 HALL, Robert: Discography of contemporary Japanese music in *Contact*, No. 8 (Summer 1974): 15-19   ((--))

MUSIC--NETHERLANDS

M-383 Records: composer's voice in Stichting Donemus: *Catalogue 1978: Dutch contemporary music.* Amsterdam: Donemus, 1978. 40 pp. ((--))

M-384 [[SMIT, Sytze: Dutch music on records in *Keynotes*, IX/1 (1979): 17-20]]

M-385 Discografie in BALFOORT, Dirk Jacobus: *Het muziekleven in Nederland in de 17de en 18de eeuw.* 's-Gravenhage: Nijhoff, 1981: 164-165   ((--))

M-386 Discografie in REESER, Eduard: *Een eeuw Nederlandse muziek, 1815-1915.* Amsterdam: Querido, 1986: 244-245   ((--))

M-387 Discografie in SAMAMA, Leo: *Zeventig jaar Nederlandse muziek, 1915-1985: voorspel tot een nieuwe dag.* Amsterdam: Querido, 1986: 291-310   ((--))

MUSIC--NEW ZEALAND

M-388 Kiwi/Pacific Records: New Zealand composer edition March 1980 in NORMAN, Philip: *Bibliography of New Zealand compositions.* Christchurch: Nota Bene Music, 1980-   ((--))

MUSIC--NORTHERN IRELAND

M-389 [[*Northern Ireland recorded music list 1982.* Belfast: Queen's University Department of Library and Information Studies, 1983. 22 pp.]]

MUSIC--NORWAY

M-390 Discography in KORTSEN, Bjarne: *Contemporary Norwegian piano music: a catalogue.* 2d ed. Bergen: forf., Ortustranden 45, 1974: 29-30   ((--))

M-391 Discography of contemporary Norwegian piano music in KORTSEN, Bjarne: *Contemporary Norwegian piano music: a catalogue.* 3d enl. ed. Bergen: forf., Ortustranden 45, 1976: 50-52 leaves   ((--))

M-392 Diskografier in *Cappelens Musikkleksikon.* Oslo: Cappelen, 1978-1980. 6 v.   ((--))

M-393 Discographies in KORTSEN, Bjarne: *Contemporary Norwegian music; a bibliography and discography.* Bergen: Kortsen, 1980. 47 pp.   ((--))

MUSIC--POLAND--RELIGIOUS

M-394 [[PRZYBYLSKA, Kazimiera: Muzyka religijna w polskich drukach i dyskografii w latach 1945-1974 in *Muzyka religijna w Polsce. Materialy i studia,* I/2 (1976): 109-322]]

M-395 Choix de musique polonaise contemporaine in COUCHOUD, Jean Paul: *La musique polonaise et Witold Lutosławski.* Paris: Stock Plus, 1981: 229-[234]   ((--))

MUSIC--PORTUGAL

M-396 Discographies in *Catálogo geral da música portuguesa: repertório contemporâneo.* Lisboa: Direcção-Geral do Património Cultural, A Secretaria, 1978-1980- 1 v.   ((5))

MUSIC--PRUSSIA

M-397 Grabaciones in VELAZCO, Jorge: *Federico II de Prussia, el rey músico.* México, D.F.: Instituto de Investigaciones Estéticas, Universidad Nacional Autónoma de México, 1985: 121-123   ((--))

MUSIC--SCANDINAVIA

M-398 Committee for Nordic Music Cooperation: *Music from Scandinavia.*
Copenhagen: NORD, 1982. 179 pp. ((--))

MUSIC--SCOTLAND

M-399 Scottish Arts Council: *Recordings of artists working in Scotland.*
Edinburgh: The Council, 1978. 34 pp. ((--))

MUSIC--SLOVAKIA

M-400 JANUŠKA, Ľudowít: *Slovenská diskografia.* V Martine, Matica
slovenská, 1959. 218 pp. ((4, 5))

M-401 YOELL, John H.: Focus on Slovak discography. Part 1: the well-
springs in *Fanfare,* X/5 (May–June 1987): 303–307; Part 2: the
ripening in XI/2 (September–October 1987): 391–398 ((--))

MUSIC--SOUTH AFRICA

M-402 [[En selektiv discografi over sydafrikansk musik in *MM* (April–May
1977)]]

MUSIC--SOVIET UNION

M-403 Státní knihovna, CSR: *Sovetski umění na českých gramofonových
deskách 1965-1972: jazykové kursy rustiny.* Praha: Národní knihovna,
1974. 95 pp. ((4, 5))

M-404 Music and the Revolution [1917] in *Music in the USSR* (October–
December 1987): 5 ((--))

MUSIC--SPAIN

M-405 TINNELL, Roger: *An annotated discography of music in Spain before
1650.* Madison [Wisconsin]: Hispanic Seminary of Medieval Studies,
1980. 145 pp. ((4))

M-406 LEMMON, Alfred E.: Spanish music of the Middle Ages and Golden Age:
a selected discography in *Anuario Musical,* XXXVII (1982): 149–179
((4))

MUSIC--SWEDEN

M-407 *Svensk ton på skiva = Swedish music on records.* Stockholm: STIMs
Informationscentral för svensk musik. Editions issued 1968, 1972 (44
pp.), 1974 (54 pp.), 1976 (79 pp.), 1978 (109 pp.), 1981. ((--))

M-408 Selective discography in Program notes for *Nine Swedish composers.*
[Sound recording] Caprice CAP 1121, 1977: 14–16 ((--))

M-409 CARLSSON, Carl: A selective discography in *Nine Swedish musicians.*
[Sound recording] Caprice CAP 1140, 1978: [7] ((--))

M-410 [Discography] in Program notes for *Contemporary music.* [Sound
recording] Caprice CAP 1183, 1981: 10 ((--))

M-411 JACOBSSON, Stig: *Svenska tonsättare diskografi*. Stockholm: Rikskonserten, 1985. 266 pp. ((4, 5))

MUSIC--SWITZERLAND

M-412 Discographies in *Schweizerisches Musik-archiv/Archives musicales suisse: ... Swiss music on records*. Editions in 1965 (28 pp.), 1973 (44 pp.), 1976 (46 pp.), 1978/9 (68 pp.), 1980 (77 pp.), 1983 (95 pp.), 1985/86 (109 pp.), 1986 (11 pp.), 1987/88 (138 pp.) ((--))

MUSIC--YUGOSLAVIA

M-413 Festivals in *Music of Yugoslav peoples and nationalities: the catalogue, the exposition of gramophone records and of scores are realized on the occasion of the 21st General Conference of the Unesco, Belgrade, Sava Centre*. Zagreb: [Savez organizacija kompozitora Jugoslavije, 1980]: [171]-187 (An identical discography is found in the same publication issued in Serbo-Croatian, pp. 171-181) ((7))

MUSIC--HISTORICAL STUDIES

M-414 Discografia sumaria in GRAU, Eduardo: *Baja edad media "ars nova" y renacimiento*. Buenos Aires: Ricordi, 1978: 135 ((--))

M-415 CROUCHER, Trevor: *Early music discography: from plainchant to the sons of Bach*. London: Library Association; Phoenix: Oryx Press, 1981. 2 v. ((4))

MUSIC--TO 500

M-416 Discography in GANGWERE, Blanche: *Music history from the late Roman through the Gothic periods, 313-1425: a documented chronology*. Westport, CT: Greenwood Press, 1986: [214]-215 ((--))

MUSIC--16TH CENTURY

M-417 Suggested list of records in BURKHALTER, A. Louis: *Music of the Renaissance*. [n.p.]: H. S. Stuttman Co.; distributed by Doubleday, 1968: 121-125 ((--))

MUSIC--17TH CENTURY

M-418 Music before Bach--Part IV, The 17th century: Foundations of the baroque in *Tarakan Music Letter*, III/4 (March-April 1982): 14-15 ((--))

MUSIC--19TH CENTURY

M-419 WINTER, Robert: An updated discography of nineteenth century music on nineteenth-century instruments in *Nineteenth Century Music*, VII/3 (1984): 262-265 ((--))

MUSIC--20TH CENTURY

M-420 Stadtbibliothek Bremen: *Neue Musik auf Schallplatten*. Bremen:

Stadtbibliothek, 1970. 35 pp. ((4))

M-421 Discographie in *Passage du XXe siècle*. Paris: IRCAM, 1976:
[187]-198 ((--))

M-422 Discography in SHEAD, Richard: *Music in the 1920's*. London:
Duckworth, 1976: [136]-144 ((--))

M-423 Discographie in XENAKIS, Iannis: *Musique, architecture*. 2d rev.
ed. Paris: Casterman, 1976: 231-234 ((7))

M-424 [[Discography in STUESSY, Clarence Joseph, Jr.: *The confluence of
jazz and classical music from 1950 to 1970*. [Dissertation,
University of Rochester, 1977] 512 pp.]]

M-425 Discography in TASKER, Howard: *Modern music*. Westport, CT:
Greenwood Press, 1979: 217-224 ((--)) [Reprinted from the 1957 ed.
published by Crowell, New York]

M-426 [[DAY, Timothy: *New music at the Henry Wood Promenade Concerts,
1981; a selected discography*. London: British Institute of
Recorded Sound, 1981. 18 pp.]]

M-427 Discographies in GRIFFITHS, Paul: *Modern music: the avant garde
since 1945*. London: Dent, 1981. 331 pp. ((-))

M-428 Choix discographie in SIRON, Paul-Louis: *Aspects de la musique
contemporaine, 1960-1981*. Lausanne: Editions de l'Aire, 1981:
126-130 ((--))

M-429 Music of the 20th century: part 2 in *Tarakan Music Letter*, II/4
(March-April 1981): [1], 8-9 ((--))

M-430 Music of the 20th century: part 3, Vienna and the avant garde in
Tarakan Music Letter, II/5 (May-June 1981): 4-5 ((--))

M-431 Music of the 20th century: Part 4, Nationalism in American music
in *Tarakan Music Letter*, III/1 (September-October 1981):
12-13 ((--))

M-432 Schallplattenverzeichnis in DIBELIUS, Ulrich: *Moderne Musik*.
München: Piper, 1984-   : v. 1, pp. [359]-368 ((--))

M-433 [[Discography in ARNOLD, Cecil Benjamin, Jr.: *War, peace, and
the apocalypse in art music since World War*. [Dissertation,
University of Kentucky, 1986] 639 pp.]]

M-434 Discographische Hinweise (Auswahl) in *fono forum* (February 1988):
30 ((--))

MUSIC--20TH CENTURY--1920-1929

M-435 Decade--music of the 1920's in *Tarakan Music Letter*, IV/4 (March-
April 1983): 13, 16 ((--))

MUSIC--20TH CENTURY--1930-1939

M-436 Decade--the 1930's in *Tarakan Music Letter*, IV/3 (January-

February 1983): 14-16   ((--))

MUSIC--20TH CENTURY--1940-1949

M-437   Decade--the 1940's in *Tarakan Music Letter*, IV/2 (November-
December 1982): 11-13   ((--))

MUSIC--STYLE OR PERIOD

MUSIC, BYZANTINE

M-438   Suggested list of records in BURKHALTER, A. Louis: *Byzantine and
medieval music.* [n.p.]: H. S. Stuttman Co. 1968: 121-125   ((--))

MUSIC, MEDIEVAL

M-439   MARINELLI, Carlo: Appendice di aggiornamento alla discografia in
REESE, Gustave: *La musica nel Medioevo.* Florence: Sansoni, 1960:
591-625   ((--))

M-440   Records [of medieval music] in *Music Teacher*, LV (November 1976):
23   ((--))

M-441   Music before Bach, Part I: Early Medieval music to the Year 1400
in *Tarakan Music Letter*, III/1 (September-October 1981): 1, 11
((--))

M-442   Records in ARNOLD, Joan: *Medieval music.* London: Oxford University
Press, 1982: 48   ((--))

M-443   Discographische Hinweise in *fono forum* (July 1988): 30; (September
1988): 32   ((--))

MUSIC, BAROQUE

M-444   Music of Bach's time--Part I, Minor composers of the high baroque
in *Tarakan Music Letter*, III/5 (May-June 1982): 13   ((--))

M-445   Music of Bach's time--Part II: Bach's major contemporaries in
Tarakan Music Letter, IV/1 (September-October 1982): 14   ((--))

M-446   Music of Bach's time--Part III, "The Big 3": Bach, Handel, Vivaldi
in *Tarakan Music Letter*, IV/2 (November-December 1982): 3   ((--))

MUSIC--PERFORMANCE

M-447   Diskographie in HARNONCOURT, Nikolaus: *Musik als Klangrede* ...
Salzburg: Residenz Verlag, 1983: 271-[284]; discography (pp.
200-205) in English ed. (Portland, OR: Amadeus Press, 1988)   ((--))

MUSIC--RELIGIOUS ASPECTS

M-448   Schallplattenaufnahmen in FREIMUTH, Heinz-Gert: *Gotteserfahrung in
der Musik.* Zürich: Benziger, 1983: 153-160   ((--))

MUSIC--TRANSCRIPTIONS, ARRANGEMENTS, ETC.

M-449   Auswahl Discographie: Transkriptionen/arrangements in *fono forum*

(February 1987): 30–31   ((−−))

MUSICAL INSTRUMENTS

M−450 Diszkográfia in DARVAS, Gábor: *Évezredek hangszerei*. Budapest: Zeneműkiadó, 1975: 333 ((−−))

M−451 Discographie in MAUMENÉ, Jean: *Construire des instruments: en jouer, en inventer d'autres*. Paris: Éditions de Scarabée, 1975: 116   ((−−))

M−452 Discography in BANEK, Reinhold: *Sound designs: a handbook of musical instrument building*. Berkeley, CA: Ten Speed Press, 1980: 203−205   ((−−))

MUSICALISCHE COMPAGNEY, West Germany

M−453 Discographische Hinweise in *fono forum* (August 1985): 36   ((−−))

(I) MUSICI, Italy

M−454 I Musici [discography] in *Record Geijutsu*, No. 276 (September 1973): 195−196   ((−−))

MUSICIANS

M−455 Recording artists of 78 rpm era in *Record Geijutsu*, No. 309 (June 1976): 188−197   ((5, 7))

M−456 Discographies in NANQUETTE, Claude: *Anthologie des interpretes*. Paris: Stock, 1979. 739 pp.   ((−−))

MUSIKVERLAG ALFRED COPPENRATH

M−457 Werke aus dem Musikverlag Alfred Coppenrath auf Schallplatten in *125 Jahre Musikverlag Alfred Coppenrath, 1855−1980*. Altötting: A. Coppenrath, 1980: 76−77   ((−−))

MUSSORGSKY, MODEST, 1839−1881   (Russian composer)

M−458 DOISY, Marcel: L'oeuvre de Moussorgsky: discographie critique in *Harmonie−Opéra−Hifi Conseil*, No. 26 (December 1982): 32−39   ((−−−))

M−459 [Mussorgsky discography] in *Stereo Geijutsu*, No. 170 (March 1981): 112−115 ((7))

INSTRUMENTAL WORKS

PICTURES FROM AN EXHIBITION (1874)

M−460   RISSIN, David: Moussorgski: Les tableaux d'une exposition: [discographie comparée] in *Harmonie*, No. 134 (February 1978): [89]−96   ((−−))

OPERAS

BORIS GODUNOV (1874)

M−461   LAWRENCE, A. F. R.: Boris Godounov: 1928 in *BIRS Bulletin*,

No. 4 (Spring 1957): 9-13   ((3, 6, 7))

M-462   MARINELLI, Carlo: [Discography] in Venezia, Gran Teatro La
Fenice, season 1972-73: program pp. 147-157   ((5))

M-463   MARINELLI, Carlo: [Discography] in Milano, Teatro alla Scala,
season 1972-73: program pp. 324-330   ((5))

M-464   PUGLIESE, Giuseppe: Melodram in discoteca: Boris le sette
edizione dell'opera di Mussorgsky in *Discoteca*, No. 124-132
(October 1972-July/August 1973)   ((--))

M-465   SIRVIN, René: Boris Godonouv: Les tribulations d'une partition:
de Moussorgsky a Moussorgsky in *Diapason*, No. 226 (March 1978):
110-113; No. 227 (April 1978): 90-93   ((--))

M-466   Discographie in LE ROUX, Maurice: *Moussorgski, Boris Godounov*.
Paris: Aubier-Montaigne, 1980: 221   ((--))

M-467   LISCHKE, André: Discographie in *L'Avant Scène Opéra*, No. 27-28
(May-August 1980): 200-203   ((1, 7))

M-468   Discography in *Boris Godunov*. London: J. Calder; New York:
Riverrun Press, 1982: 111-112   ((--))   (English National Opera
guide; 11)

M-469   HOLLAND, Dietmar: Anmerkungen zur Diskographie in *Boris Godunov:
Texte, Materialien, Kommentäre*. Reinbek bei Hamburg: Rowohlt,
1982: 244-[248]   ((1, 7))   (Rororo Opernbücher)

M-470   [[[Discography] in *Opéra International*, No. 70 (May 1984)]]

M-471   MARTIN, Serge: Discographie comparée in *Diapason*, No. 306 (June
1985): 90-92   ((--))

M-472   MARINELLI, Carlo: [Discography] in Palermo, Ente automono Teatro
Massimo, season 1986-87: program p. 8   ((5))

KHOVANTSCHINA (1886)

M-473   MARINELLI, Carlo: [Discography] in Roma, Teatro dell'Opera,
season 1970-71: program pp. 266-268   ((5))

M-474   MARINELLI, Carlo: [Discography] in Bologna, Teatro Comunale,
season 1980-81: program pp. 57-60   ((5))

M-475   MARINELLI, Carlo: [Discography] in Milano, Teatro alla Scala,
season 1980-81: program pp. 117-119   ((5))

M-476   KAMINSKI, Piotr: Discographie in *L'Avant Scène Opéra*, No.
57/58 (November-December 1983): 166-173   ((7))

SOROCHINTSY FAIR (1913)

M-477   MARINELLI, Carlo: [Discography] in Milano, Teatro alla Scala,
season 1980-81: program pp. 88-89   ((5))

MUTI, RICCARDO, 1941-   **(Italian conductor)**

M-478 Discographie de Riccardo Muti in *Harmonie-Opéra-Hifi Conseil*, No. 23 (September 1982): 17   ((--))

MUTTER, ANNE-SOPHIE, 1963-   (German violinist)

M-479 Discography, Deutsche Grammophon artist information, 1980. 1 p. ((--))

MUZIO, CLAUDIA, 1889-1936   (Italian soprano)

M-480 [Additions & corrections to discography in *Record Collector*, XVII/9-10 (February 1968)] in *Record Collector*, XXVIII/5-6 (October 1983): 120-128   ((--))

MYNBAYEV, TIMUR, 1943-   (Russian composer and conductor)

M-481 Discography in *Music in the USSR* (January-March 1986): 15   ((--))

MYSLIVEČEK, JOSEF, 1737-1781   (Bohemian composer)

M-482 Nahrávky z díla Josefa Myslivcka na deskách Supraphon in PEČMAN, Rudolf: *Josef Mysliveček*. Praha: Editio Supraphon, 1981: 258-259 ((--))

NBC SYMPHONY ORCHESTRA

See entry for

TOSCANINI, ARTURO

NADOLWITCH, JEAN, 1875-1966   (Rumanian tenor)

N-1   [[[Discography] in *Stimmen, die um die Welt gingen*, No. 6 (December 1984): 27-28]]

NASCIMBENE, MARIO, 1917-   (Italian composer)

OPERAS

FAUST A MANHATTAN (1963)

N-2   MARINELLI, Carlo: Discografie: Faust e Mefistofele nelle opere teatrali e sinfonico-vocali in *Quaderni dell'I.R.TE.M.* [Instituto di Ricerca per il Teatro Musicale] No. 3 (1986): 112-113   ((5))

NASEDKIN, ALEXEI, 1942-   (Russian pianist)

N-3   [[[Discography] in SOKOLOV, Mihail: *Aleksej Nasedkin: pianist, kompozitor, pedagog*. Moskva: Muzyka, 1983.   78 pp.]]

NASIDZE, SULKHAN, 1927-   (Georgian composer)

N-4   Discography in *Music in the USSR* (October-December 1987): 27 ((--))

NAT, YVES, 1890-1956   (French pianist)

N-5   HAMON, Jean: Discographie in *Almanach du disque*, 1957: 308-309

$((--))$

N-6   Discographie in NAT, Yves: *Carnets*. Paris: Flûte de pan, 1983:
94-96 $((--))$

NATZKE, OSCAR, 1905-1951   (New Zealand bass)

N-7   MORGAN, Charles I.: Discography in *Record Collector*, XXX/3-4
(April 1985): 91-93; additions & corrections in XXX/10-11 (October
1985): 242 $((--))$

NEBE, KARL, 1858-1908   (German bass-baritone)

N-8   Karl Nebe in *Stimmen die um Welt gingen*, No. 19 (March 1988):
24-28 $((--))$

NEDBAL, OSCAR, 1874-1930   (Czech composer)

N-9   Díla Oxkara Nedbala na gramofonvých deskách in *Metodické texty a
bibliografia městské knihovny v Praze Oskar Nedbal (26.3.1874-24.12.
1930)* Praha, 1974: 26 $((--))$

NEEL, BOYD, 1905-1981   (English conductor)

N-10   Boyd Neel discography 1934-1979 in NEEL, Boyd: *My orchestras and
other adventures: the memoirs of Boyd Neel*. Toronto; Buffalo:
University of Toronto Pres, 1985: [193]-214 $((3, 7))$

NEPOMUCENO, ALBERTO, 1864-1920   (Brazilian composer)

N-11   Discografia in CORRÊA, Sérgio Alvim: *Alberto Nepomuceno: catálogo
geral*. Rio de Janeiro: FUNARTE ..., 1985: 40-41 $((5))$

NESTERENKO, YEVGENY, 1938-   (Russian bass)

N-12   Discography in *Music in the USSR* (October-December 1985): 78 $((--))$

N-13   Discography in *Music in the USSR* (April-June 1988): 13-15 $((--))$

NEUHAUS, HEINRICH, 1888-1964   (Russian pianist)

N-14   METHUEN-CAMPBELL, James: Early Soviet pianists and their recordings:
a survey in *Recorded Sound*, No. 83 (January 1983): 1-16 $((--))$

NEUMANN, VACLAV, 1920-   (Czech conductor)

N-15   Diskographie in POSPÍŠIL, Vilém: *Václav Neumann*. Praha: Editio
Supraphon, 1981: 41-46 $((--))$

NEVEU, GINETTE, 1919-1949   (French violinist)

N-16   Ginette Neveu; Schallplattenverzeichnis in *fono forum* (January
1976): 23 $((--))$

NEW YORK CITY OPERA

N-17   Broadcasts, television, recordings, and films in SOKOL, Martin L.:
The New York City Opera: an American adventure. New York:

Macmillan, 1981: 204-214 ((1, 7))

NEW YORK PHILHARMONIC-SYMPHONY ORCHESTRA

<u>See</u> entry for

TOSCANINI, ARTURO

NEY, ELLY, 1882-1968 (German pianist)

N-18   SUGA, Hajime: Elly Ney in *LP Techno*, October 1980: 84-85 ((3))

NEZHDANOVA, ANTONIA VESILEVNA, 1873-1950 (Russian soprano)

N-19   DENNIS, J. F. E.: Antonia Vesilevna Nezhdanova discography in
        Record Collector, XXIV/1-2 (January 1978): 17-35; ((3, 4, 7));
        [DENNIS, J.]: Nezhdanova in *Record Collector*, XXVI/5-6 (December
        1980): 143 ((--))

NICHOLLS, AGNES, 1876-1959 (English soprano)

N-20   LEWIS, Paul: Agnes Nicholls: Columbia records and 78 rpm discography
        in *Record Collector*, XXX/12-13 (December 1985): 275-278 ((3, 6, 7))

NICOLAI, OTTO, 1810-1849 (German composer)

(DIE) LUSTIGEN WEIBER VON WINDSOR (1848)

N-21   THALMANN, Albert: Diskographie in *Die lustigen Weiber von Windsor*.
        München: Goldmann; Mainz: Schott, 1981: 280-281 ((--)) (Opern
        der Welt)

NIELSEN, CARL, 1865-1931 (Danish composer)

N-22   Recordings available in Great Britain in SIMPSON, Robert: *Carl
        Nielsen, symphonist, 1865-1931*. Westport, CT: Hyperion Press, 1979:
        227-230 ((--)) [Reprinted from the 1952 ed. published by Dent,
        London]

CHORAL WORKS

N-23   [[Discography in KRENEK, Thomas B.: *An examination and analysis of
        the choral music of Carl Nielsen (1865-1931)* Dissertation,
        University of Cincinnati, 1984] 96 pp.]]

NIKISCH, ARTUR, 1855-1922 (Hungarian conductor)

N-24   [Discography] in *Stimmen die um die Welt gingen*, No. 21 (September
        1988): 49-52 ((--))

NILSSON, BIRGIT, 1918-   (Swedish soprano)

N-25   Discographie de Birgit Nilsson in *Harmonie HiFi Conseil*, No. 10
        (June 1981): 27 ((--))

N-26   [[[Discography] in FÁBIÁN, Imre: *Hommage à Birgit Nillson*.
        Zürich: Orell Füssli & Friedrich, 1987: 64]]

NIVETTE, JUSTE, 1865?– ?   (French bass)

N–27 [Discography] in *Record Collector*, IX/3 (March 1954): 67 ((– –))

NOBRE, MARLOS, 1939–   (Brazilian composer)

N–28 Discographic references in *Marlos Nobre: catálogo de obras*.
[Brasília]: Ministério das Relações Exteriores, Departamento de
Cooperação Cultural, Científica e Tecnológica, 1977: [24] pp.
((– –)) (Compositores brasileiros)

NOGUEIRA, A. THEODORO, 1928–   (Brazilian composer)

N–29 Discographic references in MIGLIAVACCA, Ariede Maria: *A. Theodoro
Nogueira: catálogo de obras*. [Brasília]: Ministério das Relações
Exteriores, Departamento de Cooperação Cultural, Científica e
Tecnológica, 1977: [26] pp. ((– –)) (Compositores brasileiros)

NONO, LUIGI, 1924–   (Italian composer)

N–30 RIEHN, Rainer: Diskographie in *Luigi Nono*. München: Edition Text u.
Kritik, 1981: 127–128 ((– –)) (Musik–Konzepte; 20)

N–31 [Discography] in *Luigi Nono*. Lausanne: Éditions L'Age d'homme, 1987:
212–213 ((– –))

CONTRAPUNTO DIALETTICO ALLA MENTE

N–32 MARINELLI, Carlo: [Discography] in Roma, Teatro dell'Opera,
season 1970–71: program p. 678 ((5))

NORMAN, JESSYE, 1945–   (American soprano)

N–33 Discography [on Philips label] S.l.: [Philips, 198–?] 2 l. ((– –))

N–34 PAROUTY, Michel: Jessye Norman: discographie complète in
Diapason–Harmonie, No. 344 (December 1988): 72–73 ((– –))

NOTÉ, JEAN, 1859–1922 (Belgian baritone)

N–35 [Discography] in *Record Collector*, IX/3 (March 1954): 67–68 ((– –))

NOVÃES, GUIOMAR, 1895–1979 (Brazilian pianist)

N–36 Discography in *Records and Recording*, XXII/8 (May 1979): 28 ((– –))

NOVÁK, VÍTĔZSLAV, 1870–1949 (Czech composer)

N–37 Discographic notes in LÉBL, Vladimír: *Vítĕzslav Novák*. Prague:
Editio Supraphon, 1968: 69–83 ((– –))

NOVIK, NORA (Russian duo–pianist)

N–38 Discography in *Music in the USSR* (October–December 1987): 17
((– –))

NOVIKOV, ANATOLI GRIGOR'EVICH, 1896–   (Russian composer)

N-39   [Discography] in PERSON, David: *A. G. Novikov.* Moskva: Vses.
       izd-vo Sov. kompozitor, 1985: 65-86   ((5))

NOVOTNÁ, JARMILA, 1907-   (Czech soprano)

N-40   DENNIS, J.: Jarmila Novotná discography in *Record Collector,*
       XXV/5-6 (August 1979): 116-120; addenda in *Record Collector,*
       XXVII/7-8 (August 1982): 186-189   ((1, 3, 6, 7))

OBOE

O-1   Discography in GOOSSENS, Leon: *Oboe.* London: Macdonald & Jane's;
      New York: Schirmer Books, 1977: 221-229   ((--))   [Discography pp.
      221-232 in the New York ed.]

O-2   Discography in GOOSSENS, Leon: *Oboe.* 2d ed. London: Macdonald, 1980:
      221-229.   ((--))

OBORIN, LEV, 1907-1974   (Russian pianist)

O-3   [Discography] in OBORIN, Lev: *L.N. Oborin.* Moskva: Muzyca,
      1977: 208-[211]   ((--))

O-4   METHUEN-CAMPBELL, James: Early Soviet pianists and their recordings:
      a survey in *Recorded Sound,* No. 83 (January 1983): 1-16   ((--))

OBRAZTSOVA, ELENA, 1937-   (Russian mezzo-soprano)

O-5   [Discography] in SHEIKO, Rena: *Elena Obratzsova.* Moskva, 1984:
      349-[352]   ((5))

O-6   [[[Discography] in JIRÁSKOVÁ, Jiřina: *Jelena Obrazcovová.*
      Praha: Editio Supraphon, 1985: 55-57]]

O-7   Discography in *Music in the USSR* (April-June 1985): [73]   ((--))

OBRECHT, JACOB, 1450-1505   (Netherlands composer)

O-8   WEBER, J. F.: A discography of the music of Jacob Obrecht in
      Fanfare, IV/2 (November-December 1980): 6-9   ((5, 7))

O-9   Discography in PICKER, Martin: *Johannes Ockeghem and Jacob Obrecht:
      a guide to research.* New York: Garland Pub., 1988: 191-198   ((5))
      (Garland composer resource manuals; 13)

OCKEGHEM, JOHANNES, 1410-1496   (Flemish composer)

O-10   WEBER, J. F.: A discography of the music of Johannes Ockeghem in
       Fanfare, IV/1 (September-October 1980): 172-176   ((5, 7))

O-11   Discography in PICKER, Martin: *Johannes Ockeghem and Jacob Obrecht:
       a guide to research.* New York: Garland Pub., 1988: 191-198   ((5))
       (Garland composer resource manuals; 13)

OFFENBACH, JACQUES, 1819-1880   (German composer)

O-12   Grammophonplatten in KRISTELLER, Hans: *Katalog der Offenbach--
       sammlung.* Porto-Ronco, Schweiz, [1941]: 49-52   ((--))

O-13   Geselecteerde discografie in POURVOYUR, Robert: *Jacques Offenbach: essay in toegepaste muziek- en toneelsociologie.* Brussel: Economische Hogeschool Sint-Aloysius, 1977: 129-130   ((--))

OPERAS

CONTES D'HOFFMANN (1881)

O-14   FLINOIS, Pierre: Discographie in *L'Avant Scène Opéra*, No. 25 (January-February 1980): 120-125   ((1, 7))

O-15   HENDERSON, Robert: Les contes d'Hoffmann in *Opera*, XXI/12 (December 1980): 1173-1179; XXII/1 (January 1981): 31-39 with WALKER, Malcolm: [LP] discography, pp. 38-39   ((--)) (Opera on the gramophone; 49)

O-16   HOLLAND, Dietmar: Anmerkungen zur Diskographie in *Hoffmanns Erzählungen: Texte, Materialien, Kommentäre.* Reinbek bei Hamburg: Rowohlt, 1984: 311-314   ((1, 5)) (Rororo Opernbücher)

(LA) GRANDE-DUCHESSE DE GÉROLSTEIN (1867)

O-17   MARINELLI, Carlo: [Discography] in Palermo, Ente automono Teatro Massimo, season 1985-86: program p. 3   ((5))

ORPHÉE AUX ENFERS (1858)

O-18   MARINELLI, Carlo: [Discography] in Roma, Teatro dell'Opera, season 1970-71: program pp. 587-588   ((5))

(LA) PÉRICHOLE (1868)

O-19   MARINELLI, Carlo: [Discography] in Roma, Teatro dell'Opera, season 1982-83: program pp. 617-621   ((5))

O-20   FRAISON, Laurent: Discographie in *L'Avant Scène Opéra*, No. 66 (August 1984): 104-108   ((7))

OGDON, JOHN, 1937-   (English pianist)

O-21   ALEXANDER, John: John Ogdon--a discography in *Music & Musicians* (February 1987): 13-15   ((--))

ÖHMAN, MARTIN, 1887-1967   (Swedish tenor)

O-22   ENGLUND, Björn: Discography in *Talking Machine Review*, No. 44 (February 1977): 934-938   ((3, 6, 7))

OISTRAKH, DAVID, 1908-1974   (Russian violinist)

O-23   [Discography] in ÍAMPOLSKIĬ, Izrail Markovich. *David Oistrakh.* Moskva: Muzyka, 1964: 103-123   ((--))

O-24   Diskografie in JURÍK, Marían: *David Oistrach.*   Praha: Supraphon, 1977: 54-64   ((--))

O-25   [Discography] in IUZEFOVICH, Viktor: *David Oistrakh.* Moskva: Sov.

Kompozitor, 1978: 337–[350]   ((--))

O-26   MASINI, Umberto: Discografia di Oistrach in *Musica*, No. 6–7
(April–June 1978): 74–78   ((7))

O-27   [Discography] in SOROKER, Yakov: *David Oĭstrakh*. Ierusalim:
"Tarbut", 1981: 192–211   ((--))   [Omits record numbers]

O-28   Discography in SOROKER, Yakov: *David Oĭstrakh*. Jerusalem:
Lexicon Pub. House, 1982: 154–174   ((--))   [English version of the
item above]

O-29   [Discography] in ĬUZEFOVICH, Viktor: *David Oĭstrakh: besedy s Igorem
Oĭstrakhom*. 2d ed.   Moskva: Vses. izd-vo "Sov. kompozitor", 1985:
327–382   ((1, 7))

OLAH, GUSZTAV, 1901–1956   (Hungarian composer)

O-30   ALPÁR, Ágnes: *Oláh Gusztáv (1901–1956) Tervezési, rendezései:
adattár*.   Budapest: Magyar Színhazi Intézet, 1975.   105 pp. ((4, 7))

OLAN, DAVID, 1948–   (American composer)

O-31   Selected discography in Program notes for *Parnassus*. [Sound
recording] New World Records NW 306, 1980   ((--))

OLIVEIRA, WILLY CORREA DE, 1938–   (Brazilian composer)

O-32   Discographic references in FERREIRA, Paulo Affonso de Moura: *Willy
Correa de Oliveira: catálogo de obras*. [Brasília]: Ministério das
Relações Exteriores, Departamento de Cooperação Cultural, Científica
e Tecnológica, 1975: [10] pp.   ((--))   (Compositores brasileiros)

OLIVERO, MAGDA, 1912–   (Italian soprano)

O-33   Magda Olivero: opere intere e selezioni in *Musica*, No. 30 (October
1983): 276   ((2, 5))

OLIVEROS, PAULINE, 1932–   (American composer)

O-34   Discography in VON GUNDEN, Heidi: *The music of Pauline Oliveros*.
Metuchen, NJ: Scarecrow Press, 1983: 180   ((--))

ONDŘÍČEK, FRANTIŠEK, 1857–1922   (Czech violinist)

O-35   Diskografie in SICH, Bohuslav: *František Ondřícek, ćeský houslista*.
Praha: Supraphon, 1970: 344   ((--))

ONSLOW, GEORGE, 1784–1853   (French composer)

O-36   [[Discography in FRANKS, Richard Nelson: *George Onslow (1784–1853):
A study of his life, family, and works*. [Dissertation, University
of Texas, 1981]   422, 594 pp.]]

OPERAS

O-37   RIEMENS, L.: USSR records of opera in *Record Collector*, III/4 (April
1948): SEMEONOFF, B.: Addenda in III/8 (August 1948): 128–131

((--))

O-38   Records in GUERRE, Gisèle: *Opéra-comique in the nineteenth century*.
[n.p.], 1966: 75   ((--))

O-39   CELLETTI, Rodolfo: *Il teatro d'opera in disco*. Milano: Rizzoli,
1976. 614 pp.   ((4, 5))

O-40   Discographie in *Regards sur l'opéra: du ballet comique de la reine
à l'opera de Pékin*. Paris: Presses universitaires de France, 1976:
258   ((--))

O-41   BIELSKA, Krystyna: *Opera w partyturach, wyciagach fortepianowych
i nagraniach: katalog*. Lodz: Uniwersytet Lodzki, 1977. 247 pp.
((4))

O-42   Selected recordings in EWEN, David: *The book of European opera* ...
Westport, CT: Greenwood Press, 1977: 274-277   ((--)) [Reprinted
from the 1962 ed. published by Rinehart and Winston, New York]

O-43   [[TRANCHEFORT, François-René: *L'opera: I: D'Orfeo à Tristan. II: De
Tristan à nos jours*. Paris: Seuil, 1978. 313, 401 pp.]]

O-44   GAMMOND, Peter: *The illustrated encyclopedia of recorded opera*.
London: Salamander Books; New York: Harmony Books, 1979. 256 pp.
((4))

O-45   Ajanlo diszkografia in *Miert szep szazadunk operaja*. Budapest:
Gondolat, 1979: 461-[462]   ((--))

O-46   Discographies in PAYNE, Alexis: *Grands opéras du repertoire: resumé
des livrets, analyses, musicales, discographie*. Paris: Fayard, 1979.
574 pp.   ((--))

O-47   WALKER, Malcolm: Discographies in *Opera on record*. London:
Hutchinson, 1979; New York: Harper & Row, 1980. 663 pp.   ((5))

O-48   Discographie in SALAZAR, Philippe Joseph: *Idéologies de l'opéra*.
Paris: Presses universitaires de France, 1980: [195]-198   ((--))

O-49   MAYER, Carlo: L'opera francese dalle origini a nostri giorni in
Discoteca hi-fi, No. 210 (October 1980): [38-39]   ((--))

O-50   GUALUZZI, Giorgio and MARINELLI, Carlo: *50 anni di opera
lirica alla RAI, 1931-1980*. Torino: ERI/Edizioni RAI Radio-
televisione Italiana, 1981. 299 pp.   ((1, 4, 7))

O-51   MAYER, Carlo: L'opera tedesca dalle origini ai oggi: discografica
selezionata in *Discoteca hi fi*, No. 216 (April 1981): 14-15   ((--))

O-52   MARINELLI, Carlo: *Opere in disco: da Monteverdi a Berg: discografie
di 25 opere e di 3 balletti*. Firenze: Discanto edizioni; La Nuova
Italia Editrice, 1982. 547 pp.   ((4, 5, 7))

O-53   Orientations discographiques in TRANCHEFORT, François-René: *L'opéra*.
Paris: Seuil, 1983: 571-61   ((--))

O-54   WALKER, Malcolm: Discographies in *Opera on record 2*. London:

Hutchinson, 1983; New York: Beaufort Books, 1984. 399 pp. ((7))

O-55   Discographies in LÖBL, Karl and WERBA, Robert: *Opern auf Schallplatten; Ein Katalog der Gesamtaufnahmen. Band 1: Adolphe Adam bis Wolfgang Amadeus Mozart. Band 2: Modest Petrowitsch Mussorgsky bis Bernd Alois Zimmermann.* Düsseldorf: ECON Taschenbuch Verlag, 1984. 2 v., 288, 256 pp. ((1, 4, 7))

O-56   WALKER, Malcolm: Discographies in *Opera on record 3.* London: Hutchinson; Dover, NH: Longwood Press, 1984. 375 pp. ((1, 4, 5, 7))

O-57   Diskographie in REGLER-BELLINGER, Brigitte: *Knaurs grosser Opernführer.* Zürich: Buchclub Ex Libris, 1985: [633]-650 ((--))

O-58   CRUTCHFIELD, Will: Discography of 19th century Italian operas in *New York Times* (October 11, 1987), sec. 2, p. 31 ((--))

O-59   Discographische Hinwwise (Auswahl) in *fono forum* (March 1988): 26-27 ((--))

OPERAS--CZECHOSLOVAKIA

O-60   SYDOW, Elke: *Die national-tschechische Oper; Diskographie.* Berlin: Deutscher Biblioteksverband, Arbeitsstelle für das Bibliothekswesen, 1976. 70 pp. ((3, 4, 5))

O-61   Diskografie in ŠÍP, Ladislav: *Česká opera a její tvůrci: průvodce.* Praha: Supraphon, 1983: 362-374 ((--))

OPERAS, COMIC

O-62   Auswahl Discographie: musicalische Komödien um 1900 in *fono forum* (August 1987): 27, 29 ((--))

OPERAS, FRENCH

O-63   List of recorded music in DEMUTH, Norman: *French opera, its development to the Revolution.* New York: Da Capo Press, 1983, c1978: [323]-329 ((--)) [Reprinted from the ed. published by Artemis Press, Sussex]

ORBON, JULIAN, 1925-   (Cuban composer)

O-64   [[Discography in YEDRA, Velia: *Julián Orbón: biography and analytical study of Toccata for piano and Partitias No. 1 for harpsichord.* [DMA, University of Miami, 1986]]

ORCHESTRAL MUSIC

O-65   ARNOLD, Claude: *A discography of the orchestra, 1898-1925/26: an encyclopaedia of orchestral recording made by the acoustical process.* [Toronto]: St. Michael's College, University of Toronto, 1983. 688 pp. ((3, 4, 5, 6, 7))

ORCHESTRAS--CANADA

O-66   EDWARDS, Barry: Canadian orchestras: concealing our identity--a discography in *Musicanada*, No. 51 (June 1984): p. 5-6, 2 English section, p. 2 and 8, French section ((--))

ORCHESTRAS--UNITED STATES

O-67   HENRY, Helen and LANE, Chester: Discography of American orchestras
in *Symphony Magazine*, XXXIII/1 (1982): 24-34 ((--))

ORCHESTRE COLONNE, France

O-68   MARTIN, Odíle: Orchestre Colonne: 110 ans d'histoire de la musique
in *Harmonie Opéra hifi Conseil*, No. 38 (February 1984): 15 ((--))

ORCHESTRE DE PARIS

O-69   Discographie in *Harmonie*, No. 156 (March 1980): [20]-33 ((--))

ORCHESTRE SYMPHONIQUE DE MONTRÉAL

O-70   Liste des disques de L'Orchestre de Montréal in VAUX, Agathe de:
La petite histoire de l'Orchestre symphonique de Montréal. Montréal:
L. Courteau, 1984: 188-190 ((7))

ORFEON MURCIANO "FERNANDEZ CABALLERO", Spain

O-71   Grabaciones efectuados por el Orfeón Murciano "Fernández Caballero"
discos Columbia en 45 rpm in *Orfeón murciano "Fernández Caballero":
50 anniversario.* [Alicante?]: Caja de Ahorros de Alicante y Murcia,
1983: [243]-[247] ((--))

ORFF, CARL, 1895-1982 (German composer)

O-72   Petite discographie in *Discorama*, No. 4 (March-April 1960): 26
((--))

CARMINA BURANA (1936)

O-73   WEBER, J. F.: A discography of Carl Orff's Carmina Burana in
Fanfare, IV/6 (July-August 1981): 35-36 ((5, 7))

O-74   MARINELLI, Carlo: [Discography] in Palermo, Ente automono
Teatro Massimo, season 1983-84: program p. 13 ((5))

O-75   MARINELLI, Carlo: [Discography] in Verona, Teatro
Filharmonico, season 1984: program pp. 50-51 ((5))

ORGAN MUSIC

O-76   10. Auswahl an Schallplatten in LUTSCHEWITZ, Martin: *Neue
Orgelmusik (seit 1960).* Hamburg: Verlag der Musikalienhandel,
1969: 69 ((--))

O-77   VINEAR, Bill: *The Vinear organ library.* Ottawa: Vinear, 1981.
63 pp. ((--))

O-78   HOYLE, Terry: *The organ on record.* Tuffley, Gloucester: Hoyle,
1983. 56 pp. ((--))

O-79   [[Discographies in KRATZENSTEIN, Marilou D.: *A comprehensive performance project in organ literature with an annotated discography of historic organs and organ music from the Gothic era through the Renaissance.* [DMA Thesis, University of Iowa, 1979] 120 pp.]]

O-80   KRATZENSTEIN, Marilou and HAMILTON, Jerald: *Four centuries of organ music: from the Robertsbridge Codex through the baroque era: an annotated discography.* Detroit: Information Coordinators, 1984. 300 pp. ((--)) (Detroit studies in music bibliography; 51)

ORGAN MUSIC, AMERICAN

O-81   ROWELL, Lois: *American organ music on records.* Braintree, Mass.: Organ Literature Foundation, 1976. 105 pp. ((3, 4, 5, 7))

ORGAN MUSIC--20TH CENTURY

O-82   [[Discography in SHACKELFORD, Rudolph Owens: *Problems of editions and transcriptions in organ music of the twentieth century.* [DMA, University of Illinois, 1971] 249 pp.]]

ORGANS--CZECHOSLOVAKIA--SLOVAKIA

O-83   Diskografia/Diskographie in GERGELYI, Otmar: *Historické organy na Slovensku.* Bratislava: OPUS, 1982: 361-364 ((--))

ORGANS--FRANCE

O-84   Discographie in NOISETTE DE CRAUZAT, Claude: *L'orgue français.* Paris: Atlas, 1986: 269 ((--))

ORGANS--GERMANY, FEDERAL REPUBLIC

O-85   Wuppertaler Orgeldiscographie in DORFMÜLLER, Joachim: *300 Jahre Orgelbau im Wuppertal.* Wuppertal: Born, 1980: 195-197 ((--))

O-86   Discographies in BLARR, Oskar Gottlieb: *Orgelstadt Düsseldorf.* Düsseldorf: Trilsch Verlag, 1982. 196 pp. ((--))

ORGANS--ITALY

O-87   Discograpfia in BERTAGNA, Giancarlo: *Gli antichi organi della Diocesi di Ventimiglia-San Remo.* Savona: Liguria, 1985: 271 ((--))

ORGANS--NETHERLANDS

O-88   Diskographie in WISGERHOF, Bert: *Orgeln in den Niederlanden.* Berlin: Verlag Merseburger, 1981: 55-56 ((--))

ORGANS--SPAIN

O-89   SABATIER, François: Les disques in AUSSEIL, Louis: *L'orgue espagnol du XVIe au XIXe siècle; refléxions sur l'évolution de sa facture.* Paris: Orgue, 1980: [70]-71 ((--))

ORGANS--SWEDEN

O-90   CARLSSON, Curt: *Diskografi over alla svenska orglar som fins inspelade på skiva.* Stockholm: Proprius, 1973. 47 pp.   ((4, 7))

ORGANS--UNITED STATES--NEW ENGLAND

O-91   Discography in OWEN, Barbara: *The organ in New England.* Raleigh: Sunbury Press, 1979: 395   ((--))

ORLANDO DI LASSO, 1532-1594   (Flemish composer)

O-92   HEIN, Ulrich: Lasso-diskographie in *Orlando di Lasso: Musik der Renaissance am Münchner Fürstenhof...* Wiesbaden: Reichert, 1982: 88-115   ((7))

ORMANDY, EUGENE, 1899-1985   (Hungarian-American conductor)

O-93   TOCZEK, John: Eugene Ormandy and the Minneapolis Symphony Orchestra in *Le Grand Baton,* No. 39 (December 1977): 20-21   ((--))

ORNSTEIN, LEO, 1897-   (American composer)

O-94   Selected discography in Program notes for *Cadenza and Variations.* [Sound recording] New World Records NW 313, 1980   ((--))

OSBORNE, NIGEL, 1948-   (English composer)

O-95   HUGHES, Eric and DAY, Timothy: Nigel Osborne in *Recorded Sound,* No. 85 (January 1984): 75-78   ((1, 7))   (Discographies of British composers; 21)

OZAWA, SEIJI, 1935-   (Japanese conductor)

O-96   [Discography] in *Record Geijutsu,* No. 276 (September 1973): 185-186 ((--))

O-97   [Discography] in *Record Geijutsu,* No. 329 (February 1978): 46-50 ((4, 5, 7))

O-98   Discography [on Philips label] S.l. [Philips, 198-?] 1 leaf.   ((--))

PABLO, LUIS DE, 1930-   (Spanish composer)

P-1   Discografía y bibliografia in GARCIA DEL BUSTO, José: *Luis de Pablo.* Madrid: Espasa-Calpe, 1979: [135]   ((--))

PADEREWSKI, IGNACE JAN, 1860-1940   (Polish pianist)

P-2   Dyskografia in WŁADYSŁAW, Dulęba and SOKOŁAWSKA, Zofia: *Paderewski.* Warsaw: Polski Wydawn. Muzyczne, 1976: 178-[182]   ((5))

P-3   MASINI, Umberto: Discografia di Paderewski in *Musica,* No. 5 (February 1978): 33-35   ((7))

P-4   A list of Paderewski's recordings in PHILLIPS, Charles: *Paderewski, the story of a modern immortal.* New York: Da Capo Press, 1978: 550-552   ((--)) [Reprinted from the 1934 ed. published by Macmillan]

P-5   CARTWRIGHT, Jim: Ignace Jan Paderewski recordings in Immortal Performances 1978: List Number 1 [Dealer's List] Austin, TX:

Immortal Performances, 1978: [31]-[46]   ((3, 6, 7))   (Immortal Performances discographic data; 6)

P-6   Discography in PADEREWSKI, Ignace: *The Paderewski memoirs*. New York: Da Capo Press, 1980: 405-407 [Reprinted from the 1938 ed. published by Scribners, New York]   ((--))

PAGANINI, NICCOLO, 1782-1840   (Italian violinist)

P-7   Discography in SUGDEN, John: *Niccolo Paganini, supreme violinist or devil's fiddler?* Speldhurst, Tunbridge Wells: Midas Books, 1980: 162-164   ((--))

P-8   Discografia in BERRI, Pietro: *Paganini, la vita e le opere*. Milano: Bompiani, 1982: 557-569   ((--))

P-9   [[WARREN, George: The recorded Paganini in *Guitar and Lute*, No. 24 (September 1982): 20-21; No. 25 (November 1982): 18-20]]

CAPRICES

P-10   [[[Discography] in CANTU, Alberto: *I 24 capricci e i 6 concerti di Paganini: guida e analisi critica*. Torino: EDA, 1980: 255-262]]

PAKHMUTOVA, ALEXANDRA, 1929-   (Russian composer)

P-11   Discography in *Music in the USSR* (January-March 1986): 78-79   ((--))

PÁLENÍČEK, JOSEF, 1914-   (Czech composer)

P-12   Diskografie in POKORA, Miloš: *Josef Páleníček*. Praha: Editio Supraphon, 1982: 87-89   ((--))

PALM, SIEGFRIED, 1927-   (German cellist)

P-13   [Discography] in *Record Geijutsu*, No. 276 (September 1973): 190   ((--))

PAPINEAU-COUTURE, JEAN, 1916-   (Canadian composer)

P-14   Discographic references in MILOT, Louise Bail: *Jean Papineau-Couture; la vie, la carrière et l'oeuvre*. Ville la Salle, Québec: Hurtubise HMH, 1986: [285]-298   ((--))

PARAY, PAUL, 1886-1979   (French conductor)

P-15   BROWN, Nathan E.:   Early Paray recordings in *Le Grand Baton*, No. 46 (June 1980): 4   ((--))

P-16   KOLDYS, Mark: Paul Paray conducts the Detroit Symphony Orchestra: a discography in *American Record Guide*, XLIII/4 (February 1980): 12, 57; corrections in April 1980   ((--))

P-17   Paul Paray conducts the Detroit Symphony Orchestra: a discography in *Le Grand Baton*, No. 46 (June 1980): 6 [reprinted from *American Record Guide*, February 1980 issue, with corrections from the April issue]   ((--))

PARKER, HORATIO, 1863-1919   (American composer)

P-18   Selected discography in Program notes for *Horatio Parker: a north ballad.* [Sound recording] New World Records NW 339, 1986   ((--))

PARMEGIANI, BERNARD, 1927-   (French composer)

P-19   Discographie in THOMAS, Jean-Christophe: *L'envers d'une oeuvre: De natura sonorum de Bernard Parmegiani.* Paris: Éditions Buchet/Chastel, 1982: 204   ((--))

PASERO, TANCREDI, 1893-1983   (Italian bass)

P-20   TIBERI, Maurizio: Discografia in *Musica*, No. 18 (September 1980): 257-258   ((3, 7))

P-21   Discografia in CLERICO, Cesare: *Tancredi Pasero: voce verdiana.* [Italy]: Scomegna, [1983?]: 102-103   ((5))

PASQUIER, RÉGIS, 1945-   (French violinist)

P-22   Discographie in *Harmonie-Panorama musique*, No. 39 (February 1984): 76   ((--))

PATORZHINSKY, IVAN SERGEYEVICH, 1896-1964   (Russian bass)

P-23   [Discography] in *Ivan Sergeevich Patorzhinskii.* Moskva, 1976: 248-[256]   ((--))

PATTERSON, PAUL, 1947-   (English composer)

P-24   HUGHES, Eric and DAY, Timothy: Paul Patterson in *Recorded Sound*, No. 79 (January 1981): 121-123   ((1))   (Discographies of British composers; 10)

PATTI, ADELINA, 1843-1919   (Italian soprano)

P-25   MORAN, W. R.: The Adelina Patti recordings in KLEIN, Herman: *The reign of Patti.* New York: Arno Press, 1977: iii-v   ((3, 6, 7)) [Includes notes on playing speeds] [Originally published without discography by Century, New York, 1920]

PATY, HUBERT   (Bass)

P-26   [Discography] in *Record Collector*, IX/3 (March 1954): 68-69   ((--))

PAVAROTTI, LUCIANO, 1935-   (Italian tenor)

P-27   HOFFMAN, Keith: King of the high C's: the recordings of Luciano Pavarotti in *Tarakan Music Letter*, II/4 (March-April 1981): 6-7   ((--))

P-28   Discography in PAVAROTTI, Luciano: *Pavarotti, my own story.* Garden City, NY: Doubleday, 1981: 291-308   ((5))

P-29   Discografia essenziale in CELLETTI, Rodolfo: Pavarotti, il re della voce in *Discoteca Hifi*, No. 228 (25 April-25 May 1982): 4-9   ((--))

P-30   Pavarotti à écouter in *Diapason–Harmonie*, No. 305 (May 1985): 28
        ((--))

P-31   Recorded repertoire in MAYER, Martin: *Grandissimo Pavarotti*.
        Garden City, NY: Doubleday, 1986: 203-223   ((--))

PEARS, SIR PETER, 1910-1986   (English tenor)

P-32   Peter Pears: the recorded repertoire in *Peter Pears: a tribute on
        his 75th birthday*. London: Faber Music in association with the
        Britten Estate, Aldeburgh, Suffolk, 1985: 134-144   ((--))

PEERCE, JAN, 1904-1984   (American tenor)

P-33   PINTA, Emil R.: *A chronologic Jan Peerce discography 1932-1980*.
        Worthington, OH, 1986. 29 pp.   ((1, 3, 6, 7))

PEETERS, FLOR, 1903-1986   (Belgian composer)

P-34   Discography in HOFMANN, John: *Flor Peeters, his life and his organ
        works*. Fredonia, NY: Birchwood Press, 1978: 200-207   ((--))

PEKARSKY, MARK, PERCUSSION ENSEMBLE, USSR

P-35   Discography in *Music in the USSR* (October–December 1985): 19   ((--))

PENALVA, José, 1924-   (Brazilian composer)

P-36   Discographic notes in MIGLIAVACCA, Ariede Maria: *José Penalva:
        catálogo de obras*. [Brasília]: Ministério das Relações Exteriores,
        Departamento de Cooperação Cultural, Científica e Tecnológica,
        1978: [27] pp.   ((--)) (Compositores brasileiros)

PENDERECKI, KRZYSZTOF, 1933-   (Polish composer)

P-37   Schallplattenverzeichnis (Auswahl) in SCHWINGER, Wolfram:
        Penderecki: Begegnungen, Lebensdaten, Werkkommentäre. Stuttgart:
        Deutsche Verlags-Anstalt, 1979: 265-266   ((--))

P-38   Discography in ROBINSON, Ray: *Krzysztof Penderecki; a guide to his
        works*. Princeton: Prestige Publications, 1983: 22-27   ((--))

CHORAL WORKS

ST. LUKE PASSION (1963-65)

P-39   Discography of the St. Luke Passion in ROBINSON, Ray and WINOLD,
        Allen: *A study of the Penderecki St. Luke Passion*. Celle: Moeck
        Verlag, 1983: 118   ((--))

OPERAS

(DIE) TEUFEL VON LOUDUN (1969)

P-40   MARINELLI, Carlo: [Discography] in Roma, Teatro dell'Opera,
        season 1979-80: program p. 103   ((5))

PENTLAND, BARBARA, 1912-   (Canadian composer)

P-41   Discography in EASTMAN, Sheila and MCGEE, Timothy J.:
        Barbara Pentland. Toronto: University of Toronto Press, 1983:
        [127]-128 ((--)) (Canadian composers; 3)

PERAHIA, MURRAY, 1947-   (American pianist)

P-42   Discografia in RISALITI, Riccardo: Un poeta che viene dal Bronx
        in *Musica*, No. 17 (June 1980): [166]-168 ((--))

P-43   Discographische Hinweise in *fono forum* (January 1987): 24 ((--))

P-44   Selected discography in *Ovation*, IX/1 (February 1988): 12-16 ((--))

PERCUSSION INSTRUMENTS

P-45   Selected discography in HOLLAND, James: *Percussion.* London:
        Macdonald and Jane's, 1978: 271-277 ((--))

P-46   Discografia in CENTAZZO, Andrea: *Guida agli stumenti a percussione.*
        Milano: Il formichiere, 1979: [221]-225 ((--))

P-47   [LAYTON, Robert]: Selected discography in HOLLAND, James:
        Percussion. New York: Schirmer Books, 1981: 271-277 ((--))

P-48   Discographie de base des oeuvres contemporaines in GOLDMAN,
        Béatrice: La percussion in *Harmonie-Opéra Hi-fi Conseil*, No. 17
        (February 1982): 21 ((--))

PERGOLESI, GIOVANNI, 1710-1736 (Italian composer)

P-49   GEFFEN, Gérard: Discographie ... in *Harmonie-Panorama musique*,
        No. 42 (May 1984): 31-36 ((--))

OPERAS

(LA) SERVA PADRONA (1732)

P-50   MARINELLI, Carlo: [Discography] in Treviso, Ente Teatro
          Comunale, season 1977-78: program p. 8 ((5))

PERLE, GEORGE, 1915-   (American composer)

P-51   Selected discography in Program notes for *Exultations.* [Sound
        recording] New World Records NW 304, 1979 ((--))

P-52   Selected discography in Program notes for *Piano works.* [Sound
        recording] New World Records NW 342, 1987 ((--))

PERSICHETTI, VINCENT, 1915-1987 (American composer)

P-53   Selected discography in Program notes for *Winds of Change: music
        for wind ensemble by ... Vincent Persichetti ...* [Sound recording]
        New World Records NW 211, 1977: 3 ((--))

P-54   Selected discography in Program notes for *Vincent Persichetti choral
        works.* [Sound recording] New World Records NW 316, 1983: [2] ((--))

P-55   [[[Discography] in PATTERSON, Donald L.: *Vincent Persichetti a*

bio-bibliography. New York: Greenwood Press, 1988   (Bio-bibliographies in music; 16)]]

PERTILE, AURELIANO, 1885-1952   (Italian tenor)

P-56   Discografia in TOSI, Bruno: *Pertile; una voce, un mito.* Venezia:
CGS, 1985: 291-299   ((5))

PETKOV, DIMITUR, 1919-   (Bulgarian bass)

P-57   [Discography] in PAVLOV, Evgeni: *Dimitur Petkov: monografiia.*
Sofiia: Durzh. izd-vo "Muzika", 1987: 233-237   ((--)).

PETRASSI, GOFFREDO, 1904-   (Italian composer)

P-58   Nota discografica in *Petrassi.* Torino: EDT-/Musica, 1986: 344-348
((--))

PETRI, EGON

See entry for

BUSONI, FERUCCIO

PETROV, ANDREI, 1930-   (Russian composer)

P-59   Discography in *Music in the USSR* (October-December 1986): 5   ((--))

P-60   Discography in *Music in the USSR* (January-March 1988): 82   ((--))

PETROV, NICOLAI, 1943-   (Russian pianist)

P-61   Discography in *Music in the USSR* (January-March 1987): 26   ((--))

PETRUSENKO, OKSANA, 1900-1940   (Russian singer)

P-62   [Discography Oksana Petrusenko] in *Oksana Petrusenko: spohady,
lysty, materialy.* Kiev: "Muzychna Ukraina", 1980: 291-[295]
((3, 7))

PETTERSSON, ALLAN, 1911-1980   (Swedish composer)

P-63   Diskografi in AARE, Leif: *Allan Pettersson.* Stockholm: Norstedt,
1978: 229-231   ((--))

PFITZNER, HANS, 1869-1949   (German composer)

P-64   VOGEL, Johann Peter: Diskographie der Werke Hans Pfitzners in
Hans Pfitzner-Gesellschaft Mitteilungen, No. 37 (February 1977):
42-46; Nachtrag zur Diskographie der Werke der Hans Pfitzners in No.
38 (August 1978): 43-44   ((--))

P-65   SUGA, Hajime: Hans Pfitzner record in *LP Techno*, July 1978:
102-108   ((--))

PHILIPP, ISIDORE, 1863-1958   (French pianist)

P-66   Isidore Philipp discography in *Journal of the American Liszt*

Society, II (December 1977): 47-48   ((1, 7)) [Reprinted from
Recorded Sound, I/8 (Autumn 1962): 248]

PHILIPP, ROBERT, 1852-1933   (German tenor)

P-67   [[[Discography] in *Stimmen, die um die Welt gingen*, No. 9
(September 1985): 22-23]]

PHONOCYLINDERS

P-68   GRATTELO, Thomas and DEAKINS, Duane D.: *Comprehensive cylinder
record index.* Stockton, CA, 1956-   5 parts [pt. 1: Edison
amberol records; pt. 2: Edison standard records; pt. 3: Edison blue
amberol records; pt. 4: Indestructible records; pt. 5: U.S.
everlasting records]   ((4))

P-69   MORBY, Paul: Brown wax to Blue Amberol--and the McCormack cylinder
in *Record Collector*, XVIII/1-2 (October 1968): 5-42   ((3, 6))

P-70   GIRARD, Victor and BARNES, Harold: *Vertical-cut cylinders and
discs; a catalogue of all "Hill-&-Dale" recordings of serious worth
made and issued between 1987-1932 circa.* London: British Institute
of Recorded Sound, 1971. 196 pp.   ((4, 7))

PIANISTS

P-71   Schallplattenverzeichnis in KAISER, Joachim: *Grosse Pianisten in
unserer Zeit.* München: R. Piper, 1982: 272-[286]   ((--))

P-72   Selected discography in DUBAL, David: *The world of concert
pianists: conversations with great pianists.* New York: Summit
Books, 1984: [365]-389   ((--))

P-73   METHUEN-CAMPBELL, James: *Catalogue of recordings by classical
pianists. Volume 1 (Pianists born to 1872)* Chipping Norton [Eng.]:
Disco Epsom, 1984. 66 pp.   ((1, 3, 6, 7))

PIANISTS, FRENCH

P-74   Discographische Hinweise: französisch pianisten in *fono forum*
(September 1988): 24-25, 26-27   ((--))

PIANISTS--RUSSIA

P-75   METHUEN-CAMPBELL, James: Early Soviet pianists and their recordings:
a survey in *Recorded Sound*, No. 83 (January 1983): 1-16   ((--))

PIANO

P-76   Discography; some selected piano records in KENTNER, Louis: *Piano.*
London: Macdonald and Jane's, 1976: 191-198   ((--))

P-77   Recordings by Richard Bunger in BUNGER, Richard: *The well-prepared
piano.* San Pedro, CA: Litoral Arts Press, 1981: 93   ((--))

P-78   Discography in *The Book of the piano.* Ithaca, NY: Cornell
University Press, 1981: 281-284   ((--))

PIANO MUSIC

P-79 [[Discography in BUCCHERI, John Stephen: *An approach to twelve-tone music: articulation of serial pitch units in piano works of Schoenberg, Webern, Krenek, Dallapiccola, and Rochberg.* [Dissertation, University of Rochester, 1975] 339 pp.]]

P-80 [[Discography in BUTTARS, Jane Lurene: *Early piano discography, 1951-1983: recordings of pianos built before 1855 or modern reconstructions.* [Dissertation, University of Colorado, Boulder, 1984]   49 pp.]]

See also

KEYBOARD MUSIC

PIANO MUSIC, AMERICAN

P-81 [[Discography in BAILEY, Barbara Elliott: *A historic and stylistic study of American solo piano music published from 1956 through 1976.* [Dissertation, Northwestern University, 1980]   439 pp.]]

PIANO MUSIC, BRITISH

P-82 [[Discography in CAIRNS, Valerie: *British Romantic piano music at the beginning of the twentieth century.* [M. Litt. Musicology, Newcastle upon Tyne, 1978]   489 pp.]]

PIANO MUSIC (FOUR HANDS)

P-83 Recordings in CHANG, Frederic Ming and FAUROT, Albert: *Team piano repertoire; a manual of music for multiple players at one or more pianos.* Metuchen: Scarecrow Press, 1976: 157-184   ((5))

PIANO MUSIC (TWO PIANOS)

P-84 [[Discography in ROBERTS, Maynard Wesley: *An introduction to the literature for two pianos and orchestra, 1915-1950.* [DMA, Southern Baptist Theological Seminary, 1981]   388 pp.]]

PICCALUCA, ALBERT, 1854-?   (French baritone)

P-85 [Discography] in *Record Collector*, IX/3 (March 1954): 69-70   ((--))

PIERNÉ, Gabriel, 1863-1937   (French composer and conductor)

P-86 Discographie in MASSON, Georges: *Gabriel Pierné, musicien lorrain.* [Nancy]: Presses universitares de Nancy; [Metz]: Editions Serpenoise, 1987: 166   ((--))   [Omits record numbers]

PIJPER, WILLEM, 1894-1947   (Dutch composer)

P-87 [[Discography in RYKER, Harrison Clinton: *The symphonic music of Willem Pijper 1894-1947)* [Dissertation, University of Wisconsin, 1971]   239 pp.]]

P-88 [[Discography in HOOGERWERF, Frank W.: *The chamber music of Willem Pijper (1894-1947)* [Dissertation, University of Michigan, 1974]

469 pp.]]

PIKAISEN, VICTOR ALEXANDROVITCH, 1933–   (Russian violinist)

P–89   Discographische Hinweise: V. A. Pikaisen (Auswahl) in *fono forum*
(January 1987): 35 ((--))

PINKHAM, DANIEL, 1923–   (American composer)

P–90   Discography in DeBOER, Kee: *Daniel Pinkham, a bio-bibliography.*
New York: Greenwood Press, 1988: [117]–125 ((1, 5, 7))
(Bio-bibliographies in music; 12)

PINNOCK, TREVOR, 1946–   (English harpsichordist/conductor)

P–91   Discografia di Trevor Pinnock in *Musica*, No. 40 (March 1986): 16
((--))

P–92   Discographische Hinweise: Aktuelle veröffent lichengen mit Trevor
Pinnock in *fono forum* (November 1987): 37 ((--))

PINZA, EZIO, 1892–1957 (Italian bass)

P–93   Discography in *Record Collector*, XXVI/5–6 (December 1980): 101–137;
[Part 2–addenda] in XXIX/4–6 (August 1984): 141–143 ((3, 4, 6,7))

PIRES, MARIA JOÃO, 1944–   (Portuguese pianist)

P–94   Discographie in *Harmonie-Panorama musique*, No. 47 (November 1984):
21 ((--))

PISENDEL, JOHANN GEORG, 1687–1755 (German composer)

P–95   [[[Discography] in TREUHEIT, Albrecht: *Johann Georg Pisendel
(1687-1755), Geiger, Konzertmeister, Komponist* ... Nürnberg:
Edelmann, 1987]]

PISTON, WALTER, 1894–1976 (American composer)

P–96   Discographic references in *List of works of Walter Piston.* New York:
BMI, 1964. unpaged. ((--))

P–97   Selected discography in Program notes for *Walter Piston: String
Quartet No. 2.* [Sound recording] New World Records NW 302, 1976
((--))

P–98   CURTIS, William D.: A Piston Discography in *American Record Guide*,
XL/7 (June 1977): 38–40 ((--))

P–99   CURTIS, William David: Walter Piston (1894–1976)--a discography in
ARSC Journal, XIII/2 (1981): 76–95 ((3, 4, 5, 6, 7))

P–100   Discography in POLLACK, Howard: *Walter Piston.*   Ann Arbor, Mich.:
UMI Research Press, 1982: [195]–201 ((--))

P–101   Selected discography in Program notes for *Robert Davidovici, violin.*
[Sound recording] New World Records NW 334, 1987 ((--))

PITTSBURGH SYMPHONY ORCHESTRA

P-102 CUNNINGHAM, James: Pittsburgh Symphony Orchestra recordings in
FRANCOS, Alexis: *To research a symphony: some resources and tools
available on the Pittsburgh Symphony Orchestra.* [Pittsburgh, PA]:
A. Francos, 1982: 68-71 ((--))

PIZZETTI, ILDEBRANDO, 1880-1968 (Italian composer)

P-103 Recordings in GATTI, Guido M.: *Ildebrando Pizzetti.* Westport, CT:
Hyperion Press, 1979: 122 ((--)) [Reprinted from the 1951 ed.
published by D. Dobson, London]

P-104 MODUGNO, Maurizio: Ildebrando Pizzetti: La discografia in *Omaggio
a Ildebrando Pizzetti.* [Parma]: Grafiche STEP cooperativa editrice
[1980]: 68-74 ((1, 5))

PLAKIDIS, PETRIS, 1947-   (Latvian composer)

P-105 Discography in *Music in the USSR* (July-September 1986): 91 ((--))

PLANTÉ, FRANCIS, 1839-1934 (French pianist)

P-106 ROUSSILLON, Georges: Discographie in *Sonorités*, No. 10 (May 1984):
26 ((3, 7))

PLASSON, MICHEL, 1933-   (French conductor)

P-107 Discographie in *Harmonie-Panorama musique*, No. 38 (January 1984):
15 ((--))

PLETNYOV, MIKHAIL, 1946-   (Russian pianist)

P-108 [Discography] in *Music in the USSR* (April-June 1986): 26 ((--))

P-109 Discographische Hinweise in *fono forum* (August 1986): 26 ((--))

POLI, AFRO, 1902-1988 (Baritone)

P-110 TESORIERO, Michael: Afro Poli in *Record Collector*, XXXIII/6-7 (June
1988): 172-173 ((--))

POLLINI, MAURZIO, 1942-   (Italian pianist)

P-111 [Discography] in *Record Geijutsu*, No. 276 (September 1973): 189
((--))

P-112 LEMERY, Denis: Discographie in *Diapason*, No. 208 (June-July 1976):
7 ((--))

P-113 Discography, Deutsche Grammophon artist information, 1980. 2 pp.
((--))

P-114 LOUIS, Remy: Discographie complete in *Diapason-Harmonie*, No. 335
(February 1988): 38 ((7))

PONCE, MANUEL MARIA, 1882-1948 (Mexican composer)

P-115 Guitar discography in OTERO, Corazón: *Manuel M Ponce and the guitar.* Shaftesbury, Dorset, England: Musical New Services, 1983: 82 ((--))

PONCHIELLI, AMILCARE, 1834-1886 (Italian composer)

OPERAS

(LA) GIOCONDA (1876)

P-116 MARINELLI, Carlo: [Discography] in Roma, Teatro dell'Opera, season 1981-82: program pp. 564-572 ((5))

P-117 [[[Discography] in *Opéra International,* No. 61 (July-August 1983)]]

PONS, LILY, 1898-1976 (French soprano)

P-118 Lily Pons--Columbia recordings (1941/54) in Program notes for *Lily Pons, coloratura assoluta* [Sound recording] Columbia D3M 34394, 1976: 16 ((3, 4, 7))

PONSELLE, ROSA, 1897-1981 (American soprano)

P-119 PARK, Bill: Discography in PONSELLE, Rosa: *Ponselle, a singer's life.* Garden City, NY: Doubleday, 1982: 248-307 ((1, 3, 5, 7))

P-120 GUANDALINI, Gina: Discografia in *Musica,* No. 22 (October 1981): 252-256; addendum in *Musica,* No. 23 (November 1981): 352 ((--))

PORTER, QUINCY, 1897-1960 (American composer)

P-121 Selected discography in Program notes for *Quincy Porter: Dance in three time.* [Sound recording] New World Records NW 320, 1984 ((--))

PORTLAND YOUTH PHILHARMONIC

P-122 Discography in AVSHALOMOV, Jacob: *Music is where you make it, II: the joyful workings of America's first youth orchestra, the Portland Youth Philharmonic, 1923-1979.* [Portland, OR]: Portland Junior Symphony Association, 1979: 140 ((--))

POULENC, FRANCIS, 1899-1963 (French composer)

P-123 [[JØRGENSON, A. M. Tiedje: *Francis Poulenc. En discografi.* [Thesis, Royal Danish School of Librarianship, 1972]]]

P-124 VIDAL, Pierre: Francis Poulenc: discographie critique in *Harmonie-Panorama musique,* No. 31 (May 1983): 31-39 ((2))

P-125 BLOCH, Francine: *Francis Poulenc, 1928-1982.* Paris: Bibliothèque nationale, Departement de la phonothèque nationale et de l'audiovisuel, 1984. 253 pp. (Phonographies; 2) ((1, 3, 4, 5, 6, 7))

SONGS

P-126 SAUL, Patrick: Discographie Appendix in POULENC, Francis: *Diary of my songs = Journal des mes mélodies.* London: Gollancz, 1985:

137-160   ((--))

STAGE WORKS

(LES) BICHES (1923)

P-127   MARINELLI, Carlo: [Discography] in Roma, Teatro dell'Opera, season 1968-69: program p. 609   ((5))

P-128   MARINELLI, Carlo: [Discography] in Roma, Teatro dell'Opera, season 1984-85: program pp. 48-49   ((5))

DIALOGUES DES CARMÉLITES (1956)

P-129   Discographie in *L'Avant Scène Opéra*, No. 52 (May 1983): 113 ((7))

(LA) VOX HUMAINE (1959)

P-130   MARINELLI, Carlo: [Discography] in Roma, Teatro dell'Opera, season 1970-71: program p. 658   ((5))

P-131   MARINELLI, Carlo: [Discography] in Treviso, Ente Teatro Comunale, season 1977-78: program p. 2   ((5))

POUSSEUR, HENRI, 1929-   (French composer)

OPERAS

VOTRE FAUST (1969)

P-132   MARINELLI, Carlo: Discografie: Faust e Mefistofele nelle opere teatrali e sinfonico-vocali in *Quaderni dell'I.R.TE.M.* [Instituto di Ricerca per il Teatro Musicale] No. 3 (1986): 5-26   ((5))

POWELL, JOHN, 1882-1963   (American composer)

P-133 Selected discography in Program notes for *Works of Carpenter, Gilbert, Weiss, Powell.* [Sound recording] New World Records NW 228, 1977: 4   ((--))

POWELL, MAUD, 1868-1920   (American violinist)

P-134 CARTWRIGHT, Jim: Maud Powell [discography] in Immortal Performances LP list (July 1982) [Dealer's list]   6 pp. ((3, 6, 7))   (Immortal performances discographic data; 9)

P-135 Chronology of recording sessions [and] Discography: recordings of Maud Powell in SHAFFER, Karen A.: *Maud Powell, pioneer American violinist.* Arlington, VA: Maud Powell Foundation; Ames, IA: Iowa State University Press, 1987: 428-[446]   a((7))

POWER, LEONEL, d. 1445   (English composer)

P-136 WEBER, J. F.: A discography of the music of Leonel Power in *Fanfare*, VI/3 (January-February 1983): 229-231   ((5, 7))

PRADO, ALMEIDA   (Brazilian composer)

P-137 Discographic references in FERREIRA, Paulo Affonso de Moura: *Almeida Prado: catálogo de obras*. [Brasília]: Ministério das Relações Exteriores, Departamento de Cooperação Cultural, Científica e Tecnológica, 1976: [22] pp. ((--)) (Compositores brasileiros)

PREVIN, ANDRÉ, 1929–   **(American conductor)**

P-138 GERARDI, Carla: A music man for all seasons: the wide, wide world of André Previn in *Tarakan Music Letter*, V/1 (September–October 1983): 14–15 ((--))

PRÉVOST D'EXILES, ANTOINE–FRANÇOIS, ABBÉ, 1697–1763 (French author)

MANON LESCAUT (1731)

P-139 [[Discography in HISS, Clyde S.: *Abbé Prévost's Manon Lescaut as novel, libretto and opera*. [DMA, University of Illinois, 1967] 178 pp.]]

PREY, HERMANN, 1929–   **(German baritone)**

P-140 Diskographie in PREY, Hermann: *Premierenfieber*. München: Kindler, 1981: 345–366 ((--))

P-141 Discography in PREY, Hermann: *First night fever; the memoirs of Herman [sic] Prey*. London: Calder; New York: Riverrun Press, 1986: [277]–286 ((--))

PRICE, MARGARET, 1941–   **(British soprano)**

P-142 Discographische Hinweise: Margaret Price in *fono forum* (January 1983): 24 ((--))

PRÍHODA, VASA, 1900–1960 (Czech violinist)

P-143 Discographische Hinweise: Vasa Príhoda in *fono forum* (January 1982): 33 ((--))

PRIMROSE, WILLIAM, 1903–1982 (English violist)

P-144 Discography in PRIMROSE, William: *Walk on the north side: memoirs of a violist*. Provo, Utah: Brigham Young University Press, 1978: 223–232 ((--))

PROKOFIEV, SERGEI, 1891–1953 (Russian composer)

P-145 [[Prokofiev discography in SAMUEL, Claude: *Prokofiev*. Paris: Seuil, 1960: 179–185]]

P-146 Discography in HEERENOVÁ, Petra: *Skladatelé boje s osudem: Petr Iljič Čajkovskij, Sergej Prokofjev*. Brno: SVK, 1980: 36–38 ((--))

BALLETS

CINDERELLA (1944)

P-147 MARINELLI, Carlo: [Discography] in Roma, Teatro dell'Opera,

season 1971-72: program pp. 97-98 ((5))

ROMEO AND JULIET (1935)

P-148   MARINELLI, Carlo: [Discography] in Roma, Teatro dell'Opera,
season 1976-77: program pp. 108-111 ((5))

P-149   MARINELLI, Carlo: [Discography] in Milano, Teatro alla Scala,
season 1980-81: program p. 38 ((5))

P-150   MARINELLI, Carlo: [Discography] in Milano, Teatro alla Scala,
season 1983-84: program pp. 31-33 ((5))

STAGE WORKS

(THE) FIERY ANGEL (1925)

P-151   MARINELLI, Carlo: [Discography] in Roma, Teatro dell'Opera,
season 1965-66: program p. 565 ((5))

P-152   MARINELLI, Carlo: Discografie: Faust e Mefistofele nelle opere
teatrali e sinfonico-vocali in *Quaderni dell'I.R.TE.M.* [Instituto
di Ricerca per il Teatro Musicale] No. 3 (1986): 102-105 ((5))

(THE) LOVE FOR THREE ORANGES (1925)

P-153   MARINELLI, Carlo: [Discography] in Venezia, Gran Teatro La
Fenice, season 1970-71: program pp. 73-74 ((5))

WAR AND PEACE (1946)

P-154   MARINELLI, Carlo: [Discography] in Palermo, Ente automono
Teatro Massimo, season 1985-86: program p. 4 ((5))

SYMPHONIES

P-155   BARBIER, Pierre-E.: Discographie comparée: les symphonies de
Prokofiev in *Diapason-Harmonie*, No. 314 (March 1986): 103-106
((7))

SYMPHONY, No. 1, D Major, "Classical"

P-156   BARBIER, Pierre-E.: Discographie in *Diapason*, No. 204
(February 1976): 28 ((7)) [Includes timings]

PRYOR, ARTHUR, 1870-1942 (American trombonist, composer, conductor)

P-157   [[Discography in FRIZANE, Daniel E.: *Arthur Pryor (1870-1942),
American trombonist, bandmaster, composer.* [Dissertation, University
of Kansas, 1984] 193 pp.]]

PUCCINI, GIACOMO, 1858-1924 (Italian composer)

P-158   MARINELLI, Carlo: *La discografia, Giacomo Puccini.* Treviso: Ente
teatro comunale Autunno musicale trevigiano, [1974?]. 102 pp. ((7))

P-159   Discographie in GAUTHIER, André: *Puccini.* Paris: Seuil, 1976:
180-181 ((--)) [Originally issued 1961]

P-160 Discographies in BRAGAGLIA, Leonardo: *Personaggi ed interpreti del teatro di Puccini.* Roma: Trevi editore, 1977. 205 pp. ((--))

P-161 DE SCHAUENSEE, Max: *The Collector's Verdi and Puccini.* Westport, CT: Greenwood Press, 1978. 156 pp. ((--)) [Reprinted from the 1962 ed. published by Lippincott, New York]

P-162 Discografia essenziale in SEVERGNINI, Silvestro: *Invito all'ascolto di Giacomo Puccini.* Milano: Mursia, 1984: [189]-195 ((--))

OPERAS

(LA) BOHEME (1896)

P-163 MARINELLI, Carlo: [Discography] in Roma, Teatro dell'Opera, stagioni 1966: program pp. 699-704 ((5))

P-164 MARINELLI, Carlo: [Discography] in Treviso, Ente Teatro Comunale, Autunno Musicale Trevigiano 1977-1978: program p. 19 ((5))

P-165 [[Discography in *L'Avant Scène Opéra*, No. 20 [1978?]]]

P-166 MARINELLI, Carlo: [Discography] in Milano, Teatro alla Scala, Opera Concerto Balletto, season 1979: program pp. 66-68 ((5))

P-167 MARINELLI, Carlo: [Discography] in Milano, Teatro alla Scala, season 1980-81: pp. 66-67 ((5))

P-168 MARINELLI, Carlo: [Discography] in Palermo, Ente autonomo del Teatro Massimo, anno artistico 1981-1982: program p. 58 ((5))

P-169 SCHREIBER, Ulrich: Anmerkungen zur Diskographie in *La Bohème: Texte, Materialien, Kommentäre.* Reinbek bei Hamburg: Rowohlt, 1981: 278-280 ((5)) (Rororo Opernbücher)

P-170 HOYLE, Martin: Discography in *La Bohème.* London: J. Calder; New York: Riverrun Press, 1982: 109 ((--)) (English National Opera guide; 14)

P-171 Selected discography in *Giacomo Puccini, La Bohème.* Boston: Little, Brown [1983]: 165-171 ((5))

P-172 MARINELLI, Carlo: [Discography] in Roma, Teatro dell'Opera, season 1985-86: program pp. 50-62 ((5))

P-173 WALKER, Malcolm: Discography in GROOS, Arthur: *Giacomo Puccini, La Bohème.* Cambridge; New York: Cambridge University Press, 1986: 192-195 ((5)) (Cambridge opera handbooks)

P-174 [[[Discography] in *La Bohème: in der Originalsprache (Italienisch mit deutscher Übersetzung.* München: Goldmann; Mainz: B. Schott's Söhne, 1987: 272-277 (Opern der Welt)]]

(LA) FANCIULLA DEL WEST (1910)

P-175 MARINELLI, Carlo: [Discography] in Roma, Teatro dell'Opera,

season 1980-81: program pp. 626-636 ((5))

GIANNI SCHICCHI (1918)

P-176   MARINELLI, Carlo: [Discography] in Venezia, Teatro La Fenice, Lirica 1979-1980: program pp. 127-132 ((5))

P-177   MARINELLI, Carlo: [Discography] in Milano, Teatro alla Scala, season 1982-83: program p. 103 ((5))

P-178   CABOURG, Jean: Discographie and VOISIN, Georges and CABOURG, Jean: Airs sépares in *L'Avant Scène Opéra*, No. 82 (December 1985): 82-85 ((1, 7))

MADAMA BUTTERFLY (1904)

P-179   MARINELLI, Carlo: [Discography] in Roma, Teatro dell'Opera, season 1966-67: program pp. 121-125 ((5))

P-180   MARINELLI, Carlo: [Discography] in Venezia, Teatro La Fenice, season lirica 1971-72: program pp. 405-413 ((5))

P-181   MARINELLI, Carlo: [Discography] in Venezia, Teatro La Fenice, season lirica 1973-74: program pp. 365-382 ((5))

P-182   MARINELLI, Carlo: [Discography] in Treviso, Ente Teatro Comunale, Autunno Musicale Trevigiano, 1979: program   p. 20 ((5))

P-183   MARINELLI, Carlo: [Discography] in Venezia, Teatro La Fenice, season 1981-82: program pp. 391-401 ((5))

P-184   CABOURG, Jean: Discographie and VOISIN, Georges: Airs séparés in *L'Avant Scène Opéra*, No. 56 (October 1983): 118-[127] ((1, 7))

P-185   MARINELLI, Carlo: [Discography] in Palermo, Ente automono Teatro Massimo, season 1983-84: program p. 15 ((5))

P-186   HOYLE, Martin: Discography in *Madam Butterfly: Madama Butterfly*. London: J. Calder; New York: Riverrun Press, 1984: 126-127 ((--)) (English National Opera guide; 26)

P-187   THALMANN, Albert: Diskographie in *Madama Butterfly: in der originalsprache*. München: Goldmann; Mainz: Schott, 1984: 300-[303] ((1, 7)) (Opern der Welt)

P-188   MARINELLI, Carlo: [Discography] in Milano, Teatro alla Scala, season 1985-86: program pp. 112-117 ((5))

P-189   MARINELLI, Carlo: [Discography] in Palermo, Ente automono Teatro Massimo, season 1985-86 program pp. ((5))

MANON LESCAUT (1893)

P-190   MARINELLI, Carlo: [Discography] in Venezia, Teatro La Fenice, Opera Balletto 1977-1978: program pp. 282-290 ((5))

P-191   MARINELLI, Carlo: [Discography] in Roma, Teatro dell'Opera,

season 1978-79: program p. 716   ((5))

P-192   GUANDALINI, Gina: Le Manon di Puccini in *Musica*, No. 23
(November 1981): 369   ((3, 5))

P-193   MARINELLI, Carlo: [Discography] in Venezia, Teatro La Fenice,
season 1983: program pp. 545-547   ((5))

(LA) RONDINE (1917)

P-194   MARINELLI, Carlo: [Discography] in Roma, Teatro dell'Opera,
season 1971-72: program pp. 156-161   ((5))

P-195   MARINELLI, Carlo: [Discography] in Venezia, Teatro La Fenice,
season lirica 1972-73: program pp. 295-296   ((5))

P-196   MARINELLI, Carlo: [Discography] in Palermo, Ente automono
Teatro Massimo, season 1985-86: program p. 4   ((5))

SUOR ANGELICA (1918)

P-197   MARINELLI, Carlo: [Discography] in Milano, Teatro alla Scala,
statione d'opera e balletto 1972-1973: program pp. 538-539   ((5))

P-198   MARINELLI, Carlo: [Discography] in Milano, Teatro alla Scala,
season 1982-83: program p. 83   ((5))

(IL) TABARRO (1918)

P-199   MARINELLI, Carlo: [Discography] in Roma, Teatro dell'Opera,
season 1969-1970: program pp. 198-199   ((5))

P-200   MARINELLI, Carlo: [Discography] in Milano, Teatro alla Scala,
season 1982-83: program p. 63   ((5))

P-201   MARINELLI, Carlo: [Discography] in Milano, Teatro alla Scala,
season 1986-87: program p. 55   ((5))

TOSCA (1900)

P-202   MARINELLI, Carlo: [Discography] in Roma, Teatro dell'Opera,
season 1965-66: program pp. 37-41   ((5))

P-203   MARINELLI, Carlo: [Discography] in Venezia, Teatro La Fenice,
season lirica 1970-71: program pp. 257-264   ((5))

P-204   MARINELLI, Carlo: [Discography] in Roma, Teatro dell'Opera,
season 1970-71: program pp. 279-287   ((5))

P-205   MARINELLI, CARLO: [Discography] in Venezia, Teatro La Fenice,
season lirica 1973-74: program pp. 215-227   ((5))

P-206   MARINELLI, Carlo: [Discography] in Roma, Teatro dell'Opera,
stagione 1977-1978: program pp. 364-366   ((5))

P-207   MANNONI, Gérard: Discographie in *L'Avant Scène Opéra*, No. 11
(Sepember-October 1977): 106-116   ((1, 3, 5, 6))

P-208   MARINELLI, Carlo: [Discography] in Venezia, Teatro La Fenice,
         Opera Balletto 1978–1979: program pp. 170–184   ((5))

P-209   MARINELLI, Carlo: [Discography] in Roma, Teatro dell'Opera,
         season 1979–80: program pp. 238–240   ((5))

P-210   MARINELLI, Carlo: [Discography] in Milano, Teatro alla Scala,
         season 1979–80: program pp. 80–81   ((5))

P-211   MARINELLI, Carlo: [Discography] in Treviso, Ente Teatro
         Comunale, Autunno Musical Trevigiano 1980: program p. 29   ((5))

P-212   MARINELLI, Carlo: [Discography] in Roma, Teatro dell'Opera,
         season 1981–82: program pp. 366–372   ((5))

P-213   HOYLE, Martin: [Discography] in *Tosca*. London: J. Calder; New
         York: Riverrun Press, 1982: 78–79   ((––)) (English National
         Opera guide; 16)

P-214   MARINELLI, Carlo: [Discography] in Palermo, Ente autonomo
         Teatro Massimo, anno artistico 1982–1983: program p. 83   ((5))

P-215   THALMANN, Albert: Diskographie in *Tosca: in der original–sprache*.
         München: Goldmann; Mainz: Schott, 1984: 296–[300]   ((1, 7,))
         (Opern der Welt)

P-216   WALKER, Malcolm: Discography in CARNER, Mosco: *Giacomo Puccini,
         Tosca*. Cambridge; New York: Cambridge University Press, 1985:
         159–161   ((5)) (Cambridge opera handbooks)

P-217   Discographische Hinweise in *fono forum* (May 1987): 28   ((1, 7))

TURANDOT (1926)

P-218   MARINELLI, Carlo: [Discography] in Roma, Teatro dell'Opera,
         season 1965–66: program pp. 232–235   ((5))

P-219   [[[Discography] in *Record Geijutsu*, No. 9 (1971):]]

P-220   MARINELLI, Carlo: [Discography] in Bologna, Ente automono
         Teatro Comunale, Opera e Balletto 1978–1979: pp. 50–70   ((5))

P-221   ARNAUD, Alain: Le point sur Turandot au disque in *Diapason*, No.
         241 (July–August 1979): 36–38   ((5))

P-222   DUTRONC, Jean–Louis: Discographie in *L'Avant Scène Opéra*, No.
         33 (May–June 1981): 106–111   ((1, 7))

P-223   MARINELLI, Carlo: [Discography] in Milano, Teatro alla Scala,
         season 1983–84: program pp. 119–123   ((5))

P-224   HOYLE, Martin: Discography in *Turandot*. London: J. Calder; New
         York: Riverrun Press, 1984: 110–111   ((––)) (English National
         Opera guide; 27)

P-225   MARINELLI, Carlo: [Discography] in Milano, Teatro alla Scala,
         season 1984–85: program p. 119   ((5))

PURCELL, HENRY, ca. 1659-1695 (English composer)

P-226 GREENHALGH, Michael: *The music of Henry Purcell.* Eastcote: Greenhalgh, 1982. 40 pp. ((4))

OPERAS

DIDO AND AENEAS (1689)

P-227 [Discography in *L'Avant Scène Opéra*, No. 18 [1978]]]

P-228 [[[Discography] in HARRIS, Ellen T.: *Henry Purcell's Dido and Aeneas.* Oxford; New York: Oxford University Press, 1987]]

QUARTETTO ITALIANO

Q-1 Discography [on Philips label] S.l. [Philips, 198-?] 2 l. ((--))

Q-2 ANDREONI, Sergio: Discografia Quartetto Italiano in *Musica*, No. 37 (December 1984): 31-34 ((7))

QUILTER, ROGER, 1877-1953 (English composer)

Q-3 FOREMAN, Lewis: Discography of Quilter solo songs in HOLD, Trevor: *The walled-in garden: a study of the songs of Roger Quilter (1877-1953)* Rickmansworth: Triad Press, 1978: 57-60 ((--))

RABIN, MICHAEL, 1931-1972 (American violinist)

R-1 PAYNE, Ifan: Michael Rabin discography in *American Record Guide*, XLIV/5 (March 1981): 22-24 ((5))

RACHMANINOFF, SERGEI, 1873-1943 (Russian composer)

R-2 [[[Discography] in ZELINA, Marina and LEVINA, E. E.: *Russaia klassicheskaia muzyka.* Moskva: Isd. Kniga", 1971   174 pp.]]

R-3 WILE, Raymond R.: The Edison recordings of Sergei Rachmaninoff in *American Record Guide*, XL/3 (March 1977): 11-12 ((3, 6, 7))

R-4 Rachmaninoff discography in PALMIERI, Robert: *Sergei Vasil'evich Rachmaninoff: a guide to research.* New York: Garland Pub., 1985: 93-118 ((3, 6, 7)) (Garland composer resource manuals; 3)

CONCERTOS, PIANO

PIANO CONCERTO, No. 1, F-sharp minor, Op. 1

R-5 Diskographie in BUTZBACH, Fritz: *Studien zum Klavierkonzert Nr. 1, fis-moll, op. 1.* Regensburg: G. Bosse, 1979: 320-321 ((--))

PIANO CONCERTO, No. 3, D minor, Op. 30

R-6 LISCHKE, André: Le 3e concerto de Rachmaninov discographie in *Diapason-Harmonie*, No. 318 (July-August 1986): 87-89 ((--))

RAIMONDI, RUGGERO, 1941-   (Italian bass)

R-7   Discographie in SEGALINI, Sergio: *Ruggero Raimondi*. Paris: Fayard,
       1981: [94]-95   ((--))

R-8   Discographie in *Harmonie-Panorama musique*, No. 41 (April 1984): 19
       ((--))

RAKHMADIEV, ERKEGALI, 1932-   (Kazak composer)

R-9   [Discography] in *Music in the USSR* (April-June 1986): 91   ((--))

RAMEAU, JEAN-PHILIPPE, 1683-1764 (French composer)

R-10   ANDERSON, Nicholas: Complete discography of music from Rameau's
       stage works in *Early Music*, IV/4 (October 1976): 499-501   ((--))

R-11   [[ARNE, F.: Discographie de Rameau in *Rameau le coloriste
       instrumental*. Paris: Musée instrumental du Conservatoire, 1983:
       120-127]]

R-12   CRESTA, Michel: Rameau à écouter in *Diapason*, No. 285 (July-August
       1983): 23   ((--))

STAGE WORKS

(LES) INDES GALANTES (1735)

R-13   FAUQUET, Joël-Marie: Discographie in *L'Avant Scène Opéra*, No. 46
       (December 1982): 118-122   ((7))

KEYBOARD WORKS

PIÈCES DE CLAVECIN

R-14   HALBREICH, Harry: Rameau et le disque in *Harmonie-Opéra-Hifi
       Conseil*, No. 22 (July 1982): 42-50   ((--))

RAMEY, SAMUEL, 1942-   (American bass)

R-15   Discography [on Philips label] S.l. [Philips, 198-?] 1 leaf.
       ((--))

RAMOVS, PRIMOZ, 1921-   (Yugoslav composer)

R-16   Zvocni zapisi del Primoza Ramovsa na ploscah in kasetah in RAMOVS,
       Primoz: *Biti skladatelj: pogovori s Primozem Ramovsem*.
       Ljubljana: Slovenska matica, 1984: 269-271   ((--))

RATTLE, SIMON, 1955-   (English conductor)

R-17   Discographische Hinweise in *fono forum* (July 1985): 30   ((--))

R-18   Discography in KENYON, Nicholas: *Simon Rattle; the making of a
       conductor*. London; Boston: Faber & Faber, 1987: 237-240   ((7))

RAUCH, FRANTIŠEK, 1910-   (Czech pianist)

R-19   Diskografie in KŘÍŽ, Jaromír: *František Rauch*. Praha: Editio
       Supraphon, 1985: 86-[87]   ((--))

RAVEL, MAURICE, 1875-1937   (French composer)

R-20   A selected discography from Great Britain and America in
        JANKÉLÉVITCH, Vladimir: *Ravel*. Westport, CT: Greenwood
        Press, 1975: 190-191 ((--)) [Reprinted from the 1959 ed. published
        by Grove Press, New York]

R-21   Diszkografia in PANDI, Marianne: *Maurice Ravel*. Budapest:
        Gondolat, 1978: 196-[203] ((--))

BALLETS

DAPHNIS ET CHLOÉ (1912)

R-22   MARINELLI, Carlo: [Discography] in Venezia, Teatro La Fenice,
        season 1970-71: program pp. 176-180 ((5))

ORCHESTRAL WORKS

BOLÉRO (1927)

R-23   MARINELLI, Carlo: [Discography] in Roma, Teatro dell'Opera,
        season 1968-69: program pp. 378-387 ((5))

R-24   FANTAPIÉ, Alain: Le point sur Le boléro de Maurice Ravel in
        Diapason, No. 247 (February 1980): 44-45 ((--))

R-25   Discografia in TOZZI, Lorenzo: *Bolero: storia di un'ossessione*.
        Roma: Di Giacomo, 1981: 132 ((--))

PIANO WORKS

R-26   SAINT-PULGENT, Maryvonne de: Le piano de Ravel: discographie
        critique in *Harmonie-Opéra-Hifi Conseil*, No. 24 (October 1982):
        30-41 ((--))

GASPARD DE LA NUIT (1908)

R-27   WISSOTZKY, Joel: Gaspard de la nuit de Maurice Ravel: discographie
        critique in *Diapason*, No. 220 (September 1977): 36-37 ((--))

RAWSTHORNE, ALAN, 1905-1971   (English composer)

R-28   [[[Discography] in POULTON, Alan: *Alan Rawsthorne: a catalogue of
        his music*. [Kidderminster]: Bravura Publications, 1985?]]

RAYNER, SYDNEY, 1895-1981   (American tenor)

R-29   BOTT, Michael F.: Sydney Rayner--discography in *Record Collector*,
        XXVIII/1-2 (May 1983): 38-41; additions and corrections in XXX/12-13
        (December 1985): 293-295 ((1, 3, 6, 7))

REA, VIRGINIA   (American soprano)

R-30   FERRARA, Dennis E.: The Edison discography in *Record Collector*,
        XXXII/11-12 (November 1987): 259-260 ((3, 7)) [Includes unissued
        records]

R-31   FERRARA, D. E.: Neglected Edison Diamon Disc artists: Virginia Rea in *New Amberola Graphic*, No. 63 (January 1988): 11 ((3, 7))

REDDICK, WILLIAM J., 1890-1965 (American composer)

R-32   [[Discography in BRADLEY, Bonnie Cave: *William J. Reddick, composer-musician*. [Dissertation, University of Kentucky, 1986] 356 pp.]]

REGAMEY, CONSTANTIN, 1907-   (Swiss composer)

R-33   Discographie in LOUTAN-CHARBON, Nicole: *Constantin Regamey, compositeur*. Yverdon: Édition Revue musicale de Suisse romande: Éditions de la Thièle, 1978: 138 ((--))

REGENSBURGER DOMSPATZEN, West Germany

R-34   Discographische Hinweise: Regensburger Domspatzen in *fono forum* (December 1982): 76 ((--))

REGER, MAX, 1873-1916 (German composer)

R-35   Diskographie in *Diskographien herausgegeben anlässlich des 50. Todestages von Max Reger und des 100. Geburtstages von Ferruccio Busoni*. Berlin: Deutsche Musik-Phonothek, 1966: 13-77 ((4))

R-36   Discography in GRIM, William E.: *Max Reger: a bio-bibliography*. New York: Greenwood Press, 1988: [45]-59 ((--)) (Bio-bibliographies in music; 7)

REICH, STEVE, 1936-   (American composer)

R-37   [[[Discography] in *View* (September 1978: ?]]

REICHA, ANTON, 1770-1836 (Czech composer)

R-38   Diskografie in SOTOLOVA, Olga: *Antonin Rejcha*. Praha: Supraphon, 1977: 81-82 ((--))

R-39   YOELL, John H.: A Reicha discography in *Fanfare*, IX/3 (January-February 1986): 64-69 ((--))

REINER, FRITZ, 1888-1963 (Hungarian conductor)

R-40   Reiner at the Met on disc in *The Podium*, I/1 (1976): 9-10 ((7))

R-41   HELMBRECHT, Art: *Fritz Reiner: the comprehensive discography of his recordings*. Novelty, Ohio: Fritz Reiner Society, 1978. 79 pp. ((1, 5, 7)); *Supplement No. 1* (9 pp.) with corrections and amendments (4 pp.) Madison, NJ: A. J. Helmbrecht, 1981.

R-42   DETTMER, Roger: Reiner [discography] in *Fanfare*, V/2 (November-December 1981): 67-69 ((--))

REINHARDT, DELIA, 1892-1974 (German soprano)

R-43   TUBEUF, André: Delia Reinhardt discography in *Record Collector*, XXIII/7-8 (December 1976): 162-163 ((3, 6, 7))

REINMAR, HANS, 1895-1961 (German baritone)

R-44   [[[Discography] in *Stimmen, die um die Welt gingen*, No. 10 December 1985): 48-51; No. 15 (March 1987): 24-33]]

REĬZEN, MARK OSIPOVICH, 1895-   (Russian bass)

R-45   [Discography] in REĬZEN, Mark: *Mark Reĭzen*. Moskva: Vses. izd-vo "Sov. kompozitor", 1980: 265-280 ((5))

R-46   LINNELL, Norman: Discography in *Record Collector*, XXVIII/1-2 (May 1983): 12-31 ((4, 6, 7))

R-47   [Discography] in *Music in the USSR* (October-December 1985): 82 ((--))

RESPIGHI, OTTORINO, 1879-1936 (Italian composer)

R-48   MODUGNO, Maurizio: *Ottorino Respighi (1879-1936), discografia*. Roma: Comitato nazionale per le celebrazioni del centenario della nascità di Ottorino Respighi, 1979. 79 pp. ((4, 5))

R-49   Adriano Records: *An international Respighi discography*. Zürich: Adriano Records, 1980. [53 pp.] ((4, 5, 7))

R-50   MODUGNO, Maurizio: Ottorino Respighi--discografia in *Discoteca Hifi*, No. 217 (May 1981): 14-19 ((3, 5)))

R-51   Discografia in CANTÙ, Alberto: *Respighi compositore*. Torino: EDA, 1985: 220-233 ((5))

STAGE WORKS

(LA) BOUTIQUE FANTASQUE (1919)

R-52   MARINELLI, Carlo: [Discography] in Roma, Teatro dell'Opera, season 1966-67: program pp. 85-87 ((5))

R-53   MARINELLI, Carlo: [Discography] in Roma, Teatro dell'Opera, season 1981-82: program pp. 767-769 ((5))

REVEL, MARGUERITE (French soprano)

R-54   [Discography] in *Record Collector*, IX/3 (March 1954): 70 ((--))

REYNOLDS, ROGER, 1934-   (American composer)

R-55   Selected discography in Program notes for *Works of Paul Chihara, Chou Wen-Chung, Earl Kim, Roger Reynolds*. [Sound recording] New World Records NW 237, 1977: 2 ((--))

R-56   Discography in *Roger Reynolds, profile of a composer*. New York: C.F. Peters Corp., 1982: 42 ((--))

RIBERIO, AGNALDO, 1943-   (Brazilian composer)

R-57   Discographic references in MIGLIAVACCA, Ariede Maria: *Agnaldo*

Riberio: catálogo de obras. [Brasília]: Ministério das Relações
Exteriores, Departamento de Cooperação Cultural, Científica e
Tecnológica, 1979: [16] pp. ((--)) (Compositores brasileiros)

RICCI, RUGGIERO, 1918–   (American violinist)

R-58   Discography in *Records & Recording,* No. 270 (March 1980): 20-21
((--))

RICCIARELLI, KATIA, 1946–   (Italian soprano)

R-59   Discography [on Philips label] S.l. [Philips, 198-?] 1 leaf.
((--))

R-60   Discographie in *Harmonie-Panorama musique,* No. 32 (June 1983):
20 ((--))

RICHTER, KARL, 1926–1981   (German conductor)

R-61   [Discography] in *Record Geijutsu,* No. 276 (September 1973): 186-187
((--))

R-62   [Karl Richter discography] in *Record Geijutsu,* No. 367 (April 1981):
140-143 ((5, 7))

R-63   [Karl Richter discography] in *Stereo Geijutsu,* No. 173 (May 1981):
111-117 ((7))

R-64   Discographische Hinweise: Orgelaufnahmen mit Karl Richter in *fono
forum* (April 1982): 38 ((--))

RICHTER, SVIATOSLAV, 1915–   (Russian pianist)

R-65   TADAO, Koishi: Richter [Discography] in *Record Geijutsu,* No. 239
(November 1970): 252-255 ((--))

R-66   MASINI, Umberto: Richter e il disco in *Discoteca Alta Fedeltà,* No.
160 (May 1976): 8-[31] ((7))

R-67   Discographie Sviatoslav Richter in *fono forum* (August 1982): 20-27
((--))

R-68   MASINI, Umberto: Discografia di Sviatoslav Richter in *Musica,* No. 26
(October 1982): 278-280, 282, 284-286 ((7))

R-69   SCHWARZ, Falk and BERRIE, John: Sviatoslav Richter--a discography
in *Recorded Sound,* No. 84 (July 1983): 7-71 ((5, 7))

R-70   Discography in *Music in the USSR* (July-September 1985): 13-17 ((--))

RIEGGER, WALLINGFORD, 1885–1961   (American composer)

R-71   [[Discography in GATEWOOD, Dwight Dean, Jr.: *Wallingford Riegger: a
biography and analysis of selected works.* [Dissertation, Peabody
College, 1970] 305 pp.]]

RIETI, VITTORIO, 1898–   (Italian composer)

R-72   Discografia in RICCI, Franco Carlo: *Vittorio Rieti.* Napoli:
        Edizioni scientifiche italiane, 1987: [523]-530 ((--))

RIHM, WOLFGANG, 1952-   (German composer)

R-73   Discographische Hinweise: Wolfgang Rihm in *fono forum* (August 1982):
        34-36, 38 ((--))

RIMSKY-KORSAKOV, NIKOLAI, 1844-1908   (Russian composer)

STAGE WORKS

CHRISTMAS EVE (1895)

R-74   MARINELLI, Carlo: [Discography] in Bologna, Teatro Comunale,
        season 1976-77: program p. 3 ((5))

MOZART AND SALIERI (1898)

R-75   MARINELLI, Carlo: [Discography] in Venezia, Teatro La Fenice,
        season 1976-77: program pp. 194-196 ((5))

ROBIN, MADO, 1918-1960   (French soprano)

R-76   PARYLAK, Robert: Mado Robin discography in *Kastlemusik Monthly
        Bulletin,* IV/12 (December 1979): 22-23 ((3, 7))

ROCHBERG, GEORGE, 1928-   (American composer)

R-77   [[Discography in SMITH, Joan Templar: *The string quartets of George
        Rochberg.* [Dissertation, University of Rochester, 1976] 331 pp.]]

R-78   Selected discography in Program notes for *George Rochberg: Concerto
        for oboe and orchestra.* [Sound recording] New World Records NW 335,
        1986 ((--))

        See also

        PIANO MUSIC

RODE, WILHELM, 1887-1959   (German baritone)

R-79   [[[Discography] in *Stimmen, die um die Welt Gingen,* No. 12 (June
        1986): 45-50]]

RODRIGO, JOAQUÍN, 1901-   (Spanish composer)

R-80   Discografia in VAYA PIA, Vicente: *Joaquín Rodrigo: su vida y su
        obra.* Madrid: Real Musical, D.L., 1977: [229]-236 ((--))

R-81   Discografia in KAMHI, Victoria: *De la mano de Joaquín Rodrigo:
        historia de nuestra vida.* Madrid: Fundación Banco Exterior, 1986:
        421-429 ((--))

RODZINSKI, ARTUR, 1892-1958   (Polish conductor)

R-82   GRAY, Michael: Artur Rodzinski on records in RODZINSKI, Halina:
        Our two lives. New York: Scribners, 1976: 389-391 ((7))

R-83   GRAY, Michael: Artur Rodzinski: a discography in *Recorded Sound*,
        No. 73 (January 1979): 10-19   ((3, 4, 6, 7))

ROELSTRAETE, HERMAN, 1925–   **(Belgian composer)**

R-84   [[WILLAERT, Hendrik: Herman Roelstraete ein Portret in *Ons Erfdeel*,
        XXI/2 (March–April 1980): 286–289]]

RÖSEL, PETER, 1945–   **(German pianist)**

R-85   Schallplattenverzeichnis (Auswahl) in MÜLLER, Hans–Peter:
        Peter Rösel: für Sie Porträiert. Leipzig: Deutscher Verlag für
        Musik, 1986: 65–[68]   ((--))

ROGÉ, PASCAL, 1951–   **(French pianist)**

R-86   Discography in *Harmonie–Panorama musique*, No. 48 (December 1984):
        45   ((--))

ROGG, LIONEL, 1936–   **(Swiss organist)**

R-87   BRAS, Jean–Yves: Discographie in *Diapason*, No. 210 (October 1976):
        21   ((--)

ROLLA, ALESSANDRO, 1757–1841   (Italian violinist)

R-88   Discografia in INZAGHI, Luigi: *Alessandro Rolla.* [Milano]: La
        Spiga, 1984: [100]   ((--))

ROMERO Family

R-89   Los Romeros: Diskografie [auf Philips–Schallplatten] in Ein Romero
        kommt selten allein in *fono forum* (June 1978): 598   ((--))

R-90   Discography [on Philips label] S.l. [Philips, 198-] 1 leaf.   ((--))

ROMERO, PEPE, 1942–   **(Spanish guitarist)**

R-91   Discography [on Philips label] S.l. [Philips, 198-?]   2 l.   ((--))

ROPARTZ, GUY, 1864–1955   (French composer)

        See entry for

        COMPOSERS, FRENCH

ROREM, NED, 1923–   **(American composer)**

R-92   Selected discography in Program notes for *William Parker recital.*
        [Sound recording] New World Records NW 305, 1980   ((--))

ROSBAUD, HANS, 1895–1962   (German conductor)

R-93   GERBER, Leslie: Discografia Rosbaud in *Musica*, No. 30 (October
        1983): 291–293   ((3, 7))

ROSS, SCOTT, 1951–   **(American harpsichordist)**

R-94   Discographie in *Diapason-Harmonie*, No. 334 (January 1988): 55
        ((--))

ROSSINI, GIOACHINO ANTONIO, 1792-1868   (Italian composer)

R-95   MARINELLI, Carlo: La discografia rossiniana in *Bollettino del Centro
        Rossiniano di Studi*, No. 4-6 (1968): 164-177   ((--))

R-96   GARIAZZO, Aurelio: Discografia in ROGNONI, Luigi: *Gioacchino
        Rossini*. Torino: G. Einaudi, 1977: [519]-543   ((--))

R-97   Discografia essenziale in MIOLI, Piero: *Invito all'ascolto di
        Gioacchino Rossini*. Milano: Mursia, 1986: [245]-247   ((--))

OPERAS

R-98   GUANDALINI, Gina: Le opere serie di Rossini in disco in *Musica*,
        No. 26 (October 1982): 298-304   ((5))

(IL) BARBIERE DI SIVIGLIA (1816)

R-99   MARINELLI, Carlo: [Discography] in Roma, Teatro dell'Opera,
        season 1966-67: program pp. 638-641   ((5))

R-100   MARINELLI, Carlo: [Discography] in Roma, Teatro dell'Opera,
        season 1971-72: program pp. 23-28   ((5))

R-101   MARINELLI, Carlo: [Discography] in Treviso, Ente Teatro
        Comunale, season 1976: program p. 10   ((5))

R-102   MARINELLI, Carlo: [Discography] in Bologna, Teatro Comunale,
        season 1976-77: program p. 17   ((5))

R-103   MARINELLI, Carlo: [Discography] in Venezia, Teatro La Fenice,
        season 1978-79: program pp. 387-397   ((5))

R-104   SEGALINI, Sergio: Discographie in *L'Avant Scène Opéra*, No. 37
        (November-December 1981): 142-147   ((1, 7))

R-105   MARINELLI, Carlo: [Discography] in Palermo, Ente automono
        Teatro Massimo, season 1982-83: program p. 42   ((5))

R-106   Discografia selezionata in GUANDALINI, Gina: Il Barbiere di
        Siviglia--edizione 1982 in *Musica*, No. 28 (March 1983): 63-64
        ((5)) [Lacks issue numbers]

R-107   MARINELLI, Carlo: Discografia in Il Barbiere di Siviglia:
        season d'opera e balletto 1984-85. [Milano]: Teatro alla Scala:
        Mondadori, 1985: 73-75   ((5))

R-108   PETERSON, Cathy: Selective discography in *The Barber of
        Seville/Moses = Il Barbiere di Sivilgia/Moïse et Pharaon*.
        London: J. Calder; New York: Riverrun Press, 1985: 159   ((5))
        (English National Opera guide; 36)

R-109   THALMANN, Albert: Diskographie in *Der Barbier von Sevilla*.
        München: Goldmann; Mainz: Schott, 1985: 300-303   ((1, 5))

(Opern der Welt)

R-110   MARINELLI, Carlo: [Discography] in Roma, Teatro dell'Opera,
season 1985-86: program pp. 48-60 ((5))

(LA) CENERENTOLA (1817)

R-111   MARINELLI, Carlo: [Discography] in Roma, Teatro dell'Opera,
season 1967-68: program pp. 440-442 ((5))

R-112   ROSENTHAL, Harold: La Cenerentola in *Opera*, XXVII/3 (March 1976):
215-224 ((1, 5)) (Opera on the gramophone; 37)

R-113   [[[Discography] in *Gioacchino Rossini, La Cenerentola* ...
München: Bayerische Staatsoper, 1980: 78]]

R-114   Discography in *La Cenerentola = (Cinderella)* London: J. Calder;
New York: Riverrun Press, 1980: 96-97 ((--)) (English National
Opera guide; 1)

R-115   MARINELLI, Carlo: [Discography] in Bologna, Teatro Comunale,
season 1980-81: program pp. 48-57 ((5))

R-116   MARINELLI, Carlo: [Discography] in Roma, Teatro dell'Opera,
season 1983-84: program pp. 62-68 ((5))

R-117   MARTIN, Serge: Discographie in *L'Avant Scène Opéra*, No. 85
(March 1986): 100-106 ((1, 5))

(LE) COMTE ORY (1828)

R-118   MARINELLI, Carlo: [Discography] in Roma, Teatro dell'Opera,
season 1969-70: program p. 238 ((5))

R-119   MARINELLI, Carlo: [Discography] in Palermo, Ente automono
Teatro Massimo, season 1980-81: program p. 7 ((5))

(LA) GAZZA LADRA (1817)

R-120   CABOURG, Jean: La gazza ladra au disque in *L'Avant Scène Opéra*,
No. 110 (June 1988): 104-105 ((7))

L'ITALIANA IN ALGERI (1816)

R-121   MARINELLI, Carlo: [Discography] in Venezia, Teatro La Fenice,
season 1970-71: program pp. 287-288 ((5))

R-122   MARINELLI, Carlo: [Discography] in Milano, Teatro alla Scala,
season 1972-73: program pp. 606-609 ((5))

R-123   MARINELLI, Carlo: [Discography] in Treviso, Ente Teatro
Comunale, season 1975: program p. 3 ((5))

R-124   TUBEUF, André: Discographie comparée: L'Italienne à Alger in
Diapason-Harmonie, No. 315 (April 1986): 104-105 ((5))

R-125   MARINELLI, Carlo: [Discography] in Milano, Teatro alla Scala,
season 1983-84: program pp. 63-68 ((5))

R-126   MARINELLI, Carlo: [Discography] in Venezia, Teatro La Fenice, season 1984: program pp. 334-338 ((5))

R-127   MARINELLI, Carlo: [Discography] in Roma, Teatro dell'Opera, season 1986-87: program pp. 57-61 ((5))

MOSÈ IN EGITTO (1818)

R-128   MARINELLI, Carlo: [Discography] in Roma, Teatro dell'Opera, season 1970-71: program pp. 442-443 ((5))

R-129   MARINELLI, Carlo: [Discography] in Milano, Teatro alla Scala, season 1979: program pp. 60-61 ((5))

R-130   MARINELLI, Carlo: [Discography] in Treviso, Ente Teatro Comunale, season 1980: program p. 2 ((5))

(LA) PIETRA DEL PARAGONE (1812)

R-131   MARINELLI, Carlo: [Discography] in Milano, Teatro alla Scala, season 1981-82: program pp. 88-89 ((5))

R-132   MARINELLI, Carlo: [Discography] in Milano, Teatro alla Scala, season 1982-83: program pp. 67-69 ((5))

SEMIRAMIDE (1823)

R-133   MARINELLI, Carlo: [Discography] in Roma, Teatro dell'Opera, season 1982-83: program pp. 137-140 ((5))

R-134   [[MODUGNO, Maurizio and BOTTAZZI, Alberto: *Discografia. Semiramide. Giacomo Rossini.* Roma: Discoteca di stato, 1983. n.p.]]

(LE) SIÈGE DE CORINTHE (1826)

R-135   SEGALINI, Sergio: Discographie in *L'Avant-Scène Opéra*, No. 81 (November 1985): 90-92 ((1, 7))

TANDREDI (1813)

R-136   MARINELLI, Carlo: [Discography] in Roma, Teatro dell'Opera, season 1977-78: program pp. 32-34 ((5))

R-137   MARINELLI, Carlo: [Discography] in Venezia, Teatro La Fenice, season 1981-82: program pp. 140-143 ((5))

R-138   MARINELLI, Carlo: [Discography] in Palermo, Ente automono Teatro Massimo, season 1986-87: program p. 5 (5))

(IL) TURCO IN ITALIA (1814)

R-139   MARINELLI, Carlo: [Discography] in Roma, Teatro dell'Opera, season 1968-69: program pp. 134-136 ((5))

R-140   MARINELLI, Carlo: [Discography] in Venezia, Teatro La Fenice, season 1979-80: program pp. 35-37 ((5))

R-141   MARINELLI, Carlo: [Discography] in Roma, Teatro dell'Opera, season 1982-83: program pp. 550-553 ((5))

ROSTROPOVICH, MSTISLAV, 1927-   (Russian cellist)

R-142 Discography, Deutsche Grammophon artist information, 1980. 2 pp. ((--))

R-143 Discographie in ROSTROPOVITCH, Mstislav: *Entretiens avec Mstislav Rostropovitch et Galina Vichnevskaïa sur la Russie, la musique, la liberté.* Paris: Éditions R. Laffont, 1983: 195-[206] ((--))

R-144 Rostropovitch; une discographie in *Diapason-Harmonie*, No. 340 (July-August 1988): 32-34 ((7))

ROSVAENGE, HELGE, 1897-1972 (Danish tenor)

R-145 DENNIS, J.: Helge Rosvaenge-discography in *Record Collector*, XXIII/5-6 (September 1976): 118-140; MORTENSEN, Erik B.: Rosvaenge addenda in *Record Collector*, XXVI/9-10 (May 1981): 235-236 ((3, 4, 6, 7))

R-146 COLLINS, William J.: Rosvaenge on LP in *Record Collector*, XXV/5-6 (August 1979): 123-140; additions & corrections in XXVI/9-10 (May 1981): 235-236; addendum in XXXIII/8-10 (August 1988): 249 ((1, 4, 5, 7))

R-147 Rosvaenge in *fono forum* (July 1982): 68-73 ((--))

ROUSSEL, ALBERT, 1869-1937 (French composer)

R-148 HUGHES, Eric: A selected discography of Albert Roussel in DEANE, Basil: *Albert Roussel.* Westport, CT: Greenwood Press, 1980: 173-176 ((--)) [Reprinted from the 1961 ed. published by Barrie and Rockliff, London]

R-149 [[Discograpy] in FOLLET, Robert: *Albert Roussel, bio-bibliography.* New York: Greenwood Press, 1988: (Bio-bibliographies in music; 19)]]

ROZDESTVENSKY, GENNADY, 1931-   (Russian conductor)

R-150 Discography [with the USSR Ministry of Culture Symphony Orchestra] in *Music in the USSR* (April-June 1988): 5, 59 ((--))

RÓZSA, MIKLÓS, 1907-   (Hungarian composer)

R-151 [Discographies of film and concert music] in RÓZSA, Miklós: *Double life: the autobiography of Miklós Rózsa.* Tunbridge Wells, Kent: Midas Books; New York: Hippocrene Books, 1982: 210-219 ((--))

RUBBRA, EDMUND, 1901-1986 (English composer)

R-152 FOREMAN, Lewis: Discography in *Edmund Rubbra, composer: Essays.* Richmansworth: Triad Press, 1977: 102-107 ((1, 7))

R-153 HUGHES, Eric and DAY, Timothy: Edmund Rubbra in *Recorded Sound,*

No. 79 (January 1981): 99-115; addendum in No. 80 (July 1981):
149-151   ((1))   (Discographies of British composers; 8)

RUBIN, MARCEL, 1905-   **(Austrian composer)**

R-154 [[[Discography] in BROSCHE, Günter: *Marcel Rubin*. Wien: Doblinger,
1981]]

RUBINSTEIN, ANTON, 1829-1894   (Russian composer)

R-155 Discografía in VELAZCO, Jorge: *Dos músicos eslavos*. México:
Universidad Nacional Autónma de México, 1981: 67   ((--))

RUBINSTEIN, ARTUR, 1887-1982   (Polish pianist)

R-156 Discographie in LIPMANN, Eric: *Arthur Rubinstein: ou, L'amour de
Chopin*. Paris: Éditions de Messine, 1980: 194-197   ((--))

R-157 [Rubinstein discography] in *Record Geijutsu*, No. 390 (March 1983):
235   ((7))

R-158 MANILDI, Donald: The Rubinstein discography in *Le Grand Baton*, No.
56 (Special annual edition, Dec. 1983): 56-100   ((3, 7))

R-159 Rubinstein, discografia cameristica in *Musica*, No. 31 (December
1983): 422   ((--))

R-160 CAMACHO-CASTILLO, Mildred: A selection of Rubinstein reissues in
High Fidelity, XXXIV/9 (September 1984): 62   ((7))

R-161 CALENCO, Franco: Discografia in *Musica*, No. 48 (February-March
1988): 34-59   ((1, 5, 7))

RUDY, MICHAEL, 1947-   **(French pianist)**

R-162 A écouter in *Diapason*, No. 289 (December 1983): 9   ((--))

RUFFO, TITTA, 1877-1953   (Italian baritone)

R-163 MATHEWS, Emrys A.: *Titta Ruffo: a centenary discography*.
Llandeilo, Dyfed, Wales: Mathews, 1977. 26 pp.   ((3, 4, 6, 7))

R-164 Appendice C/Discografia (aggiornata al 31 marzo 1977) con la
collaborazioni di M. Tiberi in RUFFO, Titta: *La mia parabola:
memorie*. Roma: Staderini, 1977: [411]-431   ((3, 4, 6, 7))

R-165 MORAN, W. R.: The recordings of Titta Ruffo (1877-1953) - a discography in RUFFO, Titta: *La mia parabola: memorie: Titta Ruffo*.
New York: Arno Press, 1977: i-xiv   ((3, 6, 7)) [Includes notes on
playing speeds] [Originally published without discography by
Fratelli Treves Editori, Milano, 1937]

R-166 MORAN, William R.: Discography in *Titta Ruffo: an anthology*.
Westport, CT: Greenwood Press, 1984: [251]-269   ((3, 6, 7))

RUGGLES, CARL, 1876-1971   (American composer)

R-167 CURTIS, William D.: Carl Ruggles (1876-1971)--a comprehensive

discography in *Fanfare*, IV/1 (September–October 1980): 191–193
((3, 5, 7))

RUSS, GIANNINA, 1873–1951   (Italian soprano)

R-168   WILLIAMS, Clifford and RICHARDS, John B.: Discography in *Record Collector*, XXVII/5-6 (May 1982): 130–140; Addenda in XXVII/7-8 (August 1982): 185–186; XXVII/11-12 (March 1983): 276–277, 295 ((3, 4, 6, 7))

RUST, FRIEDRICH WILHELM, 1739–1796   (German composer)

R-169   [[Discography in RIDGWAY, Paul Campbell: *The keyboard sonatas of Friedrich Wilhelm Rust*. [Dissertation, Peabody Institute, 1981] 162 pp.]]

RYBNIKOV, ALEXEI, 1945–   (Russian composer)

R-170   Discography in *Music in the USSR* (October–December 1987): 93   ((--))

RYSANEK, LEONIE, 1926–   (Austrian soprano)

R-171   Discographie in *fono forum* (November 1986): 38   ((7))

R-172   Discographie in *Diapason-Harmonie*, No. 335 (February 1988): 47 ((1, 7))

SAAR CHAMBER ORCHESTRA, West Germany

S-1   [[MARSHALL, Andrew: *Andrew Marshall's Chamber Orchestra of the Saar discography*. Toronto: Canadian Broadcasting Corp., 1979]]

SACHER, PAUL, 1906–   (Swiss conductor)

S-2   Schallplatten unter Leitung von Paul Sacher in ROSTROPOVITCH, Mstislav, ed.: *Dank an Paul Sacher*. Zürich; Freiburg i. Br.: Atlantis Musikbuch-Verlag, [1976?]: 121–126   ((5))

S-3   Aufnahmen: Radio, Fernsehen, Schallplatte in *Paul Sacher als Gastdirigent: Dokumentation und Beiträge zum 80. Geburtstag*. Zürich: Atlantis Musikbuch-Verlag, 1986: 228–249   ((1, 7))

SACK, ERNA, 1898–1972   (German soprano)

S-4   [Discography] in *Erna Sack*. [Hamburg: Jürgen Schäfer, 1973]: 13–23 ((1, 7))

SACRED MUSIC

S-5   Recordings of sacred music in *Music in the USSR* (April–June 1988): 65   ((--))

SACRED MUSIC--ENGLAND

S-6   [[Discography in ANDERSON, Ronald Eugene: *Richard Alison's Psalter (1599) and devotional music in England to 1640*. [Dissertation, University of Iowa, 1974] 2 v. 440, 266 pp.]]

SACRED MUSIC--FRANCE

S-7   [[Discography in LABELLE, Nicole: *Les différents styles de la musique religeuse en France. Le psaume de 1539 à 1572.* [Dissertation, Paris, 1978] 2 v. 300, 500 pp.]]

SACRED VOCAL MUSIC

S-8   GARAVAGLIA, Renato: Discografia selezionata musica antica, dal canto gregoriano al Monteverdi profano in *Discoteca alta fedeltà*, No. 189 (December 1978): 196, 198, 200 ((--))

SÁDLO, MILOŠ, 1912-   (Czech cellist)

S-9   [[[Discography] in SMOLKA, Jaroslav: *Miloš Sádlo: rozhovory z českým violoncellistou.* Praha: Editio Supraphon, 1983: 88-91]]

SÆVERUD, HARALD, 1897-   (Norwegian composer)

S-10   Plateinnspillinger-recordings in LI, Bjørn: *Harald Sæverud.* Oslo: Aventura, 1986: 131-132 ((--))

SAINT-GEORGE, JOSEPH BOULOGNE, CHEVALIER DE, 1739-1799 (West Indian composer)

S-11   Discographie in *Harmonie-Panorama musique*, No. 29 (March 1983): 33 ((--))

ST. LOUIS SYMPHONY ORCHESTRA

S-12   Discography of the orchestra in WELLS, Katherine Gladney: *Symphony and song: The Saint Louis Symphony Orchestra: the first hundred years.* Taftsville, VT: Countryman Press, 1980: 177-183 ((7))

SAINT-SAËNS, CAMILLE, 1835-1921 (French composer)

S-13   PERKINS, John F. and KELLY, Alan: The Gramophone & Typewriter ltd records of Camille Saint-Saëns (1835-1921) in *Recorded Sound*, No. 79 (January 1981): 25-27 ((--))

OPERAS

SAMSON ET DALILA (1877)

S-14   DUTRONC, Jean-Louis: Discographie in *L'Avant Scène Opéra*, No. 15 (March-April 1977): 92-[95] ((1, 5))

S-15   WALKER, Malcolm: LP discography in BLYTH, Alan: Samson et Dalila in *Opera*, XXIII/10 (October 1981): 1004-1009; XXIII/11 (November 1981): 1125-1132 ((7)) (Opera on the gramophone; 51)

SALMINEN, MATTI, 1945-   (Finnish bass)

S-16   Discographie Hinweise in *fono forum* (March 1986): 22 ((--))

SALONEN, ESA-PEKKA, 1958-   (Swedish conductor)

S-17   Discographische Hinweise in *fono forum* (February 1986): 21 ((--))

(I) SALONISTI, West Germany

S-18   Discographische Hinweise in *fono forum* (January 1988):   23
((--))

SAMOSUD, SAMUIL, 1884-1964   (Russian conductor)

S-19   [Discography Samuil S. Samosud] in *S. A. Samosud: Stati,
vospominariia pisma.* Moskva: Vses. izd. Sov. Kompozitor, 1984:
203-225   (1, 7))

SAN FRANCISCO SYMPHONY ORCHESTRA

S-20   LEDIN, Victor: San Francisco Symphony discography in SCHNEIDER,
David: *The San Francisco Symphony Orchestra music, maestros, and
musicians.* Novato, CA: Presidio Press, 1987: 282-310   ((7))

S-21   LEDIN, Victor and MATTHEW-WALKER, Robert: San Francisco Symphony
discography in *Music & Musicians* (February 1987): 24-28   ((7))

SANDERLING, KURT, 1927-   (German conductor)

S-22   [[[Discography] in BITTERLICH, Hans: *Kurt Sanderling: für Sie
porträtiert.* Leipzig: VEB Deutscher Verlag für Musik, 1987]]

SANTLEY, SIR CHARLES, 1834-1922   (English baritone)

S-23   MORAN, W. R.: The recordings of Sir Charles Santley (28 Feb., 1834-
22 Sept., 1922) in SANTLEY, Charles: *Reminiscences of my life.* New
York: Arno Press, 1977: i-ii   ((3, 7))   [Includes notes on playing
speeds] [Reprinted from the 1909 ed. published by Pitman, London]

SANTORO, CLAUDIO, 1919-   (Brazilian composer)

S-24   Discographic notes in *Cláudio Santoro: catálogo de obras.*
[Brasília]: Ministério das Relações Exteriores, Departamento de
Cooperação Cultural, Científica e Tecnológica, 1977: [22] pp.
((--))   (Compositores brasileiros)

SATIE, ERIK, 1866-1925   (French composer)

S-25   Discographie in *HiFi Stereophonie*, XV/11 (November 1976): 1262
((--))

S-26   Discographie in VOLTA, Ornella: *Erik Satie.* Paris: Seghers,
1979: 151-155   ((--))

S-27   Auswahldiskographie in *Erik Satie.* München: Edition Text u. Kritik,
1980: [110]-111   ((--))   (Musik-Konzepte; 11)

S-28   Erik Satie: a discography in TEMPLIER, Pierre-Daniel: *Satie.* New
York: Da Capo Press, 1980, c1969: [117]-127   ((--))   [Reprinted from
the ed. published by MIT Press, Boston]

S-29   Discographie sélective in LAJOINIE, Vincent: *Erik Satie.* [Lausanne]:
L'Age d'homme, [1985]: 439-443   ((--))

S-30   Discographie in *Harmonie-Panorama musique*, No. 49 (January 1985):

36-37 ((--))

S-31   Discographie in *Horoskop für Erik Satie erstellt zu seinem 120. Geburtstag.* Linz: Linzer Veranstaltungsgellschaft, 1986: 79 ((--))

STAGE WORKS

(LA) BELLE EXCENTRIQUE (1920)

S-32   MARINELLI, Carlo: [Discography] in Venezia, Teatro La Fenice, season 1980: program pp. 133-134 ((5))

GENEVIÈVE DE BRABANT (1899)

S-33   MARINELLI, Carlo: [Discography] in Venezia, Teatro La Fenice, season 1983: program p. 409 ((5))

MERCURE (1924)

S-34   MARINELLI, Carlo: [Discography] in Roma, Teatro dell'Opera, season 1976-77: program pp. 531-532 ((5))

SOCRATE (1919)

S-35   MARINELLI, Carlo: [Discography] in Venezia, Teatro La Fenice, season 1980: program pp. 135-138 ((5))

SAUER, EMIL VON, 1862-1942 (German pianist)

S-36   [[Discography in RENFROE, Anita Boyle: *Emil von Sauer: a catalogue of his piano works.* [DMA, Southern Baptist Theological Seminary, 1981] 76 pp.]]

SAUGUET, HENRI, 1901-   (French composer)

S-37   Discographie in *Revue Musicale*, No. 361/3 (1983): 274-278 ((--))

SAVILLE, FRANCES, 1865-1935 (American soprano)

S-38   DAVIS, Nathan B.: Frances Saville, a discography in *Record Collector*, XXXII/6-7 (June 1987): 133-138 ((3, 6, 7)) [Includes notes on playing speeds]

SAWALLISCH, WOLFGANG, 1923-   (German conductor)

S-39   SABLICH, Sergio: Discografia in *Musica*, No. 21 (June 1981): 141-142 ((--))

S-40   Diskographie in *Stationen eines Dirigenten, Wolfgang Sawallisch.* München: Bruckmann, 1983: 215-222 ((7))

SAXOPHONE MUSIC

S-41   SCHLEUTER, Stanley L.: *Discography of saxophone music: a comprehensive listing of recorded recital and concert music.* Clear Lake: Meadow Lark, 1977. 54 pp. ((--))

S-42   Discographic notes in GEE, Harry R.: *Saxophone players and their music, 1844-1985: an annotated bibliography.* Bloomington: Indiana University Press, 1986.   300 pp.   ((--))

SCARLATTI, DOMENICO, 1685-1757   (Italian composer)

S-43   Discographische Hinweise in *fono forum* (October 1985): 32   ((--))

S-44   MARINELLI, Carlo: Scarlatti dimenticato in Ente autonomo Teatro Massimo, Palermo Quaderni 1985: 46-50   ((--))

SCELSI, GIACINTO, 1905-1988   (Italian composer)

S-45   RIEHN, Rainer: Diskographie in *Giacinto Scelsi.* München: Edition Text und Kritik, 1983: [117]   ((--))   (Musik-Konzepte; 31)

SCHAER, HANNA   (Contralto)

S-46   Discographie in *Harmonie-Panorama musique,* No. 46 (October 1984): 20-21   ((--))

SCHAFER, R. MURRAY, 1933-   (Canadian composer)

S-47   [[[Discography] in ADAMS, Stephen: A bibliography of R. Murray Schafer in *Open Letter,* IV/4-5 (Fall 1979): 235-244]]

S-48   Discography in ADAMS, Stephen: *R. Murray Schafer.* Toronto: University of Toronto Press, 1983: [207]-208   ((--))   (Canadian composers; 4)

SCHALK, FRANZ, 1863-1931   (Austrian conductor)

S-49   SUGA, Hajime: Franz Schalk in *LP Techno,* March 1979: 94-95   ((7))

SCHEIDL, THEODOR, 1880-1959   (Austrian baritone)

S-50   [[[Discography] in *Stimmen, die um die Welt gingen,* No. 1 (1983): 21; No. 5 (September 1984): 7-19; No. 6 (December 1984): 20-21]]

SCHELLENBERG, ARNO, 1903-1983   (German baritone)

S-51   [[[Discography] in *Stimmen, die um die Welt gingen,* No. 9 (September 1985): 10-14]]

SCHICKELE, PETER, 1935-   (American composer)

S-52   Discography in SCHICKELE, Peter: *The definitive biography of P.D.Q. Bach.* New York: Random House, 1976: 225-226   ((--))

SCHIFF, ANDRAS, 1953-   (Hungarian pianist)

S-53   Andras Schiff discografia in *Musica,* No. 46 (October 1987): 18   ((--))

SCHIØTZ, AKSEL, 1906-1975   (Danish tenor)

S-54   Diskographische Hinweise za Aksel Schiøtz in *fono forum* (March 1976): 228   ((--))

SCHIPA, TITO, 1888-1965 (Italian tenor)

S-55   RUBBOLI, Daniele: Discografia in D'ANDREA, Renzo: *Tito Schipa.*
Fasano di Puglia: Schena editore, 1981: [225]-240   ((5))

SCHIPPERS, THOMAS, 1930-1977 (American conductor)

S-56   GUANDALINI, Gina and MODUGNO, Maurizio: Discografia di Thomas
Schippers in *Musica,* No. 5 (February 1978): 10-11   ((7))

SCHLUSNUS, HEINRICH, 1888-1952 (German baritone)

S-57   [[[Discography] in *Stimmen, die um die Welt gingen,* No. 9 (September
1985): 41-58; No. 21 (September 1988: 23-29]]

SCHMEDES, ERIK, 1868-1931 (Danish tenor)

S-58   NORTON-WELSH, Christopher: Erik Schmedes 1868-1931 in *Record
Collector,* XXVII/1-2 (December 1981): 38-47   ((3, 4, 7))

SCHMIDT, ANNEROSE, 1936-   (German pianist)

S-59   Schallplattenverzeichnis (Auswahl) in WINKLER, Franz: *Annerose
Schmidt: für Sie porträtiert.* Leipzig: VEB Deutscher Verlag für
Musik, 1981: 59   ((--))

SCHMIDT, FRANZ, 1874-1939 (Austrian composer)

S-60   LA MIRANDE, Arthur: Discography in *Diapason,* LXVII/4 (March 1976):
18   ((--))

SCHMIDT, JOSEF, 1904-1942 (Romanian tenor)

S-61   Josef Schmidt en de grammofoonplaat in BREDSCHNEYDER, Fred: *Ik hov
van Holland; een Levensbeeld van Josef Schmidt.* Nieuwkoop:
Uitgeverij Hevff, 1981: 95-[105]   ((7))

S-62   [[[Discography] in *Stimmen, die um die Welt gingen,* No. 4 (June
1984): 5-13; No. 6 (December 1984): 63-66]]

SCHMIDT, YVES R., 1933-   (Brazilian composer)

S-63   Discographic references in FERREIRA, Paulo Affonso de Moura: *Yves
R. Schmidt: catálogo de obras.* [Brasília]: Ministério das Relações
Exteriores, Departamento de Cooperação Cultural, Científica e
Tecnológica, 1977: [34] pp.   ((--))   (Compositores brasileiros)

SCHMIDT-ISSERSTEDT, HANS, 1900-1973 (German conductor)

S-64   [Discography] in *Record Geijutsu,* No. 275 (August 1973): 269   ((--))

SCHMITT-WALTER, KARL, 1900-1985 (German baritone)

S-65   [[[Discography] in *Stimmen, die um die Welt gingen,* No. 2 (December
1983): 8-19; No. 3 (March 1984): 33-39]]

S-66   VÖLMECKE, Uwe: Karl Schmitt-Walter discography in *Record Collector,*
XXIX/7-8 (October 1984): 153-182; additions in XXX/3-4 (April 1985):

81-83   ((1, 3, 4, 6, 7))

SCHNABEL, ARTUR, 1882-1951   (Austrian pianist)

S-67   BLOESCH, David: Artur Schnabel: a discography in *ARSC Journal*,
XVIII/1-3 (1986): 33-143   ((1, 3, 4, 5, 6, 7))

SCHNABEL, KARL ULRICH, 1909-   (German pianist)

S-68   Discografia di Karl Ulrich Schnabel in *Musica*, No. 10 (December
1978): 223   ((--))

SCHNEBEL, DIETER, 1930-   (German composer)

S-69   RIEHN, Rainer: Schallplatten in *Dieter Schnebel*. München: Edition
Text u. Kritik, 1980: 133-136   ((--))   (Musik-Konzepte; 16)

S-70   BACHMANN, Claus-Henning: Discographie Dieter Schnebel in *fono forum*
(April 1981): 48-50   ((--))

SCHNITTKE, ALFRED, 1934-   (Russian composer)

S-71   Discography in *Music in the USSR* (January-March 1988): 79   ((--))

SCHOCK, RUDOLF, 1915-1988   (German tenor)

S-72   HOLLE, Friedhelm: Verzeichnis der auf erschienen Schallplatten
Aufnahmen in SCHOCK, Rudolf: *Ach, ich hab in meinem Herzen*.
München: Herbig, 1985: 410-472   ((1, 7))

SCHOECK, OTHMAR, 1886-1957   (Swiss composer)

S-73   Diskothek in *Othmar Schoeck: Leben und Schaffen im Spiegel von
Selbstzeugnissen und Zeitgenossenberichten*. Zürich: Atlantis-
Verlag, 1976: 348-349   ((--))

S-74   A Othmar Schoeck discography in *Fanfare*, VII/4 (1984): 242-243
((--))

SONGS

S-75   Discography in PUFFETT, Derrick: *The song cycles of Othmar
Schoeck*. Bern: P. Haupt, 1982: 457   ((--))

SCHOENBERG, ARNOLD, 1874-1951   (Austrian composer)

S-76   [[Discography in AVSHALOMOV, David: *Arnold Schoenberg's Five
Pieces for Orchestra, Op. 16: the story of the music and its
revisions, with a critical study of his 1949 revision*. [DMA,
University of Washington, 1976]   300 pp.]]

S-77   CLOUD, David: Schoenberg recordings in *Bulletin of the Arnold
Schoenberg Institute*, No. 3 (June 1976); 2; Update in *Journal of the
Arnold Schoenberg Institute*, I/3 (June 1977): 179-180   ((--))

S-78   [[SATOH, Tetsuo: et al.: *A bibliographic catalog with
discography and comprehensive bibliography of Arnold Schönberg*.
Tokyo: Kunitachi Music College Library, 1978.   156 pp.]]

S-79   STEURMANN, Clara: From the archives: recorded sound on discs in
        Journal of the Arnold Schoenberg Institute, III/1 (March 1979):
        93-107; Additions and amplifications in IV/1 (June 1980): 99-103
        ((1, 3, 7))

S-80   [[[Discography] in LEIBOWITZ, René: *Schoenberg.* Paris: Seuil,
        1980. 191 pp.]]

S-81   THIEL, Gordon: Recent recordings of Schoenberg's music in *Journal
        of the Arnold Schoenberg Institute*, VI/1 (June 1982): 116-125
        ((5))

S-82   HALBREICH, Harry: Arnold Schonberg: discographie critique et
        l'elements bibliographie in *Harmonie*, X (September 2, 1984): 29-44
        ((3, 5))

S-83   HAMILTON, David: The challenge of Schoenberg in *Opus* (April 1985):
        16-21; Part 2 in Opus (June 1985): 23-24   ((--))

S-84   SHOAF, R. Wayne: *The Schoenberg discography.* Berkeley: Fallen Leaf
        Press, 1986. 200 pp.   ((4, 5, 7))

        See also

        PIANO MUSIC

        CHORAL WORKS

        GURRE-LIEDER (1900-01)

S-85   MARINELLI, Carlo: [Discography] in Venezia, Teatro La Fenice,
        season 1971: program pp. 59-61   ((5))

        OPERAS

        ERWARTUNG (1924)

S-86   MARINELLI, Carlo: [Discography] in Roma, Teatro dell'Opera,
        season 1966-67: program pp. 594-595   ((5))

S-87   MARINELLI, Carlo: [Discography] in Milano, Teatro alla Scala,
        season 1979-80: program pp. 59-61   ((5))

S-88   MARINELLI, Carlo: [Discography] in Milano, Teatro alla Scala,
        season 1982-83: program p. 30   ((5))

        VOCAL WORKS

        PIERROT LUNAIRE (1912)

S-89   MARINELLI, Carlo: Discografia ragionata del Pierrot Lunaire in
        Musica, No. 26 (October 1982): 320-325   ((5))

S-90   MARINELLI, Carlo: [Discography] in Milano, Teatro alla Scala,
        season 1982-83: program p. 29   ((5))

S-91   SHOAF, R. Wayne: [Discography] in "From Pierrot to Marteau", USC
        School of Music, concert program of Mar. 14-16, 1987: p. 50

((7))

SCHREIER, PETER, 1935–   (German tenor/conductor)

S-92   Schallplattenverzeichnis (Auswahl) in SCHMIEDEL, Gottfried: *Peter
        Schreier.* Leipzig: Deutscher Verlag fur Musik, 1976: 71   ((−−)

S-93   Discographie in SCHMIEDEL, Gottfried: *Peter Schreier.* Berlin:
        Henschel, 1979: 167–173   ((−−))

S-94   SEIBERT, Hannelore: Discographie in SCHREIER, Peter: *Aus meiner
        Sicht: Gedanken und Erinnerungen.* Wien; Hamburg: P. Zsolnay, 1983:
        [178]–[206]   ((−−))

SCHRÖDER, JAAP, 1925–   (Dutch violinist/conductor)

S-95   Jaap Schröder selected discography in *Records & Recording,* XXIII/9
        (June 1980): 21   ((−−))

SCHUBERT, FRANZ, 1797–1828   (Austrian composer)

S-96   Discographie in SCHNEIDER, Marcel: *Schubert.* Paris, Seuil, 1977:
        184–191   ((−−))

S-97   [Schubert discography] in *Record Geijutsu,* No. 334 (July 1978):
        [183]–210; No. 337 (October 1978): 202–238   ((4, 5, 7))

VOCAL WORKS

S-98   BOLLERT, Werner: Discographie: Schubertiade in *fono forum*
        (December 1980): 32–33, 36, 38, 40, 42   ((3, 4))

S-99   GILBERT, Richard: Going on record: on the Shepherd on the Rock in
        Clarinet, VI/3 (1979): 28   ((−−))

LAZARUS, D. 689

S-100   MARINELLI, Carlo: [Discography] in Venezia, Teatro La Fenice,
        season 1983: program pp. 22–24   ((5))

INSTRUMENTAL WORKS

QUARTET, STRINGS, D. 810, D MINOR (1824)

S-101   LEWINSKI, Wolf-Eberhard von: Schuberts D-moll-Quartet auf
        Schallplatten (Der Tod und das Mädchen) in *fono forum* (April
        1980): 34–37   ((−−))

PIANO WORKS

S-102   [[Discography in WEEKLEY, Dallas Joseph: *The one-piano, four-hand
        compositions of Franz Schubert: a historical and interpretive
        analysis.* [DMA, Indiana University, 1968] 301 pp.]]

SCHÜTZ, HEINRICH, 1585–1672   (German composer)

S-103   Grammofoonplaten van het Heinrich Schütz Choir (& chorale) op Argo
        in Festival of Flanders, Louvair: *Heinrich-Schütz.* Louvain: Festival

of Flanders, 1972: 100   ((--))

S-104   Schallplattenverzeichnis in KÖHLER, Siegfried: *Heinrich Schütz;
        Anmerkungen zu Leben und Werk.* Leipzig: VEB Deutsche Verlag für
        Musik, 1985: 237-239   ((--))

S-105   MÜLLER, Reinhard: Heinrich Schütz in Italien in *fono forum* (November
        1985): 28-32   ((--))

SCHÜTZENDORF, LEO, 1886-1931   (German bass-baritone)

S-106   [[[Discography] in *Stimmen, die um die Welt gingen,* No. 1 (1983):
        1-7]]

SCHULLER, GUNTHER, 1925-   (American composer/conductor)

S-107   Discography in CARNOVALE, Norbert: *Gunther Schuller, a
        bio-bibliography.* Westport, CT: Greenwood Press, 1987: [132]-154
        ((7))   (Bio-bibliographies in music; 6)

S-108   Selected discography in Program notes for *Robert Davidovici, violin.*
        [Sound recording] New World Records NW 334, 1987   ((--))

SCHUMAN, WILLIAM, 1910-   (American composer)

S-109   [[[Discography] in KEATS, Sheila, ed.: *William Schuman;
        biographical and professional data, including chronological listing
        of works with background data, listing of works by performance
        medium.* September 1970.   19 leaves]]   [In the collections of the
        Rodgers and Hammerstein Archives, New York Public Library]

S-110   WEBER, J. F.: A William Schuman discography in *ARSC Journal,*
        VIII/2-3 (1976): 74-82   ((1, 5, 7))

S-111   WEBER, J. F.: *Carter and Schuman.* Utica, NY: Weber, 1978. 20 pp.
        ((4, 5, 7))   (Weber discography series; 19)

S-112   Discography in ROUSE, Christopher: *William Schuman, documentary.*
        S.l.: Theodore Presser Co., 1980: 43-47   ((--))

S-113   HALL, David: A bio-discography of William Schuman: in *Ovation,* VI/7
        (August 1985): 8-14; VI/8 (September 1985): 18-22   ((--))

S-114   Selected discography in Program notes for *Three colloquies for horn
        and orchestra.* [Sound recording] New World Records NW 326, 1985
        ((--))

S-115   Selected discography in Program notes for *Schuman Symphony No. 7.*
        [Sound recording] New World Records NW 348, 1987   ((--))

SCHUMANN, CLARA, 1819-1896   (German composer)

S-116   [[Discography in SUSSKIND, Pamela Gertrude: *Clara Wieck Schumann
        as a pianist and composer: a study of her life and works.*
        [Dissertation, University of California at Berkeley, 1977]   306,
        277 pp.]]

S-117   [[Discography in FANG, Siu-Wan Chair: *Clara Schumann as teacher.*

[DMA, University of Illinois, 1978]   96 pp.]]

SCHUMANN, ELISABETH, 1888-1952   (German soprano)

S-118   JUYNBOLL, Floris and SEDDON, James: Elisabeth Schumann discography in *Record Collector*, XXXIII/3-5 (March 1988): 54-116; additions & corrections in XXXIII/8-10: 247-249   ((1, 3, 4, 5, 6, 7))

SCHUMANN, ROBERT, 1810-1856   (German composer)

S-119   VITTOZ, Jean: Sélection des enregistrements de Schumann in *Almanach du disque*, 1956: 244-245   ((--))

S-120   A selected discography from Great Britain and America in BOURCOURECHLIEV, André: *Schumann*. Westport, CT: Greenwood Press, 1976: 190-192   ((--))   [Reprinted from the 1959 ed. published by Grove Press, New York]

S-121   SCHONBERG, Harold C.: *The collector's Chopin and Schumann*. Westport, CT: Greenwood Press, 1978.   256 pp. ((--))   [Reprinted from the 1959 ed. published by Lippincott, New York]

S-122   Discographie in STRICKER, Rémy: *Robert Schumann: le musicien et la folie*. [Paris]: Gallimard, 1984: [225]-231   ((--))   [Omits record numbers]

CHORAL WORKS

SCENES FROM FAUST (1853)

S-123   MARINELLI, Carlo: [Discography] in Venezia, Teatro La Fenice, season 1984: program pp. 612-614   ((5))

PIANO WORKS

S-124   Discographie in BEAUFILS, Marcel: *La musique pour piano de Schumann*. Paris: Phebus, 1979: 177-190   ((--))

CARNAVAL, Op. 9 (1835)

S-125   ESCUDIER, Monique: Le Carnaval de Schumann: discographie comparée in *Harmonie*, No. 124 (February 1977): 92-97   ((--))

STAGE WORKS

GENOVEVA (1850)

S-126   Diskographie in OLIVER, Willie-Earl: *Robert Schumann vergessene Oper "Genoveva"*. Freiburg i. Br.: [s.n.], 1978: 236   ((--))

S-127   FLINOIS, Pierre: Discographie in *L'Avant Scène Opéra*, No. 71 (January 1985): 108-109   ((1, 7))

SCHUMANN-HEINK, ERNESTINE, 1861-1936   (Contralto)

S-128   MORAN, W. R.: The recordings of Ernestine Schumann-Heink in LAWTON, Mary: *Schumann-Heink, the last of the titans*.

New York: Arno Press, 1977: [399]-[428]   ((1, 3, 6, 7))   [Includes notes on playing speeds]

SCHURICHT, CARL, 1880-1967   (German conductor)

S-129 Discografia in *Musica*, No. 22 (October 1981): 276-284   ((7))

SCHWARZ, GERARD, 1947-   (American trumpeter/conductor)

S-130 LOWREY, Alvin L.: A chronological list of recordings by Gerard Schwarz in *International Trumpet Guild Journal*, VII/1 (September 1982): 52-58   ((4, 5))

SCHWARZ, HANNA, 1943-   (German mezzo-soprano)

S-131 SCHAUMKELL, Claus-Dieter: Gesamt-discographie Hanna Schwarz in *fono forum* (June 1987): 30   ((--))

SCHWARZ, JOSEPH, 1880-1926   (German baritone)

S-132 NORTON-WELSH, Christopher: The records of Joseph Schwarz in *Record Collector*, XXVI/9-10 (May 1981): 231-234   ((--))

S-133 WALTER, Günter: Joseph Schwarz discography in *Record Collector*, XXVI/9-10 (May 1981): 223-231   ((3, 4, 6, 7))

SCHWARZ, RUDOLF, 1905-   (Austrian conductor)

S-134 [Discography] in UPTON, Stuart: *Sir Dan Godfrey & the Bournemouth Symphony Orchestra*. London: Vintage Light Music Society, 1979: 18   ((--))

SCHWARZKOPF, ELISABETH, 1915-   (German soprano)

S-135 TUBEUF, André: [Discographie commentée] in *Harmonie Hi-fi Conseil*, No. 8 (April 1981): [26]-33   ((--))

S-136 Discographie in SEGALINI, Sergio: *Elisabeth Schwarzkopf*. Paris: Fayard, 1983: [151]-156   ((7))

SCHWER, STEFAN, 1902-   (German tenor)

S-137 [[[Discography] in *Stimmen, die um die Welt gingen*, No. 3 (March 1984): 51-]]

SCIORTINO, PATRICE, 1922-   (French composer)

S-138 Discographie de Patrice Sciortino in *Courrier Musical de France*, No. 54 (Second Quarter, 1976): 81   ((--)

SCOTT, CYRIL, 1879-1970   (English composer)

S-139 Cyril Scott discography in *Recorded Sound*, No. 61 (January 1976): 506-510   ((1, 3, 6 ,7))

SCOTT, HENRI, 1876-1942   (American bass)

S-140 BRYANT, William R.: The recordings of Henri Scott in *New Amberola*

Graphic, No. 25: 4-8   ((3, 5, 6, 7))

SCOTTI, ANTONIO, 1866-1936   (Italian baritone)

S-141   HOGARTH, Will: Discography in *Record Collector*, XXVIII/9-10
(February 1984): 220-227   ((1, 3, 6, 7))

SCOTTO, RENATA, 1934-   (Italian soprano)

S-142   Discografia in BONAFINI, Umberto: *Perchè sono Renata Scotto*.
Mantove: [s.n.], 1976: 197-199   ((--))

S-143   Discography in SCOTTO, Renata and ROCA, Octavio: *Scotto; more than a
diva*. Garden City: NY: Doubleday, 1984: [181]-220   ((1))

SCRIABIN, ALEXANDER, 1872-1915   (Russian composer)

S-144   [[Discography in GUENTHER, Roy James: *Varvara Dernova's
Garmoniia Skriabina: a translation and critical commentary*.
[Dissertation, Catholic University, 1979]   455 pp.]]

S-145   Selected discography in *Music in the USSR* (April-June 1988): 5, 58
((--))

SEGOVIA, ANDRÉS, 1893-1987

S-146   Segovia discography in PURCELL, Ronald C.: *Andrés Segovia:
contributions to the world of the guitar*. Sherman Oaks, CA: Purcell,
1973: 23-35   ((--))

S-147   Segovia discography in PURCELL, Ronald C.: *Andrés Segovia:
contributions to the world of the guitar*. 2d ed. Melville, NY:
Belwin-Mills, 1975: 29-42   ((--))

S-148   [Discography] in VASBORD, M.: *Andrés Segovia*.   Moskva: Muzyka,
1981: 120-[125]   ((--))

S-149   Discography in WADE, Graham: *Segovia, a celebration of the man and
his music*. London; New York: Allison & Busby; New York: Schocken
Books, 1983: 121-132   ((--))

SEIDER, AUGUST, 1901-   (German tenor)

S-150   [[[Discography] in *Stimmen die um die Welt gingen*, No. 11 (March
1986): 27-34]]

SERAFIN, TULLIO, 1878-1968   (Italian conductor)

S-151   TARTONI, Guido: La discografia in CELLI, Teodoro: *Tullio
Serafin: il patriarca del melodramma*. Venezia: Corbo e Fiore,
[1985]: 192-200   ((1, 7))

SERKIN, RUDOLF, 1903-   (Austrian pianist)

S-152   [Rudolf Serkin discography] in *Record Geijutsu*, No. 311) August
1976): 215   ((--))

S-153   Rudolf Serkin on Columbia Records in Program notes for *Rudolf Serkin on Television* [Sound recording] Columbia M2 34596, 1978: 13-15 ((7))

SESSIONS, ROGER, 1896-1985   (American composer)

S-154 Selected discography in Program notes for *Roger Sessions: When lilacs last in the dooryard bloom'd.* [Sound recording] New World Records NW 296, 1977: 4 ((--))

S-155 RAPOPORT, Paul: Roger Sessions: a discography in *Tempo*, No. 127 (December 1978): 17-20 ((--))

S-156 Selected discography in Program notes for *Roger Sessions: String Quartet No. 1.* [Sound recording] New World Records NW 302, 1979 ((--))

S-157 Selected discography in Program notes for *Roger Sessions: Piano sonata No. 3.* [Sound recording] New World Records NW 307, 1980: [2-3] ((--))

S-158 Selected discography Roger Sessions's piano music in Program notes for *Quincy Porter: Dance in three time.* [Sound recording] New World Records NW 320, 1984 ((--))

S-159 Chronological discography in OLMSTEAD, Andrea: *Roger Sessions and his music.* Ann Arbor: UMI Research Press, 1985: [191]-194 ((--))

S-160 Selected discography [Orchestral works] in Program notes for *Roger Sessions: Symphonies No. 4 and 5.* [Sound recording] New World Records NW 345, 1987 ((--))

S-161 List of works and recordings in SESSIONS, Roger: *Conversations with Roger Sessions.* Boston: Northeastern University Press, 1987: 249-254 ((5))

SETTI, KILZA, 1932-   (Brazilian composer)

S-162 Discographic references in FERREIRA, Paulo Affonso de Moura: *Kilza Setti: catálogo de obras.* [Brasília]: Ministério das Relações Exteriores, Departamento de Cooperação Cultural, Científica e Tecnológica, 1976: [13] pp. ((--)) (Compositores brasileiros)

SHAFRAN, DANIEL, 1923-   (Russian cellist)

S-163 Discography in *Music in the USSR* (July-September 1985): 88 ((--))

SHAKESPEARE, WILLIAM--MUSICAL SETTINGS

S-164 Borrowing from the Bard: music inspired by the plays of Shakespeare in *Tarakan Music Letter*, III/4 (March-April 1981): 1, 16 ((--))

SHAKHIDY, TOBIB, 1946-   (Tajik composer)

S-165 Discography in *Music in the USSR* (April-June 1985): 11 ((--))

SHAKHIDY, ZIYADULLO, 1914-1985 (Tajik composer)

S-166 Discography in *Music in the USSR* (April-June 1987): 11 ((--))

SHANKAR, RAVI, 1920–   (Indian sitarist)

S-167 Discography, Deutsche Grammophon artist inforamtion, 1980. 1 p.
       ((--))

SHAW, ROBERT, 1916–   (American conductor)

S-168 Selected discography in MUSSULMAN, Joseph A.: *Dear people ... Robert Shaw: a biography.* Bloomington: University of Indiana Press, 1979: 251-256 ((5))

SHCHEDRIN, RODION KONSTANTINOVICH, 1932–   (Russian composer)

S-169 [[CANFIELD, David DeBoor: Discography in *Kastlemusick* (January 1983):]]

S-170 [Discography] in *Music in the USSR* (April–June 1985): 17 ((--))

CARMEN BALLET (1968)

S-171   MARINELLI, Carlo: [Discography] in Roma, Teatro dell'Opera, season 1984-85: program pp. 28-29 ((5))

SHEPHERD, ARTHUR, 1880-1958 (American composer)

S-172 Selected discography in Program notes for *Works by Arthur Shepherd, Henry Cowell, Roy Harris.* [Sound recording] New World Records NW 218, 1977: 4 ((--))

S-173 Selected discography in Program notes for *Henry Herford, baritone.* [Sound recording] New World Records NW 327, 1985 ((--))

SHERIDAN, MARGARET, 1889-1958 (Irish soprano)

S-174 KELLY, Alan: Margaret Sheridan, a discography in *Record Collector,* XXXIII/8-10 (August 1988): [201]-213 ((1, 3, 6, 7))

SHIFRIN, SEYMOUR J., 1926-1979 (American composer)

S-175 Selected discography in Program notes for *Choral works by Randall Thompson, Elliott Carter, Seymour Shifrin.* [Sound recording] New World Records NW 219, 1977: 4 ((--))

SHOSTAKOVITCH, DMITRI, 1906-1975 (Russian composer)

S-176 Recommended recordings in BLOKKER, Roy: *The music of Dmitri Shostakovich, the symphonies.* London: Tantivy Press; Rutherford, NJ: Fairleigh Dickinson University Press, 1979: [167]-175 ((--))

S-177 WEBER, Jan: Schallplattenverzeichnis in MEYER, Krzysztof: *Dmitri Schostakowitsch.* Leipzig: Verlag Philipp Reclam, 1980: 297-[328] ((--))

S-178 Discographic references in HULME, Derek C.: *Dmitri Shostakovitch: a catalogue, bibliograpy & discography.* Muir of Ord, Rossshire: Kyle & Glen Music, 1982. 248 pp. ((5))

S-179   [[[Discography] in JACOBSSON, Stig: *Dimitrij Sjostakovitj.* Borås:
        Norma, 1983.   216 pp.]]

S-180   Discografie in *Dimitri Schostakowitsch, 1984/5.* [Duisberg]: Stadt
        Duisberg, 1984: 200-203   ((--))   [Omits record numbers]

S-181   Diskographie in SEEHAUS, Lothar: *Dmitrij Schostakowitsch, Leben
        und Werk.* Wilhelmshaven: F. Noetzel, 1986: 219-224   ((--))

S-182   Selected discography in *Music in the USSR* (January-March 1987):
        6-7   ((--))

OPERAS

(THE) NOSE (1930)

S-183   MARINELLI, Carlo: [Discography] in Bologna, Teatro Comunale,
        season 1978-79: program pp. 41-43   ((5))

S-184   MARINELLI, Carlo: [Discography] in Venezia, Teatro La Fenice,
        season 1978-79: program pp. 109-111   ((5))

SYMPHONIES

S-185   Discographie in *Harmonie-Panorama musique*, No. 45 (September
        1984): 54-60   ((7))

S-186   [[Discography in MECHELL, Harry Anthony: *Dmitri Shostakovitch
        (1906-1975): a critical study of the Babi Yar symphony with a
        survey of his works involving chorus.* [DMA, University of Illinois
        Urbana-Champaign, 1985]   106 pp.]]

SIBELIUS, JEAN, 1865-1957   (Finnish composer)

S-187   VIDAL, Pierre: Jean Sibelius: discographie critique in *Harmonie-
        Opéra Hi-Fi Conseil*, No. 16 (January 1982): 38-48   ((--))

SIDELNIKOV, NIKOLAI, 1930-   (Russian composer)

S-188   Discography in *Music in the USSR* (July-September 1986): [83]   ((--))

SILVESTROV, VALENTIN, 1937-   (Russian composer)

S-189   Discography in *Music in the USSR* (April-June 1988): 17   ((--))

SINGERS

S-190   CELLETTI, Rodolfo: *Le grandi voci.* Roma: Instituto per la
        collaborazione culturale, 1964.   1044 pp.   ((5))

S-191   GRAY, Sid: Edison concert and opera singers in *Hillandale News*, No.
        18 (April 1964): 32; No. 20 (August 1964): 67-68   ((--))

S-192   ROBERTS, Charles: Edison concert and opera singers in
        Hillandale News, No. 1-12 (1960-1963), reprinted 1967: p. 21-32
        ((7))

S-193   Discographies in KESTING, Jürgen: *Die grossen Sänger.* Düsseldorf:

Claassen, 1986. 3 v., 2094 pp. ((--))

S-194 Discographies in KUTSCH, K. J. and RIEMENS, Leo: *Grosses Sängerlexikon.* Bern: Francke, 1987. 2 v. ((--)) [Omits record numbers]

See also

VOCAL MUSIC

SINGERS, SWEDISH

S-195 [[AHLÉN, Carl-Gunnar: *Röster på Stockholmsoperan hundra år Historik. Sångtexter. Biografier.* Stockholm: Kungliga teater, 1977. 84 pp.]]

SINGERS, WOMEN

S-196 Discographies in TUBEUF, André: *Le chant retrouvé: sept divas: renaissance de l'opéra.* Paris: Fayard, 1979: [256]-[270] ((--))

SINGERS--ITALY

S-197 BERGAMASCO, Gino: Discografie in RUBBOLI, Daniele: *Le voci raccontate: (Ferrara, 1200-1977)* Bologna: Bongiovanni, 1976: 187-202 ((3, 6, 7))

S-198 Discografia dell'epoca Rossiniana in DELLA CROCE, Vittorio: *Una giacobina piemontese alla Scala: la primadonna Teresa Belloc.* Torino: Eda, 1978: 193-198 ((--))

S-199 [[RUBBOLI, Daniele: Cantanti lirici Veneti: discografia in PADOAN, Paolo: *Profili di cantanti lirice Veneti.* Bologna: Bongiovanni, 1978: 169-205]]

SINGING

S-200 Discography in *Voice.* London: Macdonald & Jane's, 1983: 291-307 ((--))

SINOPOLI, GIUSEPPE, 1946-   (Italian composer/conductor)

S-201 Discografia in *Musica,* No. 38 (October 1985): 16 ((--))

SKILONDZ, ANDREWJEWA VON, 1882-1968 (Russian soprano)

S-202 ENGLUND, Björn: Andrewjewa von Skilondz in *Talking Machine Review International,* No. 39 (April 1976): 616-619 ((3, 6, 7))

SLOBODSKAYA, ODA, 1888-1970 (Russian soprano)

S-203 Discography in LEONARD, Maurice: A singer's art in *Records and Recording,* XXI/9 (June 1979): 54-57 ((5))

S-204 Discography in LEONARD, Maurice: *Slodbodskaya: a biography of Oda Slobodskaya.* London: Gollancz, 1979: 126-128 ((5))

SLONIMSKY, SERGEI, 1932-   (Russian composer)

S-205 [Discography] in *Music in the USSR* (January–March 1986): 86   ((--))

SMALL, WINIFRED, 1896–1979 (English violinist)

S-206 PAIN, Derek: Discography in *Talking Machine Review*, No. 70
(December 1985): 1964   ((1, 3, 7))

SMALLEY, ROGER, 1943–   (English composer)

S-207 HUGHES, Eric and DAY, Timothy: Roger Smalley in *Recorded Sound*,
No. 83 (January 1983): 101–104   ((1, 3, 7))   (Discographies of
British composers; 17)

SMETANA, BEDŘICH, 1824–1884 (Czech composer)

OPERAS

(THE) BARTERED BRIDE (1866)

S-208   THALMANN, Albert: Diskographie in *Die verkaufte Braut*. München:
Goldmann; Mainz: Schott, 1983: 201   ((7))   (Opern der Welt)

PIANO WORKS

S-209   [[[Discography] in OČADLÍK, Mirko: *Klavirní dílo Bedricha Smetany
vydáno ke kompletu gramofonových desek klavírniho díla Bedricha
Smetany*. Praha, SHV, 1961. 99 pp.]]

SMETANA STRING QUARTET, Czechoslovakia

S-210 [Discography] in *Stereo Geijutsu*, No. 52 (August 1972): 156–159
((--))

SOBINOV, LEONID, 1872–1934 (Russian tenor)

S-211 DENNIS, J.: Leonid Vitalevich Sobinov discography in *Record
Collector*, XXIV/7–8 (September 1978): 181–190   ((3, 4, 6, 7))

SOCIEDAD CORAL POLIFÓNICA DE PONTEVEDRA, Spain

S-212 Discografia in *50 aniversario de su fundación (1925–1975)*
Pontevedra: Excma. Diputación Provincial, [1975]: 129–131   ((--))

SOFRONITSKY, VLADIMIR, 1901–1961 (Russian pianist)

S-213 [Discography] in *Vospominaniĩa o Sofroniẗskom*. Moskva: "Sov.
kompozitor", 1982: 466–473   ((7))

S-214 METHUEN-CAMPBELL, James: Early Soviet pianists and their recordings
in *Recorded Sound*, No. 83 (January 1983): 1–16   ((--))

SOLESMES, MONKS OF

S-215 WEBER, J. F.: A checklist of chant recordings by the monks of
Solesmes in *Fanfare*, IV/1 (September–October 1980): 255–256
((5, 7))

SOLLBERGER, HARVEY, 1938–   **(American composer)**

S-216 Selected discography in Program notes for *Double music*. [Sound recording] New World Records NW 330, 1985 ((--))

SOLOMON, 1902–1988 (English pianist)

S-217 GRAY, Michael H.: A Solomon discography in *ARSC Journal*, X/2-3 (1979): 188-209; addenda in XI/2-3 (1980): 263-264 ((3, 4, 5, 6, 7))

SOLOVIANENKO, ANATOLI, 1932–   **(Russian tenor)**

S-218 [Discography] in TERESHCNENKO, Alla: *Anatolii Solovianenko: tvorcheskii portret*. Kiev: "Mystetstvo", 1982: 163-[164] ((--))

SOLTI, SIR GEORG, 1912–   **(Hungarian conductor)**

S-219 Solti discography in *Record Geijutsu*, No. 277 (October 1973): 186-194 ((--))

S-220 [Georg Solti discography] in *Georg Solti and the Chicago Symphony Orchestra* in Record Geijutsu, No. 321 (June 1977): 81-93 ((5, 7))

S-221 SURTEES, Bruce: Discography in ROBINSON, Paul: *Solti*. Toronto: Lester and Opern, 1979: 151-164 ((1, 7))

S-222 Discographie Solti-Chicago in *Harmonie*, No. 10 (Sept. 2, 1984): ((--))

S-223 MARSH, Robert C.: Solti in Chicago: a critical discography in *Ovation* (December 1984): 26-29, 35 ((7))

S-224 WORMS, Laurent: Discographie in *Diapason-Harmonie*, No. 322 (December 1986): 46, 48 ((5))

SOMERS, HARRY, 1925–   **(Canadian composer)**

S-225 [[Discography in HOUGHTON, Diane: *The solo vocal works of Harry Somers*. [DMA, University of Missouri, 1980] 145 pp.]]

SONATAS (VIOLIN AND HARPSICHORD)

S-226 Phonographic music reproductions in PEDIGO, Alan: *International encyclopedia of violin-keyboard sonatas and composer biographies*. Boonville, Ark.: Arriaga Publications, 1979: 116-124 ((--))

SONGS

S-227 [[[Discography] in CASPARI, Rolf: *Lied Tradition im Stilwandel um 1600. Das Nachleben des deutschen Tenorliedes in den gedruckten Liedersammlungen von Le Maistre (1566) bis Schein (1626)* [Dissertation, Kiel, 1970] 290, 33 pp.]]

S-228 [[Discography in DOBBINS, F.: *The Chanson at Lyons in the sixteenth century*. [Dissertation, New College, Oxford, 1972] 393, 234 pp.]]

S-229 Discography in LANDAU, Anneliese: *The lied: the unfolding of its style*. Washington, D.C.: University Press of America, 1980: 123-133 ((--))

S-230 [Discography] in MOORE, Gerald: *Singer and accompanist: the performance of fifty songs.* London: Hamilton, 1982: 225-229   ((--))

S-231 STAHL, Dorothy: *A selected discography of solo song: supplement 1971-1974.* Detroit: Information Coordinators, 1976. 99 pp.   ((4))
(Detroit studies in music bibliography; 34)

S-232 STAHL, Dorothy: *A selected discography of solo song. Supplement, 1975-1982.* Detroit: Information Coordinators, 1984.   236 pp.   ((4))

S-233 BLYTH, Alan: *Song on record: v. 1 Lieder.* Cambridge; New York: Cambridge University Press, 1986.   357 pp.; *Song on record 2.* Cambridge; New York: Cambridge University Press, 1988.   286 pp.   ((4))

SONGS, AMERICAN

S-234 CARMAN, Judith Elaine: The song cycle in the United States: 1900-1970 in *NATS Bulletin*, XXXIII/3 (1977): 19-24; XXXIII/4 (1977): 10-17   ((--))

SONGS, ENGLISH

S-235 SWANEKAMP, Joan: *English ayres: a selectively annotated bibliography and discography.* Westport, CT: Greenwood Press, 1984. 141 pp.   ((--))

SONGS, GERMAN

S-236 TUBEUF, André: Discographie comparée: le lied alemand in *Harmonie*, No. 126 (April 1977): 37-43   ((--))

S-237 CANTAGREL, Gilles: Discographie in BEAUFILS, Marcel: *Le lied romantique allemand.* [Paris]: Gallimard, 1982: [315]-346   ((--))

SONGS--20TH CENTURY

S-238 [[Discography in CARMAN, Judith Elaine: *Twentieth-century American song cycles: a study in circle imagery.* [Dissertation, University of Iowa, 1973]   311 pp.]]

SORABJI, KAIKHOSRU SHAPURJI, 1892-1988   (Indian composer)

S-239 [[[Discography] in ROBERGE, Marc-André: Kaikhosru Shapurji Sorabji, compositeur sui generis in *Sonances, r.m. québécoise*, II/3 (April 1983): 17-21]]

SOROZABAL, PABLO, 1887-   (Spanish composer)

S-240 Discografia de Pablo Sorozábal in SOROZABAL, Pablo: *Mi vida y mi obra.* Madrid: España: Fundación Banco Exterior, 1986: 361-363   ((--))

SOTTOLANA, EDUARDO, 1865-?   (Baritone)

S-241 [Discography] in *Record Collector*, IX/3 (March 1954): 70   ((--))

SOUND RECORDINGS

S-242 DARRELL, R. D.: *The Gramophone shop encyclopedia of recorded music.*

New York: Gramophone Shop, 1936. 574 pp. ((4))

S-243   HAGGIN, Bernard H.: *Music on records.* New York: Oxford University
Press, 1938. 164 pp. [and] Supplement [records issued between
October 1938 and September 1939]: 41 pp. (New York: Oxford
University Press, 1939) ((4))

S-244   HAGGIN, Bernard H.: *Music on records; a new guide to the music,
performances, the recordings.* New York: Knopf, 1941. 245 pp. ((4))

S-245   KOLODIN, Irving: *A guide to recorded music.* Garden City, NY:
Doubleday, 1941. 495 pp. ((4))

S-246   [DARRELL, R. D.]: *The Gramophone shop encyclopedia of recorded
music.* New York: Simon and Schuster, 1942. 558 pp. ((--))

S-247   HALL, David: *The record book.* New York: Smith & Durrell, 1940.
771 pp. ((4)) With supplement 1 (1941): pp. 777-886 and supplement
2 (1943): pp. 891-1013.

S-248   HAGGIN, Bernard H.: *Music on records; a new guide to the music,
the performances, the recordings.* 2d ed. New York: Knopf, 1942.
243 pp. ((4))

S-249   HALL, David: *The record book: a music lover's guide to the world of
the phonograph.* New York: Smith & Durrell, 1942. 886 pp. ((--))

S-250   HAGGIN, Bernard H.: *Music on records, a new guide to the music,
the performances, the recordings.* 3d. ed. New York: Knopf, 1943.
262 pp. ((4))

S-251   HAGGIN, Bernard H.: *Music on records; a new guide to the music,
the performances, the recordings.* 4th ed. New York: Knopf, 1946.
279 pp. ((4))

S-252   HALL, David: *The record book: a music lover's guide to the world of
the phonograph.* New York: Citadel Press, 1946. 1063 pp. ((4))

S-253   KOLODIN, Irving: *New guide to recorded music.* Garden City, NY:
Doubleday, 1947. 382 pp. ((4))

S-254   HALL, David: *The record book: a guide to the world of the
phonograph.* New York: O. Durrell, 1948. 1394 pp. ((--))

S-255   [REID, Robert H.]: *The Gramophone shop encyclopedia of recorded
music.* 3d ed. New York: Crown Publishers, 1948. 639 pp. ((4))

S-256   HALL, David: *Records: 1950 edition.* New York: Knopf, 1950. 524 pp.
((--))

S-257   KOLODIN, Irving: *The new guide to recoded music.* Garden City, NY:
Doubleday, 1950. 524 pp. ((4))

S-258   CLOUGH, Francis F. and CUMING, G. J.: *The world's encyclopaedia
of recorded music.* London: Sidgwick & Jackson, 1952. 890 pp. *Second
Supplement, 1951/2.* London: Sidgwick & Jackson, 1952. 262 pp. and
Third Supplement, 1953/55. London: Sigwick & Jackson, 1957. 564 pp.
All reprinted by Greenwood Press, 1970. ((--))

S-259 HALL, David and LEVIN, Abner: *The disc book.* New York: Long Player
Publications, 1955. 471 pp. ((4))

S-260 DELICATA, A. A. G.: Actual performance recordings [mostly of
performances at the Royal Opera House, Covent Garden] in *Record
Collector,* XIV/7-8: 174-178   ((3, 6, 7))

S-261 BESCOBY-CHAMBERS, John: *The archives of sound, including a selective
catalogue of historical violin, piano, spoken, documentary,
orchestra, composer's own recordings.* Lingfield, Surrey: Oakwood
Press, 1964. 153 pp. ((--))

S-262 HALL, David: *The record book: a guide to the world of the
phonograph.* Westport, CT: Greenwood Press, 1970. 1397 pp.
[Reprinted from the 1948 ed.]

S-263 [REID, Robert H.]: *The Gramophone shop encyclopedia of recorded
music.* 3d ed. Westport, CT: Greenwood Press, 1970. 639 pp. ((4))
[Reprinted from the 1948 ed.]

S-264 [[IDEYA, K.: On location recordings in *Record Geijutsu,* No. 5
(1970):]]

S-265 [[Classical four-channel discography in *Record Geijutsu,* No. 283
(May 1974):]]

S-266 [Live recording discography] in *Record Geijutsu,* No. 285 (June
1974): 236-240 ((1))

S-267 [Digital record discography] in *Stereo Geijutsu,* No. 147 (August
1979): 50-53 ((--)) [Classical recordings only]

SOUND RECORDINGS--SCANDINAVIA

S-268 LILIEDAHL, Karleric: *The Gramophone Co.: Scandinavian recordings
and recordings for the Scandinavian market (and other recordings of
some prominent Scandinavians)* Trelleborg [Sweden]: Liliedahl,
1973- ((3, 4, 6, 7)) [Mostly pop recordings]

S-269 LILIEDAHL, Karleric: *The Gramophone Co.: acoustic recordings in
Scandinavia and for the Scandinavian market.* Helsinki: Finnish
Institute of recorded sound, 1977. 564 pp. ((3, 4, 6, 7))
[Mostly pop music]

SOUSA, JOHN PHILIP, 1854-1932 (American composer/conductor)

S-270 MITZIGA, Walter: *The sound of Sousa: John Philip Sousa
compositions recorded.* [S.l.: s.n., 1986] (Chicago, IL: South Shore
Printers) 206 pp. ((1))

SOUSA BAND

S-271 SMART, James R.: *The Sousa Band, a discography.* Washington:
Library of Congress, 1970. 123 pp. ((3, 4, 6, 7))

SPALDING, ALBERT, 1888-1953 (American violinist)

S-272 FERRARA, D. E.: A Spalding Centenary [Edison records] in *New Amberola Graphic*, No. 65 (July 1988): 14-15 ((3, 6, 7))

SPIVAKOV, VLADIMIR, 1944-   **(Russian violinist)**

S-273 Discography in *Music in the USSR* (July-September 1987): 88-89 ((--))

SPOHR, LUDWIG, 1784-1859   (German composer)

S-274 JORDAN, Robert: *A discography of the music of Louis Spohr (1784-1859)* Vancouver, B.C.: Jordan, 1985. 23 pp. ((5, 7))

CONCERTOS, CLARINET

S-275 [[Discography in JOHNSTON, Stephen Keith: *The clarinet concertos of Louis Spohr.* [Dissertation, University of Maryland, 1972] 164 pp.]]

OPERAS

FAUST (1816)

S-276 MARINELLI, Carlo: Discografie: Faust e Mefistofele nelle opere teatrali e sinfonico-vocali in *Quaderni dell'I.R.TE.M.* [Instituto di Ricerca per il Teatro Musicale] No. 3 (1986): 1-5 ((5))

SPONTINI, GASPARO, 1774-1851   (Italian composer)

OPERAS

AGNES VON HOHENSTAUFEN (1829)

S-277 MARINELLI, Carlo: [Discography] in Roma, Teatro dell'Opera, season 1986-87: program pp. 82-83 ((5))

STADER, MARIA, 1911-   (Swiss soprano)

S-278 GREINNER, Hanes E.: Schallplattenverzeichnis in STADER, Maria: *Nehmt meinen Dank: Erinnerungen.* München: Kindler, 1979: 444-[452] ((--))

STAMPACONI, MR.   (Spanish tenor)

S-279 [Discography] in *Record Collector*, IX/3 (March 1954): 71 ((--))

STANLEY, JOHN, 1712-1786   (English composer)

S-280 [[Discography in WILLIAMS, Alfred Glyn: *The life and works of John Stanley (1712-1786)* [Dissertation, Reading, 1977]   209, 48 pp.]]

STARER, ROBERT, 1924-   (American composer)

S-281 [[[Discography] in LEWIS, Dorothy E.: *The major piano solo works of Robert Starer.* [Dissertation, Peabody Conservatory, 1978]   164 pp.]]

STARKER, JANOS, 1924-   (Hungarian cellist)

S-282 SMART, James R.: *The recordings of Janos Starker; a discography.* Bloomington, IN: Smart, 1987. [26 pp.] ((4, 5, 7))

STEIBELT, DANIEL, 1765-1823 (German composer)

S-283 [[Discography in HAGBERG, Karen A.: _Cendrillon by Daniel Steibelt: an edition with notes on Steibelt's life and operas._ [Dissertation, University of Rochester, 1976] 190, 499 pp.]]

STENHAMMER, WILHELM, 1871-1927 (Swedish composer)

S-284 WISER, John: Wilhelm Stenhammer on records in _Fanfare_, VII/4 (March-April 1984): 90-94 ((--))

S-285 [[Discography in program notes for _Wilhelm Stenhammar String Quartets_ [Sound recording] Caprice CAP 21337/9, 1988]]

STEPHAN, RUDI, 1887-1915 (German composer)

S-286 Diskographie in BRAND, Juliane: _Rudi Stephan._ Tutzing: H. Schneider, 1983: 125 ((--)) (Komponisten in Bayern; 2)

STERN, ISAAC, 1920-   (American violinist)

S-287 [Discography] in _Record Geijutsu_, No. 276 (September 1973): 190-191 ((--))

S-288 [Discography] in _Record Geijutsu_, No. 395 (August 1983): 202-205; No. 396 (September 1983): 180-183 ((7))

STICH-RANDALL, TERESA, 1927-   (American soprano)

S-289 DUPECHEZ, Charles-F.: Teresa Stich-Randall le disque in _Diapason_, No. 244 (November 1979): 94-95 ((7))

STILL, WILLIAM GRANT, 1895-1978 (American composer)

S-290 Discography in ARVEY, Verna: _In one lifetime._ Fayetteville: University of Arkansas, 1984: 358-360 ((--))

STOCK, FREDERICK, 1872-1942 (American conductor)

S-291 SUGA, Hajime: Frederick Stock in _LP Techno_, May 1979: 81-85; addendum in LP Techno, May 1980: 98 ((--))

STOCKHAUSEN, KARLHEINZ, 1928-   (German composer)

S-292 [[[Discography] in HENCK, Herbert: _Karlheinz Stockhausens Klavierstück IX: eine analytische Betrachtung._ Bonn-Bad Godesberg: Verlag für Systematische Musikwissenschaft, 1978:]]

S-293 Diskographie in HENCK, Herbert: _Karlheinz Stockhausens Klavierstück X: Histoire, Theorie, Analyse, Praxis, Dokumentation._ Herrenberg: G. F. Doring, 1978: 83-92 ((--))

S-294 Discography in HENCK, Herbert: _Karlheinz Stockhausen's Klavierstück X: a contribution toward understanding serial technique: history, theory, analysis, practice, documentation._ Köln: Neuland Musikverlag Herbert Henck, 1980: 93-96 ((--))

S-295   *Karlheinz Stockhausen: Werke auf Schallplatten (List of records)*
Münster, West Germany: Discoteca Schallplatten-versand, [1980?]
One pamphlet, [4] pp. ((--))

S-296   HANSEN, Ivan: Stockhausen på plade in *Dansk Musiktidsskrift*,
LVII/3 (1982-3): 134   ((--))

KONTAKTE (1960)

S-297   MARINELLI, Carlo: [Discography] in Roma, Teatro dell'Opera,
season 1970-71: program p. 642   ((5))

STOKOWSKI, LEOPOLD, 1882-1977   (American conductor)

S-298   Diskografie in BURIAN, K. V.: *Leopold Stokowski*. Praha:
Supraphon, 1976: 74-[78]   ((--))

S-299   SURTEES, Bruce: Discography in ROBINSON, Paul: *Stokowski*.
Toronto: Lester and Orpen, 1977: 123-152   ((7))

S-300   [Leopold Stokowski discography] in *Record Geijutsu*, No. 327
(December 1977): 216-225   ((7))

S-301   CARTWRIGHT, Jim: Leopold Stokowski acoustical recordings in Immortal
Performances Auction List [Dealer's List] Austin, TX: Immortal
Performances, 1978: [29]-42]   ((3, 6, 7))   (Immortal Performances
discographic data; 5)   [Includes unissued performances]

S-302   BRAGALINI, Robert: Selective discography of available Stokowski
recordings in CHASINS, Abram: *Leopold Stokowski, a profile*. New
York: Hawthorn Books; London: Dutton, 1979; New York: Da Capo Press,
1981: 278-296   ((--))

S-303   JOHNSON, Edward: Stokowski's recorded repertoire in DANIEL, Oliver:
Stokowski: a counterpoint of view. New York: Dodd, Mead & Co.,
1982: 993-1039   ((1, 5, 7))

S-304   [Selected current discography] in VROON, Don: Leopold Stokowski,
1882-1977 in *Le Grand Baton*, No. 52 (March 1982): 16-19   ((--))

STOLZ, ROBERT, 1880-1975   (Austrian composer)

S-305   Auswahl-Discographie in STOLZ, Robert: *Servus Du: Robert Stolz und
sein Jahrhundert*. München: Blanvlet, 1980: 543-551   ((--))

S-306   Robert Stolz op de grammofoonplaat in BREDSCHNEYDER, Fred: *Robert
Stolz in Holland*. Bussum: Gooise Uitgeverij, 1980: [106]-111   ((--))

S-307   Diskographie in PFLICHT, Stephan: *Robert Stolz: Werkverzeichnis =
Catalogue of works*. München: Musikverlag B. Katzbichler; Berlin:
Dreiklang-Dreimasken Bühen-und Musikverlag, 1981: 419-471   ((--))

STOLZE, GERHARD, 1926-   (German tenor)

S-308   [Discography] in *Stereo Geijutsu*, No. 46 (March 1972): 156-159
((--))

STRACCIARI, RICCARDO, 1875-1955   (Italian baritone)

S-309   PEEL, Tom and WILLIAMS, Cliff: The discography in *Record Collector*,
        XXX/1-2 (February 1985): 39-53; additions & corrections in XXXI/8-10
        (September 1986): 239   ((3, 4, 6, 7))

STRAUSS, JOHANN, JR., 1825-1899   (Austrian composer)

OPERAS

(DIE) FLEDERMAUS (1874)

S-310   MARINELLI, Carlo: [Discography] in Bologna, Teatro Comunale,
        season 1980-81: program pp. 76-93   ((5))

S-311   BLYTH, Alan: Die Fledermaus in *Opera*, XXIX/1 (January 1978):
        22-34; with WALKER, Malcolm: Die Fledermaus--LP discography,
        pp. 33-34   ((5)) (Opera on the gramophone; 42)

S-312   TUBEUF, André: Discographie comparée in *L'Avant Scène Opéra*, No.
        49 (February 1983): 146-148   ((7))

S-313   MARINELLI, Carlo: [Discography] in Venezia, Teatro La Fenice,
        season 1984: program pp. 233-237   ((5))

STRAUSS, RICHARD, 1864-1949   (German composer)

S-314   Richard Strauss; a centennial discography in *Saturday Review* (May
        30, 1964): 62f   ((--))

S-315   [Discography] in *Stereo Geijutsu*, No. 80 (October 1974): 153-160;
        No. 81 (November 1974): 152-159; No. 82 (December 1974): 168-172
        ((5, 7))

S-316   MORSE, Peter: Richard Strauss's recordings: a complete discography
        in *ARSC Journal*, IX/1 (1977): 6-65; supplement in X/2-3 (1979):
        210-215   ((1, 3, 4, 5, 6, 7))

CHORAL WORKS

S-317   Diskographie in WAJEMANN, Heiner: *Die Chorkompositionen von
        Richard Strauss*. Tutzing: H. Schneider, 1986: 335-347   ((--))

OPERAS

S-318   JEFFERSON, Alan: *Richard Strauss operas*. Utica, NY: J. F. Weber,
        1977. 51 pp.   ((1, 3, 4, 5, 6, 7))   (Weber discography series;
        17)

S-319   [Discography] in *fono forum* (June 1988): 20-26; (August 1988):
        26-32; (October 1988): 30-36   ((5))

ÄGPYTISCHE HELENA (1924-7)

S-320   [[[Discography] in *Richard Strauss, die Ägyptische Helena*.
        München: Bayerische Staatsoper, 1981: 109]]

ARABELLA (1933)

S-321   PETERSON, Cathy: Discography in *Arabella*. London: Calder; New

York: Riverrun Press, 1985: 111   ((--))   (English National Opera guide; 30)

ARIADNE AUF NAXOS (1912)

S-322   MARINELLI, Carlo: [Discography] in Milano, Teatro alla Scala, season 1983-84: program p. 30   ((5))

S-323   TUBEUF, André: Discographie in *L'Avant Scène Opéra*, No. 77 (July 1985): 120-127   ((1, 7))

ELEKTRA (1909)

S-324   MARINELLI, Carlo: [Discography] in Venezia, Teatro La Fenice, season 1971-72: program pp. 75-77   ((5))

S-325   MARINELLI, Carlo: [Discography] in Roma, Teatro dell'Opera, season 1979-80: program pp. 543-552   ((5))

S-326   GUEULLETTE, Alain: Discographie in *L'Avant Scène Opéra*, No. 92 (November 1986): 112-119   ((1, 5))

S-327   [[[Discography] in *Salome; &, Elektra*. London: J. Calder; New York: Riverrun Press, 1988:   (English National Opera guide; 37)

FEUERSNOT (1900-1)

S-328   SCHAUMKELL, Claus-Dieter: Gesamtaufnahmen auf Schallplatte in *Richard Strauss, Feuersnot*. München: Bayerische Staatsoper, 1980: 109   ((5))

(DIE) FRAU OHNE SCHATTEN (1919)

S-329   MARINELLI, Carlo: [Discography] in Roma, Teatro dell'Opera, season 1967-68: program pp. 702-704   ((5))

S-330   MARINELLI, Carlo: [Discography] in Milano, Teatro alla Scala, season 1985-86: program pp. 118-119   ((5))

(DER) ROSENKAVALIER (1917)

S-331   Discography in *Der Rosenkavalier*. London: J. Calder; New York: Riverrun Press, 1981: 126-128   ((--))   (English National Opera guide; 8)

S-332   Selected discography in *Der Rosenkavalier*. Boston: Little, Brown, 1982:   ((4, 7))

S-333   WERBA, Robert: Die Gesaumtaufnahmen des "Rosenkavalier" in *Österreichische Musikzeitschrift*, XXXVIII/7-8 (July-August 1983): 455-457   ((5))

S-334   SCHAUMKELL, Claus-Dieter: Ist ein Traum, kann doch wirklich sein (Vergleichende Discographie) in *fono forum* (October 1984): 28-30   ((7))

S-335   Discography in JEFFERSON, Alan: *Richard Strauss, Der Rosenkavalier*. Cambridge; New York: Cambridge University Press,

1985: 146-150   ((1, 7))   (Cambridge opera handbooks)

S-336   THALMANN, Albert: Diskographie in *Der Rosenkavalier*. München:
Goldmann; Mainz: Schott, 1985: 422-425   ((1, 5)) (Opern der Welt)

SALOME (1905)

S-337   MARINELLI, Carlo: [Discography] in Roma, Teatro dell'Opera,
season 1965-66: program pp. 610-611   ((5))

S-338   MARINELLI, Carlo: [Discography] in Milano, Teatro alla Scala,
season 1973-74: program pp. 33-41   ((5))

S-339   MARINELLI, Carlo: [Discography] in Roma, Teatro dell'Opera,
season 1976-77: program pp. 196-205   ((5))

S-340   GUEULLETTE, Alain: Discographie comparée in *L'Avant Scène Opéra*,
No. 47 (January 1983): 184-189   ((7))

S-341   MARINELLI, Carlo: [Discography] in Milano, Teatro alla Scala,
season 1986-87: program pp. 71-74   ((5))

S-342   [[[Discography] in *Salome; &, Elektra*. London: J. Calder; New
York: Riverrun Press, 1988:   (English National Opera guide; 37)

ORCHESTRAL WORKS

(EINE) ALPENSINFONIE, Op. 64   (1915)

S-343   Discographische Hinweise in *fono forum* (April 1986): 28-29   ((7))

ALSO SPRACH ZARATHUSTRA, Op. 30   (1896)

S-344   PHILIPPOT, Michel-P.: Discographie in *Diapason*, No. 205 (March
1976): 43   ((--))

JOSEPHSLEGENDE, Op. 60   (1914)

S-345   MARINELLI, Carlo: [Discography] in Milano, Teatro alla Scala,
season 1981-82: program p. 47   ((5))

SONGS

S-346   MORSE, Peter and NORTON-WELSH, Christopher: Die Lieder von Richard
Strauss - eine Diskographie in *Richard Strauss-Blätter*, No. 5
(August 1974): 81-123   ((--))

VIER LETZTE LIEDER (1948)

S-347   DUPECHEZ, Charles-F.: Le point sur Les derniers lieder de Richard
Strauss in *Diapason*, No. 243 (October 1979): 58-59   ((--))

STRAVINSKY, IGOR FEDOROVICH, 1882-1971   (Russian composer)

S-348 DERRIEN, Jean-Pierre and ARNOL, André: Igor Stravinsky:
orientation discographie et bibliographie in *Musique en jeu*,
No. 4 (1971): [48]-51   ((--))

S-349   [[LORCEY, Jacques: Discographie critique in STRAVINSKY, Igor: *Chronique de ma vie*.   Paris: Denoël, 1971]]

S-350   [[[Stravinsky discography] in *Record Geijutsu*, (No. 6, 1971):]]

S-351   [[FREDERICHSEN, Ebbe: *Igor Stravinskij. En diskografi 1962-1972*. [Thesis, Royal Danish School of Librarianship, 1973]]]

S-352   List of recordings in WHITE, Eric Walter: *Stravinsky: a critical survey*. Westport, CT: Greenwood Press, 1979: 182-186 ((--)) [Reprinted from the 1948 ed. published by Philosophical Press, NY]

S-353   HALBREICH, Harry: Discographie critique [d'Igor Stravinsky] in *Harmonie Hi-fi Conseil*, No. 16 (September 1980): 38-42, 44, 46-62 ((--))

S-354   MORIN, Philippe: Stravinsky dirige Stravinsky in *Diapason*, No. 254 (October 1980): 42-44 ((7))

S-355   Diskographie in HIRSBRUNNER, Theo: *Igor Strawinsky in Paris*. [Laaber]: Laaber-Verlag, 1982: [243]-255 ((--))

S-356   VROON, Don: Igor Stravinsky: a look at some recordings in *Le Grand Baton*, No. 53 (June 1982): 5-7 ((--))

BALLETS

AGON (1957)

S-357   MARINELLI, Carlo: [Discography] in Bologna, Teatro Comunale, season 1978-79: program pp. 17-18 ((5))

APOLLON MUSAGÈTE (1928)

S-358   MARINELLI, Carlo: [Discography] in Bologna, Teatro Comunale, season 1978-79: program pp. 18-23 ((5))

(LE) BAISER DE LA FÉE (1928)

S-359   MARINELLI, Carlo: [Discography] in Venezia, Teatro La Fenice, season 1971-72: program pp. 205-208 ((5))

JEU DE CARTES (1937)

S-360   MARINELLI, Carlo: [Discography] in Roma, Teatro dell'Opera, season 1970-71: program pp. 92-94 ((5))

S-361   MARINELLI, Carlo: [Discography] in Bologna, Teatro Comunale, season 1978-79: program pp. 24-27 ((5))

L'OISEAU DE FEU (1910)

S-362   MARINELLI, Carlo: [Discography] in Roma, Teatro dell'Opera, season 1971-72: program pp. 79-84   ((5))

S-363   MARINELLI, Carlo: [Discography] in Roma, Teatro dell'Opera, season 1979-80: program pp. 1017-1021 ((5))

S-364   Discografia in MARUCCI, Francesco M.: La gloria arriva con
        L'Uccello di fuoco in *Discoteca Hifi*, No. 231 (25 July-1
        September 1982): 32-34   ((--))

ORPHEUS (1947)

S-365   MARINELLI, Carlo: [Discography] in Palermo, Ente automono
        Teatro Massimo, season 1981-82: program p. 4   ((5))

PETROUSHKA (1911)

S-366   MARINELLI, Carlo: [Discography] in Roma, Teatro dell'Opera,
        season 1970-71: program pp. 64-70   ((5))

S-367   Petroushka de Stravinski: discographie critique in *Diapason*, No.
        215 (March 1977): 66-67   ((--))

S-368   Discografia in LEPIDO, Bruno: Petrouschka una 'vera' rivoluzione
        musicale in *Discoteca Hifi*, No. 231 (25 July-1 September 1982):
        57-58   ((--))

S-369   MARINELLI, Carlo: [Discography] in Roma, Teatro dell'Opera,
        season 1984-85: program pp. 40-47   ((5))

PULCINELLA (1920)

S-370   MARINELLI, Carlo: [Discography] in Venezia, Teatro La Fenice,
        season 1971-72: program pp. 199-204   ((5))

(LE) SACRE DU PRINTEMPS (1913)

S-371   MARINELLI, Carlo: [Discography] in Milano, Teatro alla Scala,
        season 1972-73: program pp. 84-91   ((5))

S-372   Die besprochenen Aufnahmen in *fono forum* (February 1976): 121
        ((--))

S-373   MARINELLI, Carlo: [Discography] in Milano, Teatro alla Scala,
        season 1980-81: program pp. 1144-1151   ((5))

S-374   Discografia in LEPIDO, Bruno: Il vento nuovo dalla Sagra della
        primavera in *Discoteca Hifi*, No. 231 (25 July-1 September 1982):
        55-56   ((--))

INSTRUMENTAL WORKS

HISTOIRE DU SOLDAT (1918)

S-375   Discografia in GAVEZZOTTI, Emilio: L'Histoire du soldat tra
        guerra e fantasia in *Discoteca Hifi*, No. 231 (25 July-1 September
        1982): 35-36   ((--))

ORCHESTRAL WORKS

CHANT DU ROSSIGNOL (1919)

S-376   MARINELLI, Carlo: [Discography] in Venezia, Teatro La Fenice,
        season 1971-72: program pp. 456-458   ((5))

S-377   MARINELLI, Carlo: [Discography] in Roma, Teatro dell'Opera,
             season 1981-82: program pp. 764-767 ((5))

FEU D'ARTIFICE (1908)

S-378   MARINELLI, Carlo: [Discography] in Roma, teatro dell'Opera,
             season 1976-77: program pp. 500-502 ((5))

(LES) NOCES (1917-1923)

S-379   MARINELLI, Carlo: [Discography] in Roma, Teatro dell'Opera,
             season 1967-68: program pp. 661-663 ((5))

S-380   MARINELLI, Carlo: [Discography] in Venezia, Teatro La Fenice,
             season 1970-71: program pp. 150-153 ((5))

PERSÉPHONE (1933)

S-381   MARINELLI, Carlo: [Discography] in Palermo, Ente automono
             Teatro Massimo, season 1981-82: program p. 3 ((5))

PIANO WORKS

S-382   Selected discography [piano works] in Program notes for
             Stravinsky: Serenade, Sonata. [Sound recording] New World
             Records NW 344, 1987 ((--))

STAGE WORKS

MAVRA (1922)

S-383   MARINELLI, Carlo: [Discography] in Roma, Teatro dell'Opera,
             season 1970-71: program pp. 81-82 ((5))

S-384   MARINELLI, Carlo: [Discography] in Treviso, Ente Teatro
             Comunale, season 1976: program p. 4 ((5))

OEDIPUS REX (1927)

S-385   MARINELLI, Carlo: [Discography] in Roma, Teatro dell'Opera,
             season 1971-72: program pp. 56-57 ((5))

S-386   MARINELLI, Carlo: [Discography] in Venezia, Teatro La Fenice,
             season 1971-72: program pp. 71-73 ((5))

S-387   MARINELLI, Carlo: [Discography] in Milano, Teatro alla Scala,
             season 1972-73: program pp. 89-91 ((5))

S-388   MARINELLI, Carlo: [Discography] in Venezia, Teatro La Fenice,
             season 1975-76: program pp. 490-493 ((5))

S-389   MARINELLI, Carlo: [Discography] in Milano, Teatro alla Scala,
             season 1979-80: program p. 77 ((5))

S-390   MARINELLI, Carlo: Discografia ragionata dell'Oedipus Rex in
             Musica, No. 20 (March 1981): 44-47 ((5))

(THE) RAKE'S PROGRESS (1951)

S-391   MARINELLI, Carlo: [Discography] in Roma, Teatro dell'Opera,
         season 1967-68: program p. 752   ((5))

S-392   WALKER, Malcolm: Discography in GRIFFITHS, Paul: *Igor
         Stravinsky, The Rake's progress*. Cambridge; New York: Cambridge
         University Press, 1982: 106   ((5))   (Cambridge opera handbooks)

S-393   MARINELLI, Carlo: [Discography] in Venezia, Teatro La Fenice,
         season 1986: program pp. 532-534   ((5))

S-394   MARINELLI, Carlo: Discografie: Faust e Mefistofele nelle opere
         teatrali e sinfonico-vocali in *Quaderni dell'I.R.TE.M.* [Instituto
         di Ricerca per il Teatro Musicale] No. 3 (1986): 105-112   ((5))

RENARD (1922)

S-395   MARINELLI, Carlo: [Discography] in Venezia, Teatro La Fenice,
         season 1971-72: program pp. 458-460   ((5))

S-396   [[Discography in DUNNER, Leslie Byron: *Stravinsky and dance:
         a conductor's study of "Renard"*. [DMA, University of Cincinnati,
         1982] 145 pp.]]

STRING QUARTETS

S-397 Diskographie in KONOLD, Wulf: *Das Streichquartett: von d. Anfängen
      bis Franz Schubert*. Wilhelmshaven: Heinrichshofen, 1980: 184-191;
      New York: C. F. Peters, 1984: 181-190   ((--))

STUDER, CHERYL   (American soprano)

S-398 Discographische Hinweise in *fono forum* (July 1988): 26   ((--))

STURZENEGGER, RICHARD, 1905–   (Swiss composer)

S-399 Discographie in *Richard Sturzenegger. Werkverzeichnis=Liste des
      oeuvres*. Zürich: Schweizerisches Musik-Archiv, 1970: [9-10]   ((--))

SUDER, JOSEPH, 1892–   (German composer)

S-400 [[[Discography] in *Joseph Suder*. Tutzing: H. Schneider, 1987:
      149-150   (Komponisten in Bayern; 15)]]

SULLIVAN, SIR ARTHUR, 1842–1900   (English composer)

S-401 [[REES, Terence: *A Sullivan Discography*. Saffon-Walden: The
      Arthur Sullivan Society, 1986.]]

      See also

D'OYLE CARTE OPERA COMPANY (London)

SUSA, CONRAD, 1935–   (American composer)

S-402 Selected discography in Program notes for *Henry Herford, baritone*.
      [Sound recording] New World Records NW 327, 1985: [1]   ((--))

SUTER, ROBERT, 1919–   **(Swiss composer)**

S-403 Discographie in *Werkverzeichnis Robert Suter=Liste des oeuvres Robert Suter: geboren am 30. Januar 1919.* Zürich: Schweizerisches Musik-Archiv, 1980: 14–15 ((--))

SUTHERLAND, DAME JOAN, 1926–   **(Australian soprano)**

S-404 Discography Joan Sutherland in ADAMS, Brian: *La Stupenda, a biography of Joan Sutherland.* Melbourne: Hutchinson of Australia, 1980: 299–307 ((--))

S-405 [Discography] in GAITA, Denis: Che voce, milady in *Discoteca Hifi*, No. 229 (25 May–25 June 1982): 16–18 ((--))

SVETLANOV, EVGENY, 1928–   **(Russian conductor)**

S-406 [Discography, with USSR Symphony Orchestra] in *Music in the USSR* (April–June 1986): 9–11 ((--))

SVIRIDOV, GEORGI, 1915–   **(Russian composer)**

S-407 [Discography] in PERSON, D.: *G.V. Sviridov.* Moskva: Soviet kompozitor, 1974: 82–85 ((--))

S-408 BLOIS, Louis: Selected discography of Georgi Sviridov in *Kastlemusik*, VIII/2 (February 1983): 10–11 ((3))

S-409 Discography in *Music in the USSR* (January–March 1987): 19 ((--))

S-410 Discography in *Music in the USSR* (October–December 1987): 25–26 ((--))

SWAROWSKY, HANS, 1899–1975 (Austrian conductor)

S-411 Diskographie in SWAROWSKY, Hans: *Wahrung der Gestalt.* Wien: Universal Edition, 1979: 278–292 ((1, 7))

SYLVA, MARGUERITE, 1876–1957 (Belgian soprano)

S-412 STONE, Robert B.: Discography in *New Amberola Graphic*, No. 32 (Spring 1980): 7–8 ((5))

S-413 WILE, Ray: From the Edison vaults: the Edison recordings of Marguerite Sylva in *New Amberola Graphic*, No. 34 (Fall 1980): 4 ((3, 7))

SYMPHONIES

S-414 [[Discography in SCHWARTZ, Judith Leah: *Phrase morphology in the early Classical symphony (ca. 1720–ca. 1765)* [Dissertation, New York University Graduate Center, 1973] 367 pp.]]

S-415 A symphonic Baedeker in *New York Times* (October 10, 1976), Section 2, pp. 25, 31, 34 ((--))

S-416 [Symphony catalog] in *Stereo Geijutsu*, No. 138 (October 1978):

59-82 ((5, 7))

S-417 ROCKWELL, John: Discography of the classical symphony in *New York Times* (April 26, 1987): section 2, p. 22 ((--))

SYMPHONIES, RUSSIAN

S-418 [[Discography in GREENWALT, Terrence Lee: *A study of the symphony in Russia from Glinka to the early Twentieth century.* [Dissertation, University of Rochester, 1972] 214 pp.]]

SYMPHONY ORCHESTRAS

S-419 [[[Discography] in HAFFNER, Herbert: *Sinfonieorchester der Welt: mit Diskographien historischer und akueller Einspielungen.* Wilhelmshaven: F. Netzel, 1988: 260-299]]

SZABÓ, FERENC, 1902-1969 (Hungarian composer)

S-420 Diszkografia in MAROTHY, Janos: *Zene, forradalom, szocializmus: Szabó Ferenc útja.* Budapest: Magvető, 1975: 800-[805] ((5))

SZELL, GEORGE, 1897-1970 (Hungarian conductor)

S-421 HIRSCH, Howard T. and SAUL, Jack: George Szell discography [Supplement] in *Le Grand Baton*, No. 43 (March-June 1979): S-1-10 ((7))

SZERYNG, HENRYK, 1918-1988 (Polish violinist)

S-422 Discography [on Philips label] S.l. [Philips, 198-?] 2 l. ((--))

SZIGETI, JOSEPH, 1892-1973 (Hungarian violinist)

S-423 Joseph Szigeti; Schallplattenverzeichnis (Auswahl) in *fono forum* (June 1976): 525 ((--))

S-424 A list of recordings in SZIGETI, Joseph: *With strings attached: reminiscences and reflections.* New York: Da Capo Press, 1979: 335-341 ((--)) [Reprinted from the 1947 ed. published by Knopf, New York]

SZPINALSKI, STANISŁAW, 1901-1957 (Polish pianist)

S-425 Nagrania in JADACKI, Jacek Juliusz: O Stanisławie Szpinalskim *Muzyka,* XXII/1 (1977): 36-37 ((--))

SZYMANOWSKI, KAROL, 1882-1937 (Polish composer)

S-426 List of recordings (1929-1979) in CHYLIŃSKA, Teresa: *Szymanowski.* Cracow: Polskie Wydawn. Muzyczne, 1981: 216-[225] ((5))

S-427 MICHAŁOWSKI, Korneł: Dyskografia Karola Szymanowskiego 1967-1981 in *Ruch Muzyczny,* XXVI/1 (1982): 4-5 ((5))

S-428 Discographische Hinweise: Karol Szymanowski: kleine Auswahl-Discographie zur Einführung in *fono forum* (December 1982): 36 ((--))

S-429   Discographie: de Magaloff a Rowicki ... in *Diapason-Harmonie*, No. 332 (November 1987): 72   ((--))

TACUCHIAN, RICARDO, 1939-   **(Brazilian composer)**

T-1   Discographic references in MIGLIAVACCA, Ariede Maria: *Ricardo Tacuchian: catálogo de obras*. [Brasília]: Ministério das Relações Exteriores, Departamento de Cooperação Cultural, Científica e Tecnológica, 1977: [24] pp.   ((--))   (Compositores brasileiros)

TAGLIAVINI, FERRUCCIO, 1913-   **(Italian tenor)**

T-2   SANGUINETTI, Horacio and WILLIAMS, Clifford: Discography in *Record Collector*, XXIX/9-12 (December 1984): 218-240; addenda in XXX/10-11 (October 1985): 239-241   ((1, 3, 4, 6, 7))

TAILLON, JOCELYNE, 1941-   **(French mezzo-sporano)**

T-3   Discographie in *Harmonie-Panorama musique*, No. 31 (May 1983): 18-19   ((--))

TAKEMITSU, TORU, 1930-   **(Japanese composer)**

See

PIANO MUSIC

TALICH, VÁCLAV, 1883-1961   (Czech conductor)

T-4   Prehled Talichovych gramofonovych snímků s Českou filharmonií in BARTOŠ, František: *Václav Talich; Zivot a práce*. Praha: Hudební matice umělecké besedy, 1943: 207-208   ((7))

TALMA, LOUISE, 1906-   **(American composer)**

T-5   [[Discography in TEICHER, Susan Carol: *The solo works for piano of Louise Talma*. [DMA, Peabody Conservatory, 1985]   227 pp.]]

T-6   Selected discography in Program notes for *Works for American composers*. [Sound recording] New World Records NW 317, 1984   ((--))

TALVELA, MARTTI, 1935-   **(Finnish bass)**

T-7   Martti Talvelan lveytykset in HEIKINHEIMO, Seppo: *Martti Talvela*. Helsinsiggsa: Otava, 1978: [328]   ((--))

TAMAGNO, FRANCESCO, 1850-1905   (Italian tenor)

T-8   MORAN, W. R.: The recordings of Francesco Tamagno (28 Dec., 1850-31 Aug., 1905) in CORSI, Mario: *Tamagno*. New York: Arno Press, 1977: [215]-[218]   ((3, 7))   [Includes notes on playing speeds] [Reprinted from the original ed. published without a discography by Ceschina, Milan, 1937]

TATE, JEFFREY, 1943-   **(English conductor)**

T-9   Discographie Hinweise in *fono forum* (January 1986): 29   ((--))

T-10   Discographie de Jeffrey Tate in *Diapason-Harmonie*, No. 332
(November 1987): 126   ((--))   [omits record numbers]

TAUBE, EVERT, 1889-1976   (Swedish composer)

T-11   Skivinspelningar in SVENSSON, Georg: *Evert Taube: poet, musikant,
artist.* Stockholm: Bonnier, 1976: 89-90   ((--))

TAUBER, RICHARD, 1891-1948   (Austrian tenor)

T-12   [[[Discography] in *Stimmen, die um die Welt gingen*, No. 1 (1983):
12-13]]

TAVARES, MARIO   (Brazilian composer)

T-13   Discographic references in MIGLIAVACCA, Ariede Maria: *Mario
Tavares: catálogo de obras.* [Brasília]: Ministério das Relações
Exteriores, Departamento de Cooperação Cultural, Científica e
Tecnológica, 1979: [15] pp.   ((--))   (Compositores brasileiros)

TAVENER, JOHN, 1944–   (English composer)

T-14   HUGHES, Eric and DAY, Timothy: John Tavener in *Recorded Sound*,
No. 80 (July 1981): 143-148   ((--))   (Discographies of British
composers; 13)

TCHAIKOVSKY, PETER ILICH, 1840-1893   (Russian composer)

BALLETS

SLEEPING BEAUTY, Op. 66 (1889)

T-15   MARINELLI, Carlo: [Discography] in Milano, Teatro alla Scala,
season 1982-83: program pp. 23   ((5))

SWAN LAKE, Op. 20 (1876)

T-16   MARINELLI, Carlo: [Discography] in Milano, Teatro alla Scala,
season 1973-74: program pp. 68-70   ((5))

T-17   MARINELLI, Carlo: [Discography] in Milano, Teatro alla Scala,
season 1979-80: program pp. 623-627   ((5))

T-18   MARINELLI, Carlo: [Discography] in Milano, Teatro alla Scala,
season 1984-85: program pp. 42   ((5))

T-19   MARINELLI, Carlo: [Discography] in Milano, Teatro alla Scala,
season 1985-86: program pp. 42   ((5))

T-20   MARINELLI, Carlo: [Discography] in Roma, Teatro dell'Opera,
season 1985-86: program pp. 44-48   ((5))

CHAMBER WORKS

TRIO, PIANO, Op. 50

T-21   SEIBERT, Don S. and WEBER, J. F.: The Tchaikovsky Trio: a
centennial discography in *Fanfare*, V/2 (November-December 1981):

261-262   ((3, 5, 7))

OPERAS

EUGENE ONEGIN (1879)

T-22   BLYTH, Alan: Eugene Onegin in *Opera*, XXX/2 (February 1979): 121-128; With WALKER, Malcolm: LP discography, p. 128; pt. 2 in Opera, XXX/3 (March 1979): 219-224 ((5)) (Opera on the gramophone; 46)

T-23   MARINELLI, Carlo: [Discography] in Roma, Teatro dell'Opera, season 1980-81: program pp. 794-807 ((5))

T-24   TUBEUF, André: Discographie in *L'Avant Scène Opéra*, No. 43 (September 1982): 112-114 ((1, 7))

T-25   SCHLIPPE, Alexander von: Anmerkungen zur Diskographie in *Eugen Onegin: Texte, Materialien, Kommentäre*. Reinbek bei Hamburg: Rowohlt, 1985: 228-[231] ((1, 5)) (Rororo Opernbücher)

T-26   MARINELLI, Carlo: [Discography] in Milano, Teatro alla Scala, season 1985-86: program pp. 57-61 ((5))

T-27   [[[Discograpy] in *Eugene Onegin*. London: J. Calder; New York: Riverrun Press, 1988:   (English National Opera guide; 38)]]

PIQUE DAME (1890)

T-28   MARINELLI, Carlo: [Discography] in Palermo, Ente automono Teatro Massimo, season 1983-84: program p. 16 ((5))

ORCHESTRAL WORKS

SERENADE FOR STRING ORCHESTRA, OP. 48 (1880)

T-29   MARINELLI, Carlo: [Discography] in Roma, Teatro dell'Opera, season 1976-77: program pp. 99-103 ((5))

SYMPHONIES

T-30   SEGALINI, Sergio: Les symphonies de Tchaikovski: discographie comparée in *Harmonie*, No. 136 (April 1978): 94-101 ((--))

SYMPHONY, No. 6, B Minor, Op. 74

T-31   [Discography] in *Stereo Geijutsu*, No. 149 (September 1979): 41-42 ((7))

TCHAIKOVSKY COMPETITION, MOSCOW

T-32   Discography International Tchaikovsky Competition in Moscow in *Music in the USSR* (January-March 1987): 11-13 ((7))

TCHEREPNIN, ALEXANDER, 1889-1977 (Russian composer)

T-33   Schallplatten in REICH, Willy: *Alexander Tcherepnin*. Bonn: M. P. Belaireff, 1970: 116-118 ((--))

T-34   [[[Discography] in ARIAS, Enrique Alberto: *Alexander Tcherepnin a bio-bibliography*. New York: Greenwood Press, 1988: (Bio-bibliographies in music; 8)]]

TEBALDI, RENATA, 1922–   (Italian soprano)

T-35   Discographie opere complete in CASANOVA, Carlamaria: *Renata Tebaldi: la voce d'angelo*. Milano: Electa, 1981: 246-247 ((5))

T-36   Discographie in SEGOND, André: *Renata Tebaldi*. Lyon: Laffont, 1981: 237-253 ((1, 5, 7))

T-37   [[[Discography] in CASANOVA, Carlamaria: *Renata Tebaldi, la voix d'angelo*. Paris: Chiron, 1986:]]

TE KANAWA, KIRI, 1944–   (New Zealand soprano)

T-38   Kiri Te Kanawa on London [S.l.]: London Records, 1985. 1 leaf ((--))

TELEMANN, GEORG PHILIPP, 1681-1767   (German composer)

T-39   [[[Discography] in UNFUG, D. Birch: *Twelve fantasies for solo flute by Georg Philipp Telemann*. Laramie, WY: University of Wyoming, 1983: leaf 137]]

TELMÁNYI, EMIL, 1892–   (Hungarian violinist)

T-40   Appendix II: Emil Telmányi--discografi in TELMÁNYI, Emil: *Af en musikers billedbog*. København: Nyt Nordisk Forlag, 1978: [311]-315 ((5))

TEMIRKANOV, YURI, 1938–   (Russian conductor)

T-41   Discography in *Music in the USSR* (July-September 1988): 19 ((--))

TENNSTEDT, KLAUS, 1926–   (German conductor)

T-42   [[STROFF, Stephen: Discography in *Goldmine* (April 27, 1984):]]

TERENTEV, BORIS, 1913–   (Russian composer)

T-43   [Discography] in VIKTOROV, Viktor Ilich: *Boris Terent'ev*. Moskva: "Sov. kompozitor", 1987: 100-[101] ((--))

TERRAZA, EMILIO, 1929–   (Brazilian composer)

T-44   Discographic references in FERREIRA, Paulo Affonso de Moura: *Emilio Terraza: catálogo de obras*. [Brasília]: Ministério das Relações Exteriores, Departamento de Cooperação Cultural, Científica e Tecnológica, 1976: [8] pp. ((--)) (Compositores brasileiros)

TETRAZZINI, LUISA, 1871-1940   (Italian soprano)

T-45   WADE, Philip H.: Luisa Tetrazzini; discography in *Record Collector*, (August 1949): 131-139 ((3, 6)) [Includes unissued records]

T-46   CARTWRIGHT, Jim: Luisa Tetrazzini's American recordings--Victor

Talking Machine in Immortal Performances 1976: List Number 2
[Dealer's list] Austin, TX: Immortal Performances, 1976: 13-[15]
((3, 6, 7)) (Immortal Performances discographic data; [2])

TEYTE, MAGGIE, 1888-1976 (English soprano)

T-47   TRON, David: Recordings of Maggie Teyte in TEYTE, Maggie: *Star on
the door.* New York: Arno Press, 1977: 188-192 ((1, 3, 7))
[Original ed. published without discography by Putnam, London, 1958]

T-48   Discography; Maggie Teyte in O'CONNOR, Garry: *The pursuit of
perfection: a life of Maggie Teyte.* London: Gollancz; New York:
Atheneum, 1979: [300]-314 ((1, 3, 6, 7))

THALBEN-BALL, GEORGE, 1896-1987 (British organist)

T-49   Appendix I: Discography in RENNERT, Jonathan: *George Thalben-Ball.*
North Pomfret, VT: David & Charles, 1979: [151]-156 ((--))

THIBAUD, JACQUES, 1880-1953 (French violinist)

T-50   J. Thibaud discography in *Stereo Geijutsu,* No. 163 (September
1980): 52-53 ((7))

T-51   [Thibaud discography] in *Record Geijutsu,* No. 417 (June 1985):
194-199; No. 418 (July 1985): 278-282; No. 419 (August 1985):
264-268; No. 420 (September 1985): 276-280; No. 421 (October 1985):
206-210 ((3, 6, 7))

T-52   DRIEU, Gérard: Jacques Thibaud in *Sonorités,* No. 17 (March 1987):
47-63 ((3, 6, 7))

THILL, GEORGES, 1897-1984 (French tenor)

T-53   Selected discography in TASSART, Maurice: Georges Thill: 80 ans
in *Diapason,* No. 223 (December 1977): 24-25 ((--))

T-54   Discographie in SEGOND, André: *Georges Thill.* Lyon: J.-M. Laffont,
1980: [261]-[278] ((5))

T-55   Discographie in SEGOND, André: *Georges Thill, album.* Aix au
Provence: Edisud, 1984: 83-89 ((5))

T-56   VOISIN, Georges: Discographie in *L'Avant Scène Opéra* (Special
number, September 1984): 100-103 in *Georges Thill & l'opéra
français.* [Sound recording] Pathé-Marconi EMI 290 1933, 1984.
((3, 7))

THOMAS, JOHN CHARLES, 1891-1960 (American baritone)

T-57   MORGAN, Charles I.: John Charles Thomas discography in *Record
Collector,* XXV/1-2 (March 1979): 15-31 ((1, 3, 6, 7,))

THOMAS, MOSTYN, 1896-1984 (Welsh baritone)

T-58   BOTT, Michael and GRIFFITHS, Bryan: Mostyn Thomas--discography in
Record Collector, XXXII/11-12 (November 1987): 246-247 ((1, 7))

THOMPSON, RANDALL, 1899-1984   (American composer)

T-59   Selected discography in Program notes for *Choral works by Randall Thompson, Elliott Carter, Seymour Shifrin.* [Sound recording] New World Records Records NW 219, 1977: 4   ((--))

T-60   SKINNER, Robert: A Randall Thompson discography in *ARSC Journal*, XII/3 (1980): 184-195   ((4, 5, 7))

THOMSON, VIRGIL, 1896-   (American composer)

T-61   Selected discography in Program notes for *The mother of us all.* [Sound recording] New World Records NW 288/289, 1977: 34   ((--))

T-62   Discography in MECKNA, Michael: *Virgil Thomson, a bio-bibliography.* Westport, CT: Greenwood Press, 1986: [73]-87   ((7)) (Bio-bibliographies in music; 4)

THORBORG, KERSTIN, 1896-1970   (Swedish soprano)

T-63   BRUUN, Carl L.: Kerstin Thorborg discography in *Record Collector*, XXIV/9-10 (October 1978): 205-215   ((1, 3, 4, 6, 7))

TIBBETT, LAWRENCE, 1896-1960   (American baritone)

T-64   MORAN, W. R.: Lawrence Tibbett (1896-1960)--a discography in TIBBETT, Lawrence: *The glory road.* New York: Arno Press, 1977: i-xxii   ((1, 3, 6, 7))

T-65   MORAN, W. R.: Lawrence Tibbett (1896-1960)--a discography in *Record Collector*, XXIII/11-12 (August 1977): 273-286; Listing of opera broadcasts and of recordings made from them, other broadcasts, films and other sources in XXIV/1-2 (January 1978): 36-46   ((1, 3, 6, 7))

T-66   [[MORAN, William R.: Discography in *Lawrence Tibbett, singing actor.* Portland, OR: Amadeus Press, 1988]]

TIMPANI

T-67   Nota discografica in FACCHIN, Guido: *Il timpano.* Padova: Zanibon, 1977: 75-77   ((--))

TIPPETT, SIR MICHAEL KEMP, 1905-   (English composer)

T-68   WOOLGAR, Alan: Recording of works by Michael Tippett in *A man of our time, Michael Tippett.* London: Schott, 1977: 115-119   ((1, 5))

T-69   ANDREWS, Paul D.: Sir Michael Tippett--a bibliography in *Brio*, XV/2 (Autumn 1978): 33-46   ((5)) [Includes discographic notes]

T-70   HUGHES, Eric and DAY, Timothy: Sir Michael Tippett in *Recorded Sound*, No. 78 (July 1980): 73-89   ((1)) (Discographies of British composers; 4) [Also issued as a pamphlet, 1980]

T-71   WOOLGAR, Alan: A Tippett discography in *Records & Recording*, No. 269 (February 1980): 26-28   ((1))

T-72   Selected discography in BOWEN, Meirion: *Michael Tippett.* London:

Robson Books, 1981: 186-188   ((--))

T-73   Discographie sommaire in LABIE, Jean-François: Connaissez-vous
        Michaël Tippett in *Diapason*, No. 266 (November 1981): 30-31   ((--))

T-74   OLIVER, Michael: Music of Tippett on record in *Gramophone*,
        LXII/741 (February 1985): 966   ((--))

OPERAS

T-75   PETERSON, Cathy: Discography in *The operas of Michael Tippett*.
        London: J. Calder; New York: Riverrun Press, 1985: 142-143   ((--))
        (English National Opera guide; 29)

TISHCHENKO, BORIS IVANOVICH, 1939-   (Russian composer)

T-76   [Discography] in *Music in the USSR* (April-June 1986): 83   ((--))

TITTERTON, FRANK, 1882-1956   (English tenor)

T-77   MORGAN, Charles: Frank Titterton discography in *Record Collector*,
        XXVII/11-12 (March 1983): 250-263; additions & corrections in
        XXX/12-13 (December 1985): 295   ((3, 6, 7))

TOKYO STRING QUARTET, USA

T-78   Discography, Deutsche Grammophon artist information, 1980. 1 p.
        ((--))

TOMOWA-SINTOW, ANNA, 1941-   (Bulgarian soprano)

T-79   Discographische Hinweise: Anna Tomowa-Sintow in *fono forum* (November
        1985): 36   ((--))

TORELLI, GIUSEPPE, 1658-1709   (Italian composer)

T-80   [[Discography in ENRICO, Eugene Joseph: *Giuseppe Torelli's
        instrumental ensemble music with trumpet*. [Dissertation, University
        of Michigan, 1970] 262 pp.]]

TORTELIER, PAUL, 1914-   (French cellist)

T-81   La discographie de Paul Tortelier in LABIE, Jean-François: Paul
        Tortelier: amoureux fou la musique in *Diapason*, No. 267 (December
        1981): 27   ((2))

T-82   Paul Tortelier discography in TORTELIER, Paul: *Paul Tortelier:
        a self-portrait in conversation with David Blum*. London: Heinemann,
        1984: 253-263   ((--))

TOSCANINI, ARTURO, 1867-1957   (Italian conductor)

T-83   GRÉNIER, Jean-Marie: Discographie choisie in *Almanach du disque*,
        1957: 311   ((--))

T-84   VITTOZ, Jean: Discographie Toscanini in *Almanach disque*,
        1958: 189-191   ((--))

T-85   [[[Toscanini record list] in *Record Geijutsu*, No. 3 (1967):]]

T-86   Toscanini and the NBC Symphony Orchestra in *The Maestro*, II
        (January–December 1970): 16–56 ((1)) [A list of performances and
        recording sessions]

T-87   Toscanini and the BBC Symphony Orchestra in *The Maestro*, III
        (January–December 1971): 2–7   ((7))

T-88   CARTWRIGHT, Jim: Arturo Toscanini's acoustical recordings--Victor
        Talking Machine Company in Immortal Performances 1976: List Number 1
        [Dealer's list] Austin, TX: Immortal Performances, 1976: 24–26
        ((3, 6, 7)) (Immortal Performances discographic data; [1])

T-89   Diskographie in WESSLING, Berndt W.: *Toscanini in Bayreuth*.
        München: Desch, 1976: 141–144   ((--))

T-90   VEGETO, Raffaele: Discografia in DELLA CROCE, Andrea: *Arturo
        Toscanini*. Pordenone: Studio Tesi, 1981: [451]–471   ((--))

T-91   BURFORD, Ray: Toscanini--a selected discography in MATTHEWS, Denis:
        Arturo Toscanini. Tunbridge Wells, Kent: Midas Books; New York:
        Hippocrene Books, 1982: 125–170   ((3, 7))

T-92   CARTWRIGHT, Jim: Philharmonic-Symphony in Immortal Performances
        1983 Auction List No. 1 [Dealers list] 15 pp. ((3, 6, 7))   (Immortal
        Performances discographic data; 10)

T-93   Discography in *Fanfare*, VIII/3 (January–February 1985): 99–100
        ((7))

T-94   SUGA, Hajime: Toscanini discography in *Record Geijutsu*, No. 427
        (April 1986): 216–220; No. 428 (May 1986): 204–208; No. 429 (June
        1986): 202–206; No. 430 (July 1986): 216–220; No. 431 (August 1986):
        278–282; No. 432 (September 1986): 278–282; No. 433 (October 1986):
        198–202; No. 434 (November 1986): 226–230; No. 435 (December 1986):
        230–234; No. 436 (January 1987): 220–224   ((1, 3, 6, 7))

TRIOS, PIANO

T-95   [[Discography in HORAN, Catherine Anne: *A survey of the piano
        trio from 1800 through 1860*. [Dissertation, Northwestern University,
        1983]   844 pp.]]

TROMBONE

T-96   [[Discography in SENFF, Thomas Earl: *An annotated bibliography
        of unaccompanied solo repertoire for trombone*. [Dissertation,
        University of Illinois, 1976]   317 pp.]]

T-97   Recordings in DEMPSTER, Stuart: *The modern trombone*. Berkeley:
        University of California Press, 1979: 104–105   ((--))

T-98   [[Discography in BAHR, Edward Richard: *A discography of classical
        trombone/euphonium solo and ensemble music on long-playing records
        distributed in the United States*. [DMA, University of Oklahoma,
        1980]   324 pp.]]

T-99   HANSEN, Jon E. and MCENIRY, JoDee: Discography of trombone solo
       literature in *International Trombone Association Journal*, XIII/2
       (1985): 32-34   ((--))

T-100 [[BAHR, Edward R.: *Trombone/euphonium discography*. Stevens
       Point, WI: Index House, 1988   [Published version of the author's
       dissertation, above]]]

TROUBADOURS

T-101 Discographie in BECK, Jean: *La musique des troubadours*. Paris:
       Stock, 1979: [129]-[131]   ((--))

T-102 MAILLARD, Jean: Troubadors et trouvères; pour une approche
       discographique in *Revue internationale*, I/3 (November 1980):
       414-423   ((5))

TRUMPET

T-103 A short list of LP gramophone records ... in BATE, Philip: *The
       trumpet and trombone*.   2 ed. London: E. Benn; New York: Norton,
       1978: 270-273   ((--))

T-104 The trumpet on records in BERGER, Melvin: *The trumpet book*.
       New York: Lothrop, Lee & Shepard Co., 1978: 123-126   ((--))

T-105 [[Discography in TUNNELL, Michael Hilton: *Selected trumpet
       excerpts from brass quintets by Ingolf Dahl, Gunther Schuller, Alvin
       Etler, and Jan Bach; and a bibliography of brass quintets written by
       American composers from 1938 to 1980*. [DMA, University of Southern
       Mississippi, 1982]   227 pp.]]

T-106 A discography of pioneers of trumpet LP's in *International Trumpet
       Guild Journal*, VIII/1 (September 1983): 23-25, 57   ((--))

TRUMPET MUSIC

T-107 [[[Discography] in PARKER, Craig Burwell: *A survey and analysis of
       contemporary solo literature for unaccompanied trumpet and for
       trumpet with tape*. [M.A. Thesis, University of California, Los
       Angeles, 1976]: 268-269]]

T-108 [[Discography in GARRETT, Stephen Craig: *A comprehensive
       performance project in trumpet repertoire; a discussion of the
       twentieth-century concerto for trumpet and orchestra; an
       investigative study of concertos by Alexander Arutunian, Henri
       Tomasi, Charles Chaynes, and André Jolivet; and a bibliography of
       concertos for trumpet and orchestra written and published from 1904
       to 1983*. [DMA, University of Southern Mississippi, 1984]   334 pp.]]

TRUMPET MUSIC--USSR

T-109 LAPLACE, Michel: The trumpet in the USSR-A Soviet players'
       discography in *Newsletter of the International Trumpet Guild*,
       IV/2 (1978): 20-21   ((--))

TUBB, CARRIE, 1876-1976   (English soprano)

T-110   WATTS, Ken: Carrie Tubb in *Hillandale News*, No. 93 (December 1976): 59-62   ((--))

TUCKER, RICHARD, 1913-1975   (American tenor)

T-111   KISER, Patricia Ann: Discography in DRAKE, James A.: *Richard Tucker, a biography*. New York: Dutton, 1984: 279-292   ((3, 5))

URLUS, JACQUES, 1867-1935   (Dutch tenor)

U-1   DENNIS, J.: Discography in *Record Collector*, XXVI/11-12 (September 1981): 268-281; Addenda in XXVII/3-4 (March 1982): 93-94 and XXVII/7-8 (August 1982): 183-185 ((3, 4, 7))

USSR MINISTRY OF CULTURE CHAMBER CHOIR

U-2   Discography in *Music in the USSR* (October-December 1987): 95   ((--))

USSR RADIO AND TELEVISION FULL SYMPHONY ORCHESTRA

See entry for

FEDOSEYEV, Vladimir

USSR SYMPHONY ORCHESTRA

See entry for

SVETLANOV, Yevgeni

VAN KEMPEN, PAUL, 1893-1955   (Dutch conductor)

V-1   DE KAY, Kenneth: Discography of van Kempen American label recordings in *Le Grand Baton*, No. 44 (September-December 1979): 49-51   ((--))

VANNI-MARCOUX, JEAN-ÉMILE, 1877-1962   (French baritone)

V-2   SHAWE-TAYLOR, Desmond: Vanni-Marcoux, a discography in *Recorded Sound*, No. 29-30 (January-April 1968): 269-272   ((3, 6, 7)) [Includes unissued records]

VARDANYAN, ZAVEN   (Armenian conductor)

V-3   Discography in *Music in the USSR* (July-September 1988): 71   ((--))

VARÈSE, EDGARD, 1883-1965   (French composer)

V-4   Diskographie in *Edgard Varèse, Rückblick auf die Zukunft*. München: Edition Text u. Kritik, 1978: [117]-118   ((--)) (Musik-Konzepte; 6)

V-5   Edgard-Varèse-Diskographie in *Schweizerische Musikzeitung*, CXIX/2 (March-April 1979): 101-102   ((5))

V-6   Discography in OUELLETTE, Fernand: *Edgard Varèse*. New York: Da Capo Press, 1981: 241-242   ((--)) [Reprinted from the 1968 ed. published by Orion Press, New York]

V-7   Discographie in BREDEL, Marc: *Edgard Varèse*. Paris: Mazarine,

1984: 1 leaf inserted   ((--))

V-8   Discographische Hinweise: Edgard Varèse in *fono forum* (December
       1985): 40   ((--))

VASARY, TAMAS, 1933-   (Hungarian pianist)

V-9   Discography, Deutsche Grammophon artist information, 1980.   1 p.
       ((--))

VAUGHAN-WILLIAMS, RALPH, 1872-1958   (English composer)

SYMPHONIES

V-10   OTTAWAY, Hugh: Recordings of Vaughan-Williams symphonies in
       Disc, VI (No. 22, 1953): 62   ((--))

V-11   WEBER, J. F.: The symphonies of Ralph Vaughan-Williams in *ARSC
       Journal*, XVI/1-2 (1984): 28-32   ((3, 6, 7))

VENTURA, ELVINO, 1875-1931   (Italian tenor)

V-12   [Discography] in *Record Collector*, IX/3 (March 1954): 71   ((--))

VERDI, GIUSEPPE, 1813-1901   (Italian composer)

V-13   Petite discographie in PETIT, Pierre: *Verdi*.   Paris: Seuil,
       [1976], 1958: 173-176   ((--))

V-14   FURIE, Kenneth: Verdi recordings in *AIVS* [American Institute for
       Verdi studies] Newsletter, No. 2 (December 1976): 14-15   ((1, 7))
       [Recent issues, reissues, forthcoming and planned and private
       recordings]

V-15   Discographie essentialle in BOURGEOIS, Jacques: *Giuseppe Verdi*.
       Paris: Julliard, 1978: [349]-350   ((--))

V-16   DE SCHAUENSEE, Max: *The Collector's Verdi and Puccini*. Westport, CT:
       Greenwood Press, 1978.   156 pp.   ((--)) [Reprinted from the 1962
       ed. published by Lippincott, New York]

V-17   Discographies in BRAGAGLIA, Leonardo: *Verdi e suoi interpreti
       (1839-1978)* Roma: Bulzoni, 1979.   375 pp. ((--))

V-18   CSAMPAI, Attila and HOLLAND, Dietmar: Auswahl-diskographie in
       Giuseppe Verdi. München: Edition Text u. Kritik, 1979: [115]-120
       ((7)) (Musik-Konzepte; 10)

V-19   Discografia verdiana in MARCHESI, Gustavo: *Verdi*. Milano:
       Fabbri, 1979: 129-136   ((--))

V-20   FAW, Marc Taylor: *A Verdi discography*.   Norman, OK: Pilgrim,
       1982.   214 pp.   ((3, 4, 7))

V-21   VINCENTINI, Mario: Incisioni verdiane (1977-1980) in *Studi verdiani*,
       I (1982): 130-140   ((1, 7))

V-22   Discografia essenziale in TINTORI, Giampiero: *Invito all'ascolto di*

Giuseppe Verdi. Milano: Mursia, 1983: [263]-276   ((--))

V-23   MARINELLI, Carlo: Discografia verdiana (Aggiornamenti 1981-1983)
in *Studi verdiani*, II (1983): 184-208   ((1, 7))

V-24   MARINELLI, Carlo: Discografia verdiana aggiornamenti, 1984 in *Studi
verdiani*, III (1985): 170-178   ((1, 7))

V-25   ...disques... in DUAULT, Alain: *Verdi, la musique et le drame.*
Paris: Gallimard, 1986: 182-184   ((5))

V-26   TUBEUF, André: Discographie: Verdi in *Diapason-Harmonie*, No. 322
(December 1986): 129-130   ((--))

V-27   ARDOIN, John: Verdi on record: the early years in *Opera Quarterly*,
V/2-3 (Summer-Autumn 1987): [48]-58   ((7))

OPERAS

AÏDA (1871)

V-28   MARINELLI, Carlo: [Discography] in Roma, Teatro dell'Opera
1969 season: program pp. 449-460   ((5))

V-29   MARINELLI, Carlo: [Discography] in Milano, Teatro alla Scala,
season d'opera e balletto 1972-73: program pp. 666-675   ((5))

V-30   TUBEUF, André: Discographie in *L'Avant Scène Opéra*, No. 4
(July-August 1976): 102-108   ((1, 3, 5))

V-31   CECCONI-BOTELLA, Monic: Le point sur Aïda de Giuseppe Verdi
in *Diapason*, No. 243 (October 1979): 56-57   ((--))

V-32   [[[Discography] in *Giuseppe Verdi, Aïda.* München: Bayerische
Staatsoper, 1979: 86-87]]

V-33   Discography in *Aïda.* London: J. Calder; New York: Riverrun Press,
1980: 94-96   ((--))   (English National Opera guide; 2)

V-34   TARDIF, Jean-Pierre: Aïda: discographie critique in *Harmonie-
Panorama musique*, No. 32 (June 1983): 33-39   ((3, 5))

V-35   MARINELLI, Carlo: [Discography] in Venezia, Teatro La Fenice,
season 1984: program pp. 540-551   ((5))

V-36   [[CSAMPAI, Attila and HOLLAND, Dietmar: [Discography] in
Giuseppe Verdi, Aida: Texte, Materialien, Kommentäre. Reinbek
bei Hamburg: Rowohlt, 1985: 277-282   (Rororo Opernbücher)]]

V-37   MARINELLI, Carlo: [Discography] in Milano, Teatro alla Scala,
season 1985-86: program pp. 52-58   ((5))

ATTILA (1846)

V-38   MARINELLI, Carlo: [Discography] in Roma, Teatro dell'Opera,
season 1980-81: program pp. 1299-1301   ((5))

V-39   MARINELLI, Carlo: [Discography] in Venezia, Teatro La Fenice, season 1986: program pp. 722-723　((5))

(UN) BALLO IN MASCHERA (1852)

V-40　　MARINELLI, Carlo: [Discography] in Venezia, Teatro La Fenice, season lirica 1970-71: program pp. 219-226　((5))

V-41　　MARINELLI, Carlo: [Discography] in Milano, Teatro alla Scala, season 1972-73: program pp. 32-36　((5))

V-42　　MARINELLI, Carlo: [Discography] in Venezia, Teatro La Fenice season lirica 1973-74: program pp. 420-432　((5))

V-43　　MARINELLI, Carlo: [Discography] in Treviso, Ente Teatro Comunale, season 1976: program pp. 248-260　((5))

V-44　　MARINELLI, Carlo: [Discography] in Milano, Teatro alla Scala, season 1977: program pp. 80-85　((5))

V-45　　TUBEUF, André: Un Bal masqué: discographie comparée in *Harmonie hi-fi conseil*, No. 6 (February 1981): 22-26　((3, 5))

V-46　　FANTAPIÉ, Alain: Discographie in *L'Avant Scène Opéra*, No. 32 (March-April 1981): 110-113　((1, 7))

V-47　　DUPECHEZ, Charles-F.: Un Bal masque de Verdi in *Diapason*, No. 305 (May 1985): 84-85　((--))

V-48　　MARINELLI, Carlo: [Discography] in Roma, Teatro dell'Opera, season 1985-86: program pp. 60-72　((5))

V-49　　MARINELLI, Carlo: [Discography] in Milano, Teatro alla Scala, season 1986-87: program pp. 106-107　((5))

(LA) BATTAGLIA DI LEGNANO (1849)

V-50　　MARINELLI, Carlo: [Discography] in Roma, Teatro dell'Opera, season 1983-84: program pp. 55-59　((5))

DON CARLOS (1867)

V-51　　MARINELLI, Carlo: [Discography] in Roma, Teatro dell'Opera, season 1968: program pp. 596-598　((5))

V-52　　MARINELLI, Carlo: [Discography] in Venezia, Teatro La Fenice, season lirica 1973-74: program pp. 115-122　((5))

V-53　　MARINELLI, Carlo: [Discography] in Milano, Teatro alla Scala, season 1977: program pp. 83-85　((5))

V-54　　RICHARDS, John B.: Don Carlo: Ella giammai m'amò. in *Record Collector*, XXIV/5-6 (July 1978): 130-143, 100　((--))

V-55　　MODUGNO, Maurizio: Rè, infanti, grandi di Spagna, inquisitori, frati, comprimari e generici: ovvero Il Don Carlos di Verdi (contributo per una storia discografica): discografia in *Discoteca hifi*, No. 206 (May 1980): 33-35　((5))

V-56   SIRVIN, René: Le point sur Don Carlos de Verdi in *Diapason*, No. 280 (February 1983): 43-46   ((7))

V-57   TARDIF, Jean-Pierre: Don Carlos: discographie comparée in *Harmonie-Panorama musique*, No. 44 (July-August 1984): 42-46   ((3, 5))

V-58   MARINELLI, Carlo: [Discography] in Palermo, Ente automono Teatro Massimo, season 1984-85: program p. 5   ((5))

V-59   Discografia del Don Carlo in *Musica*, No. 39 (December 1985): 50-51   ((7))

V-60   TUBEUF, André and VOISIN, Georges: Discographie [and] Airs séparés in *L'Avant Scène Opéra*, No. 90/91 (September-October 1986): 160-171   ((7))

V-61   CABOURG, Jean: Discographie--Don Carlos in *Diapason-Harmonie*, No. 319 (September 1986): 103-106   ((7))

V-62   MARINELLI, Carlo: [Discography] in Roma, Teatro dell'Opera, season 1986-87: program pp. 52-58   ((5))

(I) DUE FOSCARI (1844)

V-63   MARINELLI, Carlo: [Discography] in Milano, Teatro alla Scala, season 1979-80: program pp. 78-79   ((5))

V-64   MARINELLI, Carlo: [Discography] in Roma, Teatro dell'Opera, season 1980-81: program pp. 449-451   ((5))

ERNANI (1844)

V-65   MARINELLI, Carlo: [Discography] in Roma, Teatro dell'Opera, season 1966-67: program pp. 493   ((5))

V-66   MARINELLI, Carlo: [Discography] in Roma, Teatro dell'Opera, season 1969-70: program pp. 467-468   ((5))

V-67   MARINELLI, Carlo: [Discography] in Treviso, Ente Teatro Comunale, season 1980: program p. 6   ((5))

V-68   MARINELLI, Carlo: [Discography] in Milano, Teatro alla Scala, season 1982-83: program pp. 119-122   ((5))

FALSTAFF (1893)

V-69   MARINELLI, Carlo: [Discography] in Treviso, Ente Teatro Comunale, season 1977-78: program p. 17   ((5))

V-70   MARINELLI, Carlo: [Discography] in Milano, Teatro alla Scala, season 1980-81: program pp. 175-177   ((5))

V-71   HENRIOT, Patrice: Falstaff de Verdi in *Diapason*, No. 262 (June 1981): 36-37   ((3, 7))

V-72   MARINELLI, Carlo: [Discography] in Milano, Teatro alla Scala, season 1981-82: program pp. 174-177   ((5))

V-73   Discography in *Falstaff*. London: J. Calder; New York: Riverrun Press, 1982: 126 ((--)) (English National Opera guide; 10)

V-74   KESTING, Jürgen: Falstaff: Verdis Bestseller im Interpretations-vergleich in *HiFi Stereophonie* (May 1983): 500-503 ((--))

V-75   WALKER, Malcolm: Discography in HEPOKOSKI, James A.: *Giuseppe Verdi, Falstaff*. Cambridge; New York: Cambridge University Press, 1983: 176-177 ((5)) (Cambridge opera handbooks)

V-76   CABOURG, Jean: Discographie and VOISIN, Georges and CABOURG, Jean: Airs séparés in *L'Avant Scène Opéra*, No. 87-88 (May-June 1986): 146-157; ((1, 5, 7))

(LA) FORZA DEL DESTINO (1862)

V-77   [[Discografia] in *Guida illustrata a `La forza del destino'*. Milano: Fabbri, 1975:]]

V-78   MARINELLI, Carlo: [Discography] in Milano, Teatro alla Scala, season 1978: program pp. 88-89 ((5))

V-79   MARINELLI, Carlo: [Discography] in Roma, Teatro dell'Opera, season 1981-82: program pp. 981-992 ((5))

V-80   HOYLE, Martin: Discography in *The force of destiny = La forza del destino*. London: J. Calder; New York: Riverrun Press, 1983: 111 ((--)) (English National Opera guide; 23)

(UN) GIORNO DI REGNO (1840)

V-81   MARINELLI, Carlo: [Discography] in Verona Filharmonico, season 1985: program pp. 34-35 ((5))

GIOVANNA D'ARCO (1845)

V-82   MARINELLI, Carlo: [Discography] in Treviso, Ente Teatro Comunale, season 1979: program p. 4 ((5))

JÉRUSALEM (1847)

V-83   [[[[Discography] in *Opéra International*, No. 67 (February 1984)]]]

(I) LOMBARDI (1843)

V-84   MARINELLI, Carlo: [Discography] in Roma, Teatro dell'Opera, season 1969-70: program pp. 33-34 ((5))

V-85   OSBORNE, Conrad: I Lombardi in *Opera*, XXVII/5 (May 1976): 422-[427] ((1, 5)) (Opera on the gramophone; 38)

V-86   MARINELLI, Carlo: [Discography] in Milano, Teatro alla Scala, season 1983-84: program pp. 95-97 ((5))

V-87   [[[Discography] in *Opéra International*, No. 67 (February 1984)]]

V-88   MARINELLI, Carlo: [Discography] in Milano, Teatro alla Scala,

season 1985-86: program pp. 95-97 ((5))

LUISA MILLER (1849)

V-89   ROSENTHAL, Harold: Luisa Miller in *Opera*, XXIX/6 (June 1978): 564-573; with WALKER, Malcolm: Luisa Miller—LP discography: 573 ((3, 5)) (Opera on the gramophone; 45)

MACBETH (1847)

V-90   MARINELLI, Carlo: [Discography] in Roma, Teatro dell'Opera, 1969 Season: program pp. 412-415 ((5))

V-91   ROSENTHAL, Harold: Macbeth in *Opera*, XXVII/8 (August 1976): 703-712 ((1, 5)) (Opera on the gramophone; 39)

V-92   MARINELLI, Carlo: [Discography] in Roma, Teatro dell'Opera, season 1976-77: program pp. 153-162 ((5))

V-93   MARINELLI, Carlo: [Discography] in Treviso, Ente Teatro Comunale, season 1977-78: program p. 10 ((5))

V-94   MARINELLI, Carlo: [Discography] in Milano, Teatro alla Scala, season 1979: program pp. 109-111 ((5))

V-95   LAFON, François: Discographie in *L'Avant Scène Opéra*, No. 40 (March-April 1982): 106-111 ((1, 7))

V-96   Discografia in RESCIGNO, Eduardo: *Macbeth di Giuseppe Verdi: guida all'opera*. Milano: A. Mondadori, 1983: 280-[281] ((5))

V-97   Scheda discografia in *Musica*, No. 32 (March 1984): 44 ((7))

V-98   MARINELLI, Carlo: [Discography] in Milano, Teatro alla Scala, season 1984-85: program p. 78 ((5))

V-99   MARINELLI, Carlo: [Discography] in Venezia, Teatro La Fenice, season 1986: program pp. 212-223 ((5))

V-100   MARINELLI, Carlo: [Discography] in Roma, Teatro dell'Opera, season 1986-87: program pp. 62-71 ((5))

NABUCCO (1842)

V-101   MARINELLI, Carlo: [Discography] in Roma, Teatro dell'Opera, season 1970-1971: program pp. 26-27 ((5))

V-102   SEGALINI, Sergio: Discographie in *L'Avant Scène Opéra*, No. 86 (April 1986): 102-105 ((1, 5))

V-103   MARINELLI, Carlo: [Discography] in Milano, Teatro alla Scala, season 1986-87: program pp. 123-127 ((5))

OTELLO (1887)

V-104   MARINELLI, Carlo: [Discography] in Roma, Teatro dell'Opera, 1968 season: program pp. 26-30 ((5))

V-105   DUTRONC, Jean-Louis: Discographie in *L'Avant Scène Opéra*,
         No. 3 (May-June 1976): 98-104   ((1, 5))

V-106   SEGALINI, Sergio: Verdi--Otello: discographie comparée in
         Harmonie, No. 143 (January 1979): 94-101   ((5))

V-107   Le Edizioni complete di "Otello" in microsolco in *Musica*, No. 11
         (February 1979): 94-101   ((5))

V-108   MARINELLI, Carlo: [Discography] in Bologna, Teatro Comunale,
         season 1979-80: program pp. 57-77   ((5))

V-109   Discography in *Otello*. London: J. Calder; New York: Riverrun
         Press, 1981: 78-79   ((--))   (English National Opera guide; 7)

V-110   MARINELLI, Carlo: [Discography] in Milano, Teatro alla Scala,
         season 1981-82: program p. 111   ((5))

V-111   GREEN, London: Otello on records, a tragic vision in *Opera
         Quarterly*, IV/2 (1986): 49-56   ((7))

V-112   MARINELLI, Carlo: [Discography] in Milano, Teatro alla Scala,
         season 1986-87: program pp. 104-105   ((5))

V-113   WALKER, Malcolm: Discography in HEPOKOSKI, James A.: *Giuseppe
         Verdi, Otello*. Cambridge; New York: Cambridge University Press,
         1987: 203-205   ((1, 7))   (Cambridge opera handbooks)

V-114   [[DAHLEN, Thommy: Verdis Otello på skiva in *Musik Revy*,
         XLII/7-8 (1987): 325+]]

         RIGOLETTO (1850)

V-115   MARINELLI, Carlo: [Discography] in Roma, Teatro dell'Opera,
         season 1966-1967: program pp. 37-41   ((5))

V-116   MARINELLI, Carlo: [Discography] in Roma, Teatro dell'Opera,
         season 1970-1971: program pp. 312-323   ((5))

V-117   [[[Discography] in *Record Geijutsu*, (No. 9, 1971):]]

V-118   MARINELLI, Carlo: [Discography] in Venezia, Teatro La Fenice,
         season lirica 1971-1972: program pp. 308-324   ((5))

V-119   MARINELLI, Carlo: [Discography] in Treviso, Ente Teatro
         Comunale, Autunno Musicale Trevigiano, season lirica 1975:
         program p. 17   ((5))

V-120   SCHÖNEGGER, Hermann: Rigoletto: eine vergleichende Diskografie
         der Oper in *fono forum* (July 1978): 696-700   ((5))

V-121   GERHARTZ, Leo Karl: Anmerkungen zur Diskographie in *Rigoletto*.
         Reinbek bei Hamburg: Rowohlt, 1982: 255-[263]]]   ((1, 5))
         (Rororo Opernbücher)

V-122   HOYLE, Martin: Discography in *Rigoletto*. London: J. Calder;
         New York: Riverrun Press, 1982: 77-79   ((--))   (English National
         Opera guide; 15)

V-123   OSBORNE, Richard: Rigoletto in *Opera*, XXXIII/9 (September 1982): 890-898; XXXIII/10 (October 1982): 1016-1025 ((7)) (Opera on the gramophone; 52)

V-124   [[[Discography] in CONATI, Marcello: *Rigoletto di Giuseppe Verdi: guida all'opera*. Milano: A. Mondadori, 1983: 299-[305]]]

V-125   [[[Discography] in *Rigoletto: in der Originalsprache (Italienisch mit deutscher Übersetzung*. München: Goldmann: B. Schott's Söhne, 1986: 215-220 (Opern der Welt)]]

V-126   CABOURG, Jean and VOISIN, Georges: Discographie [and] Airs séparés in *L'Avant Scène Opéra*, No. 112/3 (September-October 1988): 144-167 ((1, 7))

SIMON BOCCANEGRA (1857)

V-127   MARINELLI, Carlo: [Discography] in Roma, Teatro dell'Opera, 1969 season: program pp. 487-488 ((5))

V-128   MARINELLI, Carlo: [Discography] in Treviso, Ente Teatro Comunale, season 1976: program p. 4 ((5))

V-129   MARINELLI, Carlo: [Discography] in Roma, Teatro dell'Opera, season 1979-80: program pp. 761-767 ((5))

V-130   MARINELLI, Carlo: [Discography] in Milano, Teatro alla Scala, season 1981-82: program pp. 100-103 ((5))

V-131   MARINELLI, Carlo: [Discography] in Palermo, Ente automono Teatro Massimo, season 1981-82: program p. 21 ((5))

V-132   PETERSON, Cathy: Selective discography in *Simon Boccanegra*. London: J. Calder; New York: Riverrun Press, 1985: 95 ((5)) (English National Opera guide; 32)

(LA) TRAVIATA (1853)

V-133   MARINELLI, Carlo: [Discography] in Roma, Teatro dell'Opera, season 1971-1972: program pp. 341-353 ((5))

V-134   MARINELLI, Carlo: [Discography] in Venezia, Teatro La Fenice, season lirica 1972-1973: program pp. 249-262 ((5))

V-135   MARINELLI, Carlo: [Discography] in Treviso, Ente Comunale, Autunno Musicale Trevigiano, season 1975: program p. 17 ((5))

V-136   MARINELLI, Carlo: [Discography] in Roma, Teatro dell'Opera, season 1976-77: program pp. 452-469 ((5))

V-137   MARINELLI, Carlo: [Discography] in Treviso, Ente Teatro Comunale, season 1978: program p. 22 ((5))

V-138   MARINELLI, Carlo: [Discography] in Roma, Teatro dell'Opera, season 1978-79: program pp. 786-789 ((5))

V-139   MARINELLI, Carlo: [Discography] in Venezia, Gran Teatro La

Fenice, season 1979–80: program pp. 250–262   ((5))

V-140   Discography in *La traviata*. London: J. Calder; New York:
Riverrun Press, 1981: 76–79 ((--)) (English National Opera
guide; 5)

V-141   Le edizioni complete de "La traviata" in disco in *Musica*, No. 20
(March 1981): [21] ((5))

V-142   CSAMPAI, Attila: Anmerkungen zur Diskographie in *La Traviata*.
Reinbek bei Hamburg: Rowohlt, 1983: 244–250 ((1, 7))
(Rororo Opernbücher)

V-143   Selected discography in *Giuseppe Verdi, La traviata*. Boston:
Little, Brown, 1983: 194–201 ((5))

V-144   MARINELLI, Carlo: [Discography] in Roma, Teatro dell'Opera,
season 1984–85: program pp. 56–69 ((5))

V-145   CABOURG, Jean: Discographie comparée in *L'Avant Scène Opéra*,
No. 51 (April 1983): 136–149 ((7))

V-146   MARINELLI, Carlo: [Discography] in Palermo, Ente automono
Teatro Massimo, season 1984–85: program p. 11 ((5))

(IL) TROVATORE (1853)

V-147   MARINELLI, Carlo: [Discography] in Roma, Teatro dell'Opera,
season 1967–1968: program pp. 14–17 ((5))

V-148   MARINELLI, Carlo: [Discography] in Treviso, Ente Comunale,
Autunno Musicale Trevigiano, season 1975: program p. 17 ((5))

V-149   MARINELLI, Carlo: [Discography] in Milano, Teatro alla Scala,
season 1978: program pp. 62–65 ((5))

V-150   WERBA, Robert: Verdi's "Troubadour" Ein Überblick über die
Gesamtaufnahmen in *Österreichische Musikzeitschrift*, XXXIII
(April–May 1978): 255–257 ((7))

V-151   MARINELLI, Carlo: [Discography] in Palermo, Ente automono
Teatro Massimo, season 1982–83: program p. 70 ((5))

V-152   HOYLE, Martin: Discography in *Il Trovatore*. London: Calder: New
York: Riverrun Press, 1983: 78–79 ((--)) (English National
Opera guide; 20)

V-153   CABOURG, Jean: Discographie in *L'Avant Scène Opéra*, No. 60
(February 1984): 106–117; with VOISIN, Georges and CABOURG, Jean
Il Trovatore et le 78 tours: 118–119 ((1, 7))

V-154   CSAMPAI, Attila: Anmerkungen zur Diskographie in *Der Troubadour*.
Reinbek bei Hamburg: Rowohlt, 1986: 212–217 (Rororo Opernbücher)

(LES) VÊPRES SICILIENNES (1853)

V-155   LORD HAREWOOD: Les Vêpres Siciliennes in *Opera*, XXXV/4 (April
1984): 357–361; XXXV/6 (May 1984): 495–498; with WALKER, Malcol

LP discography, p. 498 ((7)) (Opera on the gramophone; 54)

V-156   CABOURG, Jean and VOISIN, Georges: Discographie [and] Airs
séparés in *L'Avant Scène Opéra*, No. 75 (May 1985): 102-109
((1, 7))

MESSA DI REQUIEM (1874)

V-157   MARINELLI, Carlo: [Discography] in Roma, Teatro dell'Opera,
1965-1966 season: program pp. 500-504 ((5))

V-158   Die besprochenen Aufnahmen in *fono forum* (April 1976): 344 ((5))

V-159   Le edizioni complete della Messa da requiem in microsolco in
Musica, No. 17 (June 1980): 204 ((5))

V-160   Discographie Verdi Requiem in SCHÖNEGGER, Hermann: Verdis Missa
da Requiem in *fono forum* (February 1981): [34]-39 ((--))

V-161   MARINELLI, Carlo: [Discography] in Roma, Teatro dell'Opera,
season 1983-84: program pp. 46-57 ((5))

VERLET, ALICE, 1873-1934 (Belgian soprano)

V-162 [Discography] in *Record Collector*, IX/3 (March 1954): 71-72 ((--))

VICTORIA, TOMAS LUIS DE, 1548-1611   (Spanish composer)

V-163 Discografia in SOLER, Josep: *Victoria*. Barcelona: A. Bosch,
1983: 159-160 ((--))

VIERNE, LOUIS, 1830-1937   (French organist)

V-164 Discographie française in GAVOTY, Bernard: *Louis Vierne*. Paris:
Buchet & Chastel, 1980: 319-321 ((--))

VILLA-LOBOS, HEITOR, 1887-1959   (Brazilian composer)

V-165 Discografia in *Villa-Lobos, su obra cultura*. 2d ed. Acao: MEC,
1972: 247-331 ((-))

V-166 [[[Discography] in *Bibliografia e musicografia, Heitor Villa-Lobos
(1887-1959)* São Paulo: Prefeitura do Municipio de São Paulo,
Secretaria Municipal de Cultura, Centro Cultural São Paulo, 1987.
28 pp.]]

V-167 ALEXANDER, John: Selected discography in *Music & Musicians* (March
1987): 13-15 ((--))

V-168 Discographische Hinweise: Heitor Villa-Lobos in *fono forum* (March
1987): 26 ((--))

V-169 Discography in APPLEBY, David P.: *Heitor Villa-Lobos: a
bio-bibliography*. New York: Greenwood Press, 1988: [161]-240 ((--))
(Bio-bibliographies in music; 9)

BACHIANAS BRASILEIRAS

V-170   Discografia in COSTA PALMA, Enos da and DE BRITO CHAVES JUNIOR, Edgard: *As Bachianas brasileiras de Villa-Lobos.* Rio de Janeiro: Companhia editora Americana, 1973: 179-183   ((--))

PIANO WORKS

V-171   Discografia in LIMA, Souza: *Comentarios sobre a obra pianistica de Villa-Lobos.* 2d ed. [Rio]: MEC/DAC: Musee Villa-Lobos, 1976: 121-125   ((--))

VIOL MUSIC

V-172   [[Discography in ABBEY, Hermione: *An historical and stylistic chronology of the English fancy: music for viol consorts.* [Dissertation, University of Utah, 1974]   210 pp.]]

VIOLA MUSIC

V-173   BEAUMONT, François de: *L'alto et ses interprètes: discographie 1920-1980=Die viola und ihre Interpreten=The viola and its interpreters.* 4 ed. [Auvernier: Beaumont, 1980?]   61 pp.   ((4))

VIOLIN

V-174   Discography; some selected violin records in MENUHIN, Yehudi: *Violin and viola.* London: Macdonald and Jane's; New York: Schirmer Books, 1976: 235-243   ((--))

V-175   Discography; some selected violin records in MENUHIN, Yehudi: *Violin and viola.* New York: Schirmer Books, 1976: 233-246   ((--))

V-176   Discography in *The book of the violin.* New York: Rizzoli, 1984: 241-246   ((--))

VIOLINISTS

V-177   Schallplattenverzeichnis in HARTNACK, Joachim W.: *Grosse Geiger unserer Zeit.* Zürich; Freiburg i. Br.: Atlantis-Musikbuch-Verlag, 1977: 308-314   ((--))

V-178   Discography in CAMPBELL, Margaret: *The great violinists.* Garden City, NY: Doubleday, 1981: 333-353   ((--))

V-179   [[[Discography] in ROTH, Henry: *Great violinists in performance.* Los Angeles: Panjandrum Books, 1986:]]

V-180   Schallplattenhinweise in ROESELER, Albrecht: *Grosse Geiger unseres Jahrhunderts.* München: Piper, 1987: 373-385   ((--))

V-181   Discographische Hinweise in *fono forum* (May 1988): 29-30   ((--))

VISCHER, ANTOINETTE, 1909-   (German harpsichordist)

V-182   Die Schallplatten Antoinette Vischers in *Antoinette Vischer; Dokumente zu einem Leben für das Cembalo.* Basel: Birkhauser, 1976: 181   ((1))

VISHNEVSKAYA, GALINA, 1926-   (Russian soprano)

V-183 Discography in VISHNEVSKAYA, Galina: *Galina: a Russian story*. San Diego: Harcourt Brace Jovanovich, 1984: [497]-504 ((--))

V-184 [Discography] in VISHNEVSKAYA, Galina: *Galina: istoriia zhizni*. Paris: Izd. "La Presse Libre" i "Kontinenta", 1985: 541-546 ((--))

VIVALDI, ANTONIO, 1678-1741 (Italian composer)

V-185 [Discography] in *Stereo Geijutsu*, No. 136 (August 1978): 47-54 ((5, 7))

V-186 BELLINGARDI, Luigi: Discografia di Antonio Vivaldi in *Nuova Rivista Musicale Italiana*, XIII/1 (1979): 290-304 ((--))

V-187 Discographies in PINCHERLE, Marc: *Vivaldi: Marc Pincherle*. Paris: Éditions d'Aujourd'hui, 1981. 243 pp. ((--))

V-188 TRAVERS, Roger-Claude: Discographie Vivaldi n. 1 - 1979 in *Informazioni e studi vivaldiani*, I (1980): 63-76 ((--))

V-189 TRAVERS, Roger-Claude: Discographie Vivaldi n. 2 - 1980 in *Informazioni e studi vivaldiani*, II (1981): 96-107 ((--))

V-190 TRAVERS, Roger-Claude and WALKER, Thomas: Discographie Vivaldi 78 tours in *Informazioni e studi vivaldiani*, III (1982): 74-97 ((5))

V-191 TRAVERS, Roger-Claude: Nouvelles informations sur la discographie Vivaldi 78 tours in *Informazioni e studi vivaldiani*, IV (1983): 98-100 ((--))

V-192 TRAVERS, Roger-Claude: Discographie Vivaldi n. 4 - 1982 in *Informazioni e studi vivaldiani*, IV (1983): 101-111 ((--))

V-193 PAPINI, Maurizio: Discografia essenziale in GIAZOTTO, Remo: *Invito all'ascolto di Antonio Vivaldi*. Milano: Mursia, 1984: [147]-156 ((--))

V-194 TRAVERS, Roger-Claude: Discographie Vivaldi n. 5 - 1983 in *Informazioni e studi vivaldiani*, V (1984): 107-114 ((5))

V-195 TRAVERS, Roger-Claude: Discographie Vivaldi n. 6 - 1984 in *Informazioni e studi vivaldiani*, VI (1985): 128-137 ((5))

V-196 TRAVERS, Roger-Claude: Discographie Vivaldi n. 7 - 1985 in *Informazioni e studi vivaldiani*, VII (1986): 87-97 ((5))

V-197 TRAVERS, Roger-Claude: Discographie Vivaldi n. 8 - 1986 in *Informazioni e studi vivaldiani*, VIII (1987): 108-119 ((--))

CONCERTOS, VIOLIN

ESTRO ARMONICO, Op. 3

V-198 BRAS, Jean-Yves: L'estro armonico de Vivaldi, ou L'imagination créatrice in *Diapason*, No. 225 (February 1978): 54-56 ((7))

LA STRAVAGANZA, Op. 4

V-199   BRAS, Jean-Yves: Discographie in *Diapason*, No. 209 (September 1976): 29   ((--))

FOUR SEASONS (IL CIMENTO DELL'ARMONIA E DELL'INVENTIONE, Op. 8, No. 1-4)

V-200   FANTAPIÉ, Alain: Les 70 Quatre Saisons de Vivaldi in *Diapason*, No. 212 (December 1976): 38-41   ((5, 7))

CHORAL WORKS

GLORIA

V-201   PIEL, Jean-Marie: Vivaldi: Gloria en re majeur: discographie critique in *Diapason*, No. 225 (February 1978): 52-53   ((--))

VOCAL MUSIC

V-202   RICHARD, Jean-Roger: Les enregistrements d'oeuvres lyriques par leurs createurs in *Almanach du disque*, 1953: 194-197   ((--))

V-203   BENNETT, John R.: *A catalogue of vocal recordings from the English catalogues of the Gramophone Company, 1989-1899; the Gramophone Company Limited, 1899-1900; the Gramophone & Typewriter Company Limited 1901-1907; and the Gramophone Company Limited, 1907-1925.* Lingfield, Surrey: Oakwood Press, 1956; Westport, CT: Greenwood Press, 1978. 238 pp. ((3, 4, 5, 7)) (Voices of the past; 1)

V-204   BENNETT, John R.: *Vocal recordings, 1893-1925. Italian catalogue.* Lingfield, Surrey: Oakwood Press, 1957. 147 pp. ((3, 4, 6, 7)) (Voices of the past; 2)

V-205   BENNETT, John R.: *Supplement to "Dischi fonotipia".* Lingfield, Surrey: Oakwood Press, 1957. 72 pp. ((3, 4, 7)) (Voices of the past; 3)

V-206   BENNETT, John R. and HUGHES, Eric: *The international red label catalogue of `DB' & `DA': His master's voice recordings, 1924-1956. Bk. 1, `DB' (12 inch)* Lingfield, Surrey: Oakwood Press, 1957; Westport, CT: Greenwood Press, 1978. 400 pp. ((3, 4, 6)) (Voices of the past; 4)

V-207   SMITH, Michael: *The catalogue of `D' & `E': His master's voice recordings: straight couplings: "D," 1-1212, "E," 1-610; automatic couplings: "D,", 7000-7872, "E,", 7000-7008.* Lingfield, Surrey: Oakwood Press, [195?]; Westport, CT: Greenwood Press, 1978. 131 pp. ((4)) (Voices of the past; 5)

V-208   BENNETT, John R. and HUGHES, Eric: *The international red label catalogue of `DB' & `DA': His master's voice recordings, 1924-1956. Bk, 2 `DA'.* Lingfield, Surrey: Oakwood Press, [1964]; Westport, CT: Greenwood Press, 1978. 233 pp. ((3, 4, 5, 6)) (Voices of the past; 6)

V-209   LÉON, Jacques Alain: *Catalogo numerico dos discos vocais Victor Selo Vermelho. Numerical catalogue of Red-Seal Victor vocal records.*

Part 1 [numbers 500-9999] Printed by Batista, Brazil, 1964. 177 pp.;
Part 2: [Numbers 1000-18546] Printed by Batista, Brazil, 1968. 86
pp. ((4))

V-210 BENNETT, John R. and WIMMER, Wilhelm: *A catalogue of vocal
recordings from the 1898-1925 German catalogues of the Gramophone
Company Limited, Deutsche Grammophon A.-G..* Lingfield, Surrey:
Oakwood Press, 1967; Westport, CT: Greenwood Press, 1978. 404 pp.
((3, 4, 7)) (Voices of the past; 7)

V-211 SMITH, Michael and COSENS, Ian: *Columbia Graphophone Company,
ltd. English celebrity issues: D and LB series, L and LX series,
X and PB series, 7000 and PX series, ROX and SCX series, YB series.*
Lingfield, Surrey: Oakwood Press, 1970; Westport, CT: Greenwood
Press, 1978. 240 pp. ((3, 4, 6)) (Voices of the past; 8)

V-212 BENNETT, John R.: *A catalogue of vocal recordings from the 1898-
1925 French catalogues of the Gramophone Company Limited, Compaigne
française du gramophone.* Lingfield, Surrey: Oakwood Press, 1971;
Westport, CT: Greenwood Press, 1978. 304 pp. ((3, 4, 5))
(Voices of the past; 9)

V-213 SMITH, Michael and ANDREWS, Frank: *His master's voice recordings,
plum label "C" series (12 inch)* [Blandford]: Oakwood Press, 1974.
274 pp. ((3, 4, 6, 7)) (Voices of the past; 10)

V-214 [[Discography in BERRY, Corre Ivey: *A study of the vocal chamber
duet through the Nineteenth century.* [Dissertation, North Texas
State University, 1974] 345 pp.]]

V-215 BENNETT, John Reginald: *A catalogue of vocal recordings from the
Russian catalogue of the Gramophone Company Limited.* Dorset: Oakwood
Press, 1977. 220 pp. ((3, 4)) (Voices of the past; 11)

V-216 LASTER, James: *A discography of treble voice recordings.* Metuchen,
NJ; London: Scarecrow Press, 1985. 147 pp. ((5))

V-217 [[LYNGBYE, B.: *Renaissancens vokalmusic. Med én selektiv discografi
samt en annoteret litteraturliste.* [Thesis, Royal Danish School of
Librarianship, 1971]]

VÖLKER, FRANZ, 1899-1965 (German tenor)

V-218 [[[Discography] in *Stimmen, die um die Welt gingen,* No. 1 (1983):
21; No. 6 (December 1984): 31-50]]

VOGEL, ERNST, 1926-   (Austrian composer)

V-219 Discographic references in KLEIN, Rudolf and HASELAVER, Elisabeth:
Ernst Vogel; eine Monographie. Wien; München: Doblinger, 1986:
118-128 ((--))

VOGEL, WLADIMIR, 1896-1984 (Russian-Swiss composer)

V-220 Diskografischen Anhang in LABHART, Walter: *Wladimir Vogel.*
Zürich: Kommissionsverlag Hug, 1982: 57-58 ((--))

VON STADE, FREDERICA, 1945-   (American mezzo-soprano)

V-221 Discography [on Philips label] S.l.: [Philips, 1980-?] 1 leaf.
((--))

WAART, EDO DE, 1941-   **(Dutch conductor)**

W-1   Discography [on Philips label] S.l.: [Philips, 198-?] 3 l. ((--))

WAGNER, JOSEPH, 1900-1974 (American composer)

W-2   Discography in BOWLING, Lance: *Joseph Wagner: a retrospective
       of a composer-conductor.* Lomita, CA: Charade Record Co., 1976: 22
       ((--))

WAGNER, RICHARD, 1813-1883 (German composer)

W-3   MARINELLI, Carlo: Discografia wagneriana in *Rassegna Musicale*,
       XXX/3 (1961): 259-285 ((--))

W-4   FANTAPIÉ, Alain: Wagner, Bayreuth et le disque in *Diapason*, No.
       208 (June-July 1976): 12-15 ((7))

W-5   Discographie in Bibliothèques de la ville de Paris: *Richard Wagner.*
       Paris: Les Bibliothèques, 1977: 53-59 ((5))

W-6   Discography in MANDER, Raymond: *The Wagner companion.* New York:
       Hawthorn Books, 1978: 236-254 ((-))

W-7   Discografia wagneriana in MANDELLI, Alfredo: *Wagner.* Milano: Fabbri,
       1979: 127-134 ((--))

W-8   Selected recordings of Wagner's music in ANDERSON, Robert: *Wagner:
       a biography: with a survey cf books, editions, and recordings.*
       London: C. Bingley; Hamden, CT: Linnet Books, 1980. 154 pp. ((--))

W-9   CLYM: *Richard Wagner: La discographie idéale des oeuvres de
       jeunesse à Parsifal.* Paris: Editions Ramsey, 1982. ((3, 5))

W-10   Discografia essenziale in TEDESCHI, Rubens: *Invito all'ascolto di
       Richard Wagner.* Milano: Mursia, 1983: [211]-214 ((--))

W-11   Pour une discothèque wagnerienne in *Diapason*, No. 280 (February
       1983): 33 ((--))

W-12   FURIE, Kenneth: Wagner recordings: The early operas in *High
       Fidelity/Musical America* XXXIII/5 (May 1983): 52-57; The love
       stories in XXXIII/7 (July 1983): 62-68; Passing the torch in
       XXXIII/10 (October 1983): 86-89, 112-115 ((7))

   OPERAS

   (DER) FLIEGENDE HOLLÄNDER (1843)

W-13   MARINELLI, Carlo: [Discography] in Roma, Teatro dell'Opera,
       season 1969-70: program pp. 388-390 ((5))

W-14   MARINELLI, Carlo: [Discography] in Venezia, Teatro La Fenice,
       season 1971-72: program pp. 343-346 ((5))

W-15 [Flying Dutchman discography] in *Stereo Geijutsu*, No. 57 (January 1973): 218-219 ((5))

W-16 MARINELLI, Carlo: [Discography] in Roma, Teatro dell'Opera, season 1977-78: program pp. 398 ((5))

W-17 THALMANN, Albert: Discographie in *Der fliegende Holländer*. München: W. Goldmann; [Mainz]: B. Schott, 1979: 172-173 ((1, 5)) (Opern der Welt)

W-18 FLINOIS, Pierre: Discographie in *L'Avant Scène Opéra*, No. 30 (November-December 1980): 114-118 ((1, 7))

W-19 SCHAUMKELL, Claus-Dieter: Gesamtaufnahmen auf Schallplatten in *Richard Wagner, Der fliegende Holländer*. München: Bayerische Staatsoper, 1981: 127 ((5))

W-20 Discography in *Der fliegende Holländer = The Flying Dutchman*. London: J. Calder; New York: Riverrun Press, 1982: 78-79 ((--)) (English National Opera guide; 12)

W-21 HOLLAND, Dietmar: Anmerkungen zur Diskographie in *Fliegende Holländer: Texte, Materialen, Kommentäre*. Reinbek bei Hamburg: Rowohlt, 1982: 246-[249] ((1, 5)) (Rororo Opernbücher)

W-22 Der fliegende Holländer auf Schallplatten in SEELIG, Lutz Eberhardt: *Wagners Sehnsucht nach Kongenialität: Sentas Emanzipation im Fliegenden Holländer*. Wien: Böhlau, 1984: 160-161 ((5))

W-23 MARINELLI, Carlo: [Discography] in Palermo, Teatro Massimo, season 1985-6: program p. 6 ((5))

LOHENGRIN (1850)

W-24 Discographie sur Lohengrin in LEFRANÇOIS, André: *Lohengrin de Richard Wagner: étude thématique et analyse*. Paris: A. Lefrançois, 1980: 81-82 ((--))

W-25 MARINELLI, Carlo: [Discography] in Milano, Teatro alla Scala, season 1981-2: program pp. 192-195 ((5))

W-26 THALMANN, Albert: Diskographie in *Lohengrin*. München: Goldmann; Mainz: Schott, 1982: 298-301 ((1, 7)) (Opern der Welt)

W-27 MARINELLI, Carlo: Discografia ragionata del Lohengrin in *Musica*, No. 27 (December 1982): 428-435; No. 28 (March 1983): 68-76 ((3, 5, 7))

W-28 Discographie "Lohengrin" in *fono forum* (December 1987): 26 ((1, 7))

(DIE) MEISTERSINGER VON NÜRNBERG (1868)

W-29 LAWRENCE, A. F. R.: Die Meistersinger--1928 in *BIRS Bulletin*, No. 8 (Spring 1958): 2-5 ((3, 6, 7))

W-30 MARINELLI, Carlo: [Discography] in Venezia, Teatro La Fenice, season 1973: program pp. 317-323 ((5))

W-31   Discographie critique: Les maîtres chanteurs de Richard Wagner in
Diapason, No. 212 (December 1976): 34-37, 41 ((7))

W-32   Discographie sur les Maîtres-Chanteurs in LEFRANÇOIS, André: *Les
maîtres-Chanteurs de Nürnberg de Richard Wagner* ... Paris: A.
Lefrançois, 1978: 145-146   ((--))

W-33   MARINELLI, Carlo: [Discography] in Roma, Teatro dell'Opera
season 1978-9: program p. 344 ((5))

W-34   [[BRINKMAN, Reinhold: Diskographie in *Richard Wagner, Die
Meistersinger von Nürnberg*. München: Bayerische Staatsoper, 1979.
95 pp.]]

W-35   HOLLAND, Dietmar: Anmerkungen zur Diskographie in *Die
Meistersinger von Nürnberg*. Reinbek bei Hamburg: Rowohlt, 1981:
279-280 ((1, 7)) (Rororo Opernbücher)

W-36   THALMANN, Albert: Diskographie in *Die Meistersinger von
Nürnberg*. München: Goldmann; Mainz: Schott, 1981: 470-473 ((1, 7))
(Opern der Welt)

W-37   LAW, Richard: Die Meistersinger in *Opera*, XXXIV/3 (March 1983):
246-254; XXXIV/5 (May 1983): 490-497; XXXIV/6 (June 1983): 608-
613; with [WALKER, Malcolm]: LP Discography ((7))
(Opera on the gramophone; 53)

W-38   HOYLE, Martin: Discography in *The mastersingers of Nürnberg =
Die Meistersinger von Nürnberg*. London: J. Calder; New York:
Riverrun Press, 1983: 127 ((--)) (English National Opera
guide; 19)

PARSIFAL (1882)

W-39   MARINELLI, Carlo: [Discography] in Bologna, Teatro Comunale,
season 1978-9: program pp. 76-85 ((5))

W-40   HOLLOWAY, Robin: Parsifal in *Opera*, XXX/4 (April 1979): 318-325;
Part 2 in XX/5 (May 1979): 436-440 with [WALKER, Malcolm]: LP
discography ((5)) (Opera on the gramophone; 47)

W-41   Discographie sur Parsifal in LEFRANÇOIS, André: *Parsifal, drame
sacré de Richard Wagner*. Paris: Lefrançois, 1980: 93-94 ((--))

W-42   Discographie "Parsifal" in *fono forum* (May 1981): 35 ((--))

W-43   WALKER, Malcolm: Discography in BECKETT, Lucy: *Parsifal*.
Cambridge; New York Cambridge University Press, 1981: 158-160
((5)) (Cambridge opera handbooks)

W-44   FLINOIS, Pierre: Discographie in *L'Avant Scène Opéra*, No. 38-39
(January-February 1982): 196-205 ((1, 7))

W-45   MARTIN, Serge and QUAHYL, A.: Parsifal--discographie critique in
Harmonie-Opéra Hifi conseil, No. 17 (February 1982): 46-54 ((5))

W-46   HAMILTON, David: Echoes from the shrine (Parsifal on disc) in
        Opera News, XLVII/2 (August 1982): 12-14; More echoes from the
        shrine in XLVIII/2 (August 1983): 22-25, 46; Further echoes from
        the shrine in XLIV (August 1984): 20-24 ((--))

W-47   MARINELLI, Carlo: [Discography] in Roma, Teatro dell'Opera,
        season 1983: program pp. 792-799 ((5))

W-48   MARINELLI, Carlo: [Discography] in Venezia, Teatro La Fenice,
        season 1983: program pp. 175-181 ((5))

W-49   MATZNER, Joachim: Anmerkungen zur Diskographie in *Parsifal*.
        Reinbek bei Hamburg: Rowohlt, 1984: 278-[279] ((1, 7))
        (Rororo Opernbücher)

W-50   PETERSON, Cathy: Selected discography in *Parsifal*. London:
        Calder; New York: Riverrun Press, 1986: 1276 ((7)) (English
        National Opera guide; 34)

(DER) RING DES NIBELUNGEN

W-51   Ringen och grammofonen in *Ringen: om Richard Wagner och
        Nibelungens ring*. Stockholm: Sohlman; Solna: Seelig, 1976:
        150-163 ((--))

W-52   SCHAUMKELL, Claus-Dieter: Der "Ring" auf Schallplatten;
        Gesamtaufnahmen, Querschnitte und Einzelaufnahmen in *Oper 1976:
        "Ring"-Aspkete* (Velber: Opernwelt, 1976): 113-124 ((--))

W-53   Le tetrologie de Richard Wagner discographie comparée in
        Harmonie, No. 122 (December 1976): 124-131 ((--))

W-54   Complete operas on record BLYTH, Alan: *Wagner's Ring: an
        introduction*. London: Hutchinson, 1980: 143-146 ((7))

W-55   DIGAETANI, John Lewis: An annotated discography in *Penetrating
        Wagner's Ring: an anthology*. Rutherford, NJ: Fairleigh Dickinson
        University Press, 1978; New York: Da Capo Press, 1983: 443-445
        ((--))

W-56   Nota discografica in CELLI, Teodoro: *L'anello del Nibelungo*.
        Milano: Rusconi, 1983: 391-394 ((5))

(DAS) RHEINGOLD (1869)

W-57   MARINELLI, Carlo: [Discography] in Milano, Teatro alla Scala,
        season 1972-73: program pp. 496-497 ((5))

W-58   MARINELLI, Carlo: [Discography] in Venezia, Teatro La Fenice,
        season 1975-76: program pp. 319-327 ((5))

W-59   DUTRONC, Jean-Louis: Discographie in *L'Avant Scène Opéra*, No.
        6/7 (November-December 1976): 182-184 ((1, 3, 5))

W-60   [[[Discography] in LEFRANÇOIS, André: *L'or du Rhin de Wagner=Das
        Rheingold*. Paris: A. Lefrançois, 1976: [91]-[92]]]

W-61   THALMANN, Albert: Diskographie in *Das Rheingold: der Ring des*

Nibelungen. München: Goldmann; [Mainz]: Schott, 1982: 292-295 ((1, 7)) (Opern der Welt)

W-62   PETERSON, Cathy: Discography in *The Rhinegold = Das Rheingold.* London: J. Calder; New York: Riverrun Press, 1985: 94-95 ((--)) (English National Opera guide; 35)

(DIE) WALKÜRE (1877)

W-63   MARINELLI, Carlo: [Discography] in Milano, Teatro alla Scala, 1973-74: program pp. 58-68 ((5))

W-64   Discographie in LEFRANÇOIS, André: *"La Walkyrie", "Die Walküre", de Richard Wagner.* Paris: A. Lefrançois, 1975: [67]-[70] ((--))

W-65   MARINELLI, Carlo: [Discography] in Venezia, Teatro La Fenice, 1975-76: program pp. 423-434 ((5))

W-66   TUBEUF, André: Discographie in *L'Avant Scène Opéra*, No. 8 (January-February 1977): 114-122 ((1, 3, 5, 7))

W-67   GODEFROID, Philippe: Le point sur La Walkyrie in *Diapason*, No. 269 (February 1982): 36-38 ((5))

W-68   THALMANN, Albert: Diskographie in *Die Walküre: der Ring des Nibelungen.* München: Goldmann; [Mainz]: Schott, 1982: 347-351 ((1, 7)) (Opern der Welt)

W-69   HOYLE, Martin: Discography in *The Valkyrie = Die Walküre.* London: J. Calder; New York: Riverrun Press, 1983: 110-112 ((--)) (English National Opera guide; 21)

W-70   MARINELLI, Carlo: [Discography] in Reggio Emilia, Teatro municipale "Romolo Valli, season 1983: program pp. 76-94 ((5))

SIEGFRIED (1876)

W-71   MARINELLI, Carlo: [Discography] in Roma, Teatro dell'Opera season 1966-67: program pp. 280-282 ((5))

W-72   TUBEUF, André: Discographie in *L'Avant Scène Opéra*, No. 12 (November-December 1977): 122-125 ((1, 3, 5, 6, 7))

W-73   Discographie sur "Siegfried" in LEFRANÇOIS, André: *Siegfried de Richard Wagner.* Paris: LeFrançois, 1979: 109-110 ((1))

W-74   THALMANN, Albert: Diskographie in *Siegfried: der Ring des Nibelungen.* München: Goldmann; Mainz: Schott, 1982: 406-408 ((1, 7)) (Opern der Welt)

W-75   MARINELLI, Carlo: [Discography] in Reggio Emilia, Teatro municipale "Romolo Valli", season 1983: program pp. 76-94 ((5))

W-76   HOYLE, Martin: Selected discography in *Siegfried* London: Calder; New York: Riverrun Presss, 1984: 126 (English National Opera guide; 28)

GÖTTERDÄMMERUNG (1876)

W-77   BLYTH, Alan: Götterdämmerung in *Opera*, XXVII/9 (September 1976):
        804–815; XXVII/10 (October 1976): 898–906 ((1, 5)) (Opera on
        the gramophone; 40)

W-78   TUBEUF, André: Discographie in *L'Avant Scène Opéra*, No. 13/14
        (January–February 1978): 156–161 ((1, 3, 5, 6))

W-79   MARINELLI, Carlo: [Discography] in Roma, Teatro dell'Opera
        season 1979–80: program pp. 688–696 ((5))

W-80   THALMANN, Albert: Diskographie in *Der Ring des Nibelungen.
        Götterdämmerung*. München: Goldmann; [Mainz]: Schott, 1983:
        406–408 ((5)) (Opern der Welt)

W-81   PETERSON, Cathy: Discography in *Twilight of the Gods =
        Götterdämmerung*. London: J. Calder; New York: Riverrun Press,
        1985: 125–127 ((--)) (English National Opera guide; 31)

TANNHÄUSER (1845)

W-82   Discographie de Tannhäuser in LEFRANÇOIS, André: *Tannhäuser
        de Richard Wagner*. Paris: A. Lefrançois, 1982: 91 ((--))

W-83   GEFFEN, Gérard: Discographie de Tannhäuser in *Harmonie–Panorama
        musique*, No. 30 (April 1983): 40 ((1, 7))

W-84   MARINELLI, Carlo: [Discography] in Milano, Teatro alla Scala
        season 1983–4: program pp. 97–102 ((5))

W-85   FLINOIS, Pierre: Discographie and CABOURG, Jean and VOISIN,
        Georges: Tannhäuser et le 78 tours in *L'Avant Scène Opéra*,
        No. 63/64 (May–June 1984): 186–201 ((7))

W-86   MARINELLI, Carlo: [Discography] in Roma, Teatro dell'Opera,
        season 1984–5: program pp. 70–80 ((5))

W-87   HOLLAND, Dietmar: Anmerkungen zur Diskographie in *Tannhäuser:
        Texte, Materialien, Kommentäre*. Reinbek bei Hamburg: Rohwolt,
        1986: 279–281 ((--)) (Rororo Opernbücher)

W-88   [[[Discography] in *Tannhauser*. London: J. Calder; New York:x
        Riverrun Press, 1988 (English National Opera guide; 39)

TRISTAN UND ISOLDE (1865)

W-89   MARINELLI, Carlo: [Discography] in Venezia, Teatro La Fenice,
        season 1970–71: program pp. 402–404 ((5))

W-90   MARINELLI, Carlo: [Discography] in Roma, Teatro dell'Opera,
        season 1971–72: program pp. 188–191 ((5))

W-91   Discographie sur Tristan in LEFRANÇOIS, André: *Tristan et Isolde
        de Richard Wagner*. Paris: A. Lefrançois, 1978: 107–108
        ((--))

W-92   HOLLOWAY, Robin: Tristan und Isolde in *Opera*, XXX/12 (December
        1979): 1138–1147; XXXI/1 (January 1980): 38–42; with WALKER,
        Malcolm: LP discography ((5)) (Opera on the gramophone; 48)

W-93   MARINELLI, Carlo: [Discography] in Roma, Teatro dell'Opera, season 1980-1: program pp. 1062-1070 ((5))

W-94   MARINELLI, Carlo: [Discography] in Venezia, Teatro La Fenice, season 1981: program pp. 112-122 ((5))

W-95   Le dossier du mois: Tristan et Isolde in *Harmonie Hi-Fi conseil*, No. 10 (June 1981): 28-[37] ((3, 7))

W-96   TUBEUF, André: Discographie in *L'Avant Scène Opéra*, No. 34-35 (July-August 1981): 196-203 ((1, 7))

W-97   MARINELLI, Carlo: [Discography] in Palermo, Teatro Massimo, season 1981-2: program p. 32 ((5))

W-98   [[[Discography] in *Tristan und Isolde*. [Palermo]: Ente autonomo del Teatro massimo, Politeama Garibaldi, 1981-82:]]

W-99   Discography in *Tristan and Isolde*. London: J. Calder; New York: Riverrun Press, 1981: 94-95 ((--)) (English National Opera guide; 6)

W-100   HOLLAND, Dietmar: Anmerkungen zur Diskographie in *Tristan und Isolde: Texte, Materialien, Kommentäre*. Reinbek bei Hamburg: Rowohlt, 1983: 275-[280] ((1, 7)) (Rororo Opernbücher)

W-101   THALMANN, Albert: Diskographie in *Tristan und Isolde*. München: Goldmann; [Mainz]: Schott, 1983: 380-383 ((1, 7)) (Opern der Welt)

WESENDONK LIEDER (1858)

W-102   FANTAPIÉ, Alain: Discographie sélective in *Diapason*, No. 208 (June-July 1976): 25 ((--))

W-103   FANTAPIÉ, Alain: Discographie sélective in *Diapason*, No. 215 (March 1977): 25 ((--))

WAGNER, SIEGFRIED, 1869-1930 (German composer)

W-104 Siegfried Wagner--Diskographie in PACHL, Peter P.: *Siegfried Wagners musikdramatisches Schaffen*. Tutzing: Schneider, 1979: 184-185 ((7))

WALDEMAR, HENRIQUE (Brazilian composer)

W-105 Discographic references in MIGLIAVACCA, Ariede Maria: *Henrique Waldemar: catálogo de obras*. [Brasília]: Ministério das Relações Exteriores, Departamento de Cooperação Cultural, Científica e Tecnológica, 1979: 31 pp. ((--)) (Compositores brasileiros)

WALTER, BRUNO, 1876-1962 (German conductor)

W-106 [[UNO, Koho: *Bruno Walter record; a history of recorded performances*. Tokyo: Ongaku No-tomo sha, 1972. 47 pp.]]

W-107 GIUDICI, Elvio: Discografia di Bruno Walter in *Musica*,
No. 33 (June 1984): 32-39 ((1, 7))

W-108 SUGA, Hajime: Bruno Walter discography in *Record Geijutsu*, No.
401 (February 1984): 238-242; No. 402 (March 1984): 241-244;
No. 403 (April 1984): 267-272 ((3, 5, 7))

W-109 Discography in *Fanfare*, VIII/6 (July-August 1985): 112 ((--))

W-110 40 ans de musique (les disques de Bruno Walter in *Diapason-
Harmonie*, No. 311 (December 1985): 101-105 ((1, 7))

**WALTHER VON DER VOGELWEIDE, ca. 1170-ca. 1230   (German
Meistersinger)**

W-111 Diskographie in *Walther von der Vogelweide: Die gesamte
Überlieferung der Texte und Melodien.* Göppingen: A. Kummerle,
1977: 77-78 ((1, 4))

WALTON, SIR WILLIAM, 1902-1983   (English composer)

W-112 Discographic notes in CRAGGS, Stewart R.: *William Walton: a thematic
catalogue of his musical works.* London; New York: Oxford University
Press, 1977. 273 pp. ((7))

W-113 POULTON, Alan: *The recorded works of Sir William Walton.*
Kidderminster: Bravura Publications, 1980. 132 pp. ((3, 4, 6, 7))
(Studies in discography; 1)

W-114 [[[Discograpy] in SMITH, Carolyn J.: *William Walton: a
bio-bibliography.* New York: Greenwood Press, 1988.
(Bio-bibliographies in music; 18)]]

WAND, GÜNTER, 1912-   (German conductor)

W-115 Discographische Hi[n]weise: Günter Wand in *fono forum* (January
1982): 26 ((--))

WARD, ROBERT, 1917-   (American composer)

W-116 Selected discography in Program notes for *Works by Robert Ward.*
[Sound recording] New World Records, NW 300, 1977: [4] ((--))

W-117 [[Discography in WOLIVER, Charles Patrick: *Robert Ward's
"The Crucible": a critical commentary.* [DMA, University of
Cincinnati, 1986]

W-118 [[[Discography] in KREITNER, Kenneth: *Robert Ward, a
bio-bibliography.* New York: Greenwood Press, 1988
(Bio-bibliographies in music; 17)]]

WARREN, ELINOR REMICK, 1906-   (American composer)

W-119 Discography in BORTIN, Virginia: *Elinor Remick Warren: her life and
her music.* Metuchen, NJ: Scarecrow Press, 1987: 207-221 ((1, 7))
(Composers of North America; 5)

WEBER, BEN, 1916-1979   (American composer)

W-120 Selected discography in Program notes for *Chamber music by ... Ben Weber ...* [Sound recording] New World Records NW 281, 1977. ((--))

W-121 Selected discography in Program notes for *Henry Herford, baritone.* [Sound recording] New World Records NW 327, 1985: [1] ((--))

WEBER, CARL MARIA VON, 1786-1826 (German composer)

W-122 Discographie in LEINERT, Michael: *Carl Maria von Weber in Selbstzeugnissen und Bilddokumenten.* Reibek bei Hamburg: Rohwolt, 1978: 151-[152] ((--))

W-123 Discographie in ZSCHACKE, Günter: *Carl Maria von Weber: Romantiker im Aufbruch.* Lübeck: Schmidt Romhild, 1985: 314-317 ((--))

OPERAS

W-124 HALFT, Franz Werner: Carl Maria von Weber; eine vergleichende Diskografie der Opern zum Ausklang des Weber-Jahres in *fono forum* (December 1976): 1248-1259; Eine vergleichende Diskographie Opern (Teil II) in *fono forum* (February 1977): 124-126, 128-130 ((--))

W-125 MARTIN, Serge: Les opéras de Weber: discographie critique in *Harmonie-Panorama musique,* No. 29 (March 1983): 44-55 ((3, 5))

ABU HASSAN, J. 106 (1811)

W-126 MARINELLI, Carlo: [Discography] in Bologna, Teatro Comunale, season 1980-81: program pp. 47-50 ((5))

(DER) FREISCHÜTZ, J. 277 (1821)

W-127 MARINELLI, Carlo: [Discography] in Venezia, Gran Teatro La Fenice, season 1973-74: program pp. 300-307 ((5))

W-128 BLYTH, Alan: Der Freischütz in *Opera,* XXIX/4 (April 1978): 357-368; with WALKER, Malcolm: LP discography ((5)) (Opera on the gramophone; 44)

W-129 MARINELLI, Carlo: [Discography] in Venezia, Teatro La Fenice, season 1981-82: program pp. 691-698 ((5))

W-130 THALMANN, Albert: Diskographie in *Der Freischütz.* München: Goldmann, 1982: 270-271 ((1, 5, 7)) (Opern der Welt)

W-131 GRÄWE, Karl Dietrich: Anmerkungen zur Diskographie in *Der Freischütz: Texte, Materialien, Kommentäre.* Reinbek bei Hamburg: Rowohlt, 1987: 213-216 ((1, 7)) (Rororo Opernbücher)

W-132 TUBEUF, André: Discographie in *L'Avant Scène Opéra,* No. 105/106 (January-February 1988): 162-168 ((1, 5))

OBERON, J. 306 (1826)

W-133 TUBEUF, André: Discographie in *L'Avant Scène Opéra,* No. 74 (April 1985): 96-99 ((1, 7))

WEBER, HENRI   (Baritone)

W-134 [Discography] in *Record Collector*, IX/3 (March 1954): 72-73   ((--))

WEBERN, ANTON, 1883-1945   (Austrian composer)

W-135 Discographie in MATTER, Henri-Louis: *Anton Webern: essai.*
[Lausanne]: Age d'homme, 1981: 155-156   ((--))

W-136 Webern à écouter in *Diapason*, No. 88 (November 1983): 57   ((--))

See also

PIANO MUSIC

WEILL, KURT, 1900-1950   (German composer)

W-137 NATALETTI, Giorgio: Musicisti d'oggi e di ieri al disco: Kurt Weill
in *Musica d'oggi*, No. 16 (January 1934): 9-13   ((--))

W-138 Diskographie in KOTSCHENREUTHER, Hellmut: *Kurt Weill.*
Berlin-Halensee: M. Hesses, 1962: 98-99   ((--))

W-139 KOWALKE, Kim H.: Kurt Weill's European legacy: a critical
discography in *High Fidelity*, XXVIII/7 (July 1978): 62   ((--))

W-140 [Selected discography] in Concert stage, Broadway stage: The music
of George Gershwin and Kurt Weill in *Tarakan Music Letter*, III/4
(March-April 1982): 3   ((--))

W-141 Discography in JARMAN, Douglas: *Kurt Weill, an illustrated
biography.* Bloomington: Indiana University Press, 1982: 147   ((--))

W-142 A Kurt Weill discography in SANDERS, Ronald: *The days grow short:
the life and music of Kurt Weill.* New York: Holt, Rinehart and
Winston, 1980; Limelight Editions, 1985: 442-449   ((--))

W-143 SCHEBERA, Jürgen: Kurt Weill's early recordings, 1928-1933 in
Kurt Weill Newsletter, IV/1 (Spring 1986): 6-9   ((1, 7))

STAGE WORKS

(DIE) SIEBEN TODSÜNDEN (1933)

W-144   MARINELLI, Carlo: [Discography] in Roma, Teatro dell'Opera,
season 1977-78: program pp. 99-100   ((5))

WEINGARTNER, FELIX, 1863-1942   (German conductor)

W-145 DYMENT, Christopher: Discography in Program notes for *The art of
Felix Weingartner* [Sound recording] EMI RLS 717, 1975: 10-[12]
((3, 6, 7))

W-146 DYMENT, Christopher: The recorded legacy of Felix Weingartner in
Felix Weingartner: recollections & recordings. Rickmansworth: Triad
Press, 1976: [61]-92   ((1, 3, 4, 5, 6, 7))

W-147 Discography in Program notes for *Beethoven Nine Symphonies* [Sound recording] Toshiba-EMI EAC 60079/84, 1977 ((7))

W-148 SUGA, Hajime: Felix Weingartner discography 1910-1940 in *LP Techno*,
September 1978: 94- ((7))

W-149 DYMENT, Christopher: Discografia in Christopher Dyment: Felix
Weingartner in *Musica*, No. 17 (June 1980): 143-152 ((7))

W-150 KAWAI, Shiro: Weingartner discography in *Record Geijutsu*, No. 404
(May 1984): 268-270; No. 405 (June 1984): 260-262 ((3, 6, 7))

WEISS, ADOLPH, 1891-1971 (American composer)

W-151 [[Discography in GEORGE, William Bernard: *Adolph Weiss*.
[Dissertation, University of Iowa, 1971] 485 pp.]]

WEISSENBERG, ALEXIS, 1929-   (Bulgarian pianist)

W-152 Discographie in BREUER, Gustl: *Alexis Weissenberg*. Berlin:
Rembrandt Verlag, 1977: 60-62 ((--))

W-153 Discographie Alexis Weissenberg in *fono forum* (December 1980): 22-30
((--))

W-154 Discographie in *Harmonie-Panorama musique*, No. 31 (May 1983): 17
((--))

WESTMINSTER CHOIR, USA

W-155 BECK, Joseph G.: Westminster Choir discography 1926-1976; recordings
as history in *Choral Journal*, XVII/3 (1976): 9-11 ((1, 7))

WHITE, ROBERT, ca. 1538-1574 (English composer)

W-156 WEBER, J. F.: A discography of the music of Robert White in *Fanfare*,
V/5 (May-June 1982): 243-244 ((5, 7))

**WHITTAKER, WILLLIAM GILLIES, 1876-1944 (English composer and
conductor)**

W-157 GUYATT, Andrew: Aw. G. Whittaker discography in *British Music
Society Journal*, II (1980): 49-51 ((5))

WIDMER, ERNST, 1927-   (Brazilian composer)

W-158 Discographic references in MIGLIAVACCA, Ariede Maria: *Ernst Widmer:
catálogo de obras*. [Brasília]: Ministério das Relações Exteriores,
Departamento de Cooperação Cultural, Científica e Tecnológica,
1977: [34] pp. ((--)) (Compositores brasileiros)

WIDDOP, WALTER, 1892-1949 (English tenor)

W-159 Walter Widdop-a discography in *Talking Machine Review*, No. 43
(December 1976): 856 ((--))

WIENER, JEAN, 1896-1982 (French composer)

W-160 Discographie in WIENER, Jean: *Allegro appassionato*. Paris:

P. Belford, 1978: 213–[222]   ((--))

WIENER PHILHARMONIKER

W-161 [Wiener Philharmoniker discography] in *Record Geijutsu*, No. 295 (April 1975): [191]–211   ((5, 7))

W-162 [Discography] in *Record Geijutsu*, No. 318 (March 1977): 151–170 ((7))

WILDBERGER, JACQUES, 1922–   (Swiss composer)

W-163 Discographie in *Jacques Wildberger, geboren am 3. Januar 1922: Werkverzeichnis*. Zürich: Schweizerisches Musik–Archiv, 1982: 10 ((--))

WILLAN, HEALEY, 1880–1968   (Canadian composer)

W-164 [[Healey Willan--a discography in *Musicanada*, No. 42 (Spring 1980): 2+]]

W-165 Sound recordings/enregistrements sonores in BRYANT, Gilles: *Healy Willan catalogue: Supplement*. Ottawa: National Library of Canada, 1982: 29–45   ((1, 7))

WILLIAMSON, MALCOLM, 1931–   (Australian composer)

W-166 Discography in *Malcolm Williamson, (born 1931): a catalogue to celebrate the composer's 50th birthday*. London: Weinberger, 1981: 27–29   ((--))

WILLIAMSON-BALLOU, ESTHER, 1915–1973   (American composer)

W-167 Appendix I: Discography in HEINTZE, Jim: *Esther Williamson-Ballou*. Westport, CT: Greenwood Press, 1987: 102   ((5))   (Bio–bibliographies in music; 5)

WILSON, OLLY, 1937–   (American composer)

W-168 Selected discography in Program notes for *Olly Wilson: Sinfonia*. [Sound recording] New World Records NW 337, 1985   ((--))

WIND INSTRUMENTS

W-169 POTTER, Tully: Wind music on record in *Hi-fi News & Record Review*, XXVII/2 (February 1982): 70–71, 75   ((--))

WIND QUINTET OF THE USSR SYMPHONY ORCHESTRA

W-170 Discography in *Music in the USSR* (April–June 1987): 85   ((--))

WITKOWSKI, GEORGES-MARTIN, 1867–1943   (French composer)

W-171 Discographie in FERRATON, Yves: *Cinquante ans de vie musicale à Lyons: les Witkowski et l'Orchestre philharmonique de Lyon, 1903–1953*. Trévoux: Éditions de Trévoux, 1984: 353   ((5))

WOLF, HUGO, 1860–1903   (Austrian composer)

W-172 Discographische Hinweise: Hugo Wolf in *fono forum* (January
1983): 31   ((--))

W-173 Diskographie (Auswahl) in DORSCHEL, Andreas: *Hugo Wolf: mit
Selbstzeugnissen und Bilddokumenten.* Reibek bei Hamburg: Rowohlt,
1985: 147-[148]   ((--))

W-174 [[Discography in WHEELER, Ellen Jayne Maris: *The Mignon lieder of
Goethe's "Wilhelm Meisters Lehrjahre" a study of literary background
and musical evolution with particular emphasis on Hugo Wolf.*
[D.M., University of Oklahoma, 1987] 170 pp.]]

WOLFF, ERNEST, 1905-   **(German baritone)**

W-175 RUSSELL, Ronald: Ernest Wolff discography, 78 r.p.m. in *Record
Collector,* XXX/12-13 (December 1985): 282-286 ((3, 6, 7))

WOLF-FERRARI, ERMANNO, 1876-1948 (German-Italian composer)

W-176 ROSENDORFER, Herbert: Diskographie in *Ermanno Wolf-Ferrari.*
Tutzing: H. Schneider, 1986: 151-159 ((--)) (Komponisten in
Bayern; 8)

OPERAS

(I) QUATTRO RUSTEGHI (1906)

W-177   MARINELLI, Carlo: [Discography] in Roma, Teatro dell'Opera,
season 1968-69: program pp. 206 ((5))

W-178   MARINELLI, Carlo: [Discography] in Venezia, Teatro La Fenice,
season 1972-73: program pp. 356-357 ((5))

W-179   MARINELLI, Carlo: [Discography] in Treviso, Ente Teatro
Comunale, season 1976: program p. 2 ((5))

WOLL, ERNA, 1917-   **(German composer)**

W-180 Diskographie in *Erna Woll.* Tutzing: H. Schneider, 1987: 137-138
((5)) (Komponisten in Bayern; 12)

WOLPE, STEFAN, 1902-1972 (American composer)

W-181 Selected discography in Program notes for *Parnassus.* [Sound
recording] New World Records NW 306, 1980: [1] ((--))

W-182 Selected discography in Program notes for *Stefan Wolpe: Form.* [Sound
recording] New World Records NW 308, 1980: [2] ((--))

W-183 Selected discography in Program notes for *Pastorale, Passacaglia.*
[Sound recording] New World Records NW 344, 1987 ((--))

WOMEN COMPOSERS

W-184 Discography in LAURENCE, Anya: *Women of notes: 1,000 women composer
born before 1900.* New York: R. Rosen Press, 1978: 96-100 ((--))

W-185 POLL, Jeannie G.: Available recordings of works by American women

composers in *Music Educators Journal*, LXV (January 1979): 37–41
((--))

W-186 [Discography of women composers] in *Tarakan Music Letter*, II/2
(December 1980): 1, 8–9   ((--))

W-187 Discographies in LEPAGE, Jane Weiner: *Women composers, conductors,
and musicians of the twentieth century: selected biographies.*
Metuchen, NJ: Scarecrow Press, 1980.   293 pp.; Vol. II: Metuchen:
Scarecrow Press, 1983. 373 pp.   ((--))

W-188 Listen to Leonarda: the Leonarda catalog in *Tarakan Music Letter*,
II/5 (May–June 1981): 9   ((--))

W-189 Discography in ZAIMONT, Judith Lang: *Contemporary concert music by
women: a directory of the composers and their works.* Westport, CT:
Greenwood Press, 1981: 341–347   ((--))

W-190 FRASIER, Jane: *Women composers: a discography.* Detroit:
Information Coordinators, 1983.   300 pp.   ((4))   (Detroit studies
in music bibliography; 50)

W-191 MEGGETT, J. M.: *Keyboard music by women composers: catalog and
bibliography.* Westport, CT: Greenwood Press, 1983.   210 pp. ((5))

W-192 COHEN, Aaron I.: *International discography of women composers.*
Westport, CT: Greenwood Press, 1984. 254 pp.   ((4))

W-193 Discography in BESSIÈRES, Yves: *Women and music.* Brussels:
Commission of the European Communities, Directorate-General
Information, Information for Women's Organizations and Press, 1985:
90–92   ((--))

W-194 Discographies in COHEN, Aaron I. *International encyclopedia of
woman composers.* New York: Books & Music, 1988. 2 v., 1151 pp.
((--))

WOMEN MUSICIANS

W-195 MCHENRY, Susan, and MCMANUS, Jill: A woman's place is in the
groove [discographic essay] in *MS* (November 1979): 40   ((--))

WOOD, HUGH, 1932–   (English composer)

W-196 HUGHES, Eric and DAY, Timothy: Hugh Wood in *Recorded Sound*, No. 84
(July 1983): 77–81   ((1, 7))   (Discographies of British composers;
18)

WOODWIND INSTRUMENTS

W-197 WALN, George: Double reeds and saxophone on LP recordings in
Instrumentalist, VIII/7 (March 1954): 26–27   ((--))

WORK, JOHN WESLEY, III, 1901–1967   (American composer)

W-198 [[Discography in GARCIA, William Burres: *The life and choral music
of John Wesley Work III (1901–1967)* [Dissertation, University of
Iowa, 1973]   246 pp.]]

WOURINEN, CHARLES, 1938–   (American composer)

W–199 Selected discography in Program notes for *Parnassus*. [Sound
recording] New World Records NW 306, 1980: [2] ((--))

WUNDERLICH, FRITZ, 1930–1966 (German tenor)

W–200 SCHAUMKELL, Claus–Dieter: Diskographie in *Opern Welt*, XVII/11
(November 1976): 58–59 ((--))

WYNNE, DAVID, 1900–   (Welsh composer)

W–201 List of works and recordings in JONES, Richard Elfy: *David
Wynne*. Cardiff: University of Wales Press, 1979: 65–73 ((--))

XENAKIS, IANNIS, 1922–   (Greek composer)

X–1   Recordings in BOIS, Mario: *Iannis Xenakis: the man and his music*.
Westport, CT: Greenwood Press, 1980: 38–39 ((--)) [Reprinted from
the 1967 ed. published by Boosey & Hawkes, London]

X–2   Discographie in MATOSSIAN, Nouritza: *Iannis Xenakis*. Paris: Fayard:
Fondation SACEM, 1981: [312]–314 ((--))

X–3   Discographie in *Regards sur Iannis Xenakis*. Paris: Stock, 1981:
401–[409] ((--))

X–4   Discography in MATOSSIAN, Nouritza: *Iannis Xenakis*. London: Kahn &
Averill; New York: Taplinger Pub. Co., 1986: 261–265 ((--))

YAGLING, VICTORIA (Russian cellist)

Y–1   Discography in *Music in the USSR* (July–September 1987): 15
((--))

YAW, ELLEN BEACH, 1869–1947 (American soprano)

Y–2   ALTAMARINO, Antonio: An Ellen Beach Yaw discography in *Record
Collector*, X (December 1955): 153–161 ((3)) [Includes unissued
records]

Y–3   WILE, Raymond R.: Ellen Beach Yaw: information compiled from the
Edison files in *Vocal Record Collector's Society Bulletin*, I/3
(August 1966): 1–2 ((3, 7))

YLIOPPILASKUNNAN LAULAJAT (HELSINGIN YLIOPISTO), Finland

Y–4   [Discography] in *Sata, sata, sata--: Ylioppilaskunnan Laulajat,
1883–1983*. Helsinki: Yl, 1983: 105 ((7))

YSAŸE, EUGENE, 1858–1931 (Belgian violinist/conductor)

Y–5   Gramophone recordings by Eugene Ysaÿe for the Columbia Gramophone
Company, New York in YSAYE, Antoine: *Ysaÿe, his life, work, and
influence*. St. Clair Shores, Mich.: Scholarly Press, 1978: 245
((--)) [Reprinted from the 1947 ed. published by Heinemann]

Y–6   MALTESE, John Anthony: The recordings of Eugene Ysaÿe in GINZBURG,

L. S.: *Prof. Lev Ginsburg's Ysaÿe*. Neptune City, NJ: Paganiniana, 1980: 544-552 and The recorded compositions of Eugene Ysaÿe, pp. 552-559 ((--))

YUDINA, MARIA, 1899-1970   (Russian pianist)

Y-7   [Discography] in *Mariia Veniaminova Iudina*. Moskva: Sov. kompizitor, 1978: 384-[386] ((7))

Y-8   Discographische Hinweise in *fono forum* (January 1982): 49 ((--))

Y-9   METHUEN-CAMPBELL, James: Early Soviet pianists and their recordings: a survey in *Recorded Sound*, No. 83 (January 1983): 1-16 ((--))

YUN, ISANG, 1917-   (Korean composer)

Y-10   Diskographie in RINSER, Luise: *Der verwundete Drache Dialog uber Leben u. Werk d. Komponisten*. Frankfurt/Main: S. Fischer, 1977: 239-[240] ((--))

Y-11   Discographie in HEISTER, Hanns-Werner and SPAUER, Walter-Wolfgang: *Der Komponist Isang Yun*. München: Edition Text u. Kritik, 1987: 299-313 ((--))

See also

PIANO MUSIC

ZABALETA, NICANOR, 1907-   (Spanish harpist)

Z-1   Discography, Deutsche Grammophon artist information, 1980. 1 p. ((--))

Z-2   WEIDENSAUL, Jane: A Nicanor Zabaleta discography in *American Harp Journal*, VII/4 (1980): 6-7 ((--))

ZĀBERS, JĀNIS, 1935-1973   (Latvian tenor)

Z-3   Diskografija in *Jānis Zābers*. Rīga: Liesma, 1980: [295]-[304] ((--))

ZACHARIAS, CHRISTIAN, 1950-   (German pianist)

Z-4   Discographische Hinweise Christian Zacharias in *fono forum* (October 1984): 25 ((--))

ZACHER, GERD, 1929-   (German organist/composer)

Z-5   [Discography] in *Record Geijutsu*, No. 276 (September 1973): 189 ((--))

ZAK, IAKOV, 1913-   (Russian pianist)

Z-6   [Discography Iakov Zak] in *Iakov Zak: Stati, materialy, vospominaniia o IA. Zak*. Moskva: Sov. Kompozitor, 1980: [200] ((--))

ZANELLI, RENATO, 1892-1935   (Chilean tenor-baritone)

Z-7   DZAZOPULOS, E. Juan: [Discography] in *Record Collector*, XXXI/1-3
       (February 1986): 52-60   ((3, 4, 6, 7))

    ZECCHI, CARLO, 1903-   **(Italian conductor/pianist)**

Z-8   TESTAS, Henry Jean: Discografia di Carlo Zecchi, pianista in *Musica*,
       No. 18 (September 1980): 265-266   ((--))

    ZECHLIN, RUTH, 1926-   **(German composer)**

Z-9   Schallplattenverzeichnis in ZECHLIN, Ruth: *Situationen, Reflexionen,
       Gespräche, Erfahrungen, Gedanken*. Berlin: Neue Musik Berlin, 1986:
       149   ((--))

    ZEMLINSKY, ALEXANDER VON, 1871-1942   (Austrian composer)

Z-10   YOELL, John H.: Korngold and Zemlinsky: a selective discography
       (33 1/3 rpm) in *Fanfare*, VIII/2 (November-December 1984): 130-133
       ((--))

Z-11   Discographische Hinweise in *fono forum* (July 1987): 31   ((--))

    ZEPPILLI, ALICE, 1885-?   **(French soprano)**

Z-12   BOTT, Michael: Discography in *Record Collector*, XXVIII/3-4 (July
       1983): 68-69   ((3, 6, 7))

    ZHUKOV, SERGEI   (Ukrainian composer)

Z-13   Discography in *Music in the USSR* (January-March 1987): 92   ((--))

    ZIMMERMANN, BERND ALOIS, 1918-1970   (German composer)

Z-14   Diskographie in *Musik und Bildung*, X/10 (October 1978): 656   ((--))

Z-15   Schallplattenverzeichnis in KONOLD, Wulf: *Bernd Alois Zimmermann:
       der Komponist und sein Werk*. Köln: DuMont, 1986: 250-251   ((--))

Z-16   Schallplattenverzeichnis in *Bernd Alois Zimmermann: Dokumente und
       Interpretationen*. Köln: Wienand, 1986: 163-164   ((--))

Z-17   Diskographie in *Zeitphilosophie und Klanggestalt: Untersuchungen
       zum Werk Bernd Alois Zimmermanns*. Mainz; New York: Schott, 1986:
       143-146   ((--))

    ZIMMERMANN, FRANK PETER (German violinist)

Z-18   Discographische Hinweise: Frank Peter Zimmermann in *fono forum*
       (December 1987): 31   ((--))

    ZIMMERMANN, JOSEF, 1906-   **(German composer)**

Z-19   [Discography] in *Menus organistal: Festschr. Josef Zimmermann
       zum 80. Geburtstag*. Köln: Bachem, 1986: 137-138   ((--))

    ZINMAN, DAVID, 1936-   **(American conductor)**

Z-20   Discography [on Philips label] S.l.: [Philips, 1980-?] 1 leaf.

((--))

ZOCCHI, MR.   (Italian tenor)

Z-21   [Discography] in *Record Collector*, IX/3 (March 1954): 73   ((--))

ZUCKERMAN, PINCHAS, 1948-   **(Israeli violinist)**

Z-22   [Discography] in *Record Geijutsu*, No. 276 (September 1973): 191
((--))

Z-23   Discography, Deutsche Grammophon artist information, 1980.   1 p.
((--))

INDEX

AARE
Leif, P-63
ABADZHIEV
Aleksandur, G-64
ABBEY
Hermione, V-172
ADAM,
Theo, A-19, A-21
ADAMO
Maria Rosaria, B-176
ADAMS
Beverly Decker, M-133
ADAMS
Brian, B-332, S-404
ADAMS
Stephen, S-48
AHLÉN
Carl-Gunnar, S-195
AISTLEITNER
Peter, K-84
ALBANI
Emma, A-28
ALBRECHT
Theodore John, M-307
ALCARAZ
José, H-9
ALDER
Caine, H-142
ALEXANDER
Jesse J., F-28
ALEXANDER
John, M-2, O-21, V-167
ALEXANDRE
Ivan A., C-106, C-132
ALPÁR
Ágnes, O-30
ALTAMARINO
Antonio, Y-2
ALTMAN

Peter, B-226
AMANN
Jean-Pierre, K-74
AMSTERDAM
Ellen I., B-317
ANDERSON
Donna K., G-140
ANDERSON
Nicholas, R-10
ANDERSON
Robert, W-8
ANDERSON
Ronald Eugene, S-6
ANDREONI
Sergio, Q-2
ANDREWS
Frank, L-55, L-68, V-213
ANDREWS
Paul D., T-69
ANDRIESSEN
Pieter, H-2
ANNAND
H. H., L-15, L-34
APPLE
Linda Key, F-32
APPLEBY
David P., V-169
ARDOIN
John, C-10, C-26, M-118, V-27
ARIAS
Enrique Alberto, T-34
ARNAUD
Alain, B-187, C-28, P-221
ARNE
F., R-11
ARNOL
André, S-348
ARNOLD
Ben, L-166

John, R-69
BERRY
    Corre Ivey, V-214
BERRY
    Mary, C-100
BERTAGNA
    Giancarlo, O-87
BESCOBY-CHAMBERS
    John, S-261
BESSIERES
    Yves, W-193
BESSON
    François, F-21, F-72
BETZ
    Anneliese, M-368
BETZ
    Peter C., L-21
BIAS
    Iwona, F-43
BIELSKA
    Krystyna, O-41
Bild und Tonträgerverzeichnisse;
    7, M-368
Bio-bibliographies in music; 1,
    M-299
Bio-bibliographies in music; 2,
    C-216
Bio-bibliographies in music; 3,
    B-71
Bio-bibliographies in music; 4,
    T-62
Bio-bibliographies in music; 5,
    W-167
Bio-bibliographies in music; 6,
    S-107
Bio-bibliographies in music; 7,
    R-36
Bio-bibliographies in music; 8,
    T-34
Bio-bibliographies in music; 9,
    V-169
Bio-bibliographies in music; 10,
    L-105
Bio-bibliographies in music; 12,
    P-90
Bio-bibliographies in music; 13,
    B-310
Bio-bibliographies in music; 14,
    I-14
Bio-bibliographies in music; 15,
    C-97
Bio-bibliographies in music; 16,
    P-55
Bio-bibliographies in music; 17,
    W-118
Bio-bibliographies in music; 18,
    W-114
Bio-bibliographies in music; 19,

R-149
BIRD
    John, G-130
BISHOP
    John, B-381
BITTERLICH
    Hans, S-22
BLACKER
    George, E-36
BLARR
    Oskar Gottlieb, O-86
BLOCH
    Francine, M-156, M-159, P-125
BLOCH
    Suzanne, B-312
BLOCK
    Geoffrey Holden, I-14
BLOESCH
    David, S-67
BLOIS
    Louis, S-408
BLOKKER
    Roy, S-176
BLUM
    David, G-148
BLYTH
    Alan, S-15, S-233, S-311,
        T-22, W-54, W-77, W-128
BLYTH
    Charles, K-38
BOERO DE IZETA
    Carlota, B-326
BOIS
    Mario, X-1
BOLIG
    John R., C-66
BOLLERT
    Werner, S-98
BONAFINI
    Umberto, S-142
BORIE
    Alexandre, H-63
BOROS
    Attila, K-68, L-130
BOROVSKY
    Victor, C-94
BOROVYK
    Mykola, K-111
BORTIN
    Virginia, W-119
BOSTIC
    Ronald David, C-125
BOTT
    Michael F., C-53, F-1, G-134,
        L-106, M-52, R-29, T-58, Z-12
BOTTAZZI
    Alberto, R-134

About the Compiler

MICHAEL GRAY was born in Newcastle, Australia, in 1946. Since 1976, he has served as Music Librarian of the Voice of America in Washington, D.C. Mr. Gray is author of *Beecham: A Centenary Discography* and co-author of *Bibliography of Discographies. Volume I: Classical Music, 1925-1975*. He is past-President of the Association for Recorded Sound Collections, for which he served as Editor of the ARSC *Journal*.